QUEER NATIONS

QUEER NATIONS

Marginal Sexualities in the Maghreb

JARROD HAYES

The University of Chicago Press
Chicago & London

JARROD HAYES is Assistant Professor in the Department of
Romance Languages and Literatures at the University of Michigan.

10046268 33

The University of Chicago Press, Chicago 60637
The University of Chicago Press, Ltd., London
© 2000 by The University of Chicago
All rights reserved. Published 2000
Printed in the United States of America
09 08 07 06 05 04 03 02 01 00   1 2 3 4 5

ISBN 0-226-32105-3 (cloth)
ISBN 0-226-32106-1 (paper)

Library of Congress Cataloging-in-Publication Data

Hayes, Jarrod.
    Queer nations : marginal sexualities in the Maghreb / Jarrod
Hayes.
        p.   cm.
    Includes bibliographical references and index.
    ISBN 0-226-32106-1 (pbk. : alk. paper). — ISBN 0-226-32105-3
(cloth : alk. paper)
    1. North African fiction (French)—History and criticism.
2. Gay men's writings, North African (French)—History and
criticism. 3. Lesbians' writings, North African (French)—History
and criticism. 4. Homosexuality in literature. 5. Gender identity
in literature. 6. Homosexuality and literature—Africa, North.
I. Title.
PQ3988.5.N6H39   2000
843.009'92066420961—dc21   99-38490
                                                        CIP

for Ömür, canım, aşkım

Contents

Acknowledgments

This project began as a dissertation in the Ph.D. program in French at the Graduate School and University Center of the City University of New York. I therefore owe my greatest gratitude to my two advisers, Nancy K. Miller and Francesca Canadé Sautman. Careful readers, meticulously thorough, generous with suggestions, patient, supportive, and caring, they have been the advisers most graduate students can only dream of. They have left an indelible mark on this study, which certainly would never have made it to its present form without them. I would also like to thank my third reader, Ammiel Alcalay, for his support and suggestions. Ross Chambers read a more recent version of the manuscript from cover to cover and his commentary was crucial in revising the manuscript into its present form. Rare indeed is the page that has not benefited from his suggestions. In addition, Winifred Woodhull and the second reader for the University of Chicago Press provided thoughtful readings and suggestions, which offered much guidance in the final revisions. Domna C. Stanton also read the entire manuscript and offered helpful comments.

During the course of this project a number of people have read portions of this work, suggested corrections, offered support, and asked important questions that steered me in productive directions: Gina Fisch-Freedman, Dalila Hannouche, Ed Stein, Fazia Aïtel, Nadir Moknèche, Hédi Abdel-Jaouad, Maher Ben Moussa, Carina Yervasi, Lawrence D. Kritzman, Marie-Hélène Huet, David Caron, Frieda Ekotto, Timothy J. Reiss, Patricia Penn Hilden, Catherine Brown, and Colin Johnson.

Huma Ibrahim, Gaurav Desai, Jean-François Fourny, Eugene Rice, and Thomas Spear provided forums when it was important to share my work. Malek Chebel, Sue Houchins, Réda Bensmaïa, Ronnie Scharfman, Clarisse Zimra, Brinda J. Mehta, Sylvie Durmelat, Elisabeth Mudimbe-Boyi, Bernard Aresu, and Martin Bauml Duberman listened to and/or read previous versions of a number of chapters herein and offered support and helpful comments.

I would like to thank all of those from the University of Chicago Press who were involved in this project: Doug Mitchell, who has offered much support, guidance, and encouragement, as well as Russell Harper, Matthew Howard, Liz Demeter, and Barbara Fillon.

A number of my professors, while not directly involved in this project, have made important contributions to my intellectual formation. I would like to thank Royal S. Brown for his film classes and for reading my work in film studies. I would like to thank Mary Ann Caws for her professional and intellectual support and Marcel Gutwirth who, as Executive Officer, brought me into the program at the Graduate Center, obtained financial support so I could eat and live in the expensive city of New York, and supported this particular project. I would also like to thank Renée Waldinger for continuing that support.

Patrick Cullen and Mason Cooley have been, in addition to dear friends, invaluable mentors. The friendship of Gina, Fasia, Andrew, Toni, Frances, Marty, David, Alex, Carina, Frieda, Lucia, Jossianna, Catherine, and Juli gave me the strength to overcome the many frustrations a project such as this entails, and the necessary relief from "work" during time for "play." My parents, Wanda West Hayes and Jesse Lee Hayes, have offered unending support for my educational endeavors and loved me through my political commitments, during my migrations, and finally, when I came out. And Ömür's love provides the inspiration for all my undertakings, intellectual and other.

Many thanks to all my colleagues in the Department of Romance Languages and Literatures for their support and for contributing to one of the most collegial intellectual environments one could hope for. I also thank the office staff for their logistical support: Marlene Moore, Barbara Wexall, Judi Carothers, Jennifer Wade, Linda Weiss, Mary Fallert, and Jason Baluyut. I would like to thank the Mellon Foundation for their full support during my first two years of graduate school and for the fifth. And I would like to thank the Graduate School and University Center for their full support during my third and fourth years and for the Graduate Teaching Fellowship during my sixth year. I would like to thank the Fulbright Foundation for the opportunity to teach English in France for a year and the North Carolina School of Science and Mathematics for the most influential of my educational experiences.

A Note on Translations

Whenever possible, I have cited published translations of the material quoted herein. Any translation without a page-number reference is my own. For some secondary works, to avoid weighing the text down with too much cited material, I have only quoted the English version. If no published translation is listed in my Works Cited for the source of these citations, the translation is my own and the reference is to the French original.

INTRODUCTION

"Islam is my religion, Arabic is my language, Algeria is my fatherland."
This slogan, adopted in the 1930s by the Association of Ulema, led by
Sheikh Abd-el-Hamid Ben Badis, is perhaps the most concise expression
of Algerian nationalism. Although an effective battle cry in the Algerian
Revolution, as a definition of nationality, it is quite exclusionary; according to the formula, only Arabic-speaking Muslims can be truly Algerian, which leaves out many who have no "fatherland" other than Algeria
(Berbers and Algerian Jews, to name two of the most blatant exclusions).
Although defining Algerianness in opposition to the French colonizing
power was necessary to justify anticolonial struggle, must all discursive
deployments of the Nation exclude to be effective?[1] In literary discourses
at least, Algerian as well as Moroccan and Tunisian writers have envi-
sioned defining it as an inclusive space. In particular, sexuality—especially marginal sexualities, "sexual dissidence,"[2] and gender insubordination—plays an important role in articulating national identity in
Maghrebian novels in French.

In Arabic discourse, the Arab world was traditionally divided into
two parts, the Mashriq or eastern part and the Maghreb (literally the west
or where the sun sets), which includes Arab lands to the west of Egypt,
even Islamic Spain. This study deals specifically with North African
countries colonized by the French: Algeria, a French colony from 1830 to

1. I capitalize *Nation* whenever referring to it as an abstract concept and discursive phenomenon
and use the lowercase for specific nations or the Nation's actual embodiment as a geopolitical entity.
2. The term is Dollimore's (1991).

I

1962,[3] Tunisia, a French protectorate from 1881 to 1956, and Morocco, also a protectorate, from 1912 to 1956. Maghrebian Francophone literature began to articulate a national identity, distinguish itself from the literary conventions of metropolitan France (and Europe), and formulate an anticolonialist position in the aftermath of World War II and on the eve of the various independence struggles in the early 1950s (a full-blown revolution in Algeria's case). Regardless of policies of Arabicization in all three postindependence countries, Maghrebian literature in French continues to be written alongside a literature in Arabic.

The notion of combat literature, elaborated by Frantz Fanon in *Wretched of the Earth* (1961) and taken up by Jean Déjeux in *Littérature maghrébine de langue française* (1973), has often been limited to works about independence struggles. By stressing the continuity between combat literature and postindependence novels that challenge the very national bourgeoisies Fanon warned would replace the colonizer's oppressive rule, I argue that his critique is still alive. Combat literature can then be seen less as a category that includes some works while excluding others than as a potential within all Maghrebian literature; in addition to texts about anticolonial revolution, this rubric could also include women's struggles, critiques of postcolonial or neocolonial oppression, and resistance to sexual normativity, regardless of whether these issues are central or marginal within the text as a whole. In this conceptualization, combat literature confronts the literary with other discourses (such as official proclamations, the media, and political, academic, and religious texts) in dialogic encounters. Within this discursive field, the revelation of sexualities that should remain secret contradicts the official discourses of nationality that deny the existence of nonnormative sexualities. Examining the political role of sexuality in postindependence literature makes it possible to reread earlier novels traditionally classified as combat novels wherein sexuality always played a role, albeit more subtle. Finally, rereading even earlier novels, often classified as "ethnographic" by nationalists, allows one to find anticolonialist struggle in novels criticized for pandering to the exoticizing gaze of Western readers. This rereading can only be articulated through sexual allegories of the political.

Recently, studies on nationalism have proliferated in cultural and

---

3. Administratively, the three northern provinces of Algeria—Oran, Algiers, and Constantine—became *départements* (which were considered part of France) during the Second Republic in 1848.

postcolonial studies. In *Nationalisms and Sexualities* (Parker et al. 1992), such work overlaps with queer theory and lesbian and gay studies. This interest has coincided with a number of recent world events: the resurgence of nationalism in the former Yugoslavia and Soviet Union, the wars it has engendered, and interethnic civil strife in Somalia, Liberia, Mali, Burundi, and Rwanda. Since nationalism often involves a narrative return to national origins that justifies the geopolitical entity of a nation, the return to "pure" religious traditions exemplified in the rise of Islamic fundamentalism in Algeria and the ensuing civil war could be considered a phenomenon related to the worldwide rekindling of nationalisms. Serbian ethnic cleansing, therefore, and the assassination of those who do not fit either official or fundamentalist definitions of Algerian identity operate according to the same logic. Whereas these current events are usually described in a negative light, in the 1960s, nationalism, the hope of liberation for many colonized peoples, was viewed by many in a more positive way.

Likewise, many theorists have distinguished between positive and negative forms of national identity and nationalism. Fanon distinguishes between a national consciousness that leads to a broader sociopolitical awareness and nationalism, which serves only a national bourgeoisie; whereas national consciousness was necessary to mobilize Algerians in the war for independence and construct an independent nation, he was afraid nationalism would only pave the way for a national elite to replace the colonizer as a source of oppressive rule, a fear that turned out not to be unfounded. In his vision, the national struggle for independence should lead to a socialist revolution. In addition, Julia Kristeva (1992) distinguishes between inclusive and exclusive notions of nationhood and characterizes the latter as relying heavily on a cult of national origins.[4] In the African context, her distinction makes more sense after independence. Kristeva's Nation based on exclusion and its cult of origins, when considered alongside Fanon, can then be seen as serving the interests of the postindependence elite Fanon condemns. A similar interest in criticizing

---

4. See also *Etrangers à nous-mêmes* and *Lettre ouverte à Harlem Désir.* While Kristeva's faith in France's ability to hospitably "welcome" immigrants might seem unfounded, and her articulation of the need for immigrants to assimilate into French society might seem to parallel French racist discourse and the colonialist notion of the "évolué," I find her formulation of exclusion and inclusion and her notion of "nations without nationalism" helpful (cf. the title of the English translation of *Lettre ouverte, Nations without Nationalism*). On Kristeva's political writings, see Woodhull 1993, 90–95.

exclusion on the part of Maghrebian writers who articulate the need for a heterogeneous nation is indicated by the titles of Tahar Ben Jelloun's "Défendre la diversité culturelle du Maghreb" (1991) and Abdelkebir Khatibi's *Maghreb pluriel* (1983).

"Oriental Sex"

Sexual diversity, however, has long been a characteristic by which Western observers have produced a so-called Oriental difference. To articulate accounts of same-sex sexual practices in the "Arab or Islamic world" or the Middle East (however they choose to define the geographical or cultural domain of their generalizations), many studies have tended to combine an active/passive or sodomitical model (usually associated with pre- and early modern sexualities in a European context) and the transgenerational model of pederasty as it was practiced in the ancient world.[5] Arab men, as long as they are the penetrators, even with men, are still manly; the passive partner is either a boy or is feminized. When sodomy is used to describe Islamic or Arab "homosexualities," it becomes surprisingly medieval in its characteristics. This characterization is less surprising when one considers that the literary texts most often considered for examples of male-male love are erotic texts from the period of Arabic literature corresponding to the European Middle Ages. No sexologist of the Western world would think of using medieval texts to describe modern sexuality; the Arab world, however, is seen as static, unchanging, and incapable of adapting to outside influences. In a study of medieval sexualities in the Islamic world, for example, S. D. Goitein uses Rachid Boudjedra's *La répudiation* (1969) to make one of his points (48). When studying Arab sexuality, the researcher is permitted to move back and forth across vast spans of time.

Such social constructionist accounts presume that sexuality is a modern, Western construction and often cite Foucault's sentence (1976)—

5. Studies on Arab sexuality include: Murray and Roscoe, Schmitt and Sofer, "The House of Islam" (Greenberg 172–82), Bellamy, Goitein, Schild, and Bousquet. I do not suggest that all these works have the same implications. Greenberg's and Murray and Roscoe's works are especially valuable for their wealth of diverse examples. For studies of Maghrebian sexualities written by Maghrebians, see Serhane, Chebel 1988, Bouhdiba 1975, Aït Sabbah, "La sexualité selon le Coran" (Khatibi 1983, 147–76), Zeraoui, and Ben Jelloun 1977. While Maghrebian sexologies do not necessarily contradict those written by Westerners and in many cases even confirm their findings, they tend to be much less interested in articulating all-encompassing paradigms and asserting a difference from Western sexualities.

"Le sodomite était un relaps, l'homosexuel est maintenant une espèce" (59) ("The sodomite had been a temporary aberration; the homosexual was now a species" [43])—to justify a totalizing view that divides up all Westerners along the homo/hetero binary.[6] *Sexuality and Eroticism among Males in Moslem Societies* (Schmitt and Sofer 1992) follows this paradigm, which Arno Schmitt sums up in his introduction: "But in [Islamic] societies there are no 'homosexuals'—there is no word for 'homosexuality'—the concept is completely unfamiliar. There are no heterosexuals either" (5). In a strictly constructionist sense, this statement was true until fairly recently, as it was also once true in the West, but Stephen O. Murray and Will Roscoe (1997) have questioned such a Western monopoly on homosexuality by challenging the "the dominant, Eurocentric model of gay/lesbian history and the implicit, occasionally explicit, assertion in many social constructionist accounts that contemporary homosexuality is somehow incomparable to any other pattern (or that there are no other patterns)" (5). In other words, histories of homosexuality often read like narratives of progress towards the Western model of egalitarian homosexuality, wherein both partners can be active as well as passive regardless of any masculine or feminine identification on either's part. (In that these partners are assumed to be male and engaged in anal penetration, the constructionist model is also phallocentric.) Although such observations may have sociological or anthropological validity, they leave little room for dissidence and are remarkably similar to the narratives of progress that established between Europeans and the rest of the world a pseudoevolutionary hierarchy that justified the civilizing mission and, therefore, colonialism.

While these sexual narratives may describe dominant discourses (the only object of Foucault's study), Eve Kosofsky Sedgwick's *Epistemology of the Closet* (1990) questions the paradigm they valorize as the only possible way for Westerners to embody their sexual identities. She argues that "issues of modern homo/heterosexual definition are structured, not by the supersession of one model and the consequent withering away of another, but instead by the relations enabled by the unrationalized coexistence of different models during the times they do coexist" (47). Without rejecting what she refers to as "paradigm shifts," she suggests that these paradigms might not be as monolithic as one might believe. Her "aim,"

6. For an interesting argument as to how such uses of Foucault may be misinterpretations of his work, see Halperin 1998.

then, "is to denaturalize the present, rather than the past—in effect, to render less destructively presumable 'homosexuality as we know it to-day'" (48). In the U.S. one can think of a number of men who consider themselves straight because they are always the active partner in sexual intercourse with men. Many histories of homosexuality would claim these men are holding onto an "outdated" model of identity. Is it a coincidence that working-class men or men of color are characterized as embodying this model more often than middle-class white gay men? In the lesbian and gay community one can think of a whole range of identity positions that deviate from the dominant paradigm: top, bottom, butch, femme, drag queen, transsexual, and even femme top and butch bottom. The distinction Sedgwick refers to between past and present Western sexualities is the same others have made between Western and non-Western ones. One might thus use her critique of Western paradigms to render less destructively presumable homosexuality as we know it in the West. For often, studies of "Oriental sex" have less to do with empirical descriptions of an "Oriental" difference than with normalizing what constitutes Western sexuality.

According to the constructionist paradigm, it would be inappropriate to read sexuality into North African texts. The novels encountered in this study, however, directly contradict Schmitt's claims; many contain homosexual characters and discuss homosexuality. Although many representations might seem to confirm constructionist paradigms, others will challenge them. Whenever specific examples of "Oriental sex" are examined closely, they will always be much queerer than any paradigm could allow for. In "Something Queer about the Nation-State" (1995), Michael Warner also argues against an exportation of the term "queer" in a way remarkably similar to constructionist arguments against the universality of sexuality: "[I]t's embarrassing that both the word 'queer' and the concept of queerness turn out to be thoroughly embedded in modern Anglo-American culture. . . . The term does not translate very far with any ease, and . . . [i]n the New World Order, we should be more than usually cautious about global utopianisms that require American slang" (361). While it is important to be attentive to sexual differences between cultures, I am concerned that Warner's warning, in spite of its stated anticolonial intentions, might lead to an Anglo-American monopoly on queerness that repeats the exclusionary gestures many constructionists have used to define Western homosexuality. Though he uses the terms "seraglio spirit,"

"perversion," and "sexual marginalities,"[7] the Algerian anthropologist
Malek Chebel (1988) describes a Maghreb that seems remarkably queer
to me:

> We shall evoke . . . the mannish woman, the tomboy, drag queens, etc.,
> that is, the entire continuum of sexualities that connects the poles of ex-
> treme masculinity and total femininity. Between these extremes, vegetates
> an entire people of appreciators, enlightened amateurs, and perverts, dilet-
> tantes: they are voyeurs, inveterate exhibitionists, active bisexuals, swoon-
> ing uranists. This splendid array is just as wide here as elsewhere and noth-
> ing distinguishes one pervert from another except for the unheard-of
> situation in which their deviations are staged. (17)

However, in spite of the potential applicability of the term "queer" to the
Maghreb, I shall use it here less as an adjective to describe sexual acts than
as a verb to signify a critical practice in which nonnormative sexualities
infiltrate dominant discourses to loosen their political stronghold.

Veils

In "Défendre la diversité culturelle du Maghreb" (1991), the Moroccan
novelist Tahar Ben Jelloun explains the role of the prevalent representations of marginal sexualities in Maghrebian literature:

> En général, c'est dans le roman d'expression française qu'on trouve le plus
> d'audace dans la contestation de l'ordre social et dans la transgression des
> tabous, surtout d'ordre sexuel. . . . Cette tentative de dévoilement, cette
> porte ouverte sur un secret, sur un bien caché, est critiquée de manière
> sévère et souvent brutale par les intellectuels maghrébins arabophones.
> Cette ouverture sur l'Occident, cette main tendue vers l'échange, cette uti-
> lisation de la langue de l'Autre sont considérées par certains comme une
> trahison. (272)

> In general, the novel of French expression is where one finds the most
> audacity in contesting the social order and transgressing taboos, especially
> sexual ones. . . . This attempt to unveil, this door opening onto a secret,
> onto a hidden wealth, is severely and often brutally criticized by Arabic-
> speaking intellectuals from the Maghreb. This openness towards the West,
> this hand extended in the spirit of exchange, this use of the Other's lan-
> guage are considered by some as treason.

7. The term "sexual marginalities" appears in the title of the first edition; the revised edition
carries a slightly different title.

According to him, literary depictions of transgressions, especially sexual ones, serve a political purpose by deploying sexuality in a critique of the prevailing sociopolitical order in postindependence Maghrebian societies. It is thus not sexual ("private") acts in and of themselves that are subversive, but representations of them in a "public" discourse. In his own essay on Moroccan sexualities, *L'amour circoncis* (1995), Abdelhak Serhane writes, "All sexual deviations [déviances]: prostitution, homosexuality, zoophilia . . . exist in Moroccan society. Everyone knows it and admits it. But speaking about them remains intolerable. The weight of sexual taboo is without a doubt the most insurmountable even at the discursive level. Not speaking about them is proof that society does not suffer from any deviations. Silence in the service of social hypocrisy" (25). Likewise, Ben Jelloun's use of the word "trahison" (treason) refers to talking about sexual acts not just doing them; as long as they are committed in private, they do not necessarily threaten the status quo. His description of how Arab nationalists view novelistic representations of sexual transgressions evokes the trope of national security. McCarthy claimed that homosexuals in the State Department were a threat to national security. Lesbians and gay men in the United States have been excluded from the military, the FBI, and the CIA for similar reasons. Maghrebian literature offers numerous examples of sexual traitors, characters whose marginal sexualities or sexual transgressions place them in opposition to the hetero-Nation (based not only on a sexual normativity but also on *homo*geneity). Likewise, in the nationalisms of budding nations, as in many models of identity politics, Ben Jelloun's discussion of betrayal, especially as connected to the revelation of secrets, evokes another taboo, against washing dirty laundry before outsiders, in front of whom a movement should represent a united front. Dissension within the group and any potential embarrassment should remain secret, and skeletons should remain in their closets. Because Ben Jelloun characterizes these revelations as a form of unveiling, one might at first question the political motives of such an association, which could be seen as dissimulating the "actual" veils worn by many women. A closer examination of the figurative use of "unveiling," however, reveals a connection between what the "actual" veils are supposed to hide and what is hidden behind the more figurative one.

In French eyes, little signifies the otherness and impenetrability of Maghrebian culture more than the veil. In *A Dying Colonialism* (1959), Fanon describes how the French turned Algerian women into the symbol of all Algeria. Veiled, they remained beyond the colonizer's otherwise

ubiquitous grasp. Unveiled, they testified to the success of colonial penetration and the complete transformation of Algerian society. In colonial
discourse, an unveiled (i.e. Europeanized) woman was liberated, a veiled
woman oppressed; the veil signified the essence of Arab misogyny. Indeed, during the Algerian Revolution, French authorities staged public
unveilings of Algerian women to justify colonialism as the "liberation" of
colonized women. This colonial use of a pseudofeminist discourse to divide and conquer placed Algerian women in a double bind. By opposing
the oppression of women, feminists were seen as siding with the colonizer
against national liberation. To join ranks with the nationalist movement,
it seemed, they had to abandon, at least temporarily, a feminist agenda.
Western feminist discourses have often accepted these associations of the
veil without questioning them and have even paralleled colonial discourse
in what Assia Djebar calls "un maternalisme à relent colonial" (Mortimer
1988, 200) (maternalism with a colonial odor). Likewise, Chandra Talpade Mohanty (1984) describes "the 'third world difference'—that stable,
ahistorical something that apparently oppresses most if not all the women
in these countries. And it is in the production of this 'third world difference' that Western feminisms appropriate and 'colonize' the constitutive
complexities which characterize the lives of women in these countries"
(53–54). The veil, the *harem,* the sequestering of women have come to
stand for not only the oppression of women within societies these practices are seen to represent, but also the universal oppression of women.
Arab feminist discourses have often resisted the colonialist equation of
veil and women's oppression and attempted to "decolonize feminism,"[8]
in part by paying more attention to what Marnia Lazreg (1994) refers to
as "[w]omen's strategic uses of the veil" (14). The veil is not one but many,
ranging from the most encumbering cover for the whole body to the
lightest partial covering for only the hair and even to the transparent.
Likewise, the veil is worn to varying degrees and for various reasons in
the Maghreb: in Algeria, women are murdered for not wearing (or wearing) one; in Tunis, veiled women are a minority.

   It would thus perhaps be tempting to reject all figurative uses of the
veil as tainted with colonial fantasy. Maghrebian writers, however, have
used the notion of unveiling to describe narrative revelations of secrets,
of marginal sexualities, of a forgotten past, and of the politically embarrassing. As Djebar's novels demonstrate, it is also possible to make such

---

8. The expression is Lazreg's (1994, 6).

figurative use of the veil without losing track of its "material" importance; she also shows that equating a woman's unveiling with her liberation is not confined to colonial discourse, be it "feminist" or not. Just as some nationalist discourses have labeled homosexuality as a foreign menace or an evil introduced by colonialism, they have sometimes dismissed feminism as purely Western and as sowing dissension within the nationalist movement and detracting from the "main" task of national liberation. Maghrebian feminist writings, however, deconstruct divisions that set up nationalism and feminism or Islam and feminism as mutually exclusive. They point to the possibility of a feminist nationalism, of a nation that does not exclude women from the public sphere, and of feminist rereadings of Islam's founding texts. Through the trope of unveiling, marginal sexualities as well as gender insubordination, in their resistance to compulsory heterosexuality, are equal partners in a queering of the Nation.

Nations

In *Imagined Communities* (1983), Benedict Anderson asserts that "in the modern world everyone can, should, will, 'have' a nationality, as he or she 'has' a gender" (5). Of late, however, it has become fashionable to speak of the "transnational": transnational or multinational corporations are said to be a defining characteristic of "late capitalism." Paradoxically, however, the globalization of capital has coincided not with a withering away of nationalisms, but with their intensification. While capital is certainly transnational, therefore, in many ways identity is still rooted in the Nation. Some identities may cross national borders: for example, Muslim, Jewish, Arab, and Maghrebian identities, as well as those of various sub-Saharan ethnic groups. In that sense, they might be described as transnational identities, but nations have not disappeared under late capitalism. The term "transnational" has also tended to replace an older one, "international." In a certain Marxist discourse, nations were bourgeois constructs. They were to be eliminated in an *international* class struggle waged by the working class against the ruling one. Marxists who rejected an identification with their nation (especially its bourgeoisie) often referred to themselves as internationalists. Self-identifying as such, however, does not erase one's national identity. Even if the goals of internationalist struggle were realized, national identity would persist, if only in traces or as history. This persistence, especially as cultural differences in a global context, is not necessarily a bad thing, and one should be wary of any attempt to eradicate them. One tendency of a certain internationalist discourse argues that all national differences result from an identification with the national bourgeoisie. In a world without borders, it logically follows, these differences would wither away. How different are a political program that predicts the disappearance of differences it condemns and one that actively undertakes their eradication? If I am wary of such a suspicion of difference, it is because homosexuality has been similarly targeted. In the U.S., for example, the Revolutionary Communist Party, a Maoist organization, has argued that homosexuality would disappear after the "revolution."[9]

Internationalist organizations do not have a monopoly on attempts to exterminate difference; national struggles also have a history of singling out homosexuality for elimination.[10] While many radical movements have accepted the participation of lesbian and gay activists on a *temporary* basis, homosexuality often remained incompatible with utopian visions of the new Nation. In more extreme versions, lesbians and gays would commit suicide after liberation.[11] In most national struggles, the gains of women have been moderate at most. National struggles that have benefited sexual minorities are extremely rare and are more than counterbalanced by examples of active repression after liberation.[12] As many critics agree, there is something oppressive about the Nation. Yet national identity has fueled many struggles for decolonization that I find just. In a world of nations, of subjectivities situated in national identities, how does one locate spaces of political agency without falling prey to the exclusion and homogenization nations are based on? One is caught in a political double bind between, on the one hand, struggling in a world of nations and accepting the exclusions they involve, and on the other, rejecting the

9. For the official party line, see "On the Question of Homosexuality" (1988). The more traditional Communist Party (CPUSA) has its own history of rejection and denial of homosexuality, even though, before Stalin, the official Soviet stance opposed discrimination against homosexuals (Plant 39). For an example of a progay position of an American Communist Party, see McCubbin, which articulates the position of the Workers World Party.

10. The Cuban Revolution, first national later socialist as well, is one such example.

11. This subject was the topic of a teach-in entitled "Gays and Lesbians in Radical Struggles," which took place at the CUNY Graduate Center while the campus was occupied by striking students (16–25 April) during the 1991 student strikes. The participants were Rena Grant, Maxine Wolfe, and Jim Fouratt, who gave the example of a Québécois revolutionary group whose lesbian and gay militants were to commit suicide after the revolution.

12. The new constitution of South Africa guarantees the rights of lesbians and gay men. In practice, however, equality is still forthcoming in many domains. Sandinistas recently voted against Nicaragua's new repressive sodomy law, but did nothing in support of the budding lesbian and gay movement while in power and actually actively discouraged its organization (Bolt and Poveda).

Nation and its repressive exclusions and, at the same time, eliminating a major stage of political action. Many Maghrebian novels, however, suggest ways out of this double bind.

Allegories

A number of theorists have asserted that nations are like fictions; they are, in fact, supported by narratives: history, narratives of origin, tales of heroism. One might even consider nations to be the fictions that construct them. Many critics of poststructuralism, especially Marxist ones, have questioned this emphasis on the discursive and claim that it downplays material force, power relations, and oppression. To read the Nation as narrative, however, does not mean that it is not real or that it is more akin to a lie. To assert its discursive aspect does not deny the "realness" of power or its materiality. Discursive analysis of the Nation, however, does reveal it as contested ground; any claim to truth regarding what constitutes power, oppression, or the benefits and drawbacks of the Nation should be viewed with suspicion (though not necessarily rejected). In response to such critiques, Gayatri Chakravorty Spivak (1984) has clarified, perhaps more than any other, what poststructuralist analysis does and does not do. She describes a poststructuralist "acknowledgment [of] the impulse to narrate, [of] the impulse to think of origins and ends" (20); in other words, while it is possible to deconstruct collective narratives, these narratives, however much they are questioned, do not go away, nor does the deconstructor necessarily want them to go away. Discussing the Nation as narrative does not reduce the nation-state to "mere words"; rather, it acknowledges that without narratives of origin, the Nation could not exist. Spivak (1987) is careful to point out that "[d]econstruction cannot found a political program of any kind. . . . It is a corrective and a critical movement. . . . Politically, all this does is not allow for fundamentalisms and totalitarianisms of various kinds, however seemingly benevolent" (104). Combined with a political program, however, the deconstruction of nationalist narratives can strengthen a critique of the interests served by the formation of a particular nation. In the case of national struggles against colonialism, one might recognize the necessity of these narratives while still remaining suspicious of them, lest they fall into the hands of the new national elite Fanon warned against. The Moroccan writer Abdelkebir Khatibi acknowledges the political usefulness of such a deconstruction when arguing for "a decolonization that would be, at the same time, a deconstruction" (1983, 47).

In some respects, Maghrebian novels participated in the rise of national consciousness that led to independence struggles by writing the Nation through narrative. One technique of narrating the Nation is allegory, in which an individual's story represents that of an entire collectivity by narrating a return to the roots of identity (both individual and collective) and the birth of political consciousness. In postcolonial studies, the genre of national allegory has been a subject of prolonged debate. Fredric Jameson (1986) writes, "Third-world texts . . . necessarily project a political dimension in the form of national allegory: *the story of the private individual destiny is always an allegory of the embattled situation of the public third-world culture and society*" (69). This description of national allegory elaborates on *Marxism and Form* (1971), in which his discussion of Walter Benjamin emphasized the political potential of allegorical readings. According to Jameson, contrary to "[t]he tendency of our own criticism [which] has been to exalt symbol at the expense of allegory" (72), in Benjamin's work, "allegory is restored to us—not as . . . a sign of the medieval health of the essentially religious spirit, but rather as a pathology with which in the modern world we are only too familiar" (72). In contrast with medieval allegories, because Benjamin "replace[s] theology with politics" (61), allegory can become an important genre for Marxist criticism.

Aijaz Ahmad (1987) has critiqued Jameson's generalization by challenging a number of its assumptions, the first of which is that there is such a thing as the "Third World"—"we live not in three worlds but in one" (103)—and therefore a "Third World Literature." Ahmad also points out that Jameson's notion of national allegory privileges the Nation in a way that contradicts his discussion of multinational capitalism, which tends to de-emphasize national boundaries. The "Three Worlds Theory," Ahmad argues, assumes that capitalism is restricted to the "First World" and socialism to the "Second." According to him, however, capitalism is global (and on this point he agrees with Jameson) as is resistance to it, which he calls socialism. In addition, Ahmad maintains that not all so-called Third World Literature is necessarily allegorical and that "First World Literature," particularly subaltern "First World Literature," often is. By asserting the allegorical potential of some "First World" literature, however, Ahmad acknowledges the possibility of reading certain "postcolonial" novels as allegories of the "birth of the Nation." Deprivi/eging the national, however, he frames his notion of allegory in terms of the distinction between public and private.

Although Maghrebian novels participate in the articulation of national identity through narrative, often these national allegories question dominant narratives of the Nation by deconstructing them. In *Allegories of Reading* (1979), Paul de Man argues that "any narrative is primarily the allegory of its own reading" and also "the narrative of its own deconstruction" (76–77). While his generalization may not always hold true, it is precisely as national allegories that many Maghrebian novels contest the Nation in similar ways through national narratives that deconstruct themselves as well as offer a paradigm for their own reading. Without denying the Nation's existence or implying a desire to overcome the national framework, this deconstruction exposes the problems of official versions of national identity, which many of the Nation's citizens cannot fully and completely embody.

Roots

"Nations, like narratives, lose their origins in the myths of time and only fully realize their horizons in the mind's eye," writes Homi K. Bhabha (1990, 1). The consolidation of national consciousness that paved the way for anticolonial struggle often involved a return to precolonial traditions or origins of the Nation. The colonizers had attempted to sever colonized peoples from their precolonial past. France, for example, denied the existence of an Algerian nation and therefore history before the French conquest. To counter such justifications for colonial rule, nationalist discourses sought alternative origins, in the resistance of Abd al-Qadir, for instance.[13] After Algerian independence, the revolution became a glorified origin as streets were renamed after its heroes, and SNED, the national press, favored simplistic combat novels. In "Nationalism as Resistance and Resistance to Nationalism in the Literature of Francophone Africa" (1993), Christopher L. Miller argues that, before independence, African nationalism was a form of resistance to European colonial rule, but afterwards, represented by new national oligarchies, it became the target of resistance. One might similarly maintain that, before independence, roots or national origins were a source of resistance to colonialism.

13. Abd al-Qadir led an army against the French from 1838 to 1847.

After independence, however, the same origins justified more specific nation-states now ruled by national elites.

Many Maghrebian writers, while articulating nationalist returns to origins, also seem to recognize the problematic nature of roots. When postindependence official discourses attempt to fix a single source of national identity and legislate a people's roots, they also marginalize, exclude, and even exterminate those who cannot trace their history to these roots in order to consolidate the power of a new elite. Many novels counter these official prescriptions of national origins, not by uprooting identity, but by challenging official roots with alternative ones. Allegorical journeys of return to such origins then become allegories of the subversion of return narratives. In rewriting the Nation, many authors repeat official narratives with a difference. This proliferation of roots opens up the Nation to those who do not share the official version of identity and makes it a more heterogeneous space where marginalized citizens can also plant roots. This heterogeneity is also sexual; if there is something oppressive about the Nation, there is also something queer about it.

Queering the Nation

Lisa Duggan (1994) has written, "The time has come to think about queering the state" (1); perhaps the time has also come to queer the Nation. The basis for exclusion from the Nation has historically included not only race, ethnicity, gender norms, religion, and political beliefs and activities, but also sexual orientation, sexual behavior, and desire. There are quite a few examples in North African literature where homosexuality is associated with the colonizer or a foreign evil. (This is a trick that certainly could have been learned from the French, if not known before. In the nineteenth century, the French blamed homosexuality on the bad influence of Arabs on French soldiers in Algeria [Greenberg 353; Bleys 112, 148–49].) One might also think of McCarthyite discourse from the 1950s in which homosexuality, along with communism, was seen as a threat to the "American way." However, there is no need to exclude an outsider; one cannot exclude someone from the Nation unless she is already there. Nationalist discourses that define the Nation by positing marginal sexualities as foreign are not stating what is already the case but actively excluding. If there must be such an effort to exclude the queer from the Nation (queer in both the more recent, sexual sense and its previous meaning as anything out of the ordinary) and show she is an outsider trying to invade, the queer must always be inside already; that is, in some ways the Nation is always already queer.

One of the common themes running throughout *Nationalisms and Sexualities* is that when there is an attempt to exclude a group from the Nation or consolidate power in the hands of a ruling elite through national narratives, the policing of sexual normativity often comes into play as well. Some of the collection's essays show that when narratives attempt to consolidate national identity as stable subject positions that a nation's citizens can fully occupy, a parallel consolidation of sexual identity is also often involved. More specifically, nationalist narratives serving to consolidate power for a ruling elite often also attempt to affirm patriarchy and compulsory heterosexuality as inseparable from national identity. Likewise, counternarratives that question conceptions of a homogeneous nation often challenge sexual norms by "contaminating" national narratives with sexual transgressions. Although one might distinguish between the nationalism of established nations such as the U.S. and the nationalism that fueled the independence movements in the Maghreb and other colonized regions, relations between nationalism and sexuality tend to be the same in both budding and established nations. When Maghrebian authors formulate representations of homosexuality, sodomy, homoeroticism, lesbianism, cross-dressing, the joys of emasculation, women's resistance, public unveiling, and feminist guerrilla warfare, they do not merely challenge sexual taboos, sexual normativity, and patriarchy (which they do); they also reveal the queerness of the Nation. They articulate a heterogeneous Nation that national elites cannot use as a weapon against its own citizens. Many Maghrebian novels, while affirming the necessity to consolidate national identity, nevertheless recognize that any model of identity is impossible to embody fully. They attempt, therefore, without rejecting identity altogether, to articulate a national identity that is heterogeneous in relation to languages, ethnicities, sexualities, and religions, and that questions any totalizing binary opposition to the former colonizer.

When Duggan calls for the queering of the state, she conjures up a concept often named, but less often defined: that of queering. What would it mean to queer the Nation? According to Ben Jelloun, Francophone Maghrebian authors have a tendency to reveal what should remain secret and to wash the Nation's dirty laundry in public. The skeletons Maghrebian writers bring out of the closet are of two sorts: sexual and political. When writers include marginal sexualities or the transgression of sexual taboos in their novels, they reveal what is considered shameful in official discourse and destroy the officially propagated image of the Maghrebian nation as a nation of "good Muslims" who abide by the strictest interpretation of Islamic family values. By dragging out political skeletons, they often challenge official versions of national history, reveal a shameful past that contradicts the glorious one of nationalist myths, or disrupt narratives of national origins. Furthermore, some writers draw a parallel between these two types of secrets; the revelation of political secrets often coincides with that of sexual ones, which in turn plays a political role in writing alternative roots for national identity. This narrative technique constitutes one method of queering the Nation. Notwithstanding the novels Ben Jelloun describes, in which representations of marginal sexualities abound, this major part of Maghrebian literature has remained, until very recently, in the closet of criticism. Some of these representations are quoted here for the first time in literary criticism. What Maghrebian authors have gone to such lengths to unveil has been veiled again by literary critics (often Western). It seems to me that this silence has continued long enough.

Hauntings

There is a specter haunting the Maghrebian nation; it is a queer specter, the specter of queerness. In *The Apparitional Lesbian* (1993), Terry Castle uses the image of ghosts to describe a culturally constructed invisibility surrounding lesbianism: "Why is it so difficult to see the lesbian—even when she is there, quite plainly, in front of us? In part because she has been 'ghosted'—or made to seem invisible—by culture itself" (4). In *The Celluloid Closet* (1981), Vito Russo describes a similar ghosting of homosexuality, both male and female, in classical Hollywood cinema, which literally snuffed out homosexual characters before the end of films. Castle, however, carefully points out how lesbianism is further subjected to specific kinds of invisibility in ways that male homosexuality is not: "The lesbian is never with us, it seems, but always somewhere else: in the shadows, in the margins, hidden from history, out of sight, out of mind, a wanderer in the dusk, a lost soul, a tragic mistake, a pale denizen of the night. She is far away and she is dire. (She has seldom seemed as accessible, for instance, as her ingratiating twin brother, the male homosexual)" (2). Though Castle's readings are limited to the West, in Maghrebian literature, female homoeroticism is likewise harder to see than its male counterpart. Rare indeed is the Maghrebian writer who does not deal with male homoeroticism or same-sex sexual behavior in at least one novel, and a number of prominent writers deal with these topics in many works, which does not mean that male homosexuality and homoeroticism are without their own ghosts. Maghrebian literature is a haunted literature, and this "haunting" is an important part of "queering the Nation."

In *Specters of Marx* (1993), Jacques Derrida coins the term "hauntology," which can help specify exactly how the sexual ghosts of Maghrebian literature queer the Nation. "Hauntology" is, of course, a play on "ontology." Being, or essence, for Derrida, is never present as such; it can only haunt the present. Though Castle's notion of a lesbian existing throughout history might be criticized by some as essentialist, in that her lesbian is a ghost, her essentialism is likewise a hauntology. Derrida elaborates on his previous notion that origins are only present as traces to describe them as haunting the present. He also uses this understanding of origins to describe nationalism:

> Inter-ethnic wars (have there ever been another kind?) are proliferating, driven by an *archaic* phantasm and concept, by a *primitive conceptual phantasm* of community, the nation-State, sovereignty, borders, native soil and blood. Archaism is not a bad thing in itself, it doubtless keeps some irreducible resource. But how can one deny that this conceptual phantasm is, so to speak, made more outdated than ever, in the very *ontopology* it supposes, by tele-technic dis-location? (By *ontopology* we mean an axiomatics linking indissociably the ontological value of present-being [*on*] to its *situation,* to the stable and presentable determination of a locality, the *topos* of territory, native soil, city, body in general). (82)

Usually, after all, it is *places* that are haunted. As collective phantasms, national origins are like phantoms: they haunt; but as places they can also be haunted. In the spirit of Derrida, one might describe this hauntology of national origins as a "hauntopology." But does hauntology, as a deconstructive practice or concept, reveal a *topos* to be always already haunted? or does it conjure up ghosts itself to enact the haunting? I would suggest that these two possibilities are inseparable.

Through his notion of "hauntology," Derrida also brings back the ghost of Marx. He deconstructs Marxist ontology, but also situates deconstruction, which "has remained faithful to a certain spirit of Marxism" (75), in relation to Marxist political critique and praxis. Hauntology, as a practice, is a reading that simultaneously rewrites, a "performative interpretation . . . that transforms the very thing it interprets." This notion of interpretation deconstructs the opposition between interpretation and sociopolitical transformation implied in Marx's eleventh Thesis on Feuerbach: "The philosophers have only *interpreted* the world in various ways; the point, however, is to change it . . ." (51). The theoretical part of *Queer Nations*' interpretive narrative incorporates a number of related concepts to refine this notion of political reading as transformative rewriting: Judith Butler's subversive deployment of parody in the performance of heteronormative gender roles, Luce Irigaray's mimicry of femininity, Ross Chamber's "reading (the) oppositional (in) narrative," and Bhabha's notion of the Nation as performance. As readings of official national narratives that deconstruct and therefore rewrite the Nation, Maghrebian novels engage in a similar hauntology by representing the Nation as haunted and conjuring up ghosts to haunt the Nation.

By emphasizing "the haunting or the return of *revenants*" (46), Derrida offers a clue as to how "hauntology" is related to queering. *Revenant,* one French word for *ghost,* is also the present participle of the verb *to return* or *come back, revenir;* ghosts *return,* then, like the repressed. When this repression is that of sexuality (as it so often is, in Freudian as well as nationalist narratives), the ghosts that come back are sexual ones. Since nonnormative sexualities suffer repression to a far greater extent than normative ones, these sexual ghosts are often queer. *Queering* as a form of *hauntology* thus exposes the connection between sexual *re*pression and political *op*pression, and the *topos* of this queering/hauntology, for the purposes of this study, is the Nation. In her opening remarks, Castle claims, "My primary goal in this book has been to bring the lesbian back into focus, as it were . . ." (2). However, one of the strengths of her study is that, in foregrounding the ghosting of lesbians, it is less the case that she brings them into focus (turning them into "real people" and making their ghosts disappear) than that she encourages a haunting (leaving them out of focus, to a certain extent) that brings back lesbian ghosts to haunt the very representations that participate in the construction of heteronormativity. Maghrebian novels expose the queer ghosts that haunt the Nation; they also conjure up these ghosts to haunt it. Likewise, this study reveals the queer ghosts that haunt Maghrebian literature but also conjures them up. If there is an exclusion, an exorcism of queerness at the origin of the Nation, queering the Nation brings back what the Nation has attempted to conjure away, in order to haunt it.

The strategy of queering also informs the organization of this study. In parallel with the various returns to national origins examined herein, *Queer Nations,* as a sort of literary history of the Maghreb in reverse, returns to the queer roots of Maghrebian literature. Each chapter is a reading of an allegory of reading, and each subsequent chapter depends and builds on the interpretive narrative constituted by all previous chapters. Instead of using queer theory to queer Maghrebian literature, it suggests ways in which Maghrebian literature might also be said to queer both queer and postcolonial theories, which can then complement each other in productive ways. While Maghrebian novels articulate critiques of the sexually normative moves of Maghrebian nationalisms, *Queer Nations* also allows these works to cast a critical gaze back on the West. Tendencies of imposing Western theoretical frameworks on "postcolonial" literature are well enough known, as is the Western critic's privilege of questioning his/her cultural Others without being questioned by them. "We" do not have a monopoly on queering; through our readings of Maghrebian novels, "we" might also, in turn, be queered by them.

Part One

ALLEGORIES OF

READING THE

MAGHREB

Chapter One

READING AND TOURISM:
SEXUAL APPROACHES
TO THE MAGHREB

The Orient becomes a living tableau of queerness.

—Edward W. Said, *Orientalism*

Orientalism and Sexual Tourism

In *Orientalism* (1978), Edward W. Said discusses the sexual attraction that the "Orient" exerted on many Westerners:

> We may as well recognize that for nineteenth-century Europe, with its increasing *embourgeoisement,* sex had been institutionalized to a very considerable degree. On the one hand, there was no such thing as "free" sex, and on the other, sex in society entailed a web of legal, moral, even political and economic obligations of a detailed and certainly encumbering sort. Just as the various colonial possessions—quite apart from their economic benefit to metropolitan Europe—were useful as places to send wayward sons, superfluous populations of delinquents, poor people, and other undesirables, so the Orient was a place where one could look for sexual experience unobtainable in Europe. (190)

The colonization of the "Orient" not only provided a convenient vacation spot for Western tourists, it also provided a playground for the relief of tensions engendered by Western sexual normativity. Said thus situates sexual tourism in the context of Orientalist discourses that often reinforced colonial hegemonies. For the Western tourist, the availability of sex in the Orient can never merely be a matter of intimacy between two individuals in a vacuum (as if it ever could). Rather, sex takes place in a colonial or neocolonial context between colonizer and colonized (or former colonizer and former colonized).

As Said points out, such sex can be obtained just as easily at home:

"In time 'Oriental sex' was as standard a commodity as any other available in the mass culture, with the result that readers and writers could have it if they wished without necessarily going to the Orient" (190). Even after the large-scale independence of many formerly colonized countries, going to the Bois de Boulogne, for example, to pick up (for pay or not) *petits arabes* remains a cliché in a French gay context. "Oriental sex" is still readily available through organized tours to Thailand, and in North American gay slang, a variety of terms exists to denote similar sexual tastes in the exotic: dinge queen, bean queen, rice queen, curry queen, snow queen, potato queen. These terms in no way imply that sexual preference for the exotic is restricted to gay communities, merely that these communities have developed a vocabulary to discuss and analyze the phenomenon, sometimes in ironic and parodic ways. Given the diasporas of colonized peoples into colonizing countries, Westerners find spaces where they can be sexual tourists in their own countries.

Said also discusses the role of sexual tourism in literary discourses:

> Virtually no European writer who wrote on or traveled to the Orient in the period after 1800 exempted himself or herself from this quest: Flaubert, Nerval, "Dirty Dick" Burton, and Lane are only the most notable. In the twentieth century one thinks of Gide, Conrad, Maugham, and dozens of others. What they looked for often—correctly, I think—was a different type of sexuality, perhaps more libertine and less guilt-ridden; but even that quest, if repeated by enough people, could (and did) become as regulated and uniform as learning itself. (190)

These writers were not only sexual tourists in their visits to the "Orient," but they also incorporated their experience of sexual tourism into literature. Said thus points to "Oriental sex" as a discursive practice as well as a purely physical phenomenon. Once sexual tourism becomes literature, sexual tourists do not even need to leave their homes to be . . . sexual tourists; they can also consume literature as sexual tourists, because reading becomes another mode of tourism.

In *Les 1001 années de la nostalgie* (1979), the Algerian writer Rachid Boudjedra also suggests that Western readings of "Oriental" texts can constitute acts of sexual tourism with colonial implications. In the novel, a foreign film crew, under the auspices of the indigenous governor Bender Chah, arrives in a small North African village to produce a film version of the *Arabian Nights*. Whereas Bender Chah sees the undertaking as a means of promoting Arab culture, the rest of the population views it as a colonizing gesture: "[L]e Gouverneur y était pour quelque chose dans ce piège du cinématographe qui visait à permettre la recolonisation en douce du village" (231). (The governor had a part in this trap set by the cinematographer who aimed to allow the gradual recolonization of the village.) This colonization is literal—the film crew goes around raping villagers, expropriating whatever property they need to make the film, and even killing villagers to use as corpses in the film. When the villagers revolt against the American "invaders," armed forces bombard the village. This violent colonization also has a discursive parallel; the film is an Orientalizing or exoticizing version of the *Arabian Nights* that objectifies the local population and figures the "Orient" as Other: "Les Mille et Une Nuits sont merveilleuses. Tout n'y est pas. Les cinéastes étaient en train d'intervertir l'histoire, de la dévergonder. Juste une fantasmagorie de marins qui ont trop bu. L'essentiel était ailleurs" (251). (The Arabian Nights are marvelous. But they don't contain everything. The filmmakers were in the process of mixing up the story, of corrupting it. Just a phantasmagoria of sailors who had drunk too much. The essential was elsewhere.) Their version of the *Arabian Nights* becomes a receptacle for Orientalist fantasies, sexual and other. Yet the connection between colonialism and the exoticizing discourses of Western Orientalism consists in more than a parallel. As the filmmakers expropriate whatever they need in their colonizing cultural project, they have also stolen the very texts their film is based on: ". . . 250 000 manuscrits arabes [sont] éparpillés dans les bibliothèques d'Europe et d'Amérique. . . . Les manuscrits authentiques sont sous clés. Pillés par les Occidentaux" (222, 237). (. . . 250,000 Arabic manuscripts are scattered throughout the libraries of Europe and America. . . . The authentic manuscripts are under lock and key. Pillaged by Westerners.) This is especially the case with the *Arabian Nights*. In the introduction to his translation, René R. Khawam (1986–87) describes—in his effort to return to the source—consulting various manuscripts, all of which he found in European libraries, especially the manuscript "discovered" by the premier French translator of the text, Antoine Galland. At the origin of Western readings of the *Arabian Nights,* therefore, was the theft of a text, a cultural appropriation not unlike the colonial expropriation of lands and resources. The particular Western reading constituted by the film thus becomes an allegory for colonization and/or neocolonialism.

Théophile Gautier, in *Le roman de la momie* (1857), also allegorizes such a textual expropriation. Lord Evandale and Dr. Rumphius, an

Egyptologist, "discover" the novel's narrative in an ancient Egyptian tomb. The story that constitutes the rest of the novel is written on the cloth strips wrapped around the female mummy they find and take home to England. The story of *Le roman de la momie* thus becomes available to Western readers because it was stolen from the culture that produced it. Because the stolen body is a woman's, translating the Egyptian text and therefore reading it involve unraveling the text from her body. This cultural expropriation takes on a sexual significance, because the act of interpretive violence (undressing a woman) follows the penetration of two men into a woman's tomb, an act symbolic of both colonial invasion and heterosexual intercourse. Boudjedra's *1001 années* allegorizes Western readings of "Oriental" texts with the same sexual and colonial associations Gautier makes, because the *Arabian Nights* serves as a point of departure for exoticizing and Orientalizing approaches to the Orient. Translated by Galland into French in the eighteenth century, it was often the first glimpse into Arab culture available to French children. Long before André Gide visited North Africa, he was nourished by this collection of tales. Nerval, especially, makes reference to the *Arabian Nights* in his account of traveling through the "Orient." The fictional classic thus served as a sort of tour guide for Western travel, constructed their vision of the Maghreb, and gave meaning to their travel experiences. Travel to the "Orient" was the continuation of reading fiction.

Given the dominant paradigms of reading sexuality in Orientalist fiction and in Arabic texts known for their queerness, any study of Maghrebian literature that wishes to consider representations of marginal sexualities bears the burden of the colonial use to which similar readings have been put in the past. Sexuality aside, any text taught in a Western multicultural context risks becoming a site of reading *qua* tourism, which only looks for titillating, exotic qualities in a text. A study of sexuality in Maghrebian literature must therefore avoid sexual tourism if it wishes to contest colonial readings rather than reinforce them. In contrast, most critiques of sexual tourism, while pretending to condemn colonialism, end up being more about an anxiety about desires that cross racial, cultural, or class boundaries. These critiques often single out homosexual sexual tourism (which I shall call "homo sexual tourism" hereafter) for a particularly vehement criticism that tropes homosexuality as essentially exploitative. To avoid this heterosexism and fear of miscegenation, anti-homophobic critiques of sexual tourism must also critique critiques of sexual tourism and navigate between Scylla and Charybdis—the colonialist implications of sexual tourism and the sexual conservatism of most critiques of it. This chapter thus examines a number of texts that provide allegories of reading that negotiate this double bind and allow one to uncover what most critiques of homo sexual tourism tend to hide, the collaboration between colonialism and compulsory heterosexuality.

In "Vacation Cruises; or, The Homoerotics of Orientalism" (1995), Joseph A. Boone addresses "the way in which the public and personal texts produced by both straight and nonstraight travelers are implicated in a colonizing enterprise that often 'others' the homosexually inscribed Arab male, a condition that obtains, albeit with differing valences and contexts, whether that 'other' is perceived with dread or with desire" (90). His reading of the homoerotics of Western tourism in the "Orient" differs from many critiques of homo sexual tourism in its uncovering of many Western heterosexual tourists' homophobia. He also complicates understandings of both the colonial and sexual politics of sexual tourism:

> In accounts of orientalism that assume the heterosexuality of the erotic adventurer, for example, the confrontation with the specter of homosexuality that lurks in Western fantasies of Eastern decadence destabilizes the assumed authority of the tourist as a distant, uncontaminated spectator. In narratives where the occidental traveler by virtue of his homosexuality is already the other, the presumed *equivalence* of Eastern homosexuality and occidental personal liberation may disguise the specter of colonial privilege and exploitation encoded in the hierarchy white man/brown boy. (104)

While I agree with both of these assertions, this chapter's approach is slightly different: instead of focusing on potential heterosexist implications of Orientalist fiction written by heterosexual French writers, it considers how some of these texts reveal that, in the colonies, colonialism was reinforced through an attempted imposition of Western-style compulsory heterosexuality. At home, the colonial enterprise contributed to consolidating this institution, which was just coming into being. Instead of focusing on the colonialist implications of gay Western texts that deal with the "Orient," this chapter reveals the complexities of the interaction of colonial and sexual discourses within these texts.

Heterosexism and Critiques of Sexual Tourism

Although Boone marks his distance from "Said's failure to account for homoerotic elements in orientalist pursuits" (92), his analysis "of the complex undercurrents of those fantasized geographies of male desire that depend on, even as they resist, the homoerotics of an orientalizing discourse [with] phallocentric collusions and resistant excitations" (104) remains a part of the body of Saidian criticism of sexual tourism's colonial implications. Whereas Boone takes an antihomophobic approach, often revealing the heterosexist implications in the homoerotics deployed by many heterosexual Western writers, other critics of homo sexual tourism use anticolonial analysis as a disguise for heterosexism. Irene L. Szyliowicz's discussion of Pierre Loti's homosexuality in *Pierre Loti and the Oriental Woman* (1988) is one such critique. She begins by criticizing Loti for his representation of Oriental women, which has both sexist and colonialist implications: ". . . I perceive [Loti] as an exploiter of women, ready to use them to satisfy his various needs. . . . These women became the instruments by which he could gain a more penetrating perception of the area, and when he had to depart, he severed his emotional attachment with little thought of the consequences for his mistresses, their unhappiness and suffering" (13). She makes a Foucauldian connection between knowledge and power whereby *penetration* takes on several meanings. Said made the connection between knowing the Orient and having power over it and examined the sexual implications of colonial penetration: "The Middle East is resistant, as any virgin would be, but the male scholar wins the prize by bursting open, penetrating through the Gordian knot despite 'the taxing task'" (309). Szyliowicz combines these two associations into a penetration that is both colonial and sexual, both physical and hermeneutic. By penetrating/understanding the Oriental woman, the Orientalist penetrates/understands the Orient. As Orientalist discourse constructs a feminized Orient for Said, according to Szyliowicz, Loti sees in the Oriental woman a site of conquest and an object of the Orientalist will to knowledge. In this sexualized paradigm of colonization and of its parallel, Orientalism, colonizing and Orientalizing are acts of heterosexual penetration.

Yet, instead of making the connection between compulsory heterosexuality and colonialism, Szyliowicz blames Loti's "real-life" homosexuality for his colonizing approach to Oriental women: "Moreover, Loti frequently used women to mask a homosexual relationship or to draw attention away from an unsavoury liaison" (13). She even blames homosexuality for sexism in general: "Homosexuals (and we know that Loti was at least bisexual if not homosexual) frequently need to vilify women as a compensatory mechanism to deal with their guilt for their own sexual persuasions" (58). As her example demonstrates, critiques of sexual tourism or Orientalism have been levied against homosexual and heterosexual tourists unevenly, without any consideration of differences between dominant and marginalized Western sexualities as they are transplanted into the Orient. That homophobia should be related to homo sexual tourism is never suggested. Such critiques, often inspired by Said, are thus far less nuanced than *Orientalism,* which at least suggests a relation between sexual repression at home and tourism abroad. Often condemnations take on a puritanical tone: what is insidious about sexual tourism is that it involves sex; never is there any suggestion that tourism in itself might merit interrogation and that sexual tourism might only be a smaller part of a more general exploitation. Instead, characteristic critiques rely on a phobic reaction to homosexual encounters that cross national and racial boundaries.

In *Sexual Dissidence* (1991), Jonathan Dollimore, incorporating Said's connection between Western sexual repression and tourism, critiques such critiques of sexual tourism:

> [T]he homosexual is involved with difference . . . because, contrary to what the foregoing theory implies, she or he has, in historical actuality, embraced both cultural and racial difference. The relationship to these other kinds of difference has, for some homosexuals, constituted a crucial dimension of their culture. Sexually exiled from the repressiveness of the home culture . . . , homosexuals have searched instead for fulfilment in the realm of the foreign. Not necessarily as a second best. . . . That this has also occurred in exploitative, sentimental, and/or racist forms does not diminish its significance; if anything it increases it. Those who move too hastily to denounce homosexuality across race and class as essentially or only exploitative, sentimental, or racist betray their own homophobic ignorance. (250)

Dollimore, here, does not attempt to justify sexual tourism; rather, he places it in the context of homophobia at home and interrogates the validity of certain positions from which homo sexual tourism is critiqued.

Flaubert's Sexual Tour of Egypt

As Boone points out, one element of homo sexual tourism that critics often fail to consider is its availability to tourists who, conforming to sexual normativity at home, travel to the "Orient" to "play" so that their adventures will not endanger their heterosexual privilege. During his travels to Egypt, Gustave Flaubert was one tourist who took advantage of "Oriental sex." Said discusses at length Flaubert's liaison with the dancer Kuchuk Hanem, who is often said to have served as the model for Salammbô's dance and for Salomé's in "Hérodias" (6, 186–8, 207). Boone only slightly amends Said's account to point out that a boy dancer first caught Flaubert's eye (92). What neither critic reveals, however, is Flaubert's homosexual experience in Egypt. In a letter to Louis Bouilhet dated 15 Jan. 1850, Flaubert writes,

> Puisque nous causons de bardaches, voici ce que j'en sais. Ici c'est très bien porté. On avoue sa sodomie et on en parle à table d'hôte. Quelquefois on nie un petit peu, tout le monde alors vous engueule et cela finit par s'avouer. Voyageant pour notre instruction et chargés d'une mission par le gouvernement, nous avons regardé comme de notre devoir de nous livrer à ce mode d'éjaculation. L'occasion ne s'en est pas encore présentée, nous la cherchons pourtant. C'est aux bains que cela se pratique. On retient le bain pour soi . . . et on enfile son gamin dans une des salles. —Tu sauras du reste que tous les garçons de bain sont bardaches. (572)

> Since we're chatting about berdaches, here's what I know of them. Here it's quite well accepted. One admits one's sodomy and talks about it at the dinner table. Sometimes one denies it a bit, then everyone yells at you and it ends up getting admitted. Traveling for our learning experience and charged with a mission by the government, we see it as our duty to give in to this mode of ejaculation. The opportunity hasn't presented itself yet; nonetheless, we are looking for it. It's practiced in the baths. One reserves the bath for oneself . . . and one takes one's boy into one of the rooms. By the way, you should know that all the bath boys are berdaches.

In a later letter to Bouilhet (2 June 1850), he writes:

> A propos, tu me demandes si j'ai consommé l'œuvre des bains. Oui, et sur un jeune gaillard gravé de la petite vérole et qui avait un énorme turban blanc. Ça m'a fait rire, voilà tout. *Mais* je recommencerai. Pour qu'une expérience soit bien faite, il faut qu'elle soit réitérée. (638)

> By the way, you ask me whether I have consummated the bath project. Yes, and on a young, pockmarked lad with an enormous, white turban. It made me laugh, that's all. *But* I'll do it again. For an experience to be done well, it must be repeated.

The fact that Flaubert openly admits his homosexual experience and his desire to repeat it suggests a lack of guilt or threat to heterosexual privilege posed by Oriental homosex.

In *A la recherche du temps perdu* (1913–27), Proust describes how "certains Français, amateurs de femmes en France et vivant aux colonies . . . avai[en]t par nécessité d'abord pris l'habitude, et ensuite le goût des petits garçons" (4: 349) ("Frenchmen . . . after being womanisers in France, go to live in the colonies [and] from necessity . . . had acquired first the habit of and then the taste for little boys" [6: 116]). Oriental homosex can therefore play a specifically *hetero*sexual role in Orientalist discourse. Like Proust, Flaubert shows how Oriental homosex can serve as the escape hatch for activities Western heterosexuality abjects. In the colonies, the colonizer—a heterosexual at home—finds himself a consumer of Oriental homosex abroad. In the Orient, the Western hetero sexual tourist can engage in homosex without threatening his heterosexuality or compulsory heterosexuality in general. Or as Rudi C. Bleys writes, "the 'ethnographic gaze' provided an opportunity to produce works of male homoerotic tenor without becoming suspect" (11). Flaubert, rarely considered a homosexual, open or repressed, was one such tourist.

Balzac in the Colonial *Harem*

Honoré de Balzac exemplifies another way Western heterosexuality can appropriate Oriental homosex (colonize it, so to speak) for the benefit of its own discursive consolidation. In Balzac's *La fille aux yeux d'or* (1835), Henri de Marsay falls in love with Paquita, "the girl with the golden eyes," who is sequestered in an Orientalized *harem*. The Spanish Paquita is troped as Oriental, and she marks the availability of Oriental sex in Paris.[1] De Marsay manages to penetrate the *harem* and have an affair with Paquita in order to take her from her master. As the plot unravels, the reader, as well as de Marsay, learns that her master is not Don Hijos, the Marquis de San-Réal, owner of the house where she is kept, but the Marquise, who kills Paquita in a fit of jealousy at the end. The Oriental *harem* in Paris thus doubles as a closet enclosing lesbian intrigue. The

1. Her mother was a slave bought in Georgia; she thus "tenait aux houris de l'Asie par sa mère" (1093) ([was] linked through her mother with the houris of Asia" [372]). She herself was from Havana.

plot, however, situates this "lesbian drama" in a heterosexual narrative. It is the mystery surrounding Paquita that drives de Marsay's desire. The revelation of lesbian drama at the end of the narrative gives this mystery its full meaning. Lesbian drama in Balzac's novel thus at least partially serves to stimulate heterosexual desire and the penetration of the Oriental *harem* (a penetration sexually paralleling colonial invasion).

As Malek Alloula discusses in the section "Oriental Sapphism" of his study *The Colonial Harem* (1981), Western *heterosexual* fantasies about lesbianism within the *harem* are a trope of Orientalist discourse: "A universe of *generalized perversion* and of the *absolute limitlessness of pleasure,* the seraglio does appear as the ideal locus of the phantasm in all its contagious splendor. . . . Sapphism would thus contribute to further eroticize the idea of the harem, at least as it is constituted in Western belief. It underscores its polysexuality: to male homosexuality, to zoophilia and other vices, one can now add female homosexuality" (95–96). Thus, lesbianism is more than a mere counterpart to male homosexuality in the "living tableau of queerness" of Said's characterization of the Orient (103); it poses an extra challenge to phallic power, something Henri could interrupt if he were a real man. The Oriental *harem,* guarded as it is, is already difficult enough to penetrate (both physically and hermeneutically); as a challenge to male desire, it also stimulates that desire and increases it. Lesbianism inside the *harem,* or the male fantasy of it, drives on male desire even further. Regardless of how much de Marsay's heterosexuality is threatened inside the *harem* (as he crosses into the realm of the cultural Other, he must also cross-dress), he still penetrates the *harem* with a violence paralleling that of colonialism. In Orientalist discourse, the Orient is troped as feminine, and colonial conquest is figured as a rape; the violence of colonial penetration is heterosexual. Critiques of homosexual Orientalism, however, rarely take into consideration how representations of homosexuality in Orientalist fantasies can serve very heterosexual purposes.

Maupassant's Allegory of Hetero-Colonialism

Guy de Maupassant's *Bel-Ami* (1885) allegorizes Orientalism's contribution to the consolidation of compulsory heterosexuality. Georges Duroy, nicknamed Bel-Ami by a girl in the novel, desires to climb the social ladder of Paris. He begins as a journalist writing an account of his participation in the French military campaign in Algeria. Because he has difficulty beginning his task, his friend, Forestier, asks his wife to help Duroy. Instead of helping him articulate his own thoughts, she ends up writing the article:

> Elle imaginait maintenant les péripéties de la route, portraiturait des compagnons de voyage inventés par elle, et ébauchait une aventure d'amour avec la femme d'un capitaine d'infanterie qui allait rejoindre son mari.
>
> Puis, s'étant assise, elle interrogea Duroy sur la topographie de l'Algérie qu'elle ignorait absolument. En dix minutes, elle en sut autant que lui, et elle fit un petit chapitre de géographie politique et coloniale pour mettre le lecteur au courant et le bien préparer à comprendre les questions sérieuses qui seraient soulevées dans les articles suivants.
>
> Puis elle continua par une excursion dans la province d'Oran, une excursion fantaisiste, où il était surtout question des femmes, des Mauresques, des Juives, des Espagnoles.
>
> —Il n'y a que ça qui intéresse, disait-elle. (45–46)

> Next she invented exciting incidents on the journey, with fictitious pictures of the other passengers, sketching a flirtation with an infantry captain's wife on her way to rejoin her husband.
>
> After this, sitting down, she questioned Duroy about the geography of Algeria, of which she knew absolutely nothing. In ten minutes she knew as much about it as he did and composed a short paragraph on the political and colonial geography of the country to give readers some background knowledge and put them in a position to understand the serious problems which would be raised in subsequent articles.
>
> Next she went on an excursion into the province of Oran, an imaginary excursion, concerned mainly with the women, Moorish, Jewish, and Spanish.
>
> "Sex is the only subject that interests people," she commented. (45–46)

Though journalism is often considered among the most referential genres of writing, the most realist, accurately representing a referent is much less important here than reproducing a set of recognizable *idées reçues* concerning the Orient. In this article, Said's parallel between colonialism and Orientalist discourse is absolutely clear. The article's author (at least the person who gives it a signature) also participated in the military conquest of Algeria, and the novel thereby associates writing about Algeria with colonization. Yet the collaborative project of producing Orientalist discourse serves another function in cementing a future heterosexual union. Mme Forestier later becomes one in the series of women Duroy uses to move up the social ladder. Maupassant thus tells the tale of how colonial exploits (Duroy killed three Arabs in Algeria), when retold in narrative form, contribute to a sexual exploit, the conquest of a woman/ trophy. *Bel-Ami* suggests not only that heterosexuality served as a tool in colonization, but also that colonialism was a part of consolidating hetero- sexuality "as we know it today."

Colonialism and Heterosexuality

According to the Foucauldian chronology, homosexuality was coming into existence at approximately the same time as the scramble for Africa. Whereas Ross Chambers (1994) draws attention to "the incidences that might connect the emergence in the West over the last century or so of a gay male sexual identity with the historical apogee of colonial empires, like the British and the French" (16), Kobena Mercer and Isaac Julien (1988) claim that it was not merely the development of homosexuality that coincided with colonialism, but sexuality in general:

> Historically, the European construction of sexuality coincides with the ep-
> och of imperialism and the two inter-connect. Imperialism justified itself
> by claiming that it had a civilising mission—to lead the base and ignoble
> savages and "inferior races" into culture and godliness. The person of the
> savage was developed as the Other of civilisation and one of the first
> "proofs" of this otherness was the nakedness of the savage, the visibility of
> his sex. This led Europeans to assume that the savage possessed an open,
> frank and uninhibited "sexuality"—unlike the sexuality of the European
> which was considered to be fettered by the weight of civilisation. (106–7)

They point out that a major part of colonial discourse was to trope Afri- cans as sexually uncontrollable and polymorphously perverse. (Freud re- serves this description for children; colonial accounts of African sexuality are thus also a way of infantilizing colonized peoples.) Colonialism, then, undertook several missions, the civilizing mission, missionary evangeliza- tion, and conversion of natives to the missionary position (what Sue Houchins calls the "pressures of the missionary position"). With its own set of family values, it undertook, if not a systematic destruction of the extended family, at least a vast reduction of its important political, social, and economic functions, and one could describe this attack as heterosex- ualization. When learning about the "family" in colonial schools, chil- dren were bombarded with images of *maman* knitting in a rocking chair by the fireplace, *papa* reading the *journal* in his *fauteuil,* snow on the ground outside, and a Christmas tree by the window. That these images had no relevance in the traditional Maghrebian context was not considered by French educators; pupils were nevertheless subjected to this pedagogy whose purpose was to impose nuclear family values central to the consolidation of heterosexuality.

The general notion of sexuality used by Mercer and Julien can be further qualified: if homosexuality came to Africa with colonialism, so did homophobia. The self-proclaimed antiracist, anticolonial argument, "There is no homosexuality in Africa," can critique one aspect of colonialism only by relying on another. Nationalist rejections of homosexuality that inspire critiques of sexual tourism rely on a constructionist model of homosexuality as Western and bourgeois, which is exported to the rest of the world. This version of social construction, however, conveniently leaves out half of its implications. Sexuality in the dominant discourses of modern, capitalist society is defined by a homo/hetero binary that attempts to divide up all individuals according to what is assumed to be their exclusive sexual orientation towards members of the same or opposite sex. In this paradigm, both homosexuality and heterosexuality are constructed at the same time. (Actually, heterosexuality comes just a bit later.)[2] In a society without homosexuality, therefore, there would be no heterosexuality either. If colonialism imposed homosexuality, it also imposed heterosexuality. There are, however, no nationalist discourses that decry the colonial imposition of heterosexuality. Yet certain nationalist discourses use the constructionist paradigm with a slippery logic. A statement such as, "There is no homosexuality in Africa," once true in the constructionist sense, comes to imply, "There is no sex between members of the same sex in Africa," which blatantly denies all evidence to the contrary.[3] The homophobia brought to Africa by colonialism thus underlies nationalist discourses that definitionally exclude homosexuality from the Nation as well as critiques of sexual tourism that rely on these nationalist discourses.

2. Cf.: "Moreover, if homosexuality didn't exist before 1892, heterosexuality couldn't have existed either (it came into being, in fact, like Eve from Adam's rib, eight years later), and without heterosexuality, where would all of us be right now?" (Halperin 1990, 17). Katz describes how when the term "heterosexuality" was introduced into American medical discourse it originally meant an abnormal and excessive attraction to the opposite sex. Only later was it transformed from a pathology paralleling its same-sex counterpart into the norm.

3. See Dynes.

After *Orientalism*

Since *Orientalism,* a number of theorists have complicated Said's paradigms.[4] Some responses to his work, direct or indirect, have implications
for discussions of sexual tourism. In "Female Trouble in the Colonial
Harem" (1992), Emily Apter develops a reading strategy that uses Orientalist stereotypes to question both colonialism and Western sexual repression. She reads representations of the *harem* "to show, on the one hand,
how the sexual fantasies codified in harem texts may be used to construe
an antiphallic, gynarchic model of 'what a woman wants' mediated by
cultural difference, and, on the other, how the erotics of claustration allegorize the French enclosure and domination of North Africa" (207). In
other words, she finds in *harem* texts an example of the worst Western
fears about the Orient and what causes the undoing of Orientalist discourses; inside the *harem,* "native" women escape colonial domination. In
"Acting Out Orientalism: Sapphic Theatricality in Turn-of-the-Century
Paris" (1994), she describes "the use of Orientalism as an erotic cipher, a
genre of theatricality in which acting 'Oriental' becomes a form of outing, and outing is revealed to be thoroughly consonant with putting on
an act (each flips into the other unpredictably)" (106). Through Apter,
then, one might reread Mme Forestier's account of Duroy's sexual con-
quests as the opportunity for homoerotic fantasies about other women.[5]

   Apter's reading of Loti differs significantly from Szyliowicz's by demonstrating how he deconstructs the very gaze Szyliowicz criticized him
for: "When Loti tries to test Aziyadé's love by 'playing the sultan,' forcing
her to suffer his liaison with another Turkish woman, his cultural mas-
querade backfires as he finds himself rendered impotent by the courtesan's
Europeanized dress" (1994, 108). The Orient may have also served as the
stage for Loti's coming out:

> The masculinist demise, coinciding as it does with his inability to carry
> off the part of despotic pasha, implies that Arif-effendi's staged harem is
> really a convenient disguise for Loti's homoerotic closet. Aziyadé herself,
> childlike and subservient, emerges as the travestied stand-in for Loti's
> young servant Samuel, with whom he savors "the vices of Sodom" in the

4. Roussillon provides a synopsis of the debate among Arab intellectuals. See also Clifford; Ahmad's polemical criticism of *Orientalism* in "*Orientalism* and After" and "Marx on India" (1992,
159–242); Said's own response to criticism of his work (1986); and Behdad 1994a and b.
   5. I thank Winifred Woodhull for this idea.

brothels of the red-light district. Falling asleep on a boat with Samuel by his side, Loti floats into a wet dream punctuated by the sudden eruption of enemy fire. . . . Queered in this way, Loti's Turkophilia (acted "out" in real life, so to speak, through his propensity for cultural transvestism) gives a new twist to Said's characterization of the colonial traveler's perception of the Orient as a "living tableau of queerness." (108–9)

Apter offers, then, the possibility of queering Orientalist texts, of bringing what seemed queer about the Orient in Western clichés and fantasies back to haunt the West.

One finds another example of the Orient as *locus* for coming out in Oscar Wilde's *Salomé,* about which Regenia Gagnier has written, "[T]he daughter of Herodias promised a young captain who was loved by a page a 'little green flower' on the condition that he release to her John the Baptist." She states that Wilde wanted some men to wear green carnations (worn by homosexuals in Paris as a secret code for mutual recognition) to the first performance of the play in England. Because the English were unaware of this symbolism, the audience would see a young man wearing a carnation on stage and would realize they were participating in the performance. Gagnier remarks, "If [Wilde] was compelled to double as heterosexual, he had the pleasure at the premiere of watching straight men unwittingly bearing the emblem of homosexuality" (163–64). One could then read Salomé's unveiling as the coming out Wilde could not perform openly[6] and apply Apter's reading to much more recent texts, such as Charles Ludlam's version of Flaubert's *Salammbô,* written for the Ridiculous Theatrical Company, whose Everett Quinton performed Salammbô in drag. If for Flaubert, "Madame Bovary, c'est moi," Salomé doubled as Wilde's persona, and Salammbô for Ludlam's and Quinton's (and for many of the gay men in the audience who share this camp identification). In Flaubert's original, set in Carthage, Salammbô worships the moon goddess Tanit, whose statue in the temple is veiled. Mâtho, leader of the mercenaries in revolt against Carthage, steals the veil from the temple to harness the power it is believed to wield, and Salammbô dances with the temple snake before going to steal back the veil. (When the veil was stolen from the temple in *Salammbô,* the snake fell ill.) Though both the Derridean association of veil and hymen and the Lacanian notion

6. A few years after the publication of the play, however, Wilde was forcibly outed by the English judicial system, which tried and imprisoned him for homosexual activity.

that the phallus (i.e. the snake) must be veiled to signify are at work in Flaubert's text (or at least as twentieth-century critics read it),[7] in Ludlam's adaptation, these elements take on an added exaggeration and become camp. When Quinton dances in drag with a huge phallus, the phallus, especially as it is associated with male privilege and power, becomes a joke and is, in short, unveiled.

Though not in response to Said, Mercer also provides a revision of critiques of the exoticizing gazes at work in many examples of sexual tourism, a revision that, interestingly, also involves repositioning from an earlier position. In "Imaging the Black Man's Sex,"[8] he criticizes Robert Mapplethorpe's photographs of black men for their use of "the fetish of skin color in the codes of racial discourse" (183). According to Mercer's first reading, Mapplethorpe's photographs essentialize black bodies as purely sexual and participate in a discourse similar to Orientalism, because "each image thus nourishes the racialized and sexualized fantasy of appropriating the Other's body as a virgin territory to be penetrated and possessed by an all-powerful desire, 'to probe and explore an alien body'"[9] (177). In "Skin Head Sex Thing,"[10] however, Mercer considerably revises his first criticism of "the erotic objectification and aestheticization of racial difference by proposing an alternative reading that revises the assumption that 'fetishism' is necessarily a bad thing" (190). He points to a multiplicity of possible political interpretations of Mapplethorpe's work: "The photographs can confirm a racist reading as easily as they can produce an antiracist one . . ." (203). Revising as well the poststructuralist notion of the death of the author, Mercer argues that "certain kinds of performative utterances produce different meanings, not so much because of what is said but because of *who* is saying it" (204). Gay men, especially black gay men, because they inhabit a context of cultural signifiers Mapplethorpe draws on, have at their disposal the critical tools necessary to read his photographs less as an uncritical reiteration of racist stereotypes than as a critical rereading of them (205). His photographs then become a sort of parody of the clichés of the sexualized black male

7. For psychoanalytic readings of the veil in *Salammbô,* see Mossman, Godfrey, and especially, McKenna.

8. *Welcome to the Jungle* 171–189. First published in *Photography/Politics: Two,* ed. Jo Spence, Patricia Holland, and Simon Watney (London: Comedia, 1986).

9. The quotation is Edmund White's, in Mapplethorpe's *Black Males* (Amsterdam: Gallerie Jurka, 1983).

10. *Welcome to the Jungle* 189–219. First published in *How Do I Look? Queer Film and Video,* ed. Bad Object-Choices (Seattle: Bay Press, 1989).

body. Though Mercer does not mention Said's *Orientalism* in his readings of Mapplethorpe's work, he points to the possibility of rereading texts criticized earlier for a similar exoticizing or Orientalizing gaze.

Mommies, Pedophiles, and Sexual Tourists

A number of Maghrebian writers have also taken up, directly or indirectly, the question of sexual tourism. Though more directly a complex consideration of the relation between pedophilia, mothering, and feminism, Leïla Sebbar's *Le pédophile et la maman: L'amour des enfants* (1980) also addresses the sexual tourism that some of the novel's pedophiles engage in. By separating questions of sexual tourism, cross-racial desire, and pedophilia, Sebbar suggests the possibility of a cross-generational desire that is not exploitative, of cross-racial desire that is not tourism, and of a critique of sexual exploitation that is not sexually conservative and that affirms rather than condemns the desire for alterity. Sebbar is rapidly becoming a very prominent writer in Maghrebian studies, but literary studies of her work almost *never* mention this novel.[11] It is as if the sexual questions raised by it would violate the more prudish standards of literary studies, even though the novel may be crucial for understanding Sebbar's later work, in which the themes of sexual tourism, pornography, and prostitution constantly recur. When these themes are taken up in literary criticism, they are usually read as a flat denunciation of sexual exploitation in postcolonial contexts. Sebbar's treatment of these issues, however, is always more complicated and sophisticated than the body of criticism on her work would leave one to believe.

The narrative of *Le pédophile et la maman* consists of three parts: a pedophile's journal, a mother's journal, and an exchange of letters between two feminists of the MLF. In the introduction that frames the narrative, Sebbar begins with a juxtaposition:

On dit: une mère aime ses enfants.
            un pédophile aime les enfants, garçon ou fille.
            (13)

One says: a mother loves her children.
            a pedophile loves children, boys or girls.

---

11. The one exception to this rule is Merini, who nevertheless reads Sebbar as "an attempt to stigmatize the sexual exploitation of the children of immigrant workers" (197).

In a context where the mere mention of pedophilia often provokes panic-like reactions and calls for parents to protect their children from potential child molesters, Sebbar points out the similarities between mothers and pedophiles. In prevalent discourses the two should be enemies—pedophiles attempt to steal children from their mothers—but Sebbar disrupts this cliché by revealing what links mothers and pedophiles, their love of children. Condemnations of pedophilia have in common with critiques of homo sexual tourism the fact that both discourses often rely on visions of homosexuals as child molesters by nature in the one case and of homosexuality as essentially exploitative in the other.

A discussion of sexual tourism enters Sebbar's consideration of pedophilia because, given taboos against intergenerational sex in France, pedophiles often cross cultural boundaries at home or travel to obtain sex. The pedophile whose journal serves as the first part of the novel, however, offers a critique of sexual tourism. In one passage he quotes remarks made by one of his friends, a pedophile and sexual tourist:

> Je t'ai parlé de l'Afrique du Nord. J'ai aussi connu des enfants africains, noirs. Je les adore. Ce côté animiste, cette douceur, cette félinité. La beauté d'un jeune Noir est pour moi insurpassable. Cette grâce. Certains n'aiment pas les petits Africains. Ils préfèrent dans l'ordre: les Blancs européens, les Arabes, les Asiatiques . . . Pour ma part, je n'établis pas de hiérarchie. Un petit Africain, c'est doux et beau comme un animal. (77)

> I have spoken to you about North Africa. I have also known black African children. I adore them. Their animist side, their softness, their cat-like qualities. For me, a young black boy's beauty is unsurpassable. Such grace. Some don't like young Africans. They prefer, in this order, white Europeans, Arabs, Asians. . . . I, for one, don't have a hierarchy. A little African is as soft, sweet, and beautiful as an animal.

Although this passage reverses the dominant European standards of beauty wherein racial differences are categorized according to gradations hierarchically ranked with white on top and black on bottom, the remarks of the pedophile's friend are especially disturbing for their animalization of bodies of color. The eponymous pedophile criticizes the colonialist implications of his friend's touristic desire:

> Je lui ai expliqué combien j'étais gêné par ce mélange de primitivisme et de mysticisme, si souvent liés chez les pédophiles tiers-mondistes, et qui prend à mes yeux une coloration colonialiste: un bon colonialisme certes, non-violent . . . mais où je vois du missionnaire, malgré tout. (77)

I explained to him how much I was disturbed by this combination of primitivism and mysticism, which are so often linked in third-worldist pedophiles, and which, in my eyes, has colonialist implications: a good colonialism certainly, nonviolent . . . but in which I see a missionary attitude just the same.

His critique, however, is mitigated by a certain amount of compassion, which is paralleled by that of the mother, who, in her love for her own children, identifies with pedophiles. She reads the novels of Tony Duvert, an author of the radical French pedophile movement, keeps a collection of newspaper clippings about pedophiles, and sympathizes with the pedophile movement's critique of the heterosexual family wherein children are the private property of their biological or legal parents. She even goes so far as to ask, "Je serais une mère pédophile?" (156). (Could I be a pedophile mother?) By situating the critique of sexual tourism in the voice of a pedophile and the identification with pedophilia in the voice of the mother (who bears autobiographical resemblance to herself), Sebbar dislodges assumptions about the pedophile/sexual tourist and the pedophile as enemy of children and, therefore, as a parent's worst nightmare. She thus creates the possibility of a double-edged critical sword with which one can articulate a critique of sexual tourism without reinforcing the heterosexism of most such critiques and a critique of the colonial or neocolonial implications of some sexual encounters without the abjection of nonnormative sexualities in and of themselves.

Genet's Cross-Racial Desire as Political Solidarity

One could then apply this double-edged analysis to the writings of some sexual tourists in order to uncover ways in which these texts articulate anticolonial, anti-imperialist, and antiracist critiques. Jean Genet, himself a sexual tourist, also had two long-term relationships with North African men, neither of whom were, strictly speaking, gay-identified or exclusively homosexual. The first, Abdallah Bentaga, son of an Algerian man and a German mother, was an acrobat and committed suicide when Genet began to neglect him for a race-car driver after an accident left Bentaga unable to perform (White 442–73). The second, Mohammed El Katrani, a Moroccan, eventually married and settled down with his wife in a house Genet built for them in Larache, Morocco. When Genet died, he was buried in Larache within view of El Katrani's house, and El Katrani died within a year in an automobile accident (White 584–635).

In an interview with Hubert Fichte, Genet describes a Moroccan trick with the racist stereotypes sexual tourism can involve:

> . . . I was in Morocco. I met a young 24- or 25-year-old Moroccan man, very poor. He came up to my room every day. He stayed in my room. He left my money alone. He didn't touch anything. Do I admire him for that? No. I think it was a ploy. In short, I admire him for having tricked me to such a degree.
> H. F.—*Later, you brought him to France?*
> G.—Of course, and he was very clever, I don't regret having brought him to France. In Arab countries, in Third-World countries, a young boy, as soon as he meets a white guy who pays him a little attention, can only see in him a potential victim, a man to rob, and that's normal. (Genet 1991, 169)

Thus the former colonized are exploiting the former colonizers. In Genet's view, even when Moroccan tricks are not stealing, they are still thieves. The cliché is complicated by Genet's lifelong career as a thief and his glorification of thieves in his poems, novels, and plays, but the stereotype of the Arab as thief by nature still stands.

What most complicates Genet's career as a sexual tourist, however, is his antiracist and anticolonial political commitments. His play *Les nègres* (1958) articulates a subtle analysis of racism, and another, *Les paravents* (1961), is a complex depiction of the Algerian Revolution. When Genet gave up writing fiction, he devoted himself to two political struggles in particular, those of the American Black Panther Party and of the Palestinian Liberation Organization. He came to the U.S. illegally to speak on behalf of the Black Panthers and was given a *laissez-passer* by Yasser Arafat himself to visit the camps of the Palestinian *fedayeen* (White 549–58). He gives a poetic written account of his political commitments and the travels he undertook on their behalf in *Un captif amoureux* (1986), and his political speeches, writings, and interviews are collected in *L'ennemi déclaré* (1991). In another interview, Genet explicitly associated his political involvement with his sexual attraction for men of color: "[Homosexuality] made a writer of me and enabled me to understand human beings. I don't mean to say it was entirely that, but perhaps if I hadn't gone to bed with Algerians I might not have been in favor of the FLN. That's not so: I probably would have sided with them anyway. But perhaps it was homosexuality that made me realize Algerians are no different from other men" (Genet 1964, 47). In the interview with Fichte, he even states that he derived erotic pleasure from his political association with the Panthers and the Palestinians:

> The Panthers are black Americans, Palestinians are Arabs. I would have a hard time explaining why it's so, but these two groups have a very strong erotic charge for me. I wonder whether I would have been able to subscribe to revolutionary movements that are so just—I find them very just, the Panthers' movement and the Palestinians' movement—but this position, this sympathy, don't they at the same time depend on the erotic charge that the Arab world as a whole and the black American world represent for me, for my sexuality? (156)

Genet, perhaps more than any other French writer, has provoked a great deal of interest and a number of positive writings from Maghrebians, many of whom focus on his political commitments without mentioning his erotic attachments.[12] Mercer (1994) is perhaps the critic who has most directly asked the questions that Genet inspires in a consideration of sexual tourism:

> Under what conditions does eroticism mingle with political solidarity? When does it produce an effect of empowerment? And when does it produce an effect of disempowerment? When does identification imply objectification and when does it imply equality? . . . Genet's affective participation in the political construction of imagined communities suggests that the struggle for democratic agency always entails the negotiation of ambivalence subjectively. (219)

One might begin to seek an answer to these questions in Chamber's description (1991) of the role of seduction in oppositional reading:

> Acts of seduction *in* the text thus become, for the reader, a seductive action *of* the text. And, if narrative texts have the power to change their readers, it is because one cannot unbecome what one has become, unthink, unfeel, or undesire what one has once thought, or felt, or desired. To be seduced by a text—to identify with textual relations that exclude one as, by definition different—must logically, therefore, produce *change,* change being understood as *becoming less different* from the textual concerns than one once was. (32)

---

12. Choukri; El Maleh; Khatibi 1987, 129–200; and Ben Jelloun [1977] 1988, 1992, 1981–82, and his interview of Genet in *L'ennemi déclaré* (207–11). On Ben Jelloun's interest in Genet, see also Spear's interview and Ben Jelloun's autobiographical account of his relationship with Genet in *Eloge de l'amitié* (57–63).

Genet, however, was seduced not by texts, but by political militants of color, and this seduction led not only to an oppositional reading but also to a solidarity with revolutionary activities, a solidarity he expressed through engaged writing. According to Mercer, Genet's political solidarities with the Black Panthers led "to a radically different subject-position which does not attempt to master or assimilate difference, but which speaks from a position of equality as part of a shared struggle to decolonize inherited models of subjectivity" (304). His erotic desire thus became the basis for not only political action but also an interrogation of his own subjectivity. Since, from the beginning of his career as a writer, he had distanced himself from the French society that had marginalized him, one might situate this self-interrogation in the context of questioning even his own Frenchness and subjectivity as a white man. His erotic attachment to the Other could then be seen as leading to a consideration of how the universal model of subjectivity has been constructed as a white category and to a challenge to the white monopoly on subject positions that authorize a speaking voice.

Barthes's Deconstruction of Tourism

Roland Barthes was another twentieth-century French gay male writer who engaged in sexual tourism and articulated his experiences in writing. Barthes describes his sexual adventures in Morocco in his posthumously published *Incidents* (1987), especially in the section entitled "Incidents," which is a series of short *aperçus* of Moroccans (especially Moroccan men) and his interaction with them. Many of these *aperçus* are sexual in nature and involve Barthes's negotiations with men for sex: "Petit instituteur de Marrakech: «Je ferai tout ce que vous voudrez», dit-il, plein d'effusion, de bonté et de complicité dans les yeux. Et cela veut dire: *je vous niquerai,* et cela seulement" (53–54). ("The little Marrakesh schoolteacher: 'I'll do whatever you want,' he says, effusively, his eyes filled with kindness and complicity. Which means: *I'll fuck you,* and that's all" [36].) As in the previous citation, often Barthes's reflection focuses on the linguistic aspect of sexuality, desire, and sexual tourism: "Démonstration de la pertinence phonologique: un jeune vendeur de bazar (d'un air engageant): *tu/ti* (non pertinent) *veux tapis/taper* (pertinent)?" (31). (A demonstration of phonological pertinence: a young vendor in the bazaar (with an appealing glance): *tu/ti* (you/yuh: non-pertinent) *veux tapis/taper* (want a rug/want to fuck: pertinent)?" [19].) Procuring sexual partners as a sexual tourist is a matter of textual interpretation. But is this interpretation any different from that of cruising at home?

In "Pointless Stories, Storyless Points" (1994), Chambers articulates the difference between cruising in Morocco in "Incidents" and at home in "Soirées de Paris" (another section of *Incidents*), all the while demonstrating a parallel between the two. Chambers first contrasts "the commoditized erotic relations [that is, sex for hire] that are so prominent in the cruisy Parisian text with the striking de-emphasis of commoditization in the touristic Moroccan text" (or Barthes's denial of his own neocolonial privilege and the economic aspect of sexual exchanges) and then establishes a link between the two by arguing that "commoditization . . . function[s] as a displaced figure for the incidence of colonialism in sexual relations" (17):

> Orientalism, then, in "Incidents," can be seen as a condition of emergence of the text's gayness. As for "Soirées de Paris," without going so far as to claim it as an Orientalist text, I do want to propose that the link between its stress on commoditization in the Parisian context and the Orientalist cultivation of the "romanesque" in "Incidents" lies, again, in the incidences of colonialist power in gay desire, coloniality being repressed, *along with* commoditization in "Incidents," but *by means of* a displacement that substitutes the commoditized for the colonial in "Soirées." . . . [T]he double forgetting of the colonial . . . seems to function as a condition of the emergence of gayness in each text. . . . (19–20)

As suggested above, sexual tourists do not need to leave home to be sexual tourists; Chambers's intricate analysis of two "cruisy" texts, one set at home, the other in a former colony, works out the economy of what might be called sexual tourism at home. But linking a text's "gayness" to its participation in a colonial economy, as in many accounts of homosexual tourism (some of which self-identify as antihomophobic), may dissimulate colonialism's and compulsory heterosexuality's mutual dependence on each other.

In some passages, Barthes reproduces racist stereotypes so accurately that one can only assume that he has accepted them as "truth":

> Dans la rue Samarine, j'allais à contre-courant du fleuve humain. J'eus le sentiment (rien d'érotique) qu'ils avaient tous un zob et que tous ces zobs, au rythme de ma marche, s'égrenaient comme un objet manufacturé qui se détache en cadence du moule. Dans ce flot, mais vêtue de la même étoffe rugueuse, des mêmes couleurs, des mêmes haillons, de temps en temps, une carence de zob. (53)

> In the Rue Samarine, I was walking against the current of this human
> stream. I had the feeling (nothing erotic about it) that each one had a *zob*
> (Arab [*sic*] argot for penis) and that all these *zobs,* as I passed them, were
> lined up like a mass-produced object rhythmically stamped out by a mold.
> In this stream, but dressed in the same rough cloth, in the same colors,
> the same rags, from time to time, a *zob* missing. (35)

Were it not for its description of Arab instead of black men, this passage
could be a textbook example of Fanon's description of the racist sexualiza-
tion of black male bodies: "[O]n n'aperçoit plus le nègre, mais un membre: le nègre est éclipsé. Il est fait membre. Il *est* penis" (1952, 137). ("[O]ne
is no longer aware of the Negro but only of a penis; the Negro is eclipsed.
He is turned into a penis. He *is* a penis" [170].) Barthes uses an Arabic
word for penis, thereby strengthening the essential link between Arab and
penis and reducing human beings (and their subjectivities) to their libido.
In the section, "Soirées de Paris," where Barthes describes his evening
cruising in Paris, he repeats this stereotype: "Paradoxe pur: un Arabe pour
qui existe le zob d'un autre et non seulement le sien (qui est son ego)"
(103). ("Pure paradox: an Arab for whom someone else's cock exists
and not only his own (which is his ego)" [67].) Paradoxically, however,
Barthes also deconstructs sexual tourism by turning the stereotypes
against the sexual tourist. With a sense of humor typical of the "Incidents," Barthes describes "«Papa», vieil Anglais charmant et dingue, [qui]
supprime *by sympathy* son lunch pendant le Ramadan (*by sympathy* pour
les petits garçons circoncis)" (32) ("'Papa,' a charming and crazy old Englishman, [who] *in sympathy* gives up his lunch during Ramadan (*in sympathy* for the circumcised little boys)" [20]). Here Barthes captures the
cliché of what the logic of North American gay slang might dub a cous-
cous queen, and again, unmasking the cliché is a matter of interpretation.
The Englishman states he is going without lunch in solidarity with the
practicing Muslims around him, but Barthes decodes this seemingly
noble action as concealing the desires of a sexual tourist. Barthes's interpretation (enclosed within parentheses) of the gesture, which he reveals
to be a cliché, serves as the punch line; by unmasking the stereotype,
Barthes turns the sexual tourist into the butt of a joke. In *Incidents,* therefore, sexual tourism involves sex with a stereotype; rather than crossing
boundaries, the European tourist makes love with the cliché s/he brings
with him/her.

Barthes elaborates the notion of tourism as visiting what one knows already in *L'empire des signes* (1970), wherein he describes traveling to Japan. While one should be careful not to assimilate Japan, which is not a former colony, with the Maghreb, regardless of however both have been lumped under the vague rubric of the "Orient," Orientalist discourse has constructed Japan as sufficiently different from the West to allow a number of conclusions about sexual tourism even if the same economic disparities do not exist between the tourist and the country s/he is visiting. Barthes declares in his introduction that he is not visiting a "real" country and its culture but a fiction of his own writing:

> Si je veux imaginer un peuple fictif, je puis lui donner un nom inventé, le traiter déclarativement comme un objet romanesque, fonder une nouvelle Garabagne, de façon à ne compromettre aucun pays réel dans ma fantaisie (mais alors c'est cette fantaisie même que je compromets dans les signes de la littérature). Je puis ainsi, sans prétendre en rien représenter ou analyser la moindre réalité (ce sont les gestes majeurs du discours occidental), prélever quelque part dans le monde (*là-bas*) un certain nombre de traits (mot graphique et linguistique), et de ces traits former délibérément un système. C'est ce sytème que j'appellerai le Japon.
>
> L'Orient et l'Occident ne peuvent donc être pris ici comme des « réalités », que l'on essaierait d'approcher et d'opposer historiquement, philosophiquement, culturellement, politiquement. (7)

> If I want to imagine a fictive nation, I can give it an invented name, treat it declaratively as a novelistic object, create a new Garabagne, so as to compromise no real country by my fantasy (though it is then that fantasy itself I compromise by the signs of literature). I can also—though in no way claiming to represent or to analyze reality itself (these being the major gestures of Western discourse)—isolate somewhere in the world (*faraway*) a certain number of features (a term employed in linguistics), and out of these features deliberately form a system. It is this system which I shall call: Japan.
>
> Hence Orient and Occident cannot be taken here as "realities" to be compared and contrasted historically, philosophically, culturally, politically. (3)

In Japan, Barthes visits a set of *idées reçues*. Yet his examination of Orientalist discourse, unlike Said's, is a self-examination from within, of how he has been formed in and through colonial discourse. Like the writers who visited North Africa with the *Arabian Nights* as their tour guides, Barthes comes to Japan with the cumbersome baggage of Orientalist discourse. He examines how European subjectivity is necessarily entangled with these discourses and even seems to take pleasure in inhabiting it. *L'empire des signes* takes its title from the quasi-pornographic Japanese film *L'empire des sens;* the set of signs that constitutes Japan is thus a sensual, sexual system of signs that gives/elicits pleasure and desire.

Barthes articulates a philosophy of sexual tourism around what he labels the rendez-vous. The following passage is reproduced handwritten in the text:

> Ouvrez un guide de voyage: vous y trouverez d'ordinaire un petit lexique, mais ce lexique portera bizarrement sur des choses ennuyeuses et inutiles: la douane, la poste, l'hôtel, le coiffeur, le médecin, les prix. Cependant, qu'est-ce que voyager? Rencontrer. Le seul lexique important est celui du rendez-vous. (25)

> Open a travel guide: usually you will find a brief lexicon which strangely enough concerns only certain boring and useless things: customs, mail, the hotel, the barber, the doctor, prices. Yet what is traveling? Meetings. The only lexicon that counts is the one which refers to the rendezvous. (13)

Barthes follows up on this passage several times by making up for this lack in typical tourist guides and giving a lexicon of the rendez-vous. *L'empire des signes* thus serves as Barthes's ideal tourist guide to Japan and even suggests that any Western "study" of the Orient (supposedly academic and objective) is a potential tourist guide. Barthes first gives the Japanese words necessary for the preliminaries of suggesting a rendez-vous: the translations of "rendez-vous," "tous les deux," "où?" and "quand?" (28) ("rendezvous," "both [of us]," "where?" and "when?" [17]). Then he gives the Japanese words necessary for confirming the rendez-vous: "ici," "ce soir," "aujourd'hui," "à quelle heure?" "demain," and "quatre heures" (34) ("here," "tonight," "today," "what time?" "tomorrow," "four o'clock" [23]). The surprise (punch line?) comes when Barthes gives the necessary words for breaking or putting off the rendez-vous: "peut-être," "fatigué," "impossible," and "je veux dormir" (51) ("maybe," "tired," "impossible," "I want to sleep" [37]). The leitmotiv of the rendez-vous in *L'empire des signes* thus parallels the rendez-vous Barthes sets up then breaks off in "Soirée de Paris." In traveling to Japan, Barthes might expect a rendez-vous with the "real" Japan. The Japan of his expectation, however, is a construction of the Orientalist discourse in which he has been educated. His visit to Japan is then a *rendez-vous manqué* with another culture, a rendez-vous that cannot but fail.

Les 1001 années de la nostalgie: An Allegory of Reading the Sexual

If Boudjedra's *Les 1001 années* allegorizes Orientalist readings of Arabic texts, it also performs a counterreading that may serve as the inspiration for anticolonial resistance. The villagers, led by Mohamed, revolt against the invaders/filmmakers/readers of Arabic literature, expel them from the country, and overthrow the governor. Mohamed takes inspiration for his revolt in the texts of the past. He reads the work of the historian Ibn Khaldoun, erotic classical literature in Arabic, and the scholarly works of Arab scientists and mathematicians. In particular, he studies the histories of past revolutions in the Islamic world as a source for tactics in the armed struggle against the Americans. The nostalgia of the novel's title therefore has both colonial and anticolonial potential. It is both the Orientalizing nostalgia of the filmmakers' gaze directed at a glorious past as well as the nostalgia that leads Mohamed to study classical texts and incorporate his readings into an anti-imperialist project. *Les 1001 années* paradoxically takes inspiration from the same *Arabian Nights* that authorize the Americans' exoticizing vision of the Arab world; for Boudjedra's novel is replete with fantastical elements reminiscent of the Arabic classic: flying carpets abound, Mohamed controls his shadow's position regardless of the sun's position, women grow silkworms between their legs, and a polar iceberg is transported to North Africa to cool off the weather. Boudjedra, therefore, does not reject the texts that have inspired Orientalist readings; he rereads them, and his rereadings lead to both an anti-Orientalist criticism and an anti-imperialist politics. His counterreading serves as an example to anyone who seeks to examine sexuality within Maghrebian literature.

Chapter Two

MOHA THE THEORY MACHINE

In *Autobiographical Voices* (1989), Françoise Lionnet turns *métissage* (literally a mixing of races through sexual reproduction) into not only a cultural practice but also a textual and critical one:

> *Métissage* . . . brings together biology and history, anthropology and philosophy, linguistics and literature. . . . [I]t is a reading practice that allows me to bring out the interreferential nature of a particular set of texts, which I believe to be of fundamental importance for the understanding of many postcolonial cultures. If . . . identity is strategy, then *métissage* is the fertile ground of our heterogeneous and heteronomous identities as postcolonial subjects. (8)

With a play on words, Lionnet describes a "mé-tissage" (29), or weaving of voices, that links reading practices with the constitution of subjectivity.[1] The eponymous character of Tahar Ben Jelloun's novel *Moha le fou, Moha le sage* produces a similar *métissage* of voices that is also a theory of reading and of postcolonial subjectivity. In addition, Moha suggests that such a theoretical *métissage* can be found as much within Maghrebian literature as in the canons of literary theory. In many ways, Moha's flow of voices resembles the "machines désirantes" ("desiring-machines") described by Gilles Deleuze and Félix Guattari in *Anti-Oedipus* (1972):

---

1. Lionnet expands on Glissant's discussion of *métissage* in *Le discours antillais* (1981, 250–52, 462–63). The notion of *métissage* as a form of *tissage* is suggested in the following sentence by Glissant: "The poetics of *métissage* is exactly that of Relation: nonlinear, nonprophetic, *woven* [*tissé*] from arduous patience and incomprehensible detours" (251, my emphasis and trans.).

It is at work everywhere, functioning smoothly at times, at other times in fits and starts. It breathes, it heats [up], it eats. It shits and fucks. [Ça respire, ça chauffe, ça mange. Ça chie, ça baise.] What a mistake to have ever said *the* id [*le* ça]. Everywhere [there are] machines—real ones, not figurative ones: machines driving other machines, machines being driven by other machines, with all the necessary couplings and connections. An organ-machine is plugged into an energy-source-machine: the one produces a flow that the other interrupts [coupe]. . . . This is because there is always a flow-producing machine, and another machine connected to it that interrupts [opérant une coupure] or draws off part of this flow (the breast-the mouth). (1, 5; 7, 11 in original)

In addition to the body's excretions (or products), this flow describes the flow of discourses, textualities, and the interpretations that cut up, cut off, and interrupt the flow of literary discourses, while producing even more discourses. For literary production is yet another flow, a schizophrenic flow from desiring machines. Moha is, in short, a theory machine.

A babbling fool and madman, Moha also speaks words of wisdom as the conduit for many marginalized individuals whose silenced voices find an outlet through him. His rantings constitute a biting critique of postindependence Maghrebian governments, and he formulates his own subjectivity through the articulation of others' identities, even and especially when they should conflict with his own. It may be less surprising that a political critique can offer a model of personal subjectivity given the feminist slogan of the 1970s, "The personal is political." As in Nancy K. Miller's assertion (1991) that "eighties feminism has made it possible to see that the personal is also the theoretical" (21), *Moha* offers, through an individual's story, a theorization of the postcolonial writer's role in society and of ways of reading postcolonial texts. As in Deleuze and Guattari's description of discursive production, which flows from a "machine désirante," Moha transmits sexually marginalized voices and advances postcolonial writing as a sexual endeavor. The writer is not just any traitor to the Nation as conceived by the ruling class, s/he is a sexual traitor. Moha projects sexuality (as one projects rockets or shells) into the public sphere to air the Nation's dirty laundry.

Voices from the Margins

The voices that speak through Moha include those of the Patriarche, a personification of patriarchal authority who died during his pilgrimage to Mecca; Aïcha, a servant sold to the Patriarche by her father; Dada, a black slave bought by the Patriarche in Sudan who becomes his second wife only to be mistreated by the first; a child from the shantytowns; M. Milliard, the Patriarche's son who becomes rich after his father's death; and a Native American. The novel begins with the report of a man who was tortured to death, and is framed as his voice, which also speaks through Moha. Moha also dialogues with "son vieil ami Moché, le fou des juifs" (112) (his old friend Moché, the Jews' madman) and directs a political critique against the bank director and the psychiatrist, who do not have the privilege of speaking through Moha but argue against him.

Moha voices his political critique against the bank director, the psychiatrist, and M. Milliard, who articulate postindependence nationalist discourses that operate through exclusion. For M. Milliard, class struggle is a foreign concept: "Quant à la lutte des classes, c'est une notion importée; elle est étrangère à notre réalité, pernicieuse pour notre société" (97). (As for class struggle, it is an imported concept, foreign to our reality and pernicious for our society.) He repeats a certain tendency within many independence movements that denied the importance of any struggle other than the national one. In the Algerian context, this tendency was particularly strong; a large portion of the FLN denied the existence of classes in Algeria beyond those of colonizer and colonized, thereby rejecting the necessity of continuing class struggle after independence (Etienne 54). One effect of the doctrine (intended or not) was to cushion a newly forming elite from potential calls to class struggle. For the bank director, it is democracy and socialism that are imported ideals: "Tu me parles de démocratie. La démocratie, c'est une idée importée, comme le socialisme" (127). (You speak to me of democracy. Democracy is an imported idea, just like socialism.) The psychiatrist also rants against "toutes ces histoires importées de l'étranger" (155) (all these notions imported from abroad). Democracy, socialism, and class struggle are thus foreign notions excluded from official definitions of the Nation. In a recuperation of nationalist discourses from the time of independence struggles, these three characters argue that these notions threaten the very Nation itself and associate them with the former colonizer. Yet these articulations of menaces are situated in *Moha*, they are spoken by those whose interests they serve. It is not the entire Nation that is in danger, only its governing elite; formulations of national identity that attempt to exclude people who do not satisfy homogenizing prescriptions serve a ruling class in its attempt to consolidate power.

Madness as a Political Weapon

In Deleuze and Guattari's account, schizophrenia and the deterritorialization that characterizes it are both produced by capitalism and signify its limit and possible destruction. Literary production and criticism, as schizophrenic activities, therefore contain anticapitalist possibilities. The psychiatrist in *Moha* embodies the link between mainstream psychoanalysis and capitalism established by Deleuze and Guattari, and Moha, like their schizophrenic, resists not only the psychiatrist's attempt to control him, but also capitalism. Moha's verbal joust with the bank director coincides with a peculiar political action, tearing up money in front of the bank. By doing so, like Deleuze and Guattari's machine "opérant une coupure," he stops the flow of capital and interrupts the circulation of money: "Je suis envoyé par le Prophète pour arrêter sa circulation. Je le prends le soir et je le déchire le matin. Quand il tombe entre mes mains, c'est fini, il n'ira plus dans d'autres mains. J'arrête l'argent. J'arrête le cirque . . ." (91). (I have been sent by the Prophet to stop its circulation. I collect it in the evening and tear it up in the morning. Once it falls into my hands, that's it, it will never go into other hands. I stop the money. I stop the circus. . . .) As Moha becomes a wrench thrown in the machinery of capitalism, a man in the crowd calls for his arrest: "Arrêtez-le; il est fou; il manque de piété. Déchirer l'argent! Il devrait au moins le donner aux pauvres! Appelez la police. Il faut l'arrêter; cet homme est dangereux pour notre société et notre religion" (91). (Arrest this man; he's crazy; he has no respect for religion. Tearing up money! He should at least give it to the poor! Call the police! He must be stopped; this man is dangerous for our society and our religion.) Moha's anticapitalist politics are characterized as a threat to the Nation and to Islam, a threat that should be dealt with by confining him to the Nation's margins.

In his opposition to neocolonial capitalism and the ruling elite, Moha continues political actions he began before independence, which were also linked to his madness:

> Une fois, c'était avant l'indépendance, je hurlais dans le marché contre la présence des Français chez nous. . . . J'étais fou, alors je pouvais tout dire. . . . Il y avait un officier français qui se méfiait un peu. Il doutait de ma folie. Il travaillait avec un mouchard du quartier—tiens, aujourd'hui, il est sous-préfet ou directeur, je ne sais plus. Oui, le mouchard glissa dans l'oreille du Français que je faisais le fou et que mon langage était codé. (134–35)

> At one time, before independence, I shouted out in the market place
> against the French presence in our country. . . . I was crazy, so I could say
> anything. . . . There was a French officer who was a bit suspicious. He
> doubted my madness. He used to work with a neighborhood snitch—hey,
> today he's an assistant commissioner or director, one or the other. Yeah,
> the snitch gave word to the French man that I was only acting crazy and
> that my language was coded.

The French imprison Moha—suspected of doing the work of a spy, of
giving away secrets through secret code—for being a traitor to colonial
rule. His betrayal, however, does not require a secret code, he blurts it
out on the public square. Moha's betrayer, the traitor to the nationalist
cause (the nation here being an independent Morocco), now works for
the very nation he betrayed. Ironically, he is charged with bestowing
official national identity—"c'est lui qui délivre les passeports aujour-
d'hui" (135) (he's the one who gives out passports now)—the very identity
Moha has been refused: "C'est vrai, je n'ai pas de papiers d'identité . . ."
(166). (It's true, I don't have any identification papers. . . .) At the end of
the novel, men in white coats carry Moha away to a psychiatric hospital
where the psychiatrist interrogates him and administers the shock therapy
that finally kills him. Whereas the French imprisoned Moha for not
"really" being mad, postindependence forces, using his madness as an excuse, imprison him because of his political danger. He is first excluded
from the Nation by being locked away from the public sphere in the
margins. His final exclusion (final as in last, but also that exclusion from
which there is no return) is his own extermination. The removal of
threats to the Nation can be physical (imprisonment, internment in psychiatric hospitals, deportation, or elimination through assassination), or
they can be excluded definitionally—marginalized, defined as foreign
agents or as abnormal, or denied official papers of identification, all
methods described in many Maghrebian novels. Since Moha's confinement under colonialism parallels the one he experiences under the new
national elite, Ben Jelloun creates a Fanonian link between colonial authority and the postindependence bourgeoisie, between anticolonial
struggles and struggles against nationalized oppression.

Cross-Identifications

Unlike other voices that speak through Moha, Moché, "le fou des juifs"
(112) (the Jews' madman), dialogues with him. Moché, whose name is

not unlike Moha's, appears as his second self. With Moché, Ben Jelloun introduces the idea of physical exclusion from the Nation based on religious difference, in this case the departure of most Maghrebian Jews after independence and, especially, the Six-Days War. Whereas this departure strengthens official national identity, it destroys Moha's concept of who he is, of his identity as rooted in his nation:

> Tu sais, Moché, chaque juif qui quitte le pays, c'est un peu de moi-même qui s'en va. Un jour, je vais me retrouver sans mon corps, avec juste une ombre. Ils partent tous. Mais de quoi ont-ils peur? Quel malheur! Il paraît en plus que les juifs d'Europe et d'Amérique, tu sais, les plus riches, méprisent nos enfants. Ils ne sont pas heureux là-bas, je te jure! Alors ils arrivent avec des valises d'illusions et après ils se rendent compte que c'est difficile de vivre sans racines. Ils meurent de nostalgie et de mélancolie. Il y en a qui ne parlent pas un mot d'hébreu. Ils ne connaissent que l'arabe ou le berbère. Moi je sais qu'ils ne sont pas heureux là-bas. On ne quitte pas un pays si facilement. La terre vous habite. . . . (116–17)

> You know, Moché, each time a Jew leaves the country, a bit of myself goes with him. One day, I'll find myself without a body, with only a shadow. They're all leaving. But what are they afraid of? What a misfortune! What's more, I hear that European and American Jews, the richest, you know, look down on our children. They aren't happy there, I swear! So they arrive with suitcases full of illusions, and they later realize that it's hard to live without roots. They are dying from nostalgia and melancholia. Some of them don't speak a word of Hebrew. They only know Arabic or Berber. I know they're not happy there. You can't leave a country so easily. The land inhabits you. . . .

Moha reverses the logic of Zionist discourse whereby Israel is the homeland and promised land. For Moché and Moha, Morocco is the homeland for Arabs and Jews, and, for Moroccan Jews, Israel is a land of exile: "[S]i Moché avait été emmené en Israël? Non! Il crèverait plutôt que de partir en terre d'exil . . ." (112). (What if Moché had been taken to Israel? No! he'd rather die than go away to a land of exile. . . .) In this reversal of Zionist logic, *Moha* resembles many works written by Jewish writers from Arab countries.[2] In his consideration of the Moroccan Jewish diaspora (diaspora, here, from two different starting points, Israel, of course, and Morocco), Ben Jelloun rewrites the official history of Arab/Jewish separa-

---

2. On this point, see Alcalay. See also Shohat, "Sephardim in Israel: Zionism from the Standpoint of Its Jewish Victims."

tion in Morocco by describing a shared experience in the face of French colonialism:

> [L]es soldats français tirant sur la foule—juive et musulmane—qui mani-
> festait à l'entrée du port. C'était au début du siècle; l'armée française
> s'installait dans le pays. Il y eut beaucoup de morts. . . . A l'époque, l'ad-
> ministration coloniale ne faisait pas de différence entre les juifs et les mu-
> sulmans. (113–14)

> French soldiers firing on the crowd—Jewish and Muslim—that was
> demonstrating at the port entrance. It was at the beginning of the century;
> the French army was moving into the country. There were many
> deaths. . . . At that time, the colonial administration didn't distinguish be-
> tween Jews and Muslims.

The reference to the colonial administration's not making a distinction between Arabs and Jews at the beginning of the twentieth century in Morocco contrasts with an earlier distinction made in Algeria where all Algerian Jews were declared French citizens in 1870 as a part of the French divide-and-conquer tactic. Moha counters the French strategy by refusing the divisions that must be internalized by the colonized for the strategy to work. When he and Moché "décidèrent de former un groupe «de démence infernale» pour lutter contre l'occupant" (114) (decided to form a group of "infernal insanity" to struggle against the occupier), the border crossing involved in Moha's cross-identification is thus a source of strength not weakness and leads to anticolonial resistance.

The Feminist Menace

Another border Moha crosses in his delirium is the one separating genders. Moha voices a resistance to sexual oppression and identifies with the threat of this resistance, with the feminist menace to the Nation:

> Un peu de volonté, ô vous que la lune a damnés! un peu de volupté, ô
> vous, femmes absentes, femmes emmurées, femmes envoyées aux champs
> l'enfant dans le dos, femmes du silence; ô femmes, pourquoi vous
> cultivent-ils dans les ténèbres avec des sexes en bois, sans caresses, sans
> tendresse? Célébrées par le chant, méprisées par le temps et l'oubli. . . . O
> femmes, ils vous écartent les jambes depuis des siècles. Ils ne parlent pas.
> Ils ne murmurent rien. Votre cri est absorbé et vos jambes posées sur leurs
> épaules. Munissez-vous de lames de rasoir et déchirez sans pitié leur visage

et leurs certitudes. . . . Vous dansez pour faire bander des brutes; des gars
heureux de se masturber quand vous faites trembler le ventre et les fesses.
(46–47)

Willpower, you whom the moon has damned! a little voluptuous/sexual
pleasure, you, absent women, walled-up women, women sent to the fields
with children on your backs, women of silence; women, why do they cultivate you in the dark with wooden sexes, without caresses, without tender-
ness? Celebrated in song, scorned and forgotten by time. . . . Women, they
have been spreading your legs for centuries. They don't speak. They whis-
per nothing. Your cry is absorbed and your legs placed on their shoulders.
Arm yourselves with razor blades, and tear up their faces and certainties
without pity. . . . You dance to give bullies hard-ons; guys happy to masturbate when your bellies and butts tremble.[3]

In terms of his relation to feminism, Ben Jelloun shares many other male
Maghrebian writers' connection of patriarchy or sexism with both colonialism and the postindependence ruling elite. Feminism, then, becomes
a political weapon in national and postindependence struggles. Women,
however, have benefited far less from independence struggles, which re-
lied on their participation:

C'est vrai, vous avez fait la guerre contre les Français. Vous étiez utiles et
courageuses. Vous avez fait des opérations mémorables. Quelques pré-
noms de femmes sont restés sur front de nuage. Après la libération du
pays, ils ont fermé les murs et verrouillé les portes. Même les terrasses vous
sont à présent interdites. Zone extrêmement dangereuse pour la sécurité
du morceau de bois. (47)

It's true, you waged war against the French. You were useful and courageous. You carried out memorable operations. Some women's names have
remained on the front of clouds. After the country's liberation, they closed
the walls and bolted the doors. Even the rooftops are off-limits for you
now. Extremely dangerous zone for the security of the piece of wood.

Gains made by women during the revolution in terms of being able to
circulate freely as equals with their male comrades have been rolled back.
    The language Ben Jelloun uses to describe the "sécurité du morceau
de bois" (security of the piece of wood) invokes not only the enclosure of
women to protect male honor (which resides in the vagina of a faithful

---

3. The image of women as a field to be cultivated is found in the *Qur'an:* "Women are like fields
for you, so cultivate your fields as you like . . ." (Surah 2, 223).

wife to which the husband claims property rights), but also national security. The domestic sphere, like the Nation, has restricted zones, off-limit territories. The security of the "morceau de bois," therefore, is also a matter of national security. Indeed, the reduction of women to their "morceau de bois," kept under lock and key, directly follows the triumph of the nationalist struggle. Women, hardly a minority, are locked in the margins of the Nation, away from the public space of its citizens. Moha, by bringing voices out of the margins onto the public square, questions this marginalization and the separation of private and public as female and male spaces. When he says, "Munissez-vous de lames de rasoir" (Arm yourselves with razor blades), he advocates an armed struggle (what the French would call *la lutte des sexes* in parallel with class struggle), in which women fight for themselves instead of just for the Nation that might later exclude them. Yet, the voice of women's struggles is spoken by a man who not only expresses solidarity with their struggle but also constitutes himself as its leader: "O femmes, suivez mes pas, suivez-moi dans la folie d'amour et de rire" (46). (Women, follow in my footsteps, follow me in the madness of love and laughter.) One might even argue that his cry silences women ("femmes du silence" [women of silence], "Votre cri est absorbé" [your cry is absorbed]). In that sense, Moha takes on the role of more than a few male "feminists" of Maghrebian novels written by men, male "feminists" who criticize women for not revolting against the bad men, as if all the best feminists were men. I would include in this category the narrator of Rachid Boudjedra's *La répudiation* and Driss Ferdi in Driss Chraïbi's *Le passé simple* (though I would not necessarily blame these authors for their characters' faults). This role is conspicuously absent from women's texts. A question thus arises as to whether many male writers use feminism not in the interest of women's struggles, but merely to advance their own political agenda.

The "morceau de bois" also refers to female sexual organs that are not supposed to feel pleasure. (While the "sexes en bois" [wooden sexes] of the first passage seems to indicate erect penises, when read with the second passage, the expression becomes more ambiguous, possibly implying either sex.) On the one hand, while decrying the lack of physical or affective pleasure in marriage, Moha nonetheless contextualizes the feminist demand for women's right to sexual pleasure as part of marriage, as if pleasure for women can come only from men. On the other, he also condemns the form marriage has taken and seems to dismiss it through mockery:

Ils agitent leurs fesses, bavent par le sexe et par la bouche. Ils sont contents: le devoir conjugal accompli. Et dire qu'ils prient avant! Se mettre en direction de La Mecque pour une prière nocturne avant de pénétrer la femme qui n'ose pas se toucher. (48)

They grind their butts, drool through their penises and their mouths. They are content: conjugal duty accomplished. And to think that they pray first! Turning towards Mecca for an evening prayer before penetrating their wife who doesn't dare touch herself.

Here, Ben Jelloun associates this sexual misery or deprivation with Islam, but in an earlier passage he qualifies this association: "Il y a quelque chose de fêlé entre l'homme et la femme dans notre société. L'Islam. On dit que c'est écrit dans le Livre. Non. Ils font dire ce qu'ils veulent au Livre" (47–48). (Something tears men and women apart in our society. Islam. They say it's written in the Book. No. They make the Book say what they want it to.) The Islam that separates the sexes is a particular reading of Islam. Though, on the one hand, Moha criticizes a certain Islam, on the other, he likes to go to Mosque and is able to find the basis of his political critique in Islam: "On trouve tout dans l'Islam, même le socialisme" (79). (You can find everything in Islam, even socialism.) Like Fatima Mernissi in *The Veil and the Male Elite* (1987) and Assia Djebar in *Loin de Médine* (1991)—who, instead of denouncing Islam as inherently antifeminist, have gone back to reread the founding texts in order to uncover Islam's feminist possibilities—Moha denounces the role of Islam in official nationalist discourse. He also discloses, however, how alternative versions of Islam denounce those who deploy it to justify exclusion from the Nation.

Transgressions Unveiled

Moha's final cross-identification is with the Patriarche's resistance to the family narrative from within and to its fear of miscegenation. This identification is perhaps the strongest in the novel because it overrides the class antagonism that, given Moha's political positions, should divide the two men. The most sustained passage of unbridled sexuality is the voice given to the Patriarche's delirium when he falls in love with his second wife. At this moment of madness (which connects him to Moha), the Patriarche's words threaten to destroy his privilege:

. . . pénis énorme qui vous regarde, il vous surveille; mains . . . argent . . . couilles d'Antar . . . sexe, lèvres du sexe . . . vu . . . visage troué ce n'est pas

le mien, c'est le votre, c'est comme pour les dents du sexe . . . les dents du
vagin . . . le Prophète m'excite . . . l'anus . . . les couilles . . . les miennes,
rideau sur vos yeux . . . l'anus, mon doigt dans l'anus, je le suce, le ciel, le
cheval, la chamelle, le fleuve de gamins . . . baiser . . . baiser la va-
che . . . ma main sur ses seins . . . la roue . . . sept cent mille soleils . . . le
jour . . . trois cents milliards de sexes et moi qui danse sur les poils du
cul . . . la fenêtre . . . l'argent . . . les papillons sur mon sexe. . . . (66)

. . . enormous penis looking at you, keeping you under surveillance;
hands . . . money . . . Antar's balls . . . sex, lips of the sex . . . seen . . . faces
with holes it isn't mine, it's yours, it's like the teeth of the sex . . . the vagina's teeth . . . the Prophet excites me . . . anus . . . balls . . . urine . . . mine,
a curtain over your eyes . . . anus, my finger in my anus, I suck it, sky,
horse, camel, river of kids . . . fucking . . . fucking the cow . . . my hand
on his/her breasts . . . the wheel . . . seven hundred thousand suns . . .
day . . . three hundred billion sexes and I who dance on ass hairs . . .
window . . . money . . . butterflies on my penis . . .[4]

Here, the Patriarche fantasizes about giant penises and bestiality (cows
and butterflies—quite a range of species), is turned on by the Prophet
and excited anally and by coprophagy, and in fact, seems erotically self-
sufficient. At the beginning of the passage, he describes the penis as a
source of surveillance. The state or police that places its citizens under
surveillance is thus equipped with a phallic power. The word "argent"
shortly follows, connecting phallocracy to capitalism and the very flow
of money Moha cuts off. But, like Moha, the Patriarche distances himself
from this power. By invoking the *vagina dentata,* he raises the specter of
castration as an erotic possibility rather than an anxiety. Describing a
number of erogenous zones, he shifts the site of male pleasure from the
penis and diffuses it across the entire body in an eroticism usually more
associated with the feminine. The Patriarche's most notable site of pleasure is his anus; he thus makes himself a candidate for anal stimulation
and evokes the possibility of sodomy, in which he would most likely be
the passive partner.

Far from being the exemplary patriarch, because of his transgressive
sexual desire (which involves miscegenation at the expense of upholding

4. According to Chebel (1995), Antar was a poet of the pre-Islamic period who was in love with
his cousin Abla. Antar was the illegitimate son of a Bedouin lord and Abla was of noble birth of a
rival tribe. He wrote a mou'allaqa (pre-Islamic poem of great length) about his love, a mad love,
hence the Patriarche's identification with him (88–89).

the family values of the new Nation), he comes to occupy what Kaja Silverman calls "male subjectivity at the margins"—"[t]he kinds of male subjectivity which . . . open in a variety of ways onto the domain of femininity[,] . . . masculinities which . . . not only acknowledge but embrace castration, alterity, and specularity" (3). Maghrebian literature offers many examples of similarly marginal subjectivities, a few of which even experience the threat of castration (even physical castration) as a source of *jouissance*.[5] Because he embraces marginal sexuality (and therefore marginal subjectivity), the Patriarche can no longer be considered a model citizen who produces (reproduction *qua* economic production) new citizens (preferably not black ones) for the Nation and who makes his household a building block of the Nation. Instead of adopting the position of many nationalists who called on colonized men to be real men and stand up to their enemy, Moha embraces a subjectivity associated with the feminine and transforms it into solidarity. Moha's subjectivity, then, thrives on its emasculation.

In his discursive deluge, the Patriarche upsets the hierarchy within his household by exchanging the position of master for slave: ". . . qu'elle revienne la femme noire d'Afrique . . . je suis à elle, elle m'a acheté sur le marché . . . je suis son esclave . . . qu'elle vienne pour que je lui obéisse . . ." (68) (. . . let her come back, black, African woman . . . I am hers, she bought me at the market . . . I am her slave . . . let her come so I can obey her . . .). Here, one can see why the first wife and children have done all they could to expel Dada and her daughter from the household. She threatens to lessen each family member's share of inheritance, of course. In addition, her class lowers the family's standing; not only is she of a darker race, but through her daughter, she has also "darkened" the family through miscegenation. The father's sexual crossing of class, racial, and national boundaries has threatened the identity of all the other family members as if his deviance were contagious. The microcosm of the household, here, serves as the model for what the crossing of these boundaries does to national identities in the macrocosm of the Nation. It is between the Patriarche and Dada that the most literal *métissage* oc-

5. The French word "jouissance" may signify, in general, any intense pleasure (bliss), or more specifically, orgasm. The verb "jouir" can mean "to cum" or "to enjoy" (as one says "jouir d'une bonne santé"—"to enjoy good health"). Because of the wider connotation of the French word and because, since Barthes, it has acquired the additional meaning of discursive pleasure, I shall use the French term.

curs, in the form of the child they have together. The product of this miscegenation is but a small part of the mixings of identities, cultures, and theories the novel generates.[6]

In "Défendre la diversité culturelle du Maghreb," Ben Jelloun sets up an opposition between the language of unveiling (French) and the language of the Qur'an (Arabic), perhaps maintaining a sex/religion opposition: "Le fait d'écrire en français incite les auteurs à aller plus loin dans la critique. L'arabe—la langue du Coran—se prête moins au jeu de la dénonciation" (272). (The very fact of writing in French moves authors to go further with their criticisms. Arabic, the language of the Qur'an, lends itself less to the play of denunciation.) The Patriarche, however, experiences religion as erotically charged:

> Que Dieu maudisse la religion du vagin de ta mère . . . venez prier, ma tombe est ouverte . . . venez mourir dans ma tombe . . . on forniquera la nuit et le jour nous serons assistés des anges du paradis . . . on forniquera avec la mer et les sables . . . la nuit . . . je suis la nuit et la révélation . . . je vois le Prophète . . . non, c'est moi le Prophète, prophète des temps hideux, prophète de la haine, prophète du malheur . . . je serai le premier prophète du sexe. . . . (67–69)

> May God curse the religion of your mother's vagina . . . come and pray, my tomb is open . . . come and die in my tomb . . . we'll fornicate by night and by day we'll be assisted by angels from paradise . . . we'll fornicate with the sea and the sand . . . night . . . I am the night and the revelation . . . I see the Prophet . . . no, I am the Prophet, prophet of hideous times, prophet of hate, prophet of misfortune . . . I'll be the first prophet of sex. . . .

The Patriarche, like Moha, does not completely reject Islam (he dies on a pilgrimage, we remember, and is thus, according to Islamic teachings, guaranteed a place in paradise), but he does produce a counternarrative of it. Homi K. Bhabha (1994) has described "[c]ounter-narratives of the nation that continually evoke and erase its totalizing boundaries—both actual and conceptual—[and] disturb those ideological manoeuvres through which 'imagined communities' are given essentialist identities"

6. While the Patriarche's mad love for his slave may be transgressive in that it breaks taboos against miscegenation, it may also participate in a long tradition of racist stereotypes. Western racist discourses do not hold a monopoly on the hypersexualization of black bodies; the stereotype of the insatiable black African has a long tradition in classical Arabic literature as well. The *Arabian Nights* begin as the sultan discovers his wife having sex with a black slave. This racist stereotype also contains a sexist component since women are supposedly only satisfied by black men, with their supposedly oversized penises.

(149).[7] Moha articulates a counternarrative of Islam, which, in the Moroccan context, is also always a counternarrative of the Nation. Like many counternarratives of the Nation, this counternarrative of Islam (like many more examined in this study) is sexual. Ben Jelloun does not reject Islamic tradition; he is perfectly in keeping with an entire tradition of erotic literature written in the language of the Qur'an.

Homosexuality Unveiled

In "Jeh'a ou la saillie" (1991), Jean Déjeux describes a popular figure of Mediterranean culture, Jeh'a, a sort of trickster: "Jeh'a joue donc le fou et déclenche le fou rire, mais il n'est pas fou" (108). (Jeh'a plays the fool/madman and elicits mad laughter, but he's not crazy.) Rather, "Jeh'a est en fait un sage, un homme avisé, qui a une philosophie de la vie à sa manière. . . . Jeh'a fait donc l'idiot parce qu'il est obligé d'agir ainsi et qu'il est sage de se faire passer pour tel" (112). (Jeh'a is in fact a wise man, a sensible man who has his own particular philosophy of life. . . . Jeh'a plays the idiot because he is obliged to do so and because he is wise to pass himself off as such.) From the title of Ben Jelloun's novel, one might surmise that Moha is a Jeh'a figure. In fact, Déjeux includes the novel among literary adaptations of the Jeh'a tales (119). According to Déjeux, Jeh'a plays what one might describe as a political role: "Jeh'a astutely manipulates irony. Jeh'a is rebellious against merchants, men of religion, the wealthy, men of law, the powerful, who always want to dominate and take advantage of others" (114). So Moha's political actions of stopping the flow of money, attacking religious hypocrisy, and resisting colonial and postindependence authorities are consistent with Jeh'a's traditional function. Whereas, in "Défendre la diversité culturelle," Ben Jelloun associates such activities with the Francophone novel, Jeh'a attests to the fact that such a role can also be found in Arab and Berber popular cultures.

In *Les fourberies de Si Djeh'a,* Auguste Mouliéras translates a Kabyle version of one of the Jeh'a tales:

Si Djeh'a et ses amis au bain

Un jour, ses amis causaient et disaient entre eux: «Emmenons Si Djeh'a au bain, nous nous moquerons de lui.» Ils emportèrent tous des œufs avec eux. Si Djeh'a ne savait rien de cela. Ils partirent. Quand ils arrivèrent au bain, ils dirent: «Allons, pondons tous des œufs. Celui qui ne pondra pas

---

7. The allusion here is to Anderson.

un œuf payera le prix du bain pour nous.» L'un d'eux se leva, se mit à caqueter à la manière des poules et retira un œuf de dessous lui. Tous les autres en firent autant. Le tour de Si Djeh'a étant arrivé, il se leva, chanta comme un coq et se précipita sur ses amis qui se levèrent et s'enfuirent en disant: «Que fais-tu donc, Si Djeh'a?» — «Quoi! dit-il, vous êtes vingt poules; il faut bien qu'il y ait un coq parmi vous.» (87–88)

Si Jeh'a and His Friends at the *Hammam*

One day his friends were chatting among themselves: "Let's take Si Jeh'a to the *hammam* and take advantage of him." They all carried eggs with them, but Si Jeh'a knew nothing about it. So they left. When they got to the *hammam,* they said, "Okay, let's all lay an egg. He who can't lay an egg will pay for everyone's visit to the *hammam.* One of them got up, began cackling like a hen, and pulled an egg out from under himself. All the others did the same. When Si Jeh'a's turn came, he got up, crowed like a rooster, and flung himself at his friends, who got up and ran away, saying, "What are you doing, Si Jeh'a?"

"What!" he said, "you are twenty hens; there has to be a cock for you!"[8]

In this tale, Jeh'a resorts to the threat of sodomy to defend himself against being taken advantage of. Sodomy, therefore, becomes a political weapon, and the site for this sexual resistance is the *hammam.* Moha, as well, deploys same-sex eroticism in his resistance narrative and, in some cases, describes sexual crossings of class boundaries, as in the following case of boys from the shantytowns:

Ils s'amusent dans les champs. Ils se montrent leur sexe. Ils se caressent un peu. Des fois ils partent aux champs avec une nouvelle recrue, générale-ment un garçon de la ville, un garçon de riches qui s'ennuie dans la villa de ses parents. Vers la fin de la journée, ils lui font comprendre qu'il faut bien qu'il baisse son pantalon. L'enfant citadin se laisse faire mais leur de-mande de ne pas lui faire mal. Des caresses inégales, sans risque. C'est le prix qu'il faut payer pour passer une journée avec les gosses libres des ter-rains vagues. Les parents citadins en ont peur. Alors ils protègent leurs enfants par des distractions bien innocentes. (92)

They have fun in the fields. They show each other their genitals. They caress each other a little. Sometimes they leave for the fields with a new recruit, usually a city boy, a rich boy who gets bored in his parents' villa.

8. In "Si Djeh'a et les anecdotes qui lui sont attribuées," a study of the tales included in Moulié-ras's collection, René Basset lists Turkish and Arabic versions of the same tale (52).

Towards the end of the day, they let him know he must pull down his pants. The city boy lets them but asks them not to hurt him. Uneven caresses without risk. It's the price that must be paid for spending a day with free-spirited kids from vacant lots. City parents are afraid of them. So they protect their children with quite innocent distractions.

Here, homosexuality is described as lower-class behavior. The parents' negative reactions to such activity could be due to their disapproval of its same-sex nature, the fact that it involves their children's association with lower-class boys, or possibly a combination of both. At any rate, homosexual activity in the above passage is associated with liberty, forbidding the activity with constraint. Yet the passage also seems to share a similar tone with the passage in which Moha laments the lack of affection in conjugal relationships. The caresses described here seem insufficient, as if they should be more. More equal? more affectionate? more numerous? But what is the risk "more" would bring? The risk of enjoying the caresses as much as the sexual release (justified as biological need)? The risk of a pleasure incompatible with the boys' developing masculinity?

A possible example of homosexual desire also occurs in the bank director's remark: "Je sors aussi pour aller au hammam populaire. J'aime cette chaleur; j'aime les garçons qui y viennent s'amuser" (122). (I also go out for the working-class *hammam*. I like the warmth; I like the boys who come to have fun.) Again, if the boys are having fun sexually, and if it is for that reason the director likes to go to the *hammam,* homosexual behavior, if not a uniquely lower-class phenomenon, is associated by members of the wealthier classes with lower-class behavior. To have homosexual fun, the wealthy must go slumming. Rachida Saigh Bousta (1992), however, interprets this passage as follows: "Whenever the bank director leaves his office, it's either to succumb to artifice and the abstractions of the circus, or to give in to sodomy at the *hammam*" (48). First of all, there is no proof of any sexual desire or activity at all, much less of sodomy. For her assertion to work, she must assume sodomy is the only possible fulfillment of homosexual desire. Second, by making this remark without commenting on the other passage about the boys in the fields (more significant in my opinion), Saigh Bousta marks sodomy as an upper-class vice in a total reversal of the class associations implicit in the novel's sexual politics. She only discusses the rich banker who goes to "exploit" lower-class boys in the *hammam* and totally ignores and confines to silence the fact that lower-class boys also "corrupt" upper-class boys in the fields. In the latter case, the upper-class parents are the ones who have homophobic reactions. By associating sodomy uniquely with the banker (who collaborates with neocolonial economic oppression) and excluding lower-class same-sex pleasure from her discussion, Saigh Bousta repeats the definitional act of exclusion that informs some Marxist and nationalist discourses—homosexuality is bourgeois decadence, a Western evil imposed by colonialism—the very exclusion the novel actively resists.

Political Agents and Postcolonial Subjectivity at the Margins

For Silverman, marginal sexualities imply and/or create marginal subjectivities. Moha's marginal sexuality or embrace of the marginal sexualities of those who speak through him constitutes only one of the ways he challenges centered subjectivity. Moha is a subject who resists subjectivity; he is thus one possible paradigm of postcolonial subjectivity. Far from being depoliticized or having lost its agency, the postcolonial subjectivity Moha embodies positions him in an ideal location for acting politically. Pronounced in French, without the Arabic "h," "Moha" and "moi" are almost identical. In addition, there are several passages in the text that make a similar *rapprochement*. In one case, Moha uses the first-person emphatic pronoun in an expression almost identical to the title of the novel: "[M]oi le fou, moi le pauvre . . . moi le sage" (32). (I, the madman, I, the poor man . . . I, the wise man.) Here, the "Moha" of the title is replaced with "moi," as if the two were interchangeable. The other case is a simple juxtaposition of the pronoun and the proper name: "Moi, Moha, je vous dis . . ." (52). (I, Moha, tell you.) But this juxtaposition is strengthened by the fact that, in the French, Moha is surrounded on each side by a first-person pronoun, and the first three words are in apposition as interchangeable equivalents. Yet for "Moha" to be "moi," it must be pronounced *à la française*. Though an Arab, Moha's subjectivity is articulated, formulated in French, and as the assimilation of Moha to a subject (a *moi*) suggests, subjectivity in this context requires assimilation to the colonizing culture.[9] It requires what Bhabha (1994) has labeled "mimicry." But Bhabha's mimicry is not a total and complete assimilation; "co-

---

9. In his autobiographical *Eloge de l'amitié,* Ben Jelloun describes the *blessure* produced by the dropping of the Arabic "h" in his own first name: "[Les Françaises] qui nous approchaient un peu ne retenaient même pas nos noms, ou les écorchaient: Lotfi devenant Lofti et moi Ta Ar" (24). (The French women who had anything to do with us couldn't even remember our names, or else mutilated them, with Lotfi becoming Lofti and me Ta Ar.)

lonial mimicry is the desire for a reformed, recognizable Other, *as a subject of a difference that is almost the same, but not quite*" (86). In other
words, Moha is almost a subject but not quite. He is "not quite/not"
a subject (92). He occupies that space Bhabha characterizes as "in-
between": "It is not the colonialist Self or the colonized Other, but the
disturbing distance in-between that constitutes the figure of colonial otherness—the white man's artifice inscribed on the black man's body" (45).

Luce Irigaray (1974) describes the female subject's double bind,
which can be helpful for understanding the "in-between" occupied by
Bhabha's colonial subject: "We can assume that any theory of the subject
has always been appropriated by the 'masculine.' When she submits to
(such a) theory [A s'y assujettir], woman fails to realize that she is re-
nouncing the specificity of her own relationship to the imaginary" (133;
165 in original). Woman as Object is a male construction, but attempting
to claim the position of Subject is also to subject oneself to a male "colonization" of the mind. The space left for women, a liberating space, is to
be found behind the looking glass, the other side of the mirror in which
Lacan's prototypical Subject discovers himself.[10] (We are led to believe
this subject is not gendered, but we know from Irigaray he is actually a
little boy.) Irigaray's place for women is almost that of the Lacanian subject, but not quite. Likewise, the colonized subject is caught between the
sign of absolute difference invented by the colonizer (like Irigaray's
Other) and is denied access to the country club of universal subjectivity
(Irigaray's Self).

Writing the Queer Nation

The role *Moha* assigns to the postcolonial *écrivain engagé* might be described with Bhabha's concept of "writing the nation" (1994, 146). For
when Moha writes the Nation, he simultaneously rewrites it. As in
Barthes's notion of reading as a rewriting of the text, *Moha*'s paradigm of
postcolonial writing also offers modes of reading postcolonial texts. The
fact that Moha might articulate the role of the postcolonial writer is indicated in his exchange with M. Milliard:

> De toute façon, toi, tu t'es mis à l'écart et tu as le beau rôle: tu nous re-
> gardes et puis tu vas écrire des bouquins. La critique, c'est aisé, comme dit
> l'autre, mais la vie, la lutte pour la vie, ce n'est pas à la portée de n'importe

10. See "Le miroir, de l'autre côté" (1977, 7–20) for Irigaray's rewriting of *Alice in Wonderland*.

qui. . . . Vous vous réfugiez dans un buisson de mots et vous voulez refaire le monde, vous voulez faire la lutte des classes. Quelle illusion! Le pays n'a pas besoin de mots, surtout pas de poésie, il a besoin de progrès et de techniques nouvelles. (97)

At any rate, you have stepped aside and you have the easy part to play: you watch us and then you go and write books. As they say, criticizing is easy, but life, the struggle for life, that's not within anyone's reach. . . . You hide behind a thicket of words and you want to redo the world, you want to ignite a class struggle. What an illusion! This country does not need words, especially not poetry, it needs progress and new technologies.

In contrast with Moha's task of unveiling through writing, for M. Milliard, words hide. The character the novel places in opposition to Moha's class politics condemns postcolonial writers and situates their role within a context of class struggle. The critique they offer hinders the economic progress of the national ruling class. M. Milliard associates this cliché of the idealist socialist (who dreams up solutions to injustice that are unworkable in the "real" world) with the task of the writer, whom he describes as useless:

La poésie c'était bon du temps des Abbassides, du temps de l'Andalousie, du temps de l'accalmie et des lauriers de l'histoire. . . . Tu t'es englué dans le magma des mots et des phrases obscures. Tu as fait vœu de pauvreté. Tu n'es pas pauvre; tu es raté! voilà la vérité. Que peux-tu avec des livres, surtout dans un pays où l'écrasante majorité des gens ne sait ni lire ni écrire. (97–98)

Poetry was good in the times of the Abbassides, in the times of Andalusia, in times of peace, when history rested on its laurels. . . . You've gotten stuck in the magma of words and obscure phrases. You've made a vow of poverty. You're not poor; you're a failure! there's the truth. What can you do with books, especially in a country where the vast majority of people can't read or write.

In these passages, Ben Jelloun goes to the heart of the difficult position of postcolonial writers.

Of all Maghrebian writers writing in French, Tahar Ben Jelloun has perhaps been the one most criticized (especially since he won the Prix Goncourt for *La nuit sacrée*) for being "inauthentic."[11] Jacqueline Kaye

11. See Fayolle: "In fact, Tahar Ben Jelloun undoubtedly obtained the Prix Goncourt for *La nuit sacrée* in 1987 because he managed, in this novel as in several others, to evoke what thrills European readers: the condition of the Maghrebian woman oppressed beneath the weight of tradition, going

and Abdelhamid Zoubir (1990) have been among his harshest critics: "The pornographic thrust of Ben Jelloun's work is made possible by its transcription in an alien idiom" (43). According to them, he writes "[w]ith no other aim than providing his French readers with a cheap thrill . . ." (43). These accusations even apply to his psychological study:

> Ben Jelloun's other writing—both fiction and the texts presented as "factual" as a result of his work as a psychologist amongst Maghrebin emigrants in France, such as *La Réclusion solitaire* (1976) and *La Plus haute des solitudes* (1977)—is posited on the assumption that his fellow Maghrebins are obsessed with sex and that their exile in France causes most grief to them because of sexual deprivation. Indeed this is practically the only thing he has to say about Morocco. (42)

Their accusations slide over the fact that *La plus haute des solitudes* is about impotence imposed by psychological or physical trauma and deals with immigrant workers who, unlike the "obsessed" suggested by Kaye and Zoubir, are physically unable to satisfy even the slightest sexual desire. Their criticism seems to be levied as much against his treatment of sexuality as anything else and fails to consider the positive political effects of his representations of sexuality. It is precisely this type of criticism that Ben Jelloun addresses in "Défendre la diversité culturelle du Maghreb."

In their criticism of Ben Jelloun, Kaye and Zoubir fail to take into account the ways he himself articulates, at least in part, the same critique that they do. This self-critique is strengthened by his political commentary on the institution of psychiatry. The writer in *Moha* speaks as a madman; yet the writer Ben Jelloun has a doctorate in psychiatry and has written a psychiatric treatise in which the authority of the author depends on the truth-value of psychiatric discourse. Here he denies that authority by simultaneously rejecting the authority of the author (a rejection that might be related to what is often referred to as the death of the author). *Moha* is thus, in addition to a model for the role of postcolonial writers, a questioning of that same role, an acknowledgment that (in particular) the Francophone postcolonial writer's political efficacy is a matter of current (and often sharp) debate. Moha betrays not only the Nation and its bourgeoisie, he also betrays his own author, whose position he seems to usurp: "Mon pouvoir est dans les mots; et les mots sont traîtres" (25). (My power is in words; and words betray.) This treason is situated in the

---

to *hammams,* confessions of an erotic nature, everything being stamped with pathetic Orientalist stereotypes [le tout empreint d'un misérabilisme 'oriental'] . . ." (15).

context of others described above, especially sexual ones. Ben Jelloun places in the mouth of a millionaire an argument many nationalists, even leftist ones, have levied against Maghrebian writers in French and even more so against those who live in metropolitan France, like Ben Jelloun. What function does M. Milliard's argument play here, coming as it does from the mouth of the national bourgeoisie? Perhaps Ben Jelloun dismisses this nationalist argument as serving the ruling class. But perhaps he also uses it as another way of qualifying his own critique of postindependence power relations in the Maghreb, another way of questioning the speaking subject of the novel, of deconstructing his own subject position. Ben Jelloun's use of M. Milliard to criticize himself would thus work in the same way as his use of the psychiatrist's relation to Moha. Like a public writer, Moha speaks for many. Like a storyteller, he articulates a voice, which he hurls out onto the public square. Such is the task of the postcolonial writer—unveiling national and sexual secrets in public to rewrite the Nation of nationalist discourse as a queer nation.

Part Two

SEX AND

REVOLUTION

Chapter Three

HOMOSEXUALITY (UN)VEILED

Sexuality, brought out of the private sphere into plain view, is but one part of Moha's narrative. In many Maghrebian novels, however, one might argue that sexuality is central to the narrative economy. In an interview with Hafid Gafaïti, Rachid Boudjedra explicitly associated the inclusion of sexuality in his novels with political opposition along the same lines as those described by Ben Jelloun:

> Sexuality is an important element in my work because it is simply an important element in life, and also because it is taboo in the Arabo-Muslim world and in my country. I wanted to make it one of my central themes in order to attempt to transgress this taboo. And on that note, I could say that all my literature is a permanent transgression. That's why I think it is subversive. It transgresses all kinds of taboos, among them the sexual taboo, which is perhaps the hard kernel of all the others [le noyau dur de tous les autres tabous]. (Gafaïti 1987, 105)

Boudjedra's first novel, *La répudiation* (1969) has perhaps brought representations of homosexuality out of the closet more than any other Maghrebian novel.[1] In spite of the arrival of the openly gay Moroccan writer Rachid O. on the literary scene and Eyet-Chékib Djaziri's novels filled with erotic homosexual encounters described from a first-person perspective, many of *La répudiation*'s representations of homosexuality remain

---

1. Homosexuality also plays an important role in some of Boudjedra's other novels: *Le démantèlement* features a homosexual character, Latif. In *Les 1001 années de la nostalgie* the governor outlaws homosexual marriage to conceal, as it turns out, the fact that the sub-Saharan workers he has hired for construction work engage in the practice. The narrator of *La pluie* has a lesbian aunt.

among the most explicit in Maghrebian literature. Boudjedra's novel not only lays bare the mechanisms by which nationalism represses homosexuality to naturalize the Nation as heterosexual and homosocial, but also stages a return of this repressed to denaturalize official paradigms of national identity. The revolutionary politics such a queering makes possible become clearer in his *Les 1001 années de la nostalgie* (1979), which explicitly establishes sexual liberation as a prerequisite for successful struggle against colonial and neocolonial oppression. Whereas in *Les 1001 années de la nostalgie,* women's sexuality is seen as dangerous to male power in a national context, in *La répudiation,* homosexuality performs this function. *La répudiation* also challenges both colonial and neocolonial discourses at the level of representation insofar as its representations of homosexuality challenge the clichés that make up "Oriental sex" in Orientalizing studies of sexuality in the "Arabo-Muslim world."

Not all critics, however, have reacted positively to Boudjedra's treatment of sexuality. Kaye and Zoubir describe how "Boudjedra has been criticized as a maniac lured by Robbe-Grillet and whose sole concern is to scandalize bigots and pander to those whose tastes in literature are perverse or pornographic" (81). A number of critics have singled out his representations of homosexuality as a basis for condemnation. In *Fêtes et défaites d'éros dans l'œuvre de Rachid Boudjedra* (1994), Giuliana Toso Rodinis is far from celebrating eroticism when it comes to homosexuality: "Boudjedra will return several times to the theme of onanism and erotic disorders. In this vice-filled world, homosexuality, caught up in an infernal whirlwind, betrays the unleashing of the most ferocious irregularities" (31). She speaks of the "shameful actions" (31) of the homosexual brother in *La répudiation* and the "deviances of masturbation and homosexuality that Boudjedra painfully puts into play in his novels" (43). In her study of the representations of women in Maghrebian literature, Ahlem Mosteghanemi (1985) lists representations of homosexuality among the other crimes she uses as evidence to condemn Boudjedra, whose novel "includes five cases of rape (in which the protagonist variously rapes his cousins one minute, his step-mother another, and his step-sister yet another), six cases of homosexuality, and three cases of prostitution!" (277). In her discussion of another Maghrebian novel that represents same-sex desire (Mouloud Mammeri's *La colline oubliée* [1952]), she congratulates the author for tackling "various social ills such as homosexuality, adultery, etc." (241). Yet in his representation of the homoerotic (supposedly Platonic) relationship between the narrator's cousin Menach and his friend

Mouh, Mammeri is no more critical than Boudjedra, and when the narrator becomes very attached to Mouh himself after Menach's death, his initial objection to this relationship (due less to its homoerotic nature than to Mouh's lower-class status), is complicated. The major difference between the two novels' representations of homosexuality is not their judgment of same-sex eroticism but their explicitness (much greater in Boudjedra's case). One is thus left to wonder how much early condemnations of *La répudiation* are in fact displaced reactions to his inclusion of homosexuality.

Sexual Liberation

Because the revolt in *Les 1001 années* involves kicking out a foreign presence, one may read it as an allegory of the Algerian Revolution; because, in addition, this revolt overthrows the indigenous governor Bender Chah, who collaborates with foreign domination, one may simultaneously read it as an allegory of postindependence struggle against the national elite personified by him as well as against neocolonialism. In both allegorical readings, anti-imperialist struggle also involves sexual liberation. When freedom fighters go underground and take on false identities across gender lines, this change so confuses Messaouda S.N.P. (Sans Nom Patronymique) that, at one point, the men are afraid she will carry the reversal of sexual roles so far as to force them into seclusion every month to sit out their menstrual periods on chamber pots (302–3). National liberation, in the model presented by Boudjedra, thus threatens to turn men into women at the most biological level, thereby overturning the hierarchy between them and denaturalizing it.

In one episode, women oppose the governor's decree forcing them to shave their pubic hair, and their revolt becomes a means of opposing the regime in power, and therefore, (neo)colonialism. Their leader, Messaouda, incites rebellion by shouting, "Il n'a qu'à venir y mettre le nez lui-même . . . car mon sexe qui a déjà craché dix-neuf enfants n'a plus rien à craindre des menaces d'un vieux fou" (51–52). (All [the governor] needs to do is stick his nose up there himself, . . . because my vagina, which has already spit out nineteen children, doesn't have anything to fear from an old fool.) The women "réclamaient le droit d'entretenir leur sexe comme elles en avaient envie et proclamaient que si les exigences du Gouverneur devaient être respectées, il fallait que cette loi sur le pubis soit étendue aux hommes eux-mêmes" (52) (demanded the right to keep up their sexes the way they wanted and proclaimed that, if the governor's demands had to be obeyed, the pubic-hair law would have to be extended to men as well). Finally, the governor is forced to give in, and the women go back to shaving their hair, which they only stopped doing because it became the law:

> Seule la meneuse refusa de se raser et tint bon, malgré les supplications de ses filles qui avaient peur que sa toison ne débordât de sa culotte et n'envahît la maison comme une mauvaise broussaille pour s'en aller de proche en proche jusqu'à couvrir toutes les rues poudreuses, arriver sur la place et grimper comme un lierre tenace et entêté sur les murs extérieurs de la dizaine de cafés dont les propriétaires étaient, bien sûr, rançonnés sérieusement par Bender Chah. (52)

> Only the agitator refused to shave and dug in her heels, in spite of the pleas of her daughters, who were afraid that her fleece would spill out of her panties and invade the whole house like an evil undergrowth and go on by degrees to cover the dirt roads, reach the public square, and climb, like a stubborn and steadfast ivy, the outer walls of the ten or so cafés whose owners were, of course, royally extorted by Bender Chah.

Is it a coincidence that it is precisely a woman unmarked by the patronymic and patriarchal law who leads this movement? Later, in the revolution that will overthrow the powers that be, even the governor's wife espouses the people's cause, attacking the aggressors who try to rape her by protecting herself with a fan that cuts up their penises (305).

Dangerous Women, Dangerous Queers: Sexuality as Political Weapon

One should be wary of a premature celebration of the image of pubic hair taking over an entire village as a model of feminist struggle. At the end of the passage, one can see how, in the male imaginary, a dangerous female sexuality threatens to get out of control and invade the spaces traditionally reserved for men—the streets, public square, and cafés. In some respects, the above passage resembles the archetype of the omnisexual woman in Arabic erotic literature, who embodies the danger of women's sexuality as described by Fatna Aït Sabbah in *La femme dans l'inconscient musulman* (1985): "The omnisexual woman's nature requires her to declare war against the Muslim order and violate all rules regarding canonical sexuality; in particular, heterosexuality, fidelity, social homogeneity, and chastity, the essential virtue of a woman's life" (68). Rather than claiming women are inferior to men as much Western sexist discourse does, Aït Sabbah argues that, in a Muslim context, women are seen as a powerful threat to male privilege and the social order. This representation of female subversion, however, is not necessarily incompatible with official discourse. While the omnisexual woman overthrows the status quo ("Nothing can hold her back, she tramples on the rule of heterosexuality with the same ease as the rule of social homogeneity" [85]), dominant discourses use this representation to justify male privilege. Her danger must be controlled by veiling, confinement, enclosure. Unlike Ben Jelloun, who characterizes the articulation of threatening sexualities as subversive, Aït Sabbah maintains that it actually supports the status quo; the unveiling in the text actually strengthens calls to send women "back to the veil," as she puts it.

As Aït Sabbah demonstrates, one of the dangers Woman represents is her threat to a hegemonic heterosexuality. Although one cannot necessarily generalize from male representations of female homosexuality about the role of male homosexuality in a heterosexual imaginary, the political threat female homosexuality poses to the male imaginary in Aït Sabbah's account parallels the danger of women's sexuality in *Les 1001 années* and of the homosexuality of Zahir, the narrator's brother in *La répudiation*. Boudjedra's first novel consists of two parallel narratives: Like Moha, the narrator Rachid is interned in a psychiatric hospital either because of his political opposition to the postindependence regime or because he is mentally ill—probably for both reasons. He recounts his childhood and his mother's repudiation by his father to his French lover Céline, whom he desires, desires to veil and enclose (*cloîtrer*), and whose body (because it is female) disgusts him. Céline and Zahir occupy similar positions in his imaginary, because in an effort to define his own (hetero)-sexuality, the narrator also attempts not only to understand his brother but also to distance himself from his homosexuality and confine its threat. Both attempts fail, in the end, as Zahir resists his brother's will to knowledge.

If Aït Sabbah describes how the male imaginary must veil the danger of women's sexuality, Malek Chebel (1988), like Ben Jelloun, describes the veiling of a sexual secret, in this case, that of homosexuality: "First of all, it is essential that we fold back a thick veil with double seams [il est indispensable de replier un voile épais, aux doubles coutures]: that of a nervous silence. The Maghrebian homosexual exists and flourishes . . ." (16). Is this tendency to associate homosexuality's secret (what Anglo-

Americans call the closet) with the veiling of women merely another example of male fantasy projected onto the veil *qua* screen? Or could one find similarities between the function of "Woman" in the male imaginary and the function of homosexuality in the heterosexual imaginary, similarities in two types of hierarchies that privilege some at the expense of others? In *La sexualité en Islam* (1975), the Tunisian sociologist Abdelwahab Bouhdiba attributes to homosexuality a political subversion similar to the one with which Aït Sabbah characterizes the omnisexual woman: "[H]omosexuality contests the world as willed by God, the world founded on the harmony and radical separation of the sexes" (46). These dangers threaten not only individual male subjectivities, but also a political order of divine origin. In the modern context of the Nation as well, women's sexuality parallels homosexuality in that, as dangers, they threaten not only individual male subjectivities, but ruling classes as well.

Fanon's "Algeria Unveiled" ("L'Algérie se dévoile" in the original), a chapter of *A Dying Colonialism,* uses unveiling to unleash a similar political force. In his account, the veil that first protected women from the colonizer's invading and penetrating gaze is removed in the struggle for national liberation. Transgression of the forbidden thus plays an important role in Fanon's model of revolutionary struggle: "When colonized people undertake an action against the oppressor, and when this oppression is exercised in the form of exacerbated and continuous violence as in Algeria, they must overcome a considerable number of taboos [interdits]" (51; 39 in original). Nonetheless, the veil is put back on in the same struggle to hide weapons. Many critics have questioned Fanon's assumption that women's liberation naturally follows national independence. History offers numerous examples where such has not been the case. Winifred Woodhull (1993) has also shown how even in the title "L'Algérie se dévoile," the Nation is personified as Woman (3); the Nation's unveiling coincides with women's, and Woman, as a figment of this male imagination, is the incarnation of the Nation's virtue itself. One might even paraphrase Fanon's French title as "Algeria reveals her true nature." Because Fanon (like Aït Sabbah) describes the veil as hiding a danger, be it Woman or bomb, unveiling releases, quite literally, an explosion; he then deploys this explosion against the colonizer.

In *Les 1001 années,* Boudjedra unveils women's sexuality in much the same way. However, whereas Fanon uses this unveiling against the colonizer, Boudjedra uses it in a struggle that brings down an indigenous ruler (a personification of the national elite) in addition to driving out a (neo)colonial invader. Whereas Fanon was unaware of the danger of co-opting this danger and containing it after the revolution, Boudjedra warns against a recuperation of women's struggle by recounting a past revolt of the village's women against its men:

> En 1450, les femmes de Manama se révoltèrent contre les hommes et ga-gnèrent la guerre des sexes, après une année de batailles, d'embuscades et de guet-apens. Par la suite, confiantes et généreuses, elles furent récupérées en douce et progressivement par les vaincus qui non seulement les frustrè-rent d'une victoire éclatante, mais aussi les privèrent de la vie tout court. (334–35)

> In 1450, the women of Manama revolted against the men and won the war of the sexes, after a year of battles, traps, and ambushes. Later, trusting and generous, they were co-opted slyly and progressively by the conquered, who not only cheated them out of an overwhelming victory, but also quite simply deprived them of their lives.

Interestingly, Boudjedra uses the same expression ("en douce") to de-scribe male recuperation of women's struggles and the filmmakers' "colo-nization" of the village, thereby further strengthening his association be-tween colonial and postindependence domination and sexual repression. In *La répudiation,* homosexuality (along with women's sexuality) is the target of a similar repression. As Chebel and Ben Jelloun have associated homosexuality's threat with the one hidden beneath veils, in *La répudia-tion,* Boudjedra unveils and deploys it as a postcolonial political weapon. In contrast with Fanon's title, however, this chapter brackets the prefix *un-* to show how unveiling is not a clear and simple operation in either Fanon's or Boudjedra's imaginaries.

Representations of Homosexuality

In some ways *La répudiation* reinforces the nationalist stereotype of ho-mosexuality as a foreign vice imposed by colonialism. In the character of Heimatlos, Zahir's Jewish companion—which means in German "apa-tride" (without a country) as well as "déraciné" (uprooted)—homosexual and foreigner are combined into one. Homosexuality is also associated with the foreign in a number of passages: "Il y a autant de bateaux que de gargottes sordides; des pêcheurs y mangent du poisson, boivent du vin rouge et fument du kif. Certains soirs, ivres morts ils condescendent à faire l'amour à des marins étrangers et aux petits vendeurs de cigarettes"

(81). ("There are as many boats as sordid taverns in which the fishermen eat fish, drink red wine and smoke kif. Some evenings, dead drunk, they condescend to make love to the foreign sailors and [little] cigarette-vendors" [70].) The fishermen engage in homosexual acts not among themselves but with foreigners or boys, who are not (yet) men and are seen by men as substitutes for women. In that the boys are lower class, the passage associates homosexuality with lower-class activity similarly to certain passages in *Moha.* The fact that the fishermen choose same-sex partners who are foreign or beneath them in class position as well as younger allows them to do what would be unthinkable for them among equals. This passage, however, offers a slight variation on the nationalist association of homosexuality with a foreign evil: passive homosexuality is a necessary function relegated to those at the Nation's margins or beyond its borders. That this homosexual activity does not seem to threaten the masculinity of the men who engage in it (or their insertion into familial structures governed by sexual normativity) suggests that this paradigm of same-sex eroticism corresponds to Western clichés of "Islamic homosexuality."

One may also discern the model of transgenerational homosexuality, a recurrent theme in the novel, whose narrator even recalls several episodes of pederasty from his own childhood. One example occurs among dock workers at the port and the unemployed:

> En été, nous allions jusqu'à nous baigner dans l'eau fangeuse du port, parmi les dockers et les chômeurs venus au bord de l'eau fumer du kif et, par la même occasion, nous peloter les fesses sous prétexte de nous apprendre à nager. (57)

> In summer we even bathed in the muddy port waters amongst the dockers and the unemployed who had come down to the edge of the water to smoke kif, and, while they were at it, to fondle our behinds while pretending to teach us to swim. (53)

In this case, the adults are the lower-class partners, for the narrator's family belongs to the colonial indigenous bourgeoisie. He is upset that his parents do not let him go swimming, less because he particularly enjoys what the dock workers do to him than because their caresses are not too great a price to pay for a summer swim. When he speaks of "la sauvagerie des mâles" (57) ("the savagery of the males" [53]), he refers not to the dock workers but to male family members who punish violently for swimming. The parents object to summer bathing not because it involves satisfying the desires of older men, but because they believe the sea in itself is dangerous.

In a second example of pederasty, that which the narrator commits with the Qur'anic school master, the parents actually seem to collaborate:

> En hiver, j'aime beaucoup somnoler et le maître n'y peut rien car je lui fais du chantage: l'année dernière il m'a fait des propositions malhonnêtes et je les ai acceptées afin qu'il me laisse en paix et me donne le loisir de rêver du corps somptueux de ma marâtre. Tout le monde accepte les propositions du maître coranique! Il nous caresse furtivement les cuisses et quelque chose de dur nous brûle le coccyx. C'est tout! Je sais que ce n'est pas grave. Mon frère aîné veille au grain. Les parents, généralement au courant de telles pratiques, ferment les yeux pour ne pas mettre en accusation un homme qui porte en son sein la parole de Dieu; superstitieux, ils préfèrent ne pas être en butte aux sortilèges du maître. (94)

> In winter I enjoy snoozing a great deal and the schoolteacher can do nothing about it since I am blackmailing him: last year he made some indecent propositions which I accepted so he would leave me alone and let me [day]-dream in peace of my stepmother's opulent body. Everyone accepts the propositions of the Koranic schoolteacher. He caresses your thighs furtively and something hard burns your tail-bone. That's all. I know it isn't serious. My elder brother keeps watch. The parents, usually aware of such practices, close their eyes to them so as not to have to accuse a man carrying the word of God in his breast; being superstitious they prefer not to be exposed to the spells cast by the master. (79–80)

The juxtaposition of these two passages gives the impression that pederasty occurred all year round (summer and winter) throughout the narrator's childhood. He relates the winter incident in a rather nonchalant manner; not that he enjoys pederasty, but being left alone is well worth committing such acts, which seem to have no serious consequences here. In 1908 the anthropologist Edward Westermarck described "a common belief among the Arabic-speaking mountaineers of Northern Morocco that a boy cannot learn the Koran well unless a scribe commits pederasty with him" (quoted in Murray 218), thus suggesting that Rachid's experience at the Qur'anic school might conform to a paradigm. The association of homosexuality with the *école* or *maître coranique* also recalls the following comment from Driss Chraïbi's *Le passé simple* (1954): "Sans compter que les perversités des grands contaminent les petits et que presque toujours ces écoles servent de cours tacites de pédérastie appliquée avec ou sans le concours de l'honorable maître d'école" (39). ("That's without counting on the contamination of the younger boys by the older ones as these schools almost always serve as tacit courses in applied pederasty, with or without the tutelage of the honorable master of the school" [16].)

In Chraïbi's description, pederasty is troped as contagion. Likewise, in constructionist studies of sexuality, much is often made of the distinction between preindustrial categories of sodomy and pederasty and the more modern category of homosexuality. While, according to this view, homosexuality, thus strictly defined, is an identity more or less exclusive of heterosexuality, in contexts where the paradigm of sodomy reigns, none is immune from its temptation. The characteristic of a universal susceptibility to sodomy is often used to describe same-sex behavior (especially among men) in Arab or Muslim societies. Boudjedra's narrator himself is susceptible: "Pour arriver à la maison de Ma, il faudrait éviter les impasses urineuses—rendez-vous d'homosexuels qui se caressent dans le noir des latrines—et les cafés à rengaines. Faire de longs détours pour ne pas tomber dans la facilité!" (61). ("To return to Ma's house you would have to avoid the streets reeking of urine—meeting-places of the homosexuals caressing each other in the darkness of the latrines—and the cafés where the latest tunes were played. Make long detours to avoid taking the easy way!" [56].) In this passage, homosexuality must be avoided because it represents "une facilité," a temptation. Bouhdiba describes a similar view towards homosexual desire in classical Arabic literature: "Al Hassan Ibn Dhakwâm used to say: Don't sit next to the sons of noblemen: they have faces like virgins', and they're even more tempting than women" (46). Heimatlos, as well, seems infectious: "La mère, sitôt le professeur parti, aérait les chambres, lavait les verres dans lesquels le mécréant avait bu et récitait des formules incantatoires. Mon frère la laissait faire et restait impassible" (104). ("As soon as the teacher had left, Mother aired all the [rooms], washed the glasses from which the infidel had drunk and recited incantations. My brother let her be and remained impassive" [86].) His mother is perhaps cleansing the house of the impurity brought about in her mind by a Jewish presence, but she might also be disinfecting the house from his contagious sexuality.

While some passages characterize homosexuality as something foreign or external, the temptation that it represents, not merely to homosexuals, but to all, suggests that it is not so other, that it is a possibility inherent in everyone. In another passage the narrator says: "Dès que le marchand m'adresse la parole, je me crispe. Homosexualité latente. Tout le monde sait qu'il a des rapports maléfiques avec mon frère" (107). ("As soon as the [merchant] speaks to me I tense. Latent homosexuality. Everyone knows he has wicked relations with my brother" [89].) It is interesting to note that, in the second sentence, latent homosexuality is, in fact, attributed to no one. The reader might be justified in attributing this homosexuality to the merchant, who maintains a relationship with Zahir. But why not attribute it to the narrator, the closest grammatical antecedent? To assume the merchant is the homosexual one, the reader must read the narrator's prejudices back into the text. The latent homosexuality of the passage is actually a floating signifier that could be attached to one character or the other, which is precisely why it is so threatening.

The Abjection of Homosexuality and Women

In the passages cited above, the narrator associates homosexuality with urine, alcohol, disease, and filth. Female sexuality is represented as similarly abject in the character of Céline: "[S]on sexe bavait sur mes jambes un liquide épais et collant, coulant de l'atroce tuméfaction où j'aimais pourtant m'engloutir . . ." (10). ("[Her vagina drooled onto my legs, a thick, sticky liquid,] flowing from the atrocious swelling in which I still loved to plunge . . ." [18].) In another passage, Rachid links his desire to sequester her abject sexuality with his equally abject fantasies of his mother:

> Je savais que mon désir de la séquestrer était virulent, mais irréalisable; je ne voulais pas être en contradiction avec les principes que j'avais forgés au long de mes cauchemars et où les femmes jouaient toujours des rôles très importants (comme dans cet affreux rêve où j'avais vu un lapin écorché sur lequel on jetait des bassines de sang, alors que ma mère, à côté, agonisait par la faute de menstrues démentielles qui ne voulaient pas s'arrêter; dans mon cauchemar, je ne faisais pas la liaison entre le sang déversé sur l'animal excorié et le sang de ma mère, et ce ne fut qu'au réveil que je me rendis compte que tout le sang provenait de ma mère, vidée et râlante). (13)

> I knew my desire to lock her away was virulent but unrealistic; I did not wish to act contrary to the principles I had forged in the course of my nightmares where women were always very prominent (as in that dreadful dream where I had seen a skinned rabbit over which they were throwing basins of blood, while my mother, nearby, was bleeding to death from a raging menstrual flow which would not be staunched; in my nightmare I

did not link the blood poured over the peeled animal with my mother's blood and it was only when I awoke that I realised all the blood came from my mother, drained and at her last gasp). (20)

In *Pouvoirs de l'horreur* (1980), Kristeva attributes the abject to an imperative to separate from the maternal: "The abject confronts us . . . within our personal archeology, with our earliest attempts to release the hold of *maternal* entity even before ex-isting outside of her, thanks to the autonomy of language" (13). This separation can never be complete, which is why the male subject is constantly threatened with being absorbed back into the maternal body. He must therefore constantly assert himself through acts of masculine self-definition, whose purpose is to convince himself and others that the separation has actually already occurred.

Parenthesis as Veil

In the above passage, the narrator confines the female abject to parentheses. This confinement serves as the rhetorical equivalent of the very literal confinement he fantasizes for Céline:

> Je rêvais de la cloîtrer, non pour la garder pour moi et la préserver de la tutelle des mâles qui rôdaient dans la ville abandonnée par les femmes, à la recherche de quelque difficile et rare appât (non, je ne pouvais pas être jaloux dans l'état d'extrême confusion où je végétais depuis, ou bien avant, ma séquestration par les Membres Secrets dans une villa bien connue du peuple; non ce n'était pas du tout là mon but). . . . (12)

> I dreamed of shutting her away, not so as to keep her to myself and preserve her from the custody of the males prowling around the city abandoned by the women, looking for some difficult rare bait (no, I could not be jealous in this state of extreme confusion in which I had been vegetating ever since, or even before, I had been detained by the Secret Members inside a villa well known to the people; no, that was not my purpose at all). . . . (19)

This association of the *mise entre parenthèses* (as well as sequestering) of female sexuality and the abject serves as a strategy for asserting a male subjectivity by distinguishing it from its maternal and female others (which are perhaps not that different after all, since othering is an "active" and ongoing process that must continually be repeated to be effective). One could thus describe this use of parenthesis as a form of narrative veiling. In this passage, however, the narrator ends up sequestered, both rhetorically in his own parenthesis and literally as a prisoner of the Secret Members. In another passage, female homosexuality is enclosed in parenthesis in Rachid's response to a question from Céline: "(Des millions de gouines veulent entrer dans mon ventre. J'ai peur. Il faudrait réintroduire la mer dans mon sexe afin qu'il puisse clapoter de nouveau)" (138–39). ("(Millions of [dykes] are wanting to enter my belly. I am afraid. Sea will have to be reintroduced into my [sex] so it can [splash] once more)" [112].)[2] Whether Rachid speaks these words or merely thinks them, what is enclosed in parenthesis represents a danger for his sexuality, and the enclosure is one way to control this danger in narrative.

A similar *mise entre parenthèses* is at work in the novel's treatment of Zahir's homosexuality. In the following scene, for example, the narrator describes the entire family looking on as he has sex with another boy. Though it represents one of the longest, most explicit descriptions of same-sex sexuality in Maghrebian literature, its revelation of a sexual act that should remain unseen is simultaneously a cover-up:

> Lui que ma mère a surpris, un jour, dans une position scandaleuse, en compagnie d'un gamin du voisinage; . . . abominable, le spectacle de son enfant monté en grande pompe sur le dos légèrement duveteux de l'autre misérable avec sa sale figure de petit jouisseur; emportés tous les deux dans un monstrueux va-et-vient qui ébranlait leurs corps élancés, la tête ballottante, à la recherche d'un plaisir, somme toute, formel . . . ; . . . cette grotesque et haute pitrerie des deux garçons juchés là-haut sur la terrasse et dont on apercevait les têtes et les bustes qui gigotaient, se malmenaient et se violentaient tragiquement; nous tous, rivés à ce spectacle incroyable . . . et Zahir . . . toujours amarré à son camarade rechignant, peut-être, contre la lenteur du partenaire qui venait juste de faire l'expérience de cette déflagration au bout de son membre, non pas hideux, non pas crispé, mais simplement étonnant dans son érection sordide. . . . (210–11)

> He whom my mother once caught, in a shocking position, in the company of a boy living nearby; . . . outrageous, the sight of her child mounted with great pomp on the slightly downy back of the other poor sod with the ugly face of a minor sensualist; both carried away in a monstrous [back-and-

---

2. Lambrova translates the neutral "sexe" as "vagina." Although who is speaking in the dialogue is not entirely clear, the question preceding this comment is "Eut-elle d'autres amants mythiques?" (138) ["Did she have other mythical lovers?" (112)], which probably identifies the speaker as Céline. Therefore, in the answer to the question, "sexe," because it would be Rachid's sex, would most likely not be a vagina. Interestingly enough, however, the (mis)translation actually confirms my overall interpretation of the novel: Rachid must constantly assert his masculinity because it is not a given. One reader has even given him a vagina.

forth movement] shaking their slim bodies, heads lolling, seeking, when all is said and done, a formal pleasure . . . ; . . . th[at] grotesque high clowning of the two boys perched there on the terrace, whose heads and torsos we could see tragically juddering, man-handling, hurting each other; all of us riveted to this incredible spectacle . . . and Zahir . . . still joined to his companion jibbing, perhaps, at the slowness of the partner who had just experienced [that] violent explosion at the end of his member, not hideous, not tense but simply surprising in its sordid erection. . . . (165–66)

Here, the narrator stages for the reader a homosexual scene that becomes a spectacle before the gaze of a family that cannot understand the meaning of the act it witnesses:

[Ma] ne comprenait pas et n'en croyait pas ses yeux . . . et Ma les regardait faire, et Ma ne savait que dire; et moi derrière elle, pris entre le fou rire et la violence, et les sœurs derrière moi fixant Saïda et attendant d'elle quelque explication . . . et Ma qui ne pouvait interpeller son fils car elle n'était pas capable d'aller jusqu'au bout de l'explication à donner à cette agglomération de deux corps entrevus l'espace d'une douleur—d'autant plus âpre qu'elle n'allait pas pouvoir s'exprimer; et Ma finit par nous chasser de la pièce, ferma la porte à clef: «ce n'est rien qu'un jeu brutal», dit elle. . . . (210–12)

[Ma] did not understand and could not believe her eyes . . . and Ma watched them at it, and Ma did not know what to say; and I behind her, hovering between hysteric[al laughter] and violence and the sisters behind me staring at Saïda, expecting her to give them some explanation . . . and Ma who could not call out to her son because she was not capable of giving a full explanation of this junction of two bodies perceived in a flash of pain—all the more bitter in that she was not going to be able to express it; and finally Ma chased us out of the room, locking the door: "It is nothing but a rough game," she said. . . . (165–66)

What the narrator reveals, his mother attempts to hide, conceal, and deny by enclosing and shutting the door on this homosexual act.

In a parallel move, the author encloses the whole episode within parentheses, thereby enclosing a representation of pleasure within a scene of violence. For the revelation of Zahir's lovemaking on the rooftop is embedded in another episode of pederasty from the narrator's childhood in which an older man made a pass at him one day at the bakehouse:

Imperceptiblement, je sens sa main effleurer mes cuisses nues. Stupeur. Je ne sais que dire. Il continue à me parcourir les jambes et s'attarde de plus

en plus. Il regarde en face de lui et seule sa main tâtonne sur ma pauvre
chair. J'ai très peur. L'homme n'a pourtant pas l'air de bouger. Je regarde
de son côté. Sa tête est immobile. Seule sa main, comme une vipère aveugle, erre sur ma peau nue qui devient frileuse à ce contact visqueux et
moi˙.   ˙ panique. Là encore, l'enfance vient d'être saccagée,
trahie, violée à brûle-pourpoint par la faute d'un adulte monstrueux. Mais,
j'ai surtout peur qu'il ne meure là, sur son banc, car je ne comprends rien
à ses gestes ni à ses buts. Fuir. . . . L'homme, déjà, s'est agenouillé à mes
pieds et a sorti son membre viril, tellement énorme que j'ai tout à coup la
sensation d'avoir les dents très fraîches; il me force à le toucher et malgré
la raideur de l'organe, je pense à la cervelle de mouton . . . il a les yeux
fermés et me supplie de lui caresser l'organe raide; une envie folle d'uriner
me prend soudainement; il faut que je m'en aille . . . mais le cœur me bat
si fort que je n'ouvre pas la bouche et que j'appréhende de tituber et de
m'affaler dans les bras du satyre qui continue à balbutier et entre dans un
état second. Je me lance dans le vide de la porte ouverte sur le brasier et le
jaillissement lumineux, enfant pourchassé par la véhémence des grandes
personnes, déchiqueté déjà par les futurs sarcasmes des tantes et des voisines, miné par le silence qu'il faudra observer pour ne pas déranger les
certitudes d'une société ancrée dans ses mythes de pureté et d'abstinence.
Comment dénoncer l'ignoble personnage que tout le monde a vu, le matin même, en train d'égrener son chapelet et de sacrifier son mouton?
(209–10)

Imperceptibly I sense his hand lightly touching my bare thighs.
    Aghast. I do not know what to say. He continues to stroke my legs for
longer and longer. He is looking straight ahead; only his hand is feeling its
way around my poor flesh. I am very frightened. Still the man doesn't look
as if he is moving. I glance at him. His head is immobile. Only his hand,
like a blind viper, roves over my bare skin which breaks out in goose-
pimples at this sticky damp contact. Panic overwhelms me. There too,
childhood has just been ravaged, betrayed, violated point-blank by a depraved adult. But what I am most afraid of is that he will die there, on
his bench, because I understand nothing of his gestures nor objectives.
Escape. . . . The man is already kneeling at my feet and has brought out
his male member, so enormous that I suddenly feel all my teeth on edge;
he forces me to touch it and despite the stiffness of the organ, I think
of the brain of the sheep . . . his eyes are closed and he begs me to caress
his stiff organ; I suddenly have a desperate urge to urinate; I have to
leave . . . but my heart is beating so hard I cannot open my mouth and
am afraid to stumble and collapse in the arms of the satyr, still stuttering
and now going into a sort of trance. I rush out to the emptiness of the
door open to the brasier and the bright sparks, a child pursued by the
vehemence of grown-ups, already torn apart by the impending sarcastic

comments of aunts and neighbors, undermined by the silence which will
have to be observed so as not to trouble the certainties of a society an-
chored in its myths of purity and abstinence. How could I expose that vile
individual whom everyone had seen, that very morning, telling his beads
and sacrificing his sheep? (164–65)

Expressions such as "ma pauvre chair," "vipère aveugle," "visqueux," "saccagée, trahie, violée à brûle-pourpoint," and "adulte monstrueux" vehe-
mently emphasize that the narrator experiences being fondled by this
man next to the oven as a form of violence. As in the description of the
Qur'anic schoolmaster's pederasty, the narrator accuses all adults of being
the accomplices, as if such acts reinforced the power differences between
adults and children. The narrator's negative reaction in this passage, however, contradicts his reaction to the teacher's and dock workers' advances,
which may be accounted for by an age difference at the time of the various incidents (Rachid is probably younger in the oven episode). The two
distinct physical sensations the event provokes are oral (cold teeth) and
genital (the need to urinate, and this in a novel where urine has already
been associated with homosexuality). These sensations, whose sites are
erogenous zones, also render the narrator's characterizations of the older
man's sexual approaches as a form of violence a bit more ambiguous.

When the narrator fails to understand this incident, he attempts to
explain it through the rooftop lovemaking scene, which he introduces as
follows: "Il faut se taire; seul Zahir pourrait expliquer l'épisode du four"
(210). ("I will have to keep my mouth shut: only Zahir would be able to
explain the episode of the oven" [165].) After the rooftop sex scene in
parentheses, the narrator reiterates the epistemological justification for
comparing the two incidents of same-sex sexual behavior: "Seul Zahir
peut donc expliquer ce qui vient de se passer dans l'ombre du four" (212).
("That is why Zahir is the only one who can explain what has just happened in the darkness of the bakehouse" [166].) For the narrator, then,
the long parenthesis contains the secret, explanation, and meaning of the
first. Yet although both incidents involve sexual activity between two
members of the same sex, they are not that similar. In the oven scene,
a man demands pederastic acts from an unconsenting boy, and in the
parenthetical episode, two adolescents of approximately the same age
make love for mutual pleasure. Whereas many Western accounts of "Islamic homosexualities" have taken pains to distinguish transgenerational
homosexuality from what they have called "egalitarian homosexuality,"
Boudjedra's narrator seems to claim their affinity. Whereas many of these

accounts suggest that the West has a monopoly on homosexuality, Zahir seems to break that monopoly, and Boudjedra uses the word "homosexuality" in a more general or inclusive way than a stricter constructionist definition might allow.

My remarks on the use of the parenthesis to marginalize are inspired by a comment of Hélène Cixous (1975) in her discussion, interestingly enough, of the role of women in the Algerian Revolution: "'We' struggle together, yes, but, who is this 'we'? A man and beside him a thing, somebody—(a woman: always in her parenthesis, always repressed or invalidated as a woman, tolerated as a non-woman, 'accepted'!)—someone you are not conscious of, unless she effaces herself, acts the man, speaks and thinks that way" (75). Cixous uses the parenthesis as a grammatical marker of sexual repression. Her rhetoric of annulment or self-effacement evokes what many oppressed groups have articulated as internalized homophobia, racism, and sexism, and evokes what lesbian and gay activists have described as the invisibility imposed by the closet, or by a society's refusal to acknowledge the existence of nonnormative sexualities. The danger of what is in both Cixous's and Boudjedra's parenthesis is that it might not be all that parenthetical; what is marginalized is not totally separate from the marginalizing power but central to defining dominant identities. Likewise, Zahir's sexuality might not be as totally other as the narrator wants to make us believe.

A Heterosexual Will to Knowledge

Linked together by the narrator, the rooftop and oven episodes reveal his desire to understand at least the latter. This drive to understand the man's actions at the oven parallels other passages in the novel, such as the following description of the narrator's attempt to understand his Qur'anic schoolteacher's homosexuality:

> Ma sœur dit que c'est là une séquelle de l'âge d'or arabe. Plus tard, j'ai compris que c'est la pauvreté qui incite le «taleb» à l'homosexualité, car dans notre ville il faut avoir beaucoup d'argent pour se marier. Les femmes se vendent sur la place publique, enchaînées aux vaches, et les bordels sont inaccessibles aux petites bourses! (94–95)

> My sister says this is a throwback to the Arab Golden Age. Later I understood it was poverty driving the taleb to homosexuality since getting married in our city is extremely expensive. Women are sold in public squares,

chained to the cows, and brothels are inaccessible to small purses[/tes-
ticles]! (80)

As in other passages, here homosexuality remains an enigma for the narrator. In contrast with many Western accounts, which make no distinction between medieval and contemporary "Islamic homosexualities," his
sister suggests that only a fragment of medieval practice remains, that
pederasty is not as widespread as it once was. But the valorization implicit
in the association of pederasty with a previous age of splendor is contradicted by the negative connotation of the word "séquelle," often associated with sickness. The narrator, however, rejects this explanation in favor
of another, less troubling for his vision of sexuality: poverty.

Boudjedra's narrator also displays a rather persistent will to understand his brother's homosexuality:

> Zahir, lui, n'aimait pas les femmes. Il était amoureux de son professeur de
> physique, un juif aux yeux très bleus et très myopes qui venait souvent à
> la maison, malgré l'hostilité marquée de ma mère. Au début, je pensais
> qu'être homosexuel était quelque chose de distingué, car le juif était très
> beau, avait une voix douce et pleurait très facilement. Chaque fois que
> j'essayais de comprendre les rapports entre mon frère et son professeur,
> Zahir se mettait en colère: «Va renifler tes cousines!» hurlait-il. Pour com-
> muniquer entre eux, en présence d'un tiers, ils avaient inventé un code très
> compliqué. Le Juif répétait souvent qu'il était un «heimatlos» et comme je
> ne comprenais pas, je m'énervais tellement que j'allais me masturber dans
> les toilettes. (103)

> Zahir himself did not like women. He was in love with his physics teacher,
> a Jew with very blue shortsighted eyes who often came to the house despite
> the marked hostility of my mother. Initially I thought being homosexual
> was something very distinguished because the Jew was very handsome,
> had a soft voice and cried very easily. Every time I tried to understand the
> relationship between my brother and his teacher Zahir got very angry:
> "Go away and sniff [up] your girl cousins!" he yelled. To communicate
> between themselves when other people were present they had invented a
> very complicated code. The Jew often repeated that he was a "heimatlos"
> and as I didn't understand I got so annoyed that I went off to masturbate
> in the lavatory. (86)

One can see in Zahir's reply a rather strong scorn for the narrator's (hetero)sexuality. One may notice that a heterosexual presence in no way disturbs (mentally or physically) Zahir who ignores it just as in the rooftop
scene where he is totally impervious—"ne se rendait pas compte!" (211)

("did not realise!" [165])—to his family's gaze. This gaze, desiring to know all, focused on him, is not mutual. Though intolerant—"pris entre le fou rire et la violence" (211) ("hovering between hysteric[al laughter] and violence" [165])—the narrator does not describe his brother as submissive or weak. One may even notice a certain inchoate attraction towards homosexuality, since the narrator began by believing it was distinguished. He wants to know it, understand it, and his frustration at not being able to satisfy his curiosity about a homosexuality that resists his penetrating and invading gaze leads him to masturbate.

As opposed to other examples of same-sex erotic behavior in the novel, in his rejection of heterosexuality and the absence of any indication that he only plays the passive role, Zahir seems to resemble the modern, "Western" form of homosexuality. If the narrator does not self-identify as heterosexual, he defines his own sexuality in opposition to his brother's homosexuality. The two characters could thus be read as personifications of homo- and heterosexuality and, indeed, of the homo/hetero binary, which constitutes the modern regime of sexuality that many constructionists restrict to the West. But at the same time, the narrator's efforts to assert himself as not homosexual are not completely effective, because of his own ambivalent feelings and a somewhat "homosexual" past. Therein lies the danger of homosexuality: the impenetrable distinction between hetero and homo that is supposed to characterize modern sexual difference may not be as impermeable as some might claim. Homosexuality, like sodomy, is perhaps something anyone might be capable of, which would explain why attempts by men to deny the possibility that they might be homosexual (such as ostentatious heterosexuality and queer bashing) are in fact defining characteristics of heterosexual masculinity. In spite of a certain ambivalence on the narrator's part—or perhaps it is because of this ambivalence or on the condition that it exists—Boudjedra manages to represent a heterosexual will to knowledge directed at a homosexual character (a heterosexual gaze that reduces its Other to a spectacle) and the threat presented by the figure of the homosexual in a heterosexual imaginary. In this way, the unveiling of homosexuality as a narrative operation resembles in some respects Sedgwick's description of the closet, which is not a locus of ignorance but of knowledge, knowledge of a secret *qua* secret, an open secret. The unveiling of homosexuality in *La répudiation*, therefore, is not a revelation *tout court*, but the unveiling of a veiling where homosexuality can only be known as enigma, secret, site of continued resistance to a heterosexual will to knowledge.

Male Panic

The homosexual panic Sedgwick describes in *Epistemology* results from a similar realization. "Homosexual panic," a pathological insecurity concerning (especially male) heterosexual identity at a point of crisis, is a *hetero*sexual fear of the potential contagion of homosexuality. When the heterosexual encounters a homosexual and this fear reaches the level of panic, "homosexual panic" can actually serve as a legal excuse for acts of homophobic violence committed as a result of this panic.[3] This use of the term, however, implies that only a minority of heterosexual men are insecure about their heterosexuality. Sedgwick, however, questions whether there could ever be a secure heterosexual masculinity:

> If the new common wisdom that hotly overt homophobes are men who are "insecure about their masculinity" supplements the implausible, necessary illusion that there could be a *secure* version of masculinity (known, presumably, by the coolness of its homophobic enforcement) and a stable, intelligible way for men to feel about other men in modern heterosexual capitalist patriarchy, what tighter turn could there be to the screw of an already off-center, always at fault, endlessly blackmailable male identity ready to be manipulated into any labor of channeled violence? (84)

The "blackmailable" aspect of masculinity mentioned here refers back to her work on the homosocial in *Between Men* (1985), where she also describes "a structural residue of terrorist potential, of *blackmailability*, of Western maleness through the leverage of homophobia" (89). The homosocial, which includes what is commonly called male bonding, represents how men interact to show each other they are indeed *real* men. But because of the instability of the break in what would otherwise be a continuum between male homosocial and homosexual behavior, male bonding always runs the risk of being interpreted as homoerotic, hence the need for them to distinguish their homosocial behavior from homosexuality. This need to prove their heterosexuality gives rise to the "terrorist potential," the "blackmailability" that is always "ready to be manipulated into any labor of channeled violence," which can be verbal (gay baiting, homophobic insults, leering at women) or physical (gang rape, queer bashing, even murder). In some of the passages quoted above, Rachid might be considered to be in a similar state of panic. Unlike the dock workers, unemployed men, and fishermen he describes from his childhood—men

---

3. Cf. Sedgwick 1990, 19–21, 138–39, 182–212.

who engage in homosexual acts without panicking about their masculinity—for the narrator, the mere presence of homosexuality is enough to send his will to know into interpretive overdrive. His act of self-definition, which requires that he set his brother's sexuality in opposition to his own through a move many scholars have claimed is unique to Western sexualities, also coincides with Sedgwick's description of a supposedly Western homosexual panic.

Although Zahir's homosexuality is not revealed until page 103, one learns that he will die on page 104. In this way, any possible danger represented by his homosexuality is displaced within the narrative through the immediate articulation of its coming elimination. One of Russo's principal arguments shows how the cinematic convention of killing off all homosexual characters before the end of the film served to keep homosexuality in the closet. The fact that the homosexual is killed in the heterosexual imaginary perhaps expresses a desire that homosexuality not exist, a desire to destroy it. Rachid's representation of Zahir's homosexuality might thus be read as an act of symbolic murder. As Rachid confines his own and his brother's homosexuality to the parenthetical past, he distances himself from these activities to articulate his identity. In this respect, the narrator has the same desire to veil, enclose his brother's threatening sexuality as to veil and sequester Céline. In short, the veil and what is called the closet in English hide, contain, and control similar dangers. Boudjedra, through his panicky version of male heterosexuality and masculinity, points to a weakness in male supremacy, a potential bombsite of future political struggle. Nations sometimes experience similar periods of panic over threats to the Nation. (In the U.S., cold-war discourse would be an example of such a panic.) Are there ways of provoking a similar panic that could result in the implosion of supremacy rather than the extermination of the perceived cause of the panic? What happens to the Nation when the perceived danger breaks out of its parenthesis and the margins to which it is confined?

Queer Anti-Imperialism

Zahir is a threat, however, to more than the narrator's heterosexual self-definition. In his resistance to a will to knowledge, Zahir also represents a political challenge to both colonial and neocolonial exploitation, personified by the narrator's father, Si Zoubir, "meaning 'Mr. Prick' in the diminutive" (Abdel-Jaouad 1996, 22–23). Si Zoubir is a fairly wealthy

merchant and collaborates with the colonial French regime even though
he later becomes a nationalist: "Tous les juges français étaient des amis
de mon père, malgré ses opinions politiques nettement tranchées" (207).
("All the French judges were friends of my father, despite his very pronounced political ideas" [163].) The father is a "membre influent du Clan"
(222) ("influential member of the Clan" [173]) and is thus one of what
the novel refers to throughout as the Membres Secrets du Clan (MSC),
a barely disguised reference to the FLN. The MSC are the ones who are
responsible for Rachid's internment and who pursue and torture him
throughout the novel. In the novel's story, which parallels recent Algerian history, before independence, the Clan carried out a revolution to overthrow French rule. After independence, the MSC replace their former
oppressor: "[L]es Membres [étaient] réputés parmi le peuple pour leur
ignorance crasse et la sauvagerie de leurs méthodes héritées de l'ancienne
puissance . . ." (217). ("[T]he members [were] renowned amongst the
population for their crass ignorance and the barbarity of their methods
inherited from the former ruling power . . ." [170].) The novel therefore
makes a Fanonian association between colonial rule and the national elite
that replaces it, for Si Zoubir continues to be a part of this new elite even
as it imprisons Rachid: "[M]a mère, ne recevant pas de mes nouvelles,
ameuterait Si Zoubir qui serait très heureux de me savoir entre les mains
de ses amis et ne ferait rien pour intervenir en ma faveur et me faire
libérer . . ." (221–22). ("[M]y mother, if she heard no news of me would
rally Si Zoubir who would be delighted to know I was in the hands of
his friends and do nothing to intercede in my favour to get me released . . ." [173].)

Zahir, not the narrator, is the character who most personifies the novel's anticolonial politics. He points out that Si Zoubir collaborates with
French colonial rule (97) and even threatens to kill his own father (102).
He represents a danger to the Clan (in a manner that parallels the way
his homosexuality endangers his brother's heterosexual masculinity), and
the novel suggests that the MSC are responsible for his death: "La mort
de mon frère n'était que la conséquence normale des actes du clan qui se
préparait déjà à une vengeance longtemps attendue . . ." (152–53). ("The
death of my brother was merely the natural consequence of the acts of
the clan already preparing itself for a long-awaited vengeance . . ." [122].)
Si Zoubir perhaps even played a role in this death: "Si Zoubir [était]
responsable [aux] yeux [de ma mère] de la mort de l'être sublimé" (169).
("Si Zoubir [was] responsible in [my mother's] eyes for the death of the

one sublimated being" [134].) Therefore, as Zahir resists his brother's heterosexual will to knowledge, he also personifies resistance to colonialism (including its indigenous agents), neocolonialism, and the postindependence ruling elite. In the manner described by Ben Jelloun, homosexuality plays a political role in this allegory of anticolonial revolution and postindependence contestation. Rachid's political opposition is paralleled by his hate for his father, who collaborated with the colonizers and who hypocritically supports the new regime. The postindependence political system is thus represented as inextricably linked to a homophobic patriarchy, and Rachid's hatred of his father is allegorical of his political opposition. In this hatred, he has an ally, Zahir, who is much more effective than he. In *Les 1001 années de la nostalgie,* women's pubic hair becomes a site of resistance to colonialism, nationalized oppression, and American neocolonialism. In *La répudiation,* the same character who fucks a buddy on the rooftop, shouts from the very same rooftop his opposition to French colonial rule, neocolonialism, and the rule of a national elite that collaborates with continued foreign domination after independence. If Rachid and his mother attempt to veil this homosexuality, the novel unveils it and reveals it as a site of political resistance.

Chapter Four

S K E L E T O N S   I N   T H E   C L O S E T :
T A H A R   D J A O U T ' S   B E T R A Y A L
O F   N A T I O N A L   S E C R E T S

If Boudjedra describes the attempt to eliminate the danger of Zahir's homosexuality by relegating it to the past, Tahar Djaout has gone back to
find what was lost and bring it back. Algerian poet, journalist, and critic
of both the religious right and military ruling elite in Algeria, Djaout was
assassinated by fundamentalists in the summer of 1993.[1] In his novels *Les
chercheurs d'os* (1984) and *L'invention du désert* (1987), he uncovers the
hidden secrets of national history, secrets that must be forgotten and left
inside what one might call the Nation's closet. He insists on remembering
and revealing these secrets to challenge not only the Algerian ruling elite,
but also its fundamentalist opposition. *Les chercheurs d'os* is about, quite
literally, digging up bones. Sent by his parents, the young narrator sets
out in search of the remains of his brother, who died fighting for national
liberation in the Algerian Revolution. The quest to repatriate these bones
to their village succeeds, but this is not the only skeleton dug up over the
course of the novel's narrative itinerary. The bones of dead fighters also
come to represent skeletons in the closets of national history and the skeleton at the feast of the new elite's economic privileges. When Djaout
drags them out of the Nation's closet, however, they become the past that

---

1. It is not always clear that every attack attributed to fundamentalists is actually committed by
them. In a *New York Times* article on massacres in Algeria, presumably carried out by fundamentalists, Roger Cohen writes, "Many observers have concluded that the hard-line members of the
military-backed Government have either been prepared to tolerate the attacks or even to initiate
them" (A8). Many Algerian intellectuals have maintained for some time now that the government
could have committed any given assassination just as easily as the fundamentalist opposition. The
French government has also argued along these lines, but since it may be attempting to justify Western intervention in the Algerian conflict, its position cannot be considered disinterested.

haunts the present, the unofficial history that contests the rule of a new elite by revealing how it has betrayed the revolution. In *L'invention du désert*, the closet that holds the skeleton of national secrets turns out to be the same as the one hiding homosexuality. The narrator, charged with writing the history of the Almoravid dynasty,[2] ends up revealing the succeeding dynasty's repression of male homosexuality, a repression they used to consolidate their power. Djaout reveals these secrets through novelistic *re*writings of history by reclaiming what has been "hidden from history"[3] and bringing skeletons out of the Nation's closet, bringing history itself out of the closet.

From the very beginning of *Les chercheurs*, the young narrator questions the task he must fulfill, even going so far as to hope that his mission fails. His brother, in leaving to join the guerrillas, escaped from a "village tyrannique" (25) (tyrannical village). The narrator associates the struggle for national liberation with the quest for individual freedom and ability to leave and travel; in liberating his nation, his brother also liberated himself. The mission to repatriate his bones, however, goes against this personal liberation and borders on disrespect for the dead. Instead of resting in peace in the soil of a free country, his brother's bones are tossed about, disturbed: "Ils s'entrechoquent comme des pièces de monnaie à chaque fois que l'âne trébuche ou aborde les chemins encaissés" (147). (They rattle like coins each time the ass stumbles or approaches steeply embanked paths.) And the narrator describes this exhumation as a grave robbery: "[De] chercheurs d'os que nous avons été au départ nous étions devenus des voleurs d'os" (151). (Instead of the bone searchers we had been at first, we had become bone thieves.) His brother's skeleton is subjected to sacrilege at the hands of gravediggers who give themselves the right to disturb him:

> La famille vous harcèle de votre vivant, multiplie les entraves et les bâillons et, une fois qu'elle vous a poussé vers la tombe, elle s'arroge des droits draconiens sur votre squelette. Allez donc me chercher une contrée où l'on ne dispose même pas librement de ses os! On meurt en croyant laisser derrière soi des parents inconsolables et ce sont des vautours insatiables qui pourchassent vos os comme pour en extraire un reste de moelle. (149)

2. The Almoravid dynasty ruled what is now Morocco from the mid-1000s to the mid-1100s. Their area of control included Islamic Spain and stretched as far east as Algiers and as far south as ancient Ghana and Timbuktu. They founded the city of Marrakesh as their capital.

3. Cf. the title of Duberman, Vicinus, and Chauncey's *Hidden from History: Reclaiming the Lesbian and Gay Past*.

> The family harasses you while you're alive, multiplies the fetters and the gags, and once they have pushed you into the grave, they presumptuously assume draconian rights over your skeleton. Try and find a place where you can't even dispose freely of your own bones! You die thinking that you leave behind inconsolable relatives, and they are insatiable vultures that pursue your bones as if to suck out the last remaining bit of marrow.

Here the narrator reverses the usual relation between the living and the dead; the dead are no longer the ones who come back to haunt the living, but the living constitute a hell that disturbs, haunts the dead, who are denied the possibility of resting in peace. The vulture image says a great deal about this relationship, because these are the birds that feed on carcasses and profit from others' deaths; without even waiting for the death of their prey, they circle over it in a deathwatch.

The search for skeletons seems to benefit the living more than honor the dead: "Mais voilà, chaque famille, chaque personne a besoin de sa petite poignée d'os bien à elle pour justifier l'arrogance et les airs importants qui vont caractériser son comportement à venir sur la place du village" (21). (So there, every family, each person, needs their little handful of bones all to themselves in order to justify their arrogance and hotshot attitude that will characterize their future behavior on the village square.) Fighters' bones carry a moral authority founded on the spilt blood of guerrillas martyred while fighting against the immoral colonial system. This authority lies in relics rather than being guided by ideals or principles. Whoever possesses these relics may channel their power, regardless of how the power is used: "Des gamins . . . allaient «farfouiller dans les registres de la mort» pour lui disputer des squelettes dont les vivants avaient besoin pour atténuer l'éclat trop insolent des richesses que le nouveau monde dispensait" (10). (Children . . . went 'rummaging through the death certificates' to wrangle skeletons needed by the living to soften the all-too-insolent dazzle of wealth that the new world was handing out.)

Now, or even when the novel was published (1984), the reference to a wealth that the new government had promised to distribute and a new economic order that merely led up to the Algerian government's renunciation of socialism can only be ironic.[4] Describing a celebration at a place called La-Source-de-la-Vache, the narrator states: "Les riches de toujours que l'Indépendance du pays avait épargnés et les nouveaux notables en-

---

4. Shaaban writes, "The National Charter adopted in 1976 replaced the secular socialist principles of the State with an official commitment to Islam as the State religion . . ." (182).

richis par l'Indépendance viennent assurer et faire bénir leurs biens" (67).
(Those who'd always been rich and whom the country's independence
had spared and the new notables made rich by independence came to
secure their wealth and have it blessed.) Instead of a redistribution of
wealth, the new nation witnesses a consolidation of the old bourgeoisie
and the formation of a new elite. Yet, this consolidation does not prevent
the promise of economic equity from having a powerful hold on the national consciousness:

> Le mot a été connu: le pays possède désormais un gouvernement qui est à
> tout le monde et qui a des richesses à distribuer à pleines poignées. Alors
> beaucoup de villageois ont déserté leurs maisons, ont vendu leur paire de
> bœufs et leur maigre troupeau de chèvres ou de moutons pour être moins
> encombrés. Ils se sont entassés devant les locaux administratifs dans l'at-
> tente de la manne, y passant parfois la nuit pour ne pas rater la première
> minute d'ouverture.
>
>   Au code d'honneur et aux coutumes des ancêtres ils ont substitué un
> autre code fait de papiers, d'extraits d'actes et d'attestations divers, de
> cartes de différentes couleurs. Les portefeuilles ont commencé à se gonfler
> de paperasses et les paysans ont dû solliciter à tout moment le concours de
> personnes lettrées pour leur faire distinguer un document d'un autre.
> (36–37)

> The word was out: from here on out, the country has a government that
> belongs to everyone and wealth to distribute by the handfuls. So lots of
> villagers have deserted their homes, sold their pair of oxen and their
> skimpy troop of goats or sheep so as to be less encumbered. They have
> piled into the administrative bureaus to wait for the manna and sometimes
> even spent the night so as not to miss the first minute of opening.
>
>   In place of the ancestor's customs and code of honor, they have substi-
> tuted another code made up of papers, diverse certificates and vouchers,
> variously colored cards. Billfolds have begun to swell with paperwork, and
> at every moment, peasants have had to request the aid of educated people
> to distinguish one document from another.

In contrast with socialist principles, however, which emphasize work,
the universal right to employment, and the importance of eliminating
the class that, living like vultures off of others, does not work, here the
awaited redistribution of wealth excludes labor. This passage also juxtaposes the promise of a new economic order with the reality of a new
bureaucratic and administrative one. To be valid, membership in the new
Nation must be recognized officially from now on.

   Other Maghrebian writers have examined the significance of the identification card's relation to power. Moha's marginality, for example, is emphasized by his lack of an identification card. In his case, there is a connection between the new national elite and the former colonial power, which institutionalizes identity not (or not only) as an articulation of individual subjectivity, but as a thing, a piece of paper one must carry around, that may be inspected at any time. The protagonist of Rachid Mimouni's *Le fleuve détourné* (1982) also testifies to the power of a bureaucracy that retains the prerogative to recognize or withhold an identity and to exclude a person from the Nation by refusing her citizenship. Waking up after a long amnesia—due to an explosion during his participation in the Algerian Revolution—to discover his status as national hero and martyr, this hero cannot even get the bureaucracy to acknowledge that he is alive, so useful is his death to his family (which inherited his property), his wife (who receives a widow's pension), and the state (which is threatened by the hero's statements that he did not fight a revolution to install bureaucracy or corruption in the place of colonial rule). As far as the bureaucracy is concerned, he does not exist. In *Les chercheurs* as well, the bones of former fighters have a role to play in this reign of paperwork. With bones, one can obtain the papers necessary for an officially recognized identity within the new administrative order:

> Ces os constituent un prélude plutôt cocasse à la débauche de papiers, certificats et attestations divers qui feront quelque temps après leur apparition et leur loi intransigeante. Malheur à qui n'aura ni os ni papiers à exhiber devant l'incrédulité de ses semblables! Malheur à qui n'aura pas compris que la parole ne vaut plus rien et que l'ère du serment oral est à jamais révolue! (21)

> These bones constitute a rather laughable prelude to the deluge of various papers, certificates, and vouchers that will soon make their appearance and become an inescapable law. Woe to her who has neither bones nor papers to exhibit before incredulous neighbors. Woe to him who does not understand that the days are gone when one's word was as good as gold!

The old codes of honor, linked to orality, make way for paperwork, devalorized here less by privileging the oral over the written than because of the degradation of the written represented by bureaucracy. If the narrator seems to reject tradition (represented by his village) in favor of a so-called modernity, this rejection is far from being absolute even if, in one passage, he seems to reject all of Algeria: "Je les comprends maintenant ces fils de familles très pieuses, très respectables et très pauvres qui traversent une fois la mer et disent adieu à leur passé" (36). (I understand them now, those sons of very pious, respectable, poor families who cross the sea once and for all and say good-bye to the past.) In other passages, as we shall see, he also rejects the modern brought by colonialism or independence.

Symbols of the opposition to colonialism and of the hope of an independent nation, these bones can also testify that the distinction between the two orders is not as clear as promised. For this reason, the memory they signify, like a skeleton in the closet, constitutes a danger for power. The dead are therefore exhumed only to be buried again, this time deeper than before:

> D'un côté on respecte immodérément les morts comme pour justifier la vie impossible que l'on fait aux vivants, et de l'autre on les exhume pour vérifier si on ne peut leur soutirer encore quelque chose avant de les réenterrer plus profondément, là où même le souvenir ne pourra plus les retrouver. (149)

> On the one hand, they exaggerate their respect for the dead as if to justify making life impossible for the living, and on the other, they dig up the dead to see whether they can't suck something else out of them before burying them again, even deeper, where not even memory will be able to find them.

Instead of constituting an act of remembering or honoring him, bringing the brother back to his village is a way of forgetting him. By burying the dead again, the living are sure of not being disturbed:

> Pourquoi tient-on à déterrer à tout prix ces morts glorieux et les changer de sépulture? Veut-on s'assurer qu'ils sont bien morts et qu'ils ne viendront plus jamais exiger leur part de la fête et contester nos discours et nos démonstrations patriotiques, notre bonheur de rescapés d'une guerre pourtant aveugle et sans merci? Ou alors, tient-on, tout simplement, à ce qu'ils soient enterrés plus profondément que tous les autres morts? Allez donc comprendre les hommes! Ils pleurent des êtres qu'ils prétendent plus chers que tout au monde puis s'empressent de déterrer leurs restes pour les enfouir plus hermétiquement. (47)

> Why do they insist on digging up at any price the glorious dead and changing their tombs? Do they want to assure themselves that the dead are really dead and that they won't come back to demand their share of the feast and contest our speeches and patriotic displays, our happiness for escaping a blind war that had no mercy? Or rather, do they simply want to bury the dead again, deeper than all the others? Go, try and understand

men! They weep for those they claim to be dearer than everything else in the world, and then they trip over each other in the rush to dig up the remains in order to bury them even more hermetically.

The presence of those who fought for freedom points out how much it is lacking. Like a skeleton at the feast, the guerrillas' remains trouble and disturb celebrations of a newly acquired freedom as well as political speeches and the recuperation of the revolution into dominant discourse, which already uses the revolution to justify the consolidation of power in the hands of a new elite. Mostefa Lacheraf (1968) describes a similar "pseudopatriotic exploitation" of the Algerian Revolution in the official vision of how literature should represent the struggle for independence. Like Djaout, Lacheraf denounces this use of individualistic hero worship and accuses the national bourgeoisie—which "perpetuates an anachronistic nationalism and distracts people from new realities and the necessary struggle to transform society in a concrete way"—of using this heroism to maintain power. Like Lacheraf, Djaout refuses this vision of the revolution and seems, rather, to satisfy the role of the committed writer defined by the former in the following way:

> Novelists must not become accomplices of such a maneuver, and if they have to speak of the collective, popular epic of national liberation, which really existed, let them especially not neglect to evoke the shameful role of a bourgeoisie of traitors and vultures and explain how the revolution—for which a million peasants, workers, low-ranking clerks, and intellectuals died—was confiscated by traffickers, opportunists, and collaborators of the defunct colonial regime who have barely even repented. . . . (cited in Bonn 1974, 227)

Like the parents who had the brother's skeleton brought back, this rapacious elite survives thanks to the death of others. The bourgeoisie Lacheraf describes kidnaps the revolution and uses it discursively to justify and maintain its privilege.

Reburied, the bones in *Les chercheurs* will no longer be able to point out this "rôle honteux de la bourgeoisie traître et rapace" or trouble the party:

> Ce qui nous importe le plus, n'est-ce pas de l'enterrer une seconde fois— et plus profondément encore—afin qu'il ne s'avise plus jamais de venir troubler notre paix et notre bonne conscience? C'est comme si nous n'étions pas sûrs qu'il fût bien mort tant que nous n'avions pas à portée du regard cette nouvelle tombe sécurisante. (148)

Wasn't the most important thing for us to bury him a second time—even deeper still—so that he would never get it into his head to come disturb our peace and good conscience? It was as if we weren't sure he was good and dead as long as we didn't have within view this new reassuring tomb.

If the narrator in *Le fleuve détourné* returns like a ghost to threaten the status quo, the brother's skeleton in *Les chercheurs* represents a similar danger for the family and the state. Burying him again sets this danger aside and controls it, and burying him "hermétiquement" not only protects him from the elements, but also makes him impenetrable to knowledge. Since these bones resist a will to knowledge, they also resist being controlled by power. Those who dig up the former guerrillas control the possible meanings their bones might have in the national imaginary: "Tout ce que nous demandons désormais c'est d'en finir, d'exhumer ce squelette ubiquiste et farceur et de le ligoter solidement dans notre sac afin de nous en débarrasser une fois pour toutes" (144). (From now on, all we ask for is to get it over with, dig up that farcical, ubiquitous skeleton, and tie him up good in our bag to get rid of him once and for all.) The brother, who appreciated individual and collective freedom so much that he died for it, will soon find himself imprisoned: "Et voici que nous le ramenons, captif, les os solidement liés, dans ce village qu'il n'avait sans doute jamais aimé" (148). (And here we were bringing him back, captive, bones securely tied up, into this village, which he undoubtedly never liked.) Buried at first by chance, wherever they fell, these bones, like floating signifiers, were available for whoever wanted to articulate the hope of freedom they represented. Dug up, reburied, their semiotic strength is "ligoté," channeled into official discourse. Otherwise, the danger they represent is apt to pop up at any moment and return to haunt.

On the one hand, "les changer de sépulture" is a way of displaying them better:

> Le peuple aurait très bien pu élever une digue entre le passé et lui pour fortifier son nouveau bonheur; il aurait pu jeter ses morts avec l'eau putride de la baignoire guerrière pour savourer en bonne conscience une quiétude chèrement acquise. Mais le peuple tenait à ses morts comme à une preuve irréfutable à exhiber un jour devant le parjure du temps et des hommes. (10–11)

> The people could have very well erected a barrier between itself and the past in order to strengthen its new happiness; it could have thrown out the dead with the putrid bath water of war in order to savor in good con-

science a tranquillity acquired at great expense. But the people hung on to
its dead as to an irrefutable proof to exhibit one day before the perjury of
time and men.

Buried in his village, the brother serves as proof of his family's contribution to the revolution (even though those who live to reap the benefits of
this heroic reputation were in no way courageous). On the other hand,
this ostentatious remembering is also a way of forgetting the lack of heroism on the part of the survivors: "Ceux qui ont un fils ou petit-fils tombé
sous les balles se sentent encore plus coupables: ils n'auraient pas pu,
les pleutres, les égoïstes, les procréateurs indignes, aller eux-mêmes
au-devant de la mort les premiers comme la nature l'exige?" (18). (Those
who had a son or grandson who fell under the bullets felt even guiltier:
couldn't those wimps, those egoists, those unworthy breeders, have
braved death first as nature demands?) Pseudonationalist exhibitionism
also hides by putting the skeleton back in the closet where it can no
longer disturb the feast.

Djaout's purpose, however, is not to bury skeletons, but to dig them
up. Instead of hiding the skeleton, he prefers to bear its burden: "C'est
[l'âne] qui porte le fardeau mais le véritable poids du squelette est sur nos
épaules et dans nos têtes" (152). (It's the donkey that bears the weight, but
the skeleton's real burden rests on our shoulders and in our heads.) And
this burden is not only physical, but also psychological and even political.
The brother's skeleton is not the only one to be dug up during Djaout's
narrative: "The literal act of exhumation of *maquisard* remains is juxta-
posed with the inspiration this quest provides for the narrator's anamne-
sis, his 're-membering' of the incidents in the village before, during, and
immediately following the War of Independence" (Geesey 272). Since the
narrative of Djaout's novel therefore constitutes a rewriting of national
history, Djaout, himself, is a *chercheur d'os* who brings skeletons out from
their hiding place to bear their burden and dig up their secret. As Geesey
also points out (273), looking for bones thus becomes a metaphor for
what Michel de Certeau (1975) has called "the writing of history." By
describing "what must be *forgotten* in order to obtain the representation
of a present intelligibility" (4), de Certeau emphasizes that, in addition
to constituting a remembering of the past, history also involves forgetting. The brother's bones, along with all they represent, are precisely what
must be forgotten in Djaout's novel.

While one might think that the role of historiography is to uncover or dig up the past, de Certeau characterizes writing history as, at least in part, a burial: "Writing speaks of the past only in order to inter it. Writing is a tomb in the double sense of the word in that, in the very same text, it both honors and eliminates" (101). Thus while pretending to be a discourse about discovery, writing history simultaneously hides what it supposedly reveals: "The work of history (*Geschichte*) endlessly conceals what had been legible, and through the very gesture that reduces the simple element in order to discover it" (297). Although the brother is honored along with the other martyrs in Djaout's novel, ultimately he is eliminated, i.e. reburied. In de Certeau's account, what is buried is precisely the dead; for without death there is no history: "[H]istory becomes the myth of language. It manifests the very condition of discourse: *a death*" (46). And history "writing places a population of the dead on stage" (99). Although history offers a stage to the ghosts of the dead, it denies them a voice: "These ghosts find access through *writing* on the condition that they remain *forever silent*" (2). The ghostwriting de Certeau describes resembles the official version of the Algerian Revolution, rewritten by the elite to justify its privilege:

> During the anti-French Resistance War (1954–62) and, more particularly, following the Soummam Congress (1956), military oligarchs seized control of a revolutionary movement that began with widespread popular support. After the Algerian Independence in 1962, they sought to legitimate their own tyranny in the name of nationalism and patriarchy, a gesture which culminated in 1980 when the Algerian government launched a campaign to write—in other words, in order to falsify—the modern history of Algeria. (Gafaïti 1996, 814)

Djaout's narrator, however, contests this version of history. Although de Certeau does not seem to acknowledge the possibility of conflicting versions of history, of a counterdiscourse of historiography that would question the systemic forgetting that characterizes history writing in his account, he does state that whereas the dead may be buried, they can also return to haunt the present: "The dead souls resurge, within the work whose postulate was their disappearance and the possibility of analyzing them as an object of investigation" (36–37). The haunting that threatens even official versions of history can thus be exploited and exacerbated. Such is the task Djaout takes on in *Les chercheurs*.

In *L'invention du désert* as well, Djaout articulates a model of writing history that gives over the Nation's secrets and digs up its skeletons. In this later novel, he also uncovers sexualities previously hidden from history and extends his critique to include both the ruling elite and its fundamentalist opposition, which had already begun to gain momentum at the time of the novel's publication. *L'invention* is precisely a narrative of writing history, for its narrator is given the task of telling the story of the Almoravid dynasty. Again, Djaout uses historiography to dig up bones of the past, for the narrator/historian explicitly makes the comparison of bones to history that one finds in *Les chercheurs:* "Ma tête est semblable à ces outres où les Indiens transportent, au gré de leurs migrations, les os de leurs ancêtres. L'histoire almoravide clignote dans un lointain assoupissement, elle cliquette à l'intérieur de mon crâne . . ." (*L'invention* 26). (My head is like those leather pouches the Indians used during their migrations to transport their ancestors' bones. Almoravid history flickers in a faraway drowsiness and is clanking around in my head. . . .) And this clinking strangely recalls that of the brother's bones, which knock together during the return to his village in *Les chercheurs.* Just as the burden of the brother's skeleton is psychological as well as physical, the skeleton of Almoravid history disturbs the psychological state of the one who writes it. In another passage, the narrator uses the image of a skeleton to describe what he uncovers (digs up) during this itinerary of writing history: "On rencontre, tout au plus, les débris d'un frémissement venu d'au-delà des mémoires: squelettes pierreux, érigés comme stèles intemporelles . . ." (137). (At the most, one encounters the debris of a shiver coming from beyond memory: rocky skeletons, erected like timeless steles. . . .) Given the task of writing the Almoravids' history, *L'invention's* narrator decides to do so from the point of view of Ibn Toumert, founder of the Almohad dynasty that overthrew it. Instead of the height of the dynasty's glory, he is interested in its fall.

In *L'invention,* the narrator relates not only the origin of an Arabo-Berber dynasty, but also the sexual repression that went hand in hand with taking power. The narrator, in writing Ibn Toumert's story, states:

> Il commença par s'attaquer frénétiquement à une pratique dont il remarqua qu'elle s'exerçait en plein jour et sans aucun couvert: l'homosexualité masculine.
>
> A peine installé dans sa mosquée, l'imam descendit dans la ville et un spectacle l'arrêta puis porta son sang à ébullition: des garçons habillés en femmes, embellis et fardés comme elles, se promenaient avec coquetterie

sur l'esplanade près de la mer. Les habitants, au lieu d'être outrés, passaient leur chemin sans broncher ou alors, lorsqu'ils s'arrêtaient à proximité des garçons, c'était pour les considérer avec des airs amusés, les jaugeant avec convoitise comme on ferait d'une précieuse marchandise. (23)

He began by frantically attacking a practice that he noticed occurring in the light of day without any cover: male homosexuality.

Barely having moved into his mosque, the Imam went down into the city, and a spectacle stopped him short in his tracks and made his blood boil: boys, dressed as women, prettied up with make-up like women, coquettishly strolled about the promenade by the sea. Far from being upset, the locals went on their way without even blinking, or else, when they stopped in the boys' vicinity, it was to amuse themselves by checking them out, gauging with envy as one might do with a precious merchandise.

In the era evoked by the narrator, male homosexuality did not need unveiling; there was nothing secretive about it. Ibn Toumert is the only one who attacks and tries to eliminate it, or (since sexual repression has never managed to destroy what it targets but only to drive it underground) to force it into the closet. What is surprising is that Ibn Toumert, in his desire to annihilate homosexuality, is in the minority. When he attacks the *éphèbes* to drive them from the public square, he is the one who must flee for his life. The narrator also describes another attack by Ibn Toumert at a sumptuous circumcision celebration:

Gent mâle et gent femelle évoluaient dans le même espace, et les mêmes intraitables garçons circulaient entre les convives en faisant tinter leurs anneaux et en exhibant leurs lèvres peintes.

L'imam se précipita encore tel un forcené, usant de coups et d'imprécations, escomptant séparer les deux sexes et donner une nouvelle leçon aux jeunes hommes dépravés. (24)

Persons male and female carried on in the same space, and circulating among the guests, the same incorrigible boys made music with the rings on their fingers and showed off their painted lips.

Again, the Imam rushed in like a madman, preaching and dealing blows, determined to separate the two sexes and teach the depraved young men a lesson.

Ibn Toumert opposes male homosexuality, but especially its blatancy, which he associates with a lack of separation between the sexes. Abun-Nasr describes a similar attack carried out by the actual historical figure Ibn Toumert, this time against an unveiled woman: ". . . Ibn Tumart had had the audacity of throwing the [Almoravid] amir's sister off her horse when he saw her in the street unveiled" (104). With this historical example, the parallels between the rise of the Almohads and the fundamentalist movement's attempts to gain power become clear.

In his writing of history Djaout thus reveals a violence that, as in "Qu'est-ce qu'une nation?" (1882), Ernest Renan describes as being at every nation's origin:

> Forgetting, I would even go so far as to say historical error, is a crucial factor in the creation of a nation, which is why progress in historical studies often constitutes a danger for [the principle of] nationality. Indeed, historical enquiry brings to light deeds of violence which took place at the origin of all political formations, even those whose consequences have been altogether beneficial.[5] (11)

The forgetting Renan describes thus reveals de Certeau's notion of writing history as a nationalist project. The violence at the origin of the Almohad dynasty, however, is also a violence against sexual minorities. In this sense, the sexual secrets described by Ben Jelloun in "Défendre la diversité" are as dangerous for the Nation as the political secrets at the Nation's origin described by Renan. Again, Djaout uses writing history to dig up bones of the past and bring sexual secrets out of the Nation's closets. Bhabha, who himself has commented on Renan's essay, credits what he calls "minority discourse" with playing an especially important role in challenging official versions of national history: "Minority discourse . . . contests genealogies of 'origin' that lead to claims for cultural supremacy and historical priority. Minority discourse acknowledges the status of national culture—and the people—as a contentious, performative space of the perplexity of the living in the midst of the pedagogical representations of the fullness of life" (1994, 157). When read along with Djaout, Bhabha's minority discourse can have a special significance for sexual minorities. Revealing the sexual secrets of history

---

5. Renan wrote during the second half of the nineteenth century and is better known for his racist ideas and justification of French colonialism in North Africa. He delivered "Qu'est-ce qu'une nation?" as a speech just eleven years after France's defeat by Prussia. In spite of his insights on the Nation, he justifies the original violence rather than criticizes it. One might object that the Nation described by Renan is a uniquely European construct and that imposing such a model on a Maghrebian novel would be problematic. One of the legacies of colonialism, however, has been that, in order to decolonize themselves, colonized peoples have had to assert themselves as nations by European standards. The Nation, itself, has been a colonial imposition sometimes (especially in the case of certain parts of sub-Saharan Africa) without any correlation to the precolonial divisions or groupings combined or separated by the borders drawn up by colonial authorities.

challenges official discourses that justify rule by the national elites Fanon
warned would replace the colonizer.

For *L'invention du désert*'s narrator/historian, writing history constitutes an unveiling of sexual secrets, an unveiling that threatens. As the
novel's back cover indicates, "ressusciter le passé est une entreprise qui
peut lâcher sur le présent des hantises et des démons insoupçonnés" (resurrecting the past is an enterprise that can let loose on the present
hauntings and unsuspected demons). Unlike Ibn Toumert, who attempts
to chase homosexuality from the public sphere as the historical figure
attempted to veil women by force, the narrator returns it precisely to
that space. The Almoravids' "histoire d'une hantise et d'un dépaysement"
(107) (history of a haunting and a homesickness) also represents a
haunting for the narrator/historian of the novel's present: "Je congédie les
Almoravides pour m'engourdir sans témoins. Ils sortent lentement de ma
tête, fantômes langés de bures de laine" (41). (So as to vegetate without
witnesses, I dismiss the Almoravids. They leave my head slowly, like
phantoms swaddled in brown wool.) The skeletons dug up in writing
history are like ghosts released into the collective consciousness of the
present-day Nation. Homosexuality, in Djaout's novel, comes out of the
closet of history to haunt the Nation's present.

Djaout describes this haunting's effect by bringing Ibn Toumert into
the novel's present. The narrator imagines him as a *flâneur* in Paris who
is shocked by a lack of morals:

> Dieu est sans doute décédé—à moins qu'il n'ait été lui aussi gagné à la
> mollesse des stupres. Mais n'a-t-il pas été plutôt détrôné par Satan qui
> cultive désormais en maître sur la planète des Sodome et des Gomorrhe?
> Onan est réhabilité, il narre devant l'humanité ses ignominieuses prou-
> esses. (51)

> God must be dead—unless he too has been won over by the looseness of
> debauchery. Or rather, hasn't he been dethroned by Satan who, hereafter
> as master, has been planting Sodoms and Gomorrahs all over the planet?
> Onan is rehabilitated, and he is narrating his ignominious prowess to all
> of humanity.

His attempt to oppose this Western decadence with a so-called Muslim
purity fails because, in la Goutte-d'Or (a Parisian neighborhood with a
large immigrant population) he witnesses the same "decadence": "[O]ui,
hommes et femmes mêlés, comme les impudiques Nazaréens . . ." (54).
(Yes, men and women mixed together, like shameless Christians. . . .)

Not only is Ibn Toumert confronted with loose morals, but he also ends up being contaminated by them and participating in them: "Ibn Toumert sort en titubant, bourré d'alcool, de ressentiment et de nostalgie. . . . Il rue comme un forcené pour quitter la prison de ma tête" (56). (Ibn Toumert stumbled out, plastered drunk from alcohol, filled with resentment and nostalgia. . . . He charges like a madman to break out of the prison of my head.) What happens to Ibn Toumert as he encounters the present represents the effect of rewriting history from the margins. The hidden secret of the Nation's past is dangerous because, contagious, it threatens to infect the present. By revealing the sexual secrets of Maghrebian history and displaying the Nation's dirty laundry, Djaout commits an act of treason similar to the one described by Ben Jelloun. Like a traitor, Djaout gives over national secrets as he gives over the historical character Ibn Toumert:

> [J]e compte [le] livrer, pieds et poings liés, à la lecture irrespectueuse, à la fringale des analystes. Il ne restera rien de sa piété ni de sa folie fondatrice. Pauvre hère rêvant de prophétie, il sera offert au public avec ses burnous crasseux, sa paranoïa débusquée, son Œdipe entortillé, tous ses incestes rentrés et ses dérivatifs d'impuissant. (76)

> I count on giving him over, hands and feet bound, to a disrespectful reading, to famished analysts. Nothing will be left of his piety, nor of his founding folly. Poor wretch dreaming of prophecy, he'll be offered up to the public with his filthy robes, his ousted paranoia, his confounded Oedipus complex, his incest put back into place, and his diverted impotence.

Like the tied-up skeleton in *Les chercheurs,* here, Ibn Toumert, dug up from the past, "pieds et poings liés," is brought back to the present, where, in the narrator's imagination, he occupies the same position as the *enfant terrible,* traveler, and homosexual poet, Rimbaud: "[I]l convenait que j'arrive à déterminer qui m'habitait réellement: Ibn Toumert ou Rimbaud?" (71). (It was appropriate that I figure out who actually inhabited me: Ibn Toumert or Rimbaud?)

Ibn Toumert is brought into the present in another way as well. We learn that, whereas he came to power by attacking the preceding dynasty's moral decay, though he seems to represent innovation, he is in fact repeating history. The preceding dynasty was also based on a puritanism that disappeared as soon as it was no longer needed:

> Le tribalisme puritain qui avait constitué la charpente de la dynastie fit place au ramollissement, au désir de mieux vivre: vins, riches tables et hé-

taïres vinrent révéler et dénoncer le rigorisme mutilant; des affaires de mœurs, des bacchanales ne tardèrent pas à alimenter la chronique du royaume.

Comment en était arrivée là une dynastie dont le puritanisme avait été le motif fondateur? (16)

The puritan tribalism that made for the dynasty's rise gave way to a loosening of morals, a desire for better living: wines, succulent meals, hetaerae came to reveal and denounce the choking rigor; scandals, bacchanals wasted no time in feeding into the royal chronicles.

How had a dynasty whose puritanism had been the founding virtue come to this?

By resurrecting history repeating itself, Djaout draws attention to the fact that Algerian history is once again repeating itself and uses history as an allegory of the present. One dynasty (the religious right) is attempting to overthrow the one in place (a military ruling elite). The state Ibn Toumert is in the process of founding, like its predecessor, begins with a violence directed against sexuality, and this antisexual violence constitutes the Nation's secret described by Renan. According to Chebel, "marginal sexualities constitute an accurate indication of the moral order in place, of tolerance, and especially of a society's behavioral creativity" (1988, 17). He suggests that in a repressive society, marginal sexualities are often the first targets.[6] Djaout reveals that attacks on marginal sexualities have a political purpose in addition to attempting to legislate the Nation's family values; they are also a political weapon used to bring ruling elites to power.

However, one should not too quickly characterize this vision of writing history as purely iconoclastic. Though it is true that the author betrays national secrets, at the same time, the narrator reclaims Ibn Toumert for national history:

J'ai une admiration sans retenue pour la vigilance d'Ibn Toumert. Il arrive souvent que le mahdi fondateur m'échappe, profitant de mon surmenage ou d'une distraction salutaire pour briser les verrous de ma tête et partir sillonner en découvreur les rapides traîtres du futur. (57)

I didn't hold back in my admiration for the vigilance of Ibn Toumert. It often happens that the founding *mahdi* escapes me by taking advantage of my being overworked or healthily distracted in order to break open the

---

6. This point is made more explicitly in Chebel 1994.

locks in my head and, cutting through the future's treacherous rapids, set out for discovery.

The narrator identifies with Ibn Toumert's historical importance as the founder of an Arabo-Berber dynasty as much as he destabilizes Ibn Toumert's puritanism. Djaout, a Berber himself, by digging through Maghrebian history to find Berber sources, contradicts the government's official policies of Arabicization, which in fact, have also been taken up by the fundamentalist opposition. Although this critique conforms to a well-known Kabyle opposition to this fundamentalism, instead of reinforcing the Arab/Berber division exploited (and to a great extent created) by the colonizers in their divide-and-conquer tactics, Djaout chooses a historical figure in whom Arab and Berber cultures mix. In addition, he situates the opposition's puritanism in a long tradition wherein sexual repression serves to consolidate power. If this contextualization seems pessimistic in demonstrating that history repeats itself, it is also optimistic in envisioning for the present armed opposition a death similar to that of previous ones. Djaout, however, is far from rejecting Islam in favor of a secularism whose expression in French bourgeois philosophy coincided with the project of colonialism. One might even find his model for writing history within Islam. When he writes

$$\text{Rév}_{\text{o}\ \text{u}}^{\acute{\text{e}}\ \text{la}}\text{tion} \ (63)$$

he emphasizes the political revolution that accompanied the revelation of a new religion. But in another sense, he alludes to the political role of history as he conceives it: the revelation of what orthodoxy prefers to hide participates in the revolution begun by the brother in *Les chercheurs,* but "détourné" (or diverted, to use Mimouni's image) by a new elite. In this sense, Djaout shares Fanon's revolutionary project of a national liberation that leads directly to sociopolitical revolution.

Upon returning to the village with the skeleton in hand, the narrator of *Les chercheurs d'os* finds another source of resistance to the conformity he criticizes. This resistance occurs in the character of his uncle, within the same society the narrator characterizes as oppressive:

Mais mon oncle n'est pas malheureux. Je me rends même compte maintenant qu'il possède des privilèges, entre autres celui d'être dispensé de toutes ces corvées d'os. Il n'est importuné par aucun squelette empoisonnant qui hanterait son sommeil ou le ferait courir par monts et par vaux. Malgré sa rogne continuelle et la crainte qu'il inspire à ses vis-à-vis, c'est peut-être lui le vrai sage du village. Vu notre lien de parenté, il était tout désigné pour m'accompagner à la place de Rabah Ouali. Mais il n'a jamais eu l'air de prendre au sérieux toutes ces histoires de squelettes. (151)

> But my uncle was not unhappy. I realize now that he had the privilege, among others, of being excused from all these bone chores. He isn't bothered by any poisonous skeleton that would haunt his sleep or send him searching far and wide. In spite of his constant griping and the fear he instills in his neighbors, he is perhaps the true wise man of the village. Given how we were related, he is the one who should have come with me to Rabah Ouali. But he never seemed to take seriously all this to-do about skeletons.

The uncle's contestatory stance is also related to sexuality, for he refuses to repudiate his barren wife (is she barren or is he sterile?) and defies reproductive conformity, which inscribes pleasure in an economy of sexual (re)production. His uncle is no more threatened by the haunting of historical secrets represented by skeletons than by the demands of sexual normativity. The discovery of his uncle's resistance complicates the binary oppositions between tradition and modernity, village and city, Islam and secularism, private and public, and personal and political; it is inscribed in the in-between space located in the conflict between tradition and modernity, which is fundamental to the role of history in relation to national identity in Djaout's work.

Hédi Abdel-Jaouad, in "The Dialectics of the Archaic and the Postmodern in Maghrebian Literature Written in French" (1991), and Antoine Raybaud, in "Nomadism between the Archaic and the Modern" (1993), describe a similar tension in dealing with the past. Raybaud describes a "nomadism of nostalgia" that is a desire not to return to the past but to question the present. Beginning with a citation of Bachir Hadj-Ali ("La nostalgie du passé / n'est pas une marche arrière" [Nostalgia for the past / is not backwards]), Abdel-Jaouad describes a similar opposition. Whereas Abdel-Jaouad speaks of a "dialectic," however, and Raybaud describes a "nomadism," the former calls postmodern what the latter refers to as the modern. In contrast with Raybaud, Abdel-Jaouad associates the modern with colonization and its civilizing narratives of progress. An attempt merely to criticize traditional culture and leave it behind would be to repeat the gesture of colonizers. It is not surprising that notions of development and secular modernism would leave the bitter taste of the colonialism that introduced them. Yet most Maghrebian literature does not repeat the gesture of some nationalist discourses in seeking a return to a precolonial purity. For Abdel-Jaouad, "decolonization posits the deconstruction, in the Derridean sense, not only of Western metaphysics but also Islamic theology" (61), and setting the archaic against the postmodern produces this decolonization/deconstruction: "The problem of writing (*l'écriture*) in and of French, the *itinéraire* as form of a narrative in crisis and the return of the ancestral text are manifestations of the alliance of the post-modern and the archaic to bridge the abyss of modernity" (63). Whereas Bhabha sees the deconstruction of national narratives already within nationalist discourse, with all its contradictions, Abdel-Jaouad suggests that the postmodern deconstruction of the modern or of colonial cultures and discourses lies within the archaic:

> As a genealogy symbolic and emblematic of the quest for identity and ontology, the archaic means (in the context of Maghrebian literature) not only the tapping and using of traditional and ancient materials and forms of expression, but also the resurgence of orality and/or oral literature. As often presumed, the archaic is neither monolithic nor homogeneous. . . . This difference within the archaic is the blueprint for the post-modern discourse of plurality and alterity. (Abdel-Jaouad 59–60)

This potential for deconstruction within the archaic is made possible when the archaic returns with all its multiplicity. Similarly, Djaout subverts the opposition between a so-called Muslim purity and a Western promiscuity by bringing Ibn Toumert (the archaic) into a nightclub at la Goutte-d'Or (the postmodern). Likewise, the narrator of *Les chercheurs* does not need to leave his country to find freedom; his journey leads him to the Nation's sexual and political margins where he also finds sources of resistance.

Historical Postscript

In *Le blanc de l'Algérie* (1995), the Algerian novelist Assia Djebar, who was Djaout's professor in Algeria (Djebar 1993), perhaps gives the best demonstration of the political significance of Djaout's novelistic rewriting of history. In Algeria, as she points out, digging up heroes' bones has not been confined to the pages of novels. She describes how the Ben Bella government conceived of repatriating the remains of Abd al-Qadir, whose actual exhumation and rehumation was carried out by the Boumediène government. According to her, like the skeleton in *Les chercheurs,* Abd al-

Qadir could only be turning over in his grave at the thought of the discursive use to which his remains have been put:

> Ils ont dit qu'il était normal que le héros de l'indépendance algérienne puisse enfin se reposer dans le pays de ses ancêtres, une fois ce pays libéré. Ce n'est pas vrai: simple illusion: il ne se repose pas, et s'il est vraiment là, je sais, je suis sûre qu'il se tourne et qu'il se retourne. (266)

> They said it was only natural that the hero of Algerian independence should finally come to rest in the country of his ancestors once it was liberated. It's not true: simply an illusion: he's not resting, and if he's really there, I know, I'm sure that he is turning over and over.

As it turns out, this exhumation, like the brother's in *Les chercheurs,* only served to bury the hero again, this time even deeper than before; for Abd al-Qadir has been silenced in the process:

> En cette année 1966, on ne s'est pas hâté d'éditer les poèmes d'Abdelkader, de les chanter, de les enseigner, de rappeler le message spirituel de ses dernières méditations, et en même temps d'étudier ses stratégies de guerrier, sa technique de mobilité, sa vaillance seule contre tous! . . . Non. Les écoles partout s'ouvriront dans la jeune et nouvelle Algérie, les universités se multiplieront: mais on ne trouvera pas encore de place pour la beauté créatrice, pour l'intelligence et la sagesse d'Abdelkader!
> Seul son nom, ou tout au moins son prénom formellement confisqué. Ensuite, son corps transporté! (266–67)

> In that year of 1966, no one was in a hurry to publish Abd al-Qadir's poems, to sing them, teach them, recall the spiritual message of his last meditation, and at the same time, study his war strategies, his mobility tactics, his valor alone against all others! . . . No. Schools would open everywhere in the young, new Algeria, universities would multiply: but no place would be found for Abd al-Qadir's creative beauty, for his intelligence and wisdom.
> Only his name, or at least his first name, formally confiscated. Then, his body transported!

Djebar further points out the hypocrisy of official discourse surrounding the exhumation by telling the story of the Algerian official who goes to Damascus to negotiate the return of the remains with Abd al-Qadir's heir, who informs the official that his son, Abd al-Qadir's descendant, has been imprisoned and tortured in Algeria for a year. This son's freedom is the price the Algerian government must pay for the Amir's bones.

If the Algerian government has buried Abd al-Qadir again to control the meaning of his bones, Djebar digs him up again in *Le blanc de l'Algérie,* along with a long list of other writers and fighters:[7] "D'autres parlent de l'Algérie qu'ils aiment, qu'ils conaissent, qu'ils fréquentent. Moi, grâce à quelques-uns de mes amis couchés là dans ce texte . . . , moi, opiniâtre, je les ressuscite, ou je m'imagine le faire" (261). (Others speak of the Algeria they love, that they visit or live in. I, thanks to those of my friends at rest here in this text . . . , I, stubborn, resurrect them, or imagine myself doing so.) The other exhumation she describes is that of the revolutionary Abane Ramdane—military leader of the Algiers region and one of the masterminds of the Battle of Algiers—who was murdered during the course of the revolution by his own "comrades" for what seem to be mere differences of personality. The FLN covered up this murder by turning Abane into a hero: "His death would only be officially revealed five months after it was carried out. Issue 24 (29 May 1958) of *El Moudjahid* announced it. The martyr's photo was plastered all over the front page, where, framed by a black border, the announcement was overwhelmed by a headline in bold print proclaiming: 'Abane Ramdane gunned down in the field of battle' [Abane Ramdane est mort au champ d'honneur]" (Mameri 301). Djebar describes the same article in the following terms: "L'annonce nécrologique, dans ces termes convenus, devenait une nouvelle tentative pour étrangler cette fois le fantôme même de l'assassiné" (146). (The obituary in these agreed-upon terms, became a new attempt to strangle, this time around, the assassinated man's ghost itself.) She describes how Abane, like the narrator's brother in *Les chercheurs d'os,* is brought back after independence for reburial in his village. The government sent the "comrade" responsible for his murder, Krim Belkacem, to deliver the official eulogy. This attempt to "ligoter" the signifying potential of Abane's bones did not go uncontested, as his brother cried out: "Arrête! Arrête de pérorer sur mon frère! Vous l'avez tué vousmêmes et, à présent, vous osez pleurer sur sa tombe! C'est le comble!" (Djebar 148). (Stop! Stop pontificating about my brother! You killed him yourselves and now you have the gall to mourn him at his grave! What an outrage!) Yet as de Certeau points out, history's dead never rest in peace, but always return to haunt the living. Though the revolutionary elite attempted to stifle even Abane's ghost, he returned to exact his re-

---

7. Lauten uses the concept of exhumation to describe Assia Djebar's writing of history. In her conclusion she also discusses *Les chercheurs* (148–68).

venge. Belkacem, later a member of the opposition to Boumediène, was found strangled in a hotel room in Algeria:

> A cette occasion [1984], le corps d'Abane Ramdane eut droit à sa troisième tombe. Une troisième fois, on célébra le mort «tombé au champ d'honneur»; il y eut probablement d'autres discours, aussi pompeux. Cette fois («le comble», dirait le frère d'Abane), on l'enterra tout près . . . de Krim Belkacem, son meurtrier, et ce dernier reposa non loin de l'imposant tombeau de Boumediene, celui-ci en somme le meurtrier du meurtrier. . . . (Djebar 149)

> On this occasion in 1984, Abane Ramdane's corpse was granted a third tomb. For the third time, they honored the deceased "gunned down in the field of honor"; there were probably more speeches, just as pompous. This time ("the outrage," Abane's brother would have said), they buried him right next to . . . Krim Belkacem, his murderer, and the latter lay to rest not that far from the imposing tomb of Boumediène, himself in fact the murderer's murderer. . . .

The image of Abane's ghost returning to haunt not only his murderers but also present-day Algeria as a whole is not limited to Djebar's novelistic rewriting of Algerian history; these tropes are also present in the discourses of History itself. Abane's biographer, Khalfa Mameri (quoted already above), uses the following words to describe Abane's ghost:

> Il est incontestable que la Révolution algérienne traîne derrière elle le cadavre de Abane Ramdane. (15)

> The Algerian Revolution unquestionably drags Abane Ramdane's corpse behind it.

> Vivant ou mort, Abane Ramdane n'a jamais cessé de hanter les esprits. De son vivant, son rôle et sa place ont largement dominé le champs [*sic*] de la Révolution algérienne. Mort, son cadavre reste au travers de notre histoire et interpelle les consciences. (291)

> Dead or alive, Abane Ramdane has never ceased to haunt minds. While he was alive, his role and place widely dominated the field of the Algerian Revolution. In death, his corpse remains throughout our history and beckons our consciousness.

> Mort étranglé, Abane va se redresser, comme dans un cauchemar, pour ne jamais cesser de poursuivre ceux qui ont accompli ou laissé accomplir un tel acte. Comment leur conscience pourra-t-elle jamais trouver la paix? (298)

Killed by strangulation, Abane would rise again, as in a nightmare, to pursue ceaselessly those who accomplished or allowed to be accomplished such an act. How will their conscience ever find peace?

A peine enseveli . . . Abane ressurgit de l'au-delà et continue de donner des sueurs froides à ceux qui croyaient s'en débarrasser à bon compte. (301)

Barely buried . . . Abane rises from the hereafter and continues to give a cold sweat to those who thought they could get rid of him once and for all.

Djebar's exhumation of the rehumation of Abd al-Qadir and Abane Ramdane, paralleling as they do Djaout's novelistic rewriting of the history of the Algerian Revolution in *Les chercheurs d'os,* also have important implications for a reading of *L'invention du désert.* As the revolutionary elite attempted to cover up Abane's murder by turning him into a martyr in the pages of *El Moudjahid,* the very next dead man Djebar digs up is Jean Sénac, homosexual *pied-noir* poet and revolutionary who was a member of the Ben Bella government and whose death was reported in the same newspaper. Djebar brings Sénac back to haunt the society that censored him:

Peut-être aussi que Jean Sénac, qui signait ses poèmes, ses missives, par un soleil à cinq rayons, vivait ses amours—de la terre natale, de la vie, des garçons—dans un éblouissement qui fit ombre soudain violente à une société où l'homosexualité, si prégnante pourtant, évite de se dire haut. (153)

Perhaps as well Jean Sénac, who signed his poems, his letters, with a sun with five rays, lived his love affairs—with his native country, with life, with boys—in a splendor that suddenly cast a violent shadow over a society where homosexuality, so prominent nonetheless, dares not speak its name.

Djebar associates his love of country, what I would call his revolutionary nationalism, with his love for boys. While the elite might not necessarily have killed him, official discourse was quick to bury him, as the Boumediène government had silenced him before by shutting down his popular radio show. As Djaout brings homosexuality, hidden from history, back from history to haunt the present, Djebar resurrects Sénac with all his contestatory potential.

Mameri ends his historical biography of Abane with the following reflection:

Abane's death was perhaps necessary for Algeria's liberation. As it currently stakes a claim [elle campe] forever in our history, it must be for us and for all the generations that will follow an untarrying source of inspiration to instill forever tolerance, generosity, and freedom, the only sources of life for a political society. Only then will Abane be able to rest in peace. [Ainsi seulement Abane pourra enfin reposer en paix.] Thus may Algeria, as well, be thankful to him until the end of time. (303)

If we go digging around for Djaout's bones today, let us do so in a way that does not bury them again even more deeply than before. Let us make him the skeleton at the banquet for state power (present and potential) he was when alive, the reason for his assassination. Djaout's texts inscribe the writer in his political role in relation to national history. His death testifies to the menace to ruling powers or (in this case) to the pretenders to state power the committed writer can represent. His writings become, after his assassination, another skeleton in the closet we are left with digging up and dragging out of its hiding place.

Chapter Five

In the Nation's Closets: Sexual Marginality and the Itinerary of National Identity

While Boudjedra's narrator attempts to hide homosexuality in the closet of the past and Djaout brings it back to haunt the present, Ben Jelloun shows how a return of the repressed can challenge nationalist cults of origin. In *La prière de l'absent* (1981), the association between challenging the social order and unveiling sexual secrets plays a particularly important role. This novel narrates the journey of three marginal characters— Yamna, Sindibad, and Boby—who take a baby to Smara, a site of Moroccan resistance to French colonial penetration. Summoned by the Secret Empire, they must endow the child with both a national identity and a subjectivity in this return to the Nation's "roots" and the origins of Moroccan nationalism and identity. Ben Jelloun thereby allegorizes the coming to national identity and the "birth of a nation" through the life story of an individual and his coming to subjectivity. In this allegory, subjectivity requires a national identity in the way "by which we are marked subjects, particular subjects of particular states . . . [in] processes of subjectification that define selves and others as the subjects of nation and ethnicity" (Arteaga 1). Ben Jelloun's novel, however, is also an allegory of the failure of national allegory; for the narrative of national identity fails to produce a subject position that citizens can fully embody without contradiction. He literalizes this failure by cutting short the journey of return, which ends when a man drags a sack of rotten meat across their path and leaves a trail of blood that marks the interdiction of their contin-

A version of this chapter originally appeared in *Romanic Review*, vol. 89, no. 3, pp. 445–67, as "In the Nation's Closets: Sexual Marginality and the Itinerary of National Identity in Tahar Ben Jelloun's *La prière de l'absent*." Reprinted here by permission.

uation. Yet, this impurity is not the only obstacle to the itinerary of coming to national identity.

Ben Jelloun challenges official versions of what constitutes nationality and who should be excluded from the definition of the Nation in three ways, each of which is also a challenge to the postindependence elite. *La prière de l'absent* first combines novel, Nation, and national identities, only to overturn linear narrative, thus disrupting the version of identity articulated through this story. Second, this narrative of identity is told by marginal characters who would themselves be excluded from the Nation; telling the national story is therefore denied any grounding in the authority of its authors. Third, Sindibad's marginal sexuality or the forgotten memory of a homoerotic friendship poses a particular threat to the official version of the Nation. Whereas a discussion of the first two challenges to national identity is necessary to contextualize Sindibad's role, this chapter focuses on the way his sexuality enters into the narrative allegory of the Nation's birth only to cause its failure. His haunting secret, or closet, represents a political danger inasmuch as the secret may be revealed or he may come out at any moment. For his closet corresponds to a national secret, that of a shameful, violent history, and his coming out opens the doors to the Nation's closets. Finally, this reading of Ben Jelloun's novel offers a model for staging a conversation between queer and postcolonial theories as a way of theorizing postcolonial sexualities.

The Breakdown of Narrative

After the journey fails, Yamna associates it (especially its narrativity) with the novel it occurs in: "Un voyage rêvé, un pèlerinage inachevé, un passé impossible. Emmener un enfant au Sud pour ressourcer sa mémoire et son être! Un beau sujet de roman ou de conte, mais une illusion dans le réel" (224). (A dreamt journey, an unfinished pilgrimage, an impossible past. Taking a child to the South to re-source one's memory and one's being! A nice subject for a novel or tale, but an illusion in real life.) She points out the similarities between Nation, individual identity, and fiction, all combined here in a single book: this novel. Again, the novel's characters are aware of their participation in a narrative economy, in a story being told:

> Nous avons été désignés par la source, par l'arbre et les mains de la sage-femme, Lalla Malika, pour écrire ce livre, pour remplir toutes ces

> pages. . . . Le livre avec des pages blanches, encore intactes, c'est cet enfant. Il est l'histoire que nous vivons déjà. (56–57)

> We have been appointed by the source, the spring, the tree, and the hands of the midwife, Lalla Malika, to write this book, to fill all these pages. . . . The book with blank pages still intact is this child. He is the story and the history we live already.

Writing this book will constitute the child's being, identity (national and other), and subjectivity, which are authorized by the source/spring and by the tree, both images of allegorical significance; his subjectivity is rooted at the source/spring of national identity. Yet, the novel denies any direct access to this origin.

The deconstruction of the Nation begins by questioning the novel's narrativity. The first chapter relates the death of a philosophy teacher whose life retains only two important events, his birth (in Fès) and his death. The second chapter relates the birth of a boy (perhaps the same person as the philosophy teacher, but one cannot be sure this is the case) in Fès at the time of the birth of the Moroccan nationalist movement. *Histoire* takes on its double meaning in French as both *history* and *story* since the story of an individual's birth coincides with the history of the Nation's birth. A prayer is said that grants the child an identity, "la prière de la naissance, la prière qui donne le nom et fixe les racines de l'être" (28) (the prayer of birth, the prayer that grants a name and firmly plants the roots of being). Identity, again, has roots planted in the Nation's history. The coinciding of naming and granting identity remains important because the child taken to the South is nameless, and the goal of the journey is to confer an identity on him:

> Toi qui n'as pas de nom, tu es venu cette fois-ci au monde à l'insu du temps. . . . Je suis chargée de te transmettre tant et tant de paroles et de messages. . . . Toi, tu n'es le fils de personne! C'est un privilège que je suis chargée de confirmer en t'emmenant vers l'origine, vers les dunes du Sud, là où tu trouveras des racines et une histoire. (74–75)

> You, who have no name, you have come into the world this time without being noticed by Time. . . . I am in charge of passing on to you so many words and messages. . . . You are the son of no one! This is a privilege I have been assigned to confirm by taking you to the origin, the dunes of the South, where you will find roots and a history.

In the third chapter, Lalla Malika, the grandmother of the boy mentioned in the second and third chapters, tells him, "Va vers le Sud!" (46). (Go south!) Her imperative direction and the fact that she appears on several occasions during the journey and seems to belong to the Secret Empire suggest that the protagonists of the second and third chapters are the same person as the child carried to the South in the novel's remaining chapters.

The novel's beginning three chapters thus have a precarious relationship with the narrative journey that constitutes the greater part of the novel, and the undecidability of the novel's beginning parallels its questioning of national origins (which would be the beginning of the national narrative, the beginning of the Nation as narration). If the teacher, the child of the second and third chapters, and the baby of the rest of the novel are not the same person, the first three chapters have nothing to do with the rest of the novel. But one cannot be sure they are the same person. As Mustapha Marrouchi writes, "[a]nother remarkable aspect of Ben Jelloun's narrative technique is a spatial (as opposed to chronological) structuring of events that gives his novels the appearance of symbolic itineraries" (73). This generalization is true in the case of *La prière*, which replaces a chronological telling of events with an itinerary leading to a beginning. The purpose of the journey is to bestow an identity upon the baby and narrate a history that places him in a linear series of events that begin with the origin of his nation, include his birth and the realization of his individual subjectivity, and end with his death. Yet, this series is told in reverse order, and the narrative is fragmented. The fact that one cannot be sure whether the subject in this narrative of subjectivity is the same throughout suggests that subjectivity and identity are elusive categories; the subject can never embody her identity without contradiction, can never be identical to her identity. If the Nation is a narrative construct, the challenge to traditional narrative forms (in which the story is told from beginning to end in chronological order, which situates events in a series of cause-and-effect relationships) that this novel of nationality carries out is also a challenge to the Nation. As will become clear, Ben Jelloun disrupts the spatial itinerary (described by Marrouchi as replacing chronology) as much as he does the novel's chronology. In addition, this novel of Moroccan identity is written in French; if subjectivity is articulated through language, Moroccan identity, here, is articulated in the language of the colonizer. In this allegory, coming to national identity requires crossing linguistic borders, leaving the Nation, going outside the very national identity one is trying to embody.

In the Nation's Margins

Sindibad and Boby's marginality is the source of the novel's second challenge to identity. In a cemetery in Fès, a baby appears before these two
beggars who make a living reciting Qur'anic verses over graves. Next appears Yamna, a former prostitute, housekeeper, and beggar. During this
pilgrimage to the South of Morocco, she is the one who tells the story/
history of the mystic and military leader Ma -al-Aynayn, founder of the
city of Smara, who is buried in Tiznit. This hi/story, narrative within the
narrative of the novel, bestows both national identity and subjectivity on
the child, but those who are supposed to bestow this identity do not have
an identity themselves. Neither Yamna nor Sindibad have identification
cards (*cartes d'identité*), that is, an official identity recognized by the ruling bureaucracy; they thus have no place in the Nation as it is constructed
in official discourse. When the garbage collectors find Yamna dead, an
incident told before the journey begins (she comes back from the dead to
undertake the journey), "[i]ls essayèrent d'avertir les autorités du quartier.
Cette personne n'avait pas d'identité et avait par conséquent le privilège
de ne pas exister, de n'avoir jamais vécu!" (70) (they tried to alert the
neighborhood authorities. This person had no identity and, as a result,
had the privilege of not existing, of never having lived!). Like other Maghrebian novelists, Ben Jelloun uses the lack of a *carte d'identité* as a
marker of a character's marginal status.

When Boby asks Sindibad whether he has an identification card, the
latter answers, "Une carte, et pour quoi faire? Je m'appelle Sindibad et
tout le monde le sait. S'ils ont des doutes, ils n'ont qu'à interroger les
marins qui étaient sous mes ordres" (90). (What would I do with an ID?
My name is Sindibad, as everyone knows. If they have any doubts, they
need only question the sailors who were at my command.) Before Sindibad's bout with madness, his name was Ahmad. Afterwards, both his
name and identity are based on fiction, that of Sindbad the Sailor, a well-
known character of classical Arabic literature. The novel thus recognizes
Sindibad's identity as a narrative construct. But is there an identity that
is not a fiction, that is not always already narratively constructed? The
novel seems to suggest that coming to identity (national and sexual) and
coming to subjectivity always involve writing a fiction. On several occasions, the individual identities of Yamna, Sindibad, and Boby interrupt
the narrative of return to origins in the form of biographies, themselves
narratives marking the personal's irruption into the political. Sindibad's

story, in particular, disturbs the narrative of national identity, since the
specter of the memory of his old friend Jamal haunts the journey
throughout the novel through the threat of its revelation. Finally, the revelation of this memory and Sindibad's reconciliation with it lead directly
to the journey's failure. These marginal characters (marginal in the context of the Nation, central within the novel) therefore "contest genealogies of 'origin,'" a role Bhabha attributes to "minority discourse" (1994,
157), and cause the failure of narratives of return to these national origins,
narratives that help to consolidate power in the hands of the elite Fanon
describes. *La prière* uses its characters' marginality, or "minority discourse," to disrupt "cults of origin" and prevent the articulation of a homogeneous nation based on exclusion. Instead, the novel prefers a more
heterogeneous nation inclusive of those at the margins of its borders/
boundaries, including sexual nonconformists.

The novel's itinerary involves a search for the very same origin contested by "minority discourse": "Nous partons donc vers la source et l'origine, vers le commencement et l'arrêt du temps" (*La prière* 76). (We are
leaving for the spring, the source, the origin, for the beginning and the
end of time.) As the group approaches the South, the clear geographic
referents of Fès, Meknès, Casablanca, and Marrakesh are abandoned for
the "village de l'oubli" (village of forgetting) and the "village de l'attente"
(village of waiting), which have no clear geographic referents. As they
approach the site/source of national origins, the novel's topography becomes more fictitious:

> A partir de Marrakech, les lieux, chemins et villages, devenaient mouvants,
> des images inventées, des tourbillons et des visions absolument
> incertaines.... [I]ls apprirent qu'El Asnam venait d'être rayée de la
> carte.... Ils croyaient avoir inventé ou rêvé le village de l'attente, ils pen-
> saient l'avoir imaginé à l'aide de quelques ingrédients.... (217–18)

> After Marrakesh, the places, routes, and villages became shaky, invented
> images, whirlwinds and absolutely uncertain visions.... They learned
> that El Asnam had just been wiped off the map.... They believed they
> had made up or dreamt the *village de l'attente,* they thought they had made
> it up with the help of a few ingredients....

They also approach another uncertainty—and this is the novel's great
unspoken secret—they approach a territory over which Moroccan claims
to possession are contested, the Western Sahara, of which Morocco only
took complete possession (which is still contested) two years before the

novel's publication. Smara, the city founded by Ma -al-Aynayn, actually belongs to this territory. A successful inclusion of Smara in a narrative of *Moroccan* national origins would support Moroccan claims of territorial possession over the Western Sahara in official discourse. Ben Jelloun implicitly undermines those claims, even though "La marche verte," Polisario, and the Saharawi are never mentioned.[1] *La marche verte ou la philosophie de Hassan II,* coffee-table book and perfect example of dominant discourse in its role of propaganda supporting official Moroccan policy, includes the reproduction of a letter from the cheïkh Ma -al-Aynayn to the sultan Abdelaziz Ibn El Hassan (predecessor to the present king of Morocco), in which he recognizes the sultan as his sovereign (59). In this official version of history, Ma -al-Aynayn serves to justify Moroccan claims to the Western Sahara.[2] Ben Jelloun questions both Moroccan possession of the Western Sahara and this official version of Ma -al-Aynayn's role in Moroccan history.

The Sexual Margins of the Nation

In *La prière de l'absent,* the subversive potential of minority discourse discovers a sexual significance in the character of Sindibad. Throughout the narrative, his erotic memory haunts him with the threat of returning:

Son regard était par moments fiévreux, traversé par de l'inquiétude, celle que peut faire naître le mystère, celle aussi qui naît de la crainte de voir des événements déjà vécus se dérouler de nouveau. Dans son cas, c'était

1. The only hint of military conflict occurs in the sentence "Des camions militaires recouverts de bâches se dirigeaient vers Tan Tan" (219) (Military trucks with canvas tops drove towards Tan Tan), Tan Tan being a city just North of the contested territory. The Western Sahara was colonized by Spain, which decided to relinquish control in 1975. Polisario was the armed liberation movement in the region. In 1975, Hassan II organized a march of civilians armed only with Qur'ans and Moroccan flags to take control of the northern part of the region in spite of the presence of Polisario and its demands for a Saharawi state independent from surrounding countries. The discursive target of this action was the Spanish, who were called on to immediately relinquish control of the area. Spain's decision to leave, however, had already been made. Anticolonial discourse thus masked Morocco's expansionist policies. In 1976, the Western Sahara was divided between Morocco and Mauritania, and Algeria's support of Polisario led to border conflicts between Morocco and Algeria. Morocco gained complete control in 1979 with the withdrawal of Mauritania from the southern part of the region. A cease-fire between Morocco and Polisario was negotiated in 1989, and a referendum on Saharawi independence was scheduled to occur in 1992. The referendum was delayed, but negotiations continued. Preparations are underway for a March 2000 referendum.

2. Ma -al-Aynayn's historical role was a bit more ambiguous. When he thought the sultan was giving in too much to the French, "[p]roclaiming himself sultan, he assembled an army of Soussi and Saharawi tribesmen and marched north, but was defeated by a French force" (Hodges 212).

un passé lointain, une partie de sa vie qu'il pensait avoir définitivement enterrée et oubliée qui revenait se présenter devant son regard, image par image, recréant des sensations étranges et des émotions plutôt pénibles provoquées par des situations dont le souvenir n'était pas totalement éteint. Quelque chose s'était ranimé en lui, et la manière déroutante avec laquelle il racontait à Boby des histoires sans queue ni tête trahissait une perturbation importante qui s'était produite en lui, et qui ne devait pas avoir un lien direct avec le voyage. (78)

At times, his gaze was feverish, worried, revealing a deep concern such as the one a mystery can elicit, such as the one that comes from a fear of seeing past events happen again. In his case, it was a distant past, a part of his life he thought he had forgotten and buried for good, a part of his life coming back before his very eyes, image by image, recreating sensations and somewhat powerful emotions provoked by situations whose memory was not totally extinguished. Something in him had come back to life, and the confusing way he told Boby stories with neither head nor tail betrayed a serious disturbance that had come about within him, a disturbance that shouldn't have any connection with the journey.

The secrets of his past, which he believed buried or hidden, threaten to appear again and come out of the closet of his past. Keeping this past hidden "in the closet" contains the danger it represents. Remembering it comes with a reversal in the narrative order of his stories "sans queue ni tête," paralleling the entire novel's disruption of narrative structure. The reader discovers Sindibad's biography in chapter seven, "Sindibad": His real name is Ahmad Suleiman, he studied at the Qaraouiyine University in Fès, where he was a *contestataire,* basing his revolt against religious/academic authority on classical Arabic texts, including Ma -al-Aynayn's mystical writings. He thus gives an alternative reading of Yamna's account of Ma -al-Aynayn's life, opposing her official version of the hero's story with his own reading, which is part of his revolt against dominant academic discourses. His teacher even complained to his father that Ahmad's questioning of tradition was endangering the nationalist movement (81–82), thereby explicitly marking him as dangerous to official accounts of Moroccan national identity. Even in his youth he was seen as a threat to the Nation.

The threat of his past—which "shouldn't have any connection with the journey" but haunts it—turns out to be his friendship with Jamal, which "devint très vite un élément essentiel de leur vie et ne tarda pas à se transformer en passion, le jour où, après avoir lu un long poème de

Jamal, Ahmad, ému, ne dit rien, mais s'approcha de son ami et l'embrassa longuement en pleurant" (83) (quickly became an essential element of their lives and didn't waste any time transforming itself into a passion the day when, after reading a long poem by Jamal, Ahmad, touched, said nothing, but instead approached his friend and kissed him at length while crying). This kiss confirms "la violence de leur passion" (83) (the violence of their passion): "Leur amitié était ainsi scellée par ce long baiser silencieux. . . . Ahmad l'aimait avec la passion du secret et du silence" (83–84). (Their friendship was thus sealed by this long, silent kiss. . . . Ahmad loved him with all the passion of secrecy and silence.) Jamal's beauty is associated with femininity and upsets the masculine order that founds the academy:

> Quand il mettait du kohol autour des yeux, il donnait une légère expres-sion de cruauté à ce regard. Il en jouait discrètement dans cette société d'hommes imbus de leur force mâle où les manifestations de virilité étaient grotesques. Jamal était l'élément féminin dans cette université où les seules jeunes filles qui étudiaient, venaient tout enveloppées dans leur *haïk*, comme des momies qui auraient effacé leur corps. (83–84)

> When he put kohl around his eyes, he gave his gaze a slight expression of cruelty. He toyed with it discreetly in a society of men saturated with their male strength where manifestations of virility were grotesque. Jamal was the feminine element in this university where the only young girls who studied, came all wrapped up in their *haïks*, like mummies that would have erased their bodies.

Their passion is described as troubling or upsetting, and Sindibad has controlled this danger by confining it to a sort of closet and forgetting it. His love for Jamal, characterized by its secretiveness, and his revolt against "une société conformiste et conventionnelle" (84) (a conformist, conven-tional society) go hand in hand: "Il était possédé par cet amour fou qu'il assimilait à sa révolte" (85). (He was possessed by this mad love, which he assimilated with his revolt.) In a letter to Sindibad, Jamal reveals the dan-ger of their love: "[C]e qui nous lie . . . c'est la maladie dans ce qu'elle a de plus noble et de plus beau. Notre amitié est un feu qui est en train de nous consumer, je n'envisage pas une seconde de porter atteinte à cette flamme, mais j'ai peur et je te le dis" (86). (What ties us together . . . is a sickness in its most noble and beautiful form. Our friendship is a fire that is consuming us, I wouldn't think for a second of putting out this flame, but I am afraid and tell you so.) Just after this letter, Jamal's father takes him away, separating the two friends. Sindibad goes insane, spends some time in a psychiatric hospital, and finally becomes a beggar.

In Marrakesh, Sindibad begins to reconcile himself with his memory: "Pour la première fois, l'idée de rencontrer des images et des souvenirs venus du lointain ne l'inquiéta point. Il les laissait venir à lui, avec le sourire de celui qui venait d'abandonner en route un lourd fardeau" (150). (For the first time, the idea of coming across images and memories from afar didn't disturb him at all. He let them come to him, with the smile of someone who had just left a heavy burden by the wayside.) Sindibad remembers Jamal again, paradoxically, in the "village de l'oubli," and this time, he experiences remembering not as a haunting but as a reconciliation, a liberation:

[I]l fut aveuglé par une lumière brutale éclairant un moment précis et lointain de sa vie, un moment retenu jusqu'à ce jour par la volonté des ténèbres. Tout se déroula très vite. . . . D'abord l'image d'un jeune homme. . . . Ce visage avait un nom: Jamal. . . . Ce visage aimé puis retiré au souvenir revenait cette fois presque avec sérénité comme s'il n'avait jamais disparu. Le souvenir de cette passion s'inscrivit dans le corps de Sindibad non comme une trace mais comme une rencontre neuve avec lui-même. . . . Il était comme un morceau de terre fêlée par une longue sécheresse, et qui était tout d'un coup inondée par des fontaines et des sources d'eau pure et fraîche. . . . Il avait peur . . . de perdre le goût et le parfum de cette terre imbibée par les sources du passé. (184–85)

He was blinded by a harsh light, shining on a precise and faraway moment of his life, a moment held back until this day by the will of darkness. Everything happened very quickly. . . . First, the image of a young man. . . . This face had a name: Jamal. . . . This beloved face taken away from his memory, returned this time with a serenity as if it had never disappeared. The memory of this passion was inscribed in Sindibad's body not as a trace but as a brand-new encounter with himself. . . . He was like a parcel of earth cracked from a long drought, and flooded all at once by fountains and springs of pure, cool water. . . . He was afraid . . . of losing the taste and aroma of this earth soaked with the springs of the past.

Sindibad allows his memories to return, and the revelation of his erotic past constitutes a liberation. His refusal to keep his sexuality a secret constitutes a political act and a challenge to the discourses of sexual normativity that police the invisibility of sexualities they exclude. During a journey whose purpose is to discover an identity at the Nation's origin, Sindibad finds a *source*—both *source* and *spring* in French—for his identity in passion, in the domain of the erotic. Yamna immediately characterizes his remembering as a threat to their journey: "Je suis seule à tout décider dans cette traversée. Sindibad a retrouvé la mémoire, ou plus exactement le souvenir suprême qu'il avait perdu" (190). (I am alone in deciding everything in this trek. Sindibad has found his memory again, the supreme memory he had lost.) This remembering directly precedes the failure of the quest for national origins.

Unveiling Sexual Secrets

In Ben Jelloun's novel, one finds yet another association between the narrative articulation of sexual transgressions and unveiling. The three main characters share both a secret and a veil: "Nous sommes enveloppés par le même linceul—un voile—dans le même nuage" (56). (We are wrapped up in the same shroud—a veil—in the same cloud.) When Sindibad recovers his memory, Yamna veils her face: "Son visage était voilé, moins pour se protéger de la poussière que pour dissimuler une réelle inquiétude" (186). (Her face was veiled, less to protect herself from the dust than to hide a true anxiety.) Ma -al-Aynayn, who is also veiled—"Etrange! Il apparaissait souvent voilé en public . . ." (98) (How strange! He often appeared veiled in public . . .)—also has a secret. When Yamna reveals this secret at the end of the novel, one could say that she unveils the national hero:

> Et puis les ancêtres ne donnèrent du cheïkh Ma -al-Aynayn que l'image du héros national, celui qui résista à la pénétration coloniale. Ils oublièrent de dire qu'ils avaient fait de lui un mythe, un saint, une image, dissimulant le caractère féodal, autoritaire et même esclavagiste de ce chef de tribu qui rêvait d'être le chef de tout un Etat. (224)

> And then again, the ancestors only gave of the cheïkh Ma -al-Aynayn the image of a national hero, the one who resisted colonial penetration. They forgot to say that they had turned him into a myth, a saint, an image, hiding the feudal, authoritarian, and slave-owning character of this tribal chief who dreamt of being the head of an entire state.

The hi/story she narrated to the child glorified Ma -al-Aynayn. She undoes her own telling of the story by unveiling the hero, displaying the

Nation's dirty laundry, and revealing secrets she should have left untold. Given the role of Ma -al-Aynayn in *La marche verte,* one might assimilate her story with the official version of history.[3] The undoing of her story is also an undoing of official discourses of national history. Both the unveiling of Sindibad's sexual history and that of the Nation's secrets coincide with the failure of the return to national origins.

What, then, is the relation between the Nation's closet and Sindibad's? More particularly, how does Ben Jelloun politically use the articulation of a coming out, the revelation of the secret of the Nation's past and of Sindibad's? As in Fanon's unveiling of Algeria *qua* Woman and Boudjedra's (un)veiling of homosexuality, Ben Jelloun uses the unveiling of Sindibad's dangerous memories for the political force it unleashes. Though Fanon directs this force against the colonizer, Ben Jelloun directs it against the national elite Fanon warned might replace the colonizer after independence. Up until the point of Sindibad's remembering, the characters' secret has been well kept. The Secret Empire hovered over the characters, forbidding them to reveal their mission. When Boby gives away the secret-—the group's story and reason for the journey—in a public square in Marrakesh, he is struck mute and shackled forever. The forgotten violence Renan describes at the origin of every nation could therefore be considered its secret. For Ben Jelloun, sketching a return to this origin must end in failure, because he refuses to veil anything that, hidden, would consolidate nationality for the benefit of a national elite. Like a traitor, he gives over national secrets to the enemies of the national bourgeoisie. This deconstruction of the Nation in no way detracts from resisting colonialism; in fact, at one point, one of Lalla Malika's acts of resistance to colonialism is marked by an unveiling: "Quand je passais donc devant les Français, je baissais mon voile et les regardais droit dans les yeux. Tu comprends, une femme se voile quand elle est en face d'hommes. Les soldats français n'existaient pas!" (40). (When I passed in front of the French, I lowered my veil and looked them straight in the eyes. You have to understand, a woman veils herself when in front of men. French soldiers did not exist!) Anticolonial struggle and overthrowing the national bourgeoisie, then, involve similar unveilings.

3. Although, unlike *La marche verte,* she does include in her story the fact that Ma -al-Aynayn was about to attack Fès when it became clear that the sultanate was giving in to the French (*La prière* 192).

Theories Postcolonial and Queer

If the return to national origins represents an oppressive consolidation of
power by official discourse, what is the point of narrating a desire to seek
the source of national identity only to have the actual return blocked and
the desire for national identity frustrated? If some sort of national identity
is necessary to consolidate opposition to a colonial presence, Sindibad's
remembering constitutes for the citizen an alternative source of identity
that contests the source official discourse proposes as unique. Ben Jelloun
does not reject all claims to the roots of national identity; rather, he pro-
liferates many origins to compete with the single official one and dislodge
it from its dominant position. Sedgwick (1990) offers a useful analogy in
her discussion of the importance of multiple accounts of gay origins:

> In this unstable balance of assumptions between nature and culture, at
> any rate, under the overarching, relatively unchallenged aegis of a culture's
> desire that gay people *not be,* there is no unthreatened, unthreatening con-
> ceptual home for a concept of gay origins. We have all the more reason,
> then, to keep our understanding of gay origin, of gay cultural and material
> reproduction, plural, multi-capillaried, argus-eyed, respectful, and end-
> lessly cherished. (43–44)

If a single cause of homosexuality were ever discovered in a homophobic
society, Sedgwick warns, there would be an immediate attempt to eliminate the effect by removing the cause. The history of scientific experi-
mentation on lesbian and gay people attests to the desire to find such
a cause.

In a similar manner, Ben Jelloun seems to argue against official prescriptions of a single source of the Nation where its citizens' national
identities are firmly rooted. Rather than uprooting national identity, his
novel extends alternate and multiple roots. In this way, Ben Jelloun's
model of identity parallels Edouard Glissant's replacement of roots with
rhizomes (1990):

> Gilles Deleuze and Felix [*sic*] Guattari criticized the notions of the root
> and, even perhaps, notions of being rooted.[4] The root is unique, a stock
> [une souche] taking all upon itself and killing all around it. In opposition
> to this they propose the rhizome, an enmeshed root system [une racine
> démultipliée], a network spreading either in the ground or in the air, with

---

4. Glissant is here referring to "Introduction: Rhizome," in *Mille plateaux* (Deleuze and Guattari
1980, 9–37).

no predatory rootstock taking over permanently. The notion of the rhizome maintains, therefore, the idea of rootedness but challenges [récuse] that of a totalitarian root. (11; 23 in original)

Because any attempt to fix a single origin of national identity, to legislate a people's roots, could be used to marginalize, exclude, even exterminate those who do not share the roots, Glissant's rhizomatic identity would satisfy the need for multiple origins articulated by Sedgwick. Nevertheless, Ben Jelloun stages an official journey of national identity even while causing its failure. Sindibad bases his revolt on the texts of the same Ma -al-Aynayn government propaganda used to justify "La marche verte." The rhizomes of national identity extend from the same root that signifies the official version. One could say, then, that Ben Jelloun stages the official version to rewrite it. As Djaout articulates a strategy for rewriting History, queer theory and postcolonial theory, when read in conversation, propose one strategy for a similar rewriting of the Nation.

In *Gender Trouble* (1990), Judith Butler describes the Law of gender roles as open to such a rewriting. Following Adrienne Rich's argument (1980), Butler describes heterosexuality as a compulsory, oppressive system. The Law of gender offers two identities, Man and Woman, and the two elements of this binary are in a heterosexual relationship with one another. For Monique Wittig, "[l]esbians are not women" (1980, 32); they escape compulsory heterosexuality altogether: "Lesbians are runaways, fugitive slaves . . ." (1989, 45). For Butler, however, one can no more operate outside of gender than outside of the Nation. In the dominant discursive logic of compulsory heterosexuality, if a woman desires other women, it is because she identifies with men (such was the position of Freud). Her desire must be masculine, because identification and desire cannot have the same gender as their objects—desire must always be heterosexual. According to this logic, homosexuals can only be parodies of heterosexuals; a drag queen mimics "real" women, and butch/femme lesbian couples mimic heterosexual ones. Butler, however, turns this assumption on its head:

> [H]eterosexuality offers normative sexual positions that are intrinsically impossible to embody, and the persistent failure to identify fully and without incoherence with these positions reveals heterosexuality itself not only as a compulsory law, but as an inevitable comedy. Indeed, I would offer this insight into heterosexuality as both a compulsory system and an intrinsic comedy, a constant parody of itself, as an alternative gay/lesbian perspective. (122)

Even heterosexuals can only parody heterosexuality, and often their parody is no less laughable than that of the obvious drag queen; it is impossible to perform these roles exactly according to the ideal.

In the discrepancy between the Law of gender and the performance of gender roles, Butler articulates a strategy of not only leading gendered lives without being reduced to the roles one must perform but also of envisioning the transformation of the Law itself into a less oppressive system. She offers a way out of the double bind of the binary of heterosexual gender roles by pointing out that, since the performance is never completely faithful to the ideal, in the repetition of performances, there lies the possibility of driving a wedge between ideal and performance and widening the difference between the two, thereby creating a new ideal. Her strategy of subverting the compulsory heterosexual gender system involves parodying the very roles the system imposes: "As a strategy to denaturalize and resignify bodily categories, I describe and propose a set of parodic practices based in a performative theory of gender acts that disrupt the categories of the body, sex, gender, and sexuality and occasion their subversive resignification and proliferation beyond the binary frame" (xii). Her strategy involves repeating gender norms without being reduced to them, repeating them with a difference through such acts as butch/femme roles, drag, and camp.

Using Bhabha's terminology, one might even say that Butler's parody would be "almost the same" as ideal gender "but not quite" (1994, 86). In his writing on nationality, Bhabha has described a similar splitting between the national ideal (which he labels as pedagogy, the ideal as it is taught) and the various ways it is performed: "In the production of the nation as narration there is a split between the continuist, accumulative temporality of the pedagogical, and the repetitious, recursive strategy of the performative. It is through this process of splitting that the conceptual ambivalence of modern society becomes the site of *writing the nation*" (145–46). The pedagogical involves imparting to students national ideals and values (including but not limited to the Nation's family values) as well as teaching national identity and a sense of national belonging in the form of narratives that constitute the fiction of a nation. The repetitive recitation of these narratives constitutes nationalist pedagogy in action. Constituting oneself as a national subject, however, and performing national identity are never quite so simple. Writing the Nation is always a rewriting, and in rewriting, there is room for subversion. Butler's performance of gender roles, then, parallels Bhabha's performance of the Nation. Her parody, inserting a slight difference from the original, exploits what Bhabha characterizes as the splitting between the ideal and its performance and offers a way of transforming national identity and proliferating it beyond its narrow definition in dominant discourse. If this splitting can be used to challenge dominant models of gendered identity, perhaps it can also be exploited to challenge official models of nationality. Given the parallels between Butler's and Bhabha's deployment of the concepts of performance and excess, I suggest—and argue that the texts of Maghrebian novelists suggest—that Butler's strategy of parodic performance can also be deployed as a method of rewriting national identity in heterogeneous and inclusive ways. When Bhabha argues that "[m]inority discourse acknowledges the status of national culture . . . as a contentious, performative space . . . in the midst of the pedagogical representations of the fullness of life" (1994, 157), he also acknowledges that it is especially those at the Nation's margins who can perform such a subversive parody or rewriting of national identity.

The "subversion of identity" in the subtitle of Butler's *Gender Trouble* is not merely a deconstruction, a subversion of the system of identity, it also involves making identity subversive. It rewrites dominant narratives of sexual identity and subjectivity so that they can be deployed in acts of political struggle. In *La prière de l'absent,* Tahar Ben Jelloun exploits the difference between the ideal of national identity proposed by official discourses of nationality and its embodiment by the Nation's citizens. He takes advantage of the fact that the performance of national identity, especially in the case of the Nation's marginalized citizens, can never fully live up to the ideal standards. By unveiling Sindibad's sexual secrets, Ben Jelloun also brings national history out of the Nation's closet. He neither rejects nationalist models nor repeats them the way they are supposed to be embodied. He neither rejects a national cult of origins nor accepts the single root of identity glorified by this cult. Rather, he proposes multiple origins/rhizomes, makes the Nation heterogeneous by bringing to the center what it prefers to marginalize, by unveiling what it prefers to stash away in its closets. In his writing of the Moroccan nation, he rewrites the Nation, he subverts national identity not by destroying it but by making it subversive, available for deployment in struggles within the postcolonial context. Whereas the fictions of both gender and Nation are inescapable, neither are written in stone, and both, therefore, are subject to rewriting.

Chapter Six

SEX ON FIRE:
MOHAMMED DIB AND
THE ALGERIAN REVOLUTION

In the postindependence literature of Boudjedra, Djaout, and Ben Jelloun, sexual nonconformity functions politically as part of a struggle against the power and privilege of postindependence elites. These novels prompt another set of rereadings of earlier novels more traditionally characterized as combat literature, rereadings that reveal the revolution against colonial rule had also always been sexual. The term "littérature de combat" is often used in dividing Maghrebian literature into various categories according to the subject matter, and often according to periods. Fanon (1961) describes a "period of . . . assimilation," a "literature of just-before-the-battle," and a "third phase, . . . called the fighting phase," which includes "a [combat] literature, a revolutionary literature, and a national literature" (222–23; 162 in original). In his narrative of literary history, the development of colonial literature thus parallels that of the nationalist movements leading up to independence struggles. Jean Déjeux (1973), writing after large-scale independence, elaborates six categories: "so-called ethnographic (or documentary) literature," "aesthetic literature," "literature of refusal and opposition" (from the colonial period), "combat literature," "witness literature," and "literature of opposition and unveiling" (37–39). For Déjeux, only the last category, which associates political resistance and unveiling in the manner Ben Jelloun describes, coincides with the postindependence era. With the example of Mohammed Dib's *Qui se souvient de la mer* (1962), however, we shall see how the unveiling of sexual transgression and of women's dangerous sexuality was part and parcel of the Algerian Revolution as depicted in the novel.

Qui se souvient de la mer is perhaps the most widely acclaimed combat novel. Published in the year of the victory of the Algerian Revolution and of Algeria's independence, it describes a revolution in full swing with its narrator's wife, Nafissa, playing the role of what Djebar (1980) calls a "porteuse de feu" (60) ("fire carrier" [44]). In addition to colonial targets, her bombs blow up not only the traditional family, but also the more "modern" heterosexual monogamous couple—established by choice and out of mutual respect and love—that many nationalists have proposed to replace the traditional family as the building block of the new Nation. Nafissa's newfound freedom to circulate, to come and go independently of her husband's wishes (a necessary freedom in light of her participation in the revolution) disturbs and threatens the narrator and, in short, becomes his obsession. In Dib's vision, the Algerian Revolution is therefore a sexual revolution as well. The narrator is threatened not only because his wife's liberation (which coincides with that of the Nation) challenges his privilege as married man in a patriarchal society; he is also haunted because the bombs of national liberation threaten to explode inside the family and within his subjectivity, his very notion of who he is. The national revolution, therefore, decenters and marginalizes male subjectivity and overturns power relations within the heterosexual couple. Dib writes that, after underground explosions, "la ville fut remuée de fond en comble" (146) ("the entire city was [shaken up from top to bottom]" [93]). The colonial city, however, is not the only thing shaken up; masculinity and male subjectivity also risk exploding along with the apparatus of colonial rule.

Dib's narrator first witnesses the construction of a new city (*nouvelle cité*). In this sense, the novel's cityscape resembles the maps of many Maghrebian cities with their medinas (or precolonial cities) and the *villes nouvelles* or European quarters, constructed by the French after colonization. The novel's landscape also resembles a science fiction: the narrator circulates through the labyrinth of the old city inhabited by Minotaurs and moles beneath the ground as "spyrovirs" and "iriaces" attack from above. As Woodhull (1993) points out, "The text is structured partly by an opposition between the 'underground city' and the 'new constructions' that seem to correspond to the Algerian revolutionary movement on the one hand, and the colonial machinery on the other . . ." (59). The moles, therefore, would represent Algerian fighters, and the Minotaurs, French soldiers; the spyrovirs and iriaces would then be weapons of the French. Yet the exact allegorical correspondence between the science-fiction narrative and the Algerian Revolution eludes the critic; as Wood-hull also observes, "the text provides no specific historical or geographical reference points that allow us to determine these correspondences with any certainty" (59).

Fires begin to sweep across the novel's cityscape, but the narrator, throughout most of the novel, only observes the upheaval. His major preoccupation seems to be with making sense of the turbulence occurring around him:

> Pour chasser l'angoisse de ces journées, j'essaye de jeter les bases d'une nouvelle sorte de science que j'appellerais la théorie du comportement des iriaces. Je note la direction, le nombre, les heures de leurs sorties et de leurs retraites; j'évalue l'ampleur et la durée, ainsi que la hauteur de leurs vols; je relève les temps où ils gardent le silence et ceux où ils vocifèrent. (133)

> To drive away the anguish that fills our days, I'm attempting to lay down the basis for a new kind of science which I will call the theory of the behavior of iriace. I note the direction, the number, and the times of their attacks and retreats; I assess the amplitude and the duration, as well as the altitude of their flights; I record their periods of silence as well as those in which their calls are heard. (84)

Like the philosophers Marx criticizes, the narrator defines his purpose as being to understand his world, not to change it. His science consists in attempting to establish the causes of the effects around him and serves as a therapy to alleviate his anguish.

In the novel, therefore, the struggle for decolonization, as Judith Roumani points out, is also a "perilous transition in the national psyche" (10) or exacts what Louis Tremaine calls "the terrible cost of this triumph to the human psyche" (285). In his reading of the novel, Tremaine breaks with several previous interpretations of the ending of *Qui se souvient,* when the narrator seems to descend into the underground city. Since Nafissa disappears, seemingly for good, Charles Bonn (1974) assumes the narrator joins her in the underground. Thus, for Bonn, the revolution, once both spouses are participants, rejoins the heterosexual couple and cements their union. Tremaine also takes issue with Roumani, who thinks that the narrator, in descending into the underground city, becomes an active participant in the revolution: "[H]e is an utterly passive participant, . . . he does not *join* the underground city but merely takes refuge in it" (Tremaine 294). Here Tremaine puts his finger on something quite important; the narrator's passivity, however, is more than political (as Tremaine describes it). It is also—as we shall see in other passages—sexual. Like Boudjedra's version of revolution in *Les 1001 années,* Dib's version of the Algerian Revolution also threatens to invert the sexual order, even at the most physically sexual level, toppling the man from his dominant position onto his back, whereupon he can only wait to be penetrated. Although Tremaine goes further than many critics in understanding what the revolution does to the married couple in Dib's vision, he assumes that the "failure of language to render meaning" in *Qui se souvient* represents the "terrible cost" of the revolution and not one of its benefits (296). Rather than a "terrible cost," however, the demise of masculinity in Dib's vision of revolution could perhaps be one of its most precious benefits. As the narrator's wife detonates explosion after explosion in the novel, male subjectivity also seems to go up in flames. The de(con)struction of the subject that the narrator's wife sets off along with the explosion of colonialism does not disturb the narrator in an abstract or metaphysical way and is not merely about the "perilous transition in the national psyche"; it is male panic. To the extent that he reads the narrator's experience as a "terrible cost" of the Algerian Revolution, Tremaine shares that panic.

The narrator's observations of the political turmoil in the city begin to coincide with something rotten in the state of the household. His wife Nafissa leaves the house without telling him where she is going, what she is doing, or how long she will be gone:

> Nafissa s'absente souvent; les heures d'attente sont autant d'heures d'agonie. Par sa force, le soulagement que son retour m'apporte s'accompagne d'une souffrance plus intense. Elle a une allure méconnaissable, prudente. Elle était dehors quand quelques-unes des constructions ont sauté, ce matin, et n'est revenue qu'une heure après. (157)

> Nafissa is often away; the hours of waiting are so many hours of agony. The relief that her return brings to me is so strong that it carries with it a more intense suffering. Her bearing is unfamiliar, cautious. She was outside when some of the constructions blew up this morning, and didn't return until an hour later. (101)

Her absence provokes a panic on his part, and instead of alleviating his anguish, her return makes it worse, since her presence emphasizes the fact that he no longer controls her comings and goings. As in the above citation, her outings correspond with explosions in the new city: "Nafissa est de retour. Entre-temps, une des nouvelles constructions a explosé" (163).

("Nafissa is back. In the meantime, one of the new constructions has exploded" [104].) His own panic is therefore accompanied by and associated with the explosions of urban guerrilla warfare. His panic is not channeled into male terrorist violence (as in homosexual panic) but is the result of an anticolonial (female) terrorism, which ends up taking patriarchy, especially of the colonialist variety, as its target as well. The narrator finally gives up on trying to prevent her absences and understand them:

> Les craintes que je nourrissais pour Nafissa, le tourment où elle-même me jetait, ont changé aussi, depuis; mais plus que moi, c'est le monde qui a changé. . . . Je ne lui pose plus de questions: au moment où elle sort comme au moment où elle rentre, je regarde ailleurs, je porte mon attention sur autre chose. Une victoire sur moi que j'ai obtenue non sans peine. (143)

> The fears that I'd been having for Nafissa, the torment into which she would throw me, have since changed as well; but more than I, it's the world that has changed. . . . I don't ask her any more questions: as she leaves, and as she returns, I look away, I focus my attention on something else. A victory over myself that I have not won without cost. (91)

While the narrator seeks to understand his world, it is changing around him. Nafissa throws her husband into a torment, as she wreaks havoc on the colonial city. A change in the world brings about change in the narrator, in the narrator's *moi* ("[u]ne victoire sur moi"), self, or subjectivity. The narrator seeks to know his wife, but Nafissa resists his will to knowledge, which the passage associates with his gaze. The narrator may understand the comings and goings of the iriaces (that is, the colonialist's weapons), but he can understand (i.e. seize or penetrate) neither his wife nor the revolution. Knowing is thus associated with the weapons of the colonizer, and as the colonizer is defeated, the narrator must conquer his own curiosity and resign himself to not knowing. His own "victory," a word with its own military implications, over himself, his *moi*, foreshadows the coming victory over the colonizers. Victory over colonialism thus coincides with the defeat of male subjectivity.

In other passages as well, Nafissa escapes the narrator's desire to know her:

> A ce moment, ce qui subsistait de familier entre nous s'évanouit et c'est réellement une autre femme qui fut devant moi. J'eus presque envie de crier à cette vue. Cette autre Nafissa arborait un sourire assuré qui eût

facilement passé pour cruel—mais ne l'était pas—parce que inconce-
vable. (117)

At that moment, any familiarity that still subsisted between us vanished
and it was actually another woman who stood before me. I almost wanted
to cry out at the sight. This other Nafissa displayed an assured smile that
might easily have passed for cruel—though it wasn't—for it was so incon-
ceivable. (73)

She becomes double, the wife he has known and the militant he ceases
to understand:

Le léger bruit répandu ainsi me renvoie à l'autre, qui se présente à moi
chaque fois qu'elle s'absente. Forment-elles un couple antagoniste? Il ne
m'est jamais arrivé de les voir ensemble, mais il est certain qu'elles com-
posent une seule femme, l'une relayant l'autre au point où la distinction
n'est guère possible, où il n'y a pas de distinction. . . . J'observe Nafissa à
la dérobée. Elle ne me dit rien et je ne lui dis rien. Il me paraît l'apercevoir
à une grande distance, alors que je pourrais la toucher en étendant le bras.
Je m'abîme dans un tourment sans nom. (69)

The light sound thus given off takes me back to the other, who comes to
me each time she is absent. Do they form an antagonistic couple? I've
never seen them together, but it's clear that they comprise a single woman,
the one switching off with the other to the point where a distinction is
hardly possible, or where there is no distinction. . . . I watch Nafissa when
she's not looking. She says nothing to me and I say nothing to her. She
seems to appear to me from a great distance away, though I could reach
out my arm and touch her. I am engulfed in a nameless torment. (40–41)

Whereas usually it is women's sexuality that must be concealed in this
context because of the danger it represents, here the relation is reversed:
even just to see her, he must hide. Man, usually associated with the public, is hidden, and Woman, usually confined to the private sphere, circulates in plain view. The narrator's torment is epistemological in nature,
because his inability to control his wife's comings and goings coincides
with ignorance, power and knowledge—or the lack thereof—being
linked in a Foucauldian way.

In addition to the explosions' corresponding to Nafissa's absences, for
the narrator, she becomes an explosion, and Woman becomes fire: "Sur
les champs, dans l'atmosphère de feu, une seule femme dansait dont l'incandescence m'envahissait. J'étais sans défense contre l'illumination qui
émanait d'elle" (34). ("Over the fields, in the fiery atmosphere, there
danced a lone woman whose incandescence overwhelmed me. I was de-

fenseless against the illumination emanating from her" [18].) As for Aït Sabbah and Fanon, for Dib, the veil hides a danger, be it woman or bomb. Nafissa, "tantôt flamme, tantôt femme" (177) (a flame one minute, a woman the next [my trans.]), is described as circulating veiled: "[La mer] ne parle ni ne bouge, ce soir, mais la flamme voilée qui frémit sur elle semble dire plus nettement qu'elle ne l'a fait jusqu'à présent . . ." (176). ("[The sea] neither speaks nor moves this evening, but the veiled flame that flickers over it seems to say more clearly than it has up to now . . ." [113].) Because her flames are concealed by a veil, her unveiling releases this fire:

> Marchant et réfléchissant ainsi, je découvre devant moi Nafissa dont je reconnais l'allure rapide malgré le voile qui la dérobe aux yeux. . . . Elle entrouvre son voile d'un mouvement vif, me laisse voir son visage. Il ne règne plus autour de moi que l'éclat brûlant de ses yeux. (161)

> Walking and thinking over these things, I discover before me Nafissa, whose quick step I recognize in spite of the veil that hides her from view. . . . She draws back her veil with a quick motion, lets me see her face. Everything around me disappears in the burning glow of her eyes. (103)

And this fire, this *femme-flamme,* threatens to catch on, to spread, to burn him as well:

> J'écoutais ces mots quand une chose me foudroya: la rose de Nafissa s'était plantée dans ma main. Je contemplais son rayonnement et un sentiment de sécurité ineffable me pénétrait. . . . *Deux des nouvelles constructions explosèrent presque au même moment.* (181)

> I was listening to these words when I saw something that struck me like an electric shock: Nafissa's rose [had planted itself] in [my] hand. I gazed at its bright gleam and an inexpressible feeling of security penetrated me. . . . Two of the new constructions exploded almost at the same moment. (117)

Nafissa's rose, the poetic image for the explosions she detonates, takes root in the narrator's own flesh. Here, for some reason, the fire provides a sense of security. In most other passages, however, this fire seems more dangerous, even spreading to the conjugal bed: "A mon retour, je découvre, allongé à ma place, un fleuve d'or et de flammes sous le ciel du matin, et non plus un corps. Je contemple ce ciel, le visage blanc de cette eau que le sommeil berce. Je me recouche près d'elle, Nafissa se réveille" (105). ("On my return, I discover, lying in my place, a river of gold and flames beneath the morning sky, and no longer a body. I contemplate this sky, the blank face of this water rocked in slumber. I lie back down next to it, Nafissa awakes" [65].) The bed, place of marital coitus, of (hetero)sexual union, is engulfed in flames. Nothing in the married couple remains sacred, no part of heterosexuality cannot be sacrificed to the revolution. The conjugal bed is one more bombsite of the Algerian Revolution, which in fact, seems to sweep away the institution of heterosexual marriage along with colonialism.

At one point, the narrator is approached by a fireball. At first, he mistakes it for a spyrovir, and then he realizes it is Nafissa:

> Quand la roue de feu m'aborda comme pour me dévisager, seulement alors, je pus me retourner contre le mur. . . . Dirigeant un regard en coulisse vers elle, je reconnus, dans un cri, Nafissa! Je fis volte-face: elle se rapprocha et m'enveloppa dans une sorte de vibration infuse et légère à la fois. Toutes les serres qui étaient plantées en moi me lâchèrent. On est toujours seul au plus fort de l'intimité: là, ce fut autre chose, un sang chaud, électrisé, irrigua mes veines. Sans fin . . . Je tentai de me ressouvenir de quelque chose d'analogue et n'y parvins pas, mais mon cœur tressaillait de joie. D'un geste lent, Nafissa m'alluma la cigarette que j'avais gardée à la bouche. (103)

> When the wheel of fire came up to me as if to [stare me down], only then was I able to turn back around against the wall. . . . Peering sideways at it, I recognized, with a shout, Nafissa! I spun around: she came up to me and enveloped me in a sort of vibration, at once inward and gentle. All the claws that had [sunk into my flesh] let [me] go. One is always alone at the moment of greatest intimacy: here it was different, a warm electrified blood coursed through my veins. Endlessly . . . I sought in my memory for something analogous and could find nothing, but my heart leapt with joy. Slowly, Nafissa lit the cigarette that still dangled from my mouth. (63)

His wife, Nafissa, described again as a *femme-flamme,* is equated with the fire of her bombs. The narrator's experiments and his scientific understanding of the spyrovirs seem not to be working; colonial knowledge no longer suffices to understand the workings of the revolution. The fire engulfs him ("m'enveloppa") and even lights his cigarette. Yet being consumed by fire seems to provoke a certain *jouissance* ("mon cœur tressaillait de joie"), even a *jouissance* in the most literal sense ("au plus fort de l'intimité," which might be read as orgasm). What he describes in other passages as his torment here causes him to tremble with joy. He takes sexual pleasure in the usurpation of his male privilege and delights in his increasingly marginal status and even in his specularity ("la roue de feu m'aborda comme pour me dévisager"), the delight in specularity Silverman lists as one of the characteristics of marginal male subjectivity.

Like the Patriarche in *Moha,* Dib's narrator enjoys not only being the object of a female gaze (he is not allowed, we remember, to treat his wife as such an object since he must hide just to get a look at her) but also being penetrated. In this sexual encounter, explosive as it is, the narrator, who cannot penetrate his wife in the epistemological sense, can only be penetrated by her physically ("les serres qui étaient plantées en moi"). The image of the narrator being penetrated by his wife occurs in another passage:

> Des iriaces venaient m'assaillir en foule avec une stupéfiante audace, cherchant à s'incruster dans ma tête, à y entrer. Mais ils avaient beau s'accumuler au-dessus de moi et, pour m'atteindre, défoncer des portes, mettre des maisons à sac, semer l'effroi et la désolation, ils ne m'impressionnaient pas. La douceur, la mobilité de Nafissa me pénétraient comme une flamme. . . . (129)

> A crowd of iriace set upon me with astonishing audacity, trying to dig their way into my head. But swarm as they might overhead and, in their efforts to get at me, beat down doors, sack houses, sow fear and despair, they didn't impress me. The softness, the gentle motion of Nafissa penetrated me like a flame. . . . (80–81)

As in the above passage, in the following one as well, this penetration is described as a burning: "Mais à peine me suis-je allongé sous les couvertures qu'une autre femme se jette dans mes bras, cherche par tous les moyens une intimité étroite, violente, une autre femme qui me brûle jusqu'au fond de l'être" (85). ("But no sooner have I stretched out beneath the covers than another woman throws herself into my arms, seeking desparately [*sic*] a tight, violent intimacy, another woman who scorches me to the very depths of my being" [51].) His very being, threatened by this burning, could thus be said to be his subjectivity, conquered as it is by his wife's revolutionary activities. Though the narrator seems, in some passages, to resist both this inversion of sexual roles and even perhaps a hostility on Nafissa's part—"Je chante avec force dans l'intention de ramener Nafissa des rives incertaines d'où elle me fait face" (136) ("I sing loudly to bring Nafissa back from the uncertain shores where she stands and faces me" [85])—in other passages, where he seems to enjoy this inversion, it is hard to justify the assertion made by Tremaine that the narrator pays the "terrible cost" of the Algerian Revolution.

Fanon (1959) perhaps hinted at this cost when he wrote, "With this phase, the Algerian woman penetrates a little further into the flesh of the Revolution [s'enfonce un peu plus dans la chair de la Révolution]" (54; 42 in original). In chapter three of *A Dying Colonialism*, "The Algerian Family," devoting an entire section to "The Couple" (111–14), he describes the changes in the traditional family brought on by the revolution in a more positive light that suggests these changes are not a terrible cost, but instead, a benefit. The husband must give up his jealousy and insistence on defending his honor in the person of his wife when she participates in the revolution. For Fanon, the value of national liberation supersedes traditional values: "The Algerian couple rids itself of its traditional weaknesses at the same time that the solidarity [cohésion] of the people becomes a part of history" (114; 106). Yet Fanon expects the couple to come out of the struggle even stronger than before:

> The Algerian couple has become considerably more closely knit in the course of this Revolution. The sometimes fragile bonds, marked by the precarious nature of the present, of what could be rejected from one moment to the next, were strengthened, or at least changed character. What could formerly be defined as mere cohabitation today includes a multiplicity of points of communication. First and foremost is the fact of incurring dangers together, or turning over in the same bed, each [to] his [or her] own side, each with his [or her] fragment of a secret. It is also the consciousness of collaborating in the immense work of destroying the world of oppression. The couple is no longer shut in upon itself. It no longer finds its end in itself. It is no longer the result of the natural instinct of perpetuation of the species, nor the institutionalized means of satisfying one's sexuality. The couple becomes the basic cell of the commonwealth, the fertile nucleus of the nation. The Algerian couple, in becoming a link in the revolutionary organization, is transformed into a unit of existence. *The mingling of fighting experience with conjugal life deepens the relations between husband and wife and cements their union. There is a simultaneous and effervescent emergence of the citizen, the patriot, and the modern spouse* [*du citoyen, du patriote et d'un époux moderne*]. (113–14; 105–6)

Bonn's interpretation of the ending of *Qui se souvient* (in which the narrator joins his wife underground) would therefore uphold Fanon's hypothesis. If one considers that the notion of the couple as a basis of social organization is quite foreign to the traditional extended family in Maghrebian society, Fanon's song of praise to what seems to be a "modern," even Western, couple stands out indeed. For Fanon, though the revolution weakens the traditional family with its kinship networks, and though, like in *Qui se souvient,* the revolution even sneaks its way into the bedroom, it strengthens the heterosexual couple. In Fanon's bed, however, the dangers of revolution remain as secrets that separate the spouses ("se retourner dans le lit chacun de son côté"). His bed is thus marked by an absence of coitus at the time of revolution; sex and revolution do not mix. Though women are unveiled in his vision of revolution, political secrets remain veiled. By entering the conjugal bed, they become sexual secrets. Fanon's vision of revolution, then, maintains the marginalization of sexual secrets that many other authors seek to disclose.

If this confining of sexual secrets to the Nation's margins (i.e. its bedrooms) serves the national bourgeoisie, which maintains power through exclusion from the Nation, Fanon is not willing to go as far in transgressing taboos as he claims in "Algeria Unveiled." Although he allows women to "penetrate" the revolution, he exempts the Nation's bedrooms from revolutionary change. In addition, Fanon does not acknowledge that the couple would be an innovation. He constructs a couple that supposedly already existed, one that used to be "fermé sur lui-même," a falsification in the context of the extended family. Before, his version of the traditional couple was merely "the natural instinct of perpetuation of the species" and "the institutionalized means of satisfying one's sexuality." The only innovation he recognizes is that, through participation in the national struggle, the couple has become the most basic building block of the independent Nation, as if the great advance of the revolution were the consolidation of compulsory heterosexuality, Western style. By claiming that reproduction is a natural instinct, that this instinct was already a part of an Algerian "couple," Fanon conceals how his *version* of the couple is merely another form of social contract that institutionalizes, even constructs, sexuality and reproduction in new ways (or not really that new in the context of Western compulsory heterosexuality), of linking sexuality and power in ways that I would suggest actually reinforces the power of a national elite that he opposes in *The Wretched of the Earth.* The national bourgeoisie he wishes to eliminate thus finds itself strengthened in the very work that advocates its elimination.

Dib, on the other hand, seems to offer a different vision of what revolution should do to the couple. The narrator, like Fanon's abstract father in "The Son and the Father" (102–5) and "The Daughter and the Father" (105–10), seems to lose authority over his children:

> Dans la chambre, pas de Nafissa. Encore! Où peut-elle être allée? Je me sens inquiet; quelle habitude! Elle a laissé les enfants, que je découvre en train de jouer comme s'ils la croyaient près d'eux. Ils ne daignent pas m'accorder un regard. Avec une cruelle indifférence, une tranquillité qui semble s'amuser de mon désarroi, ils continuent à jouer. (139–40)

> In the room, no Nafissa. Again! Where can she have gone? I feel worried; what a habit! She's left the children, whom I find playing as if they thought she was nearby. They don't bother even to glance up at me. With cruel indifference, a tranquility that seems amused at my distress, they go on playing. (88)

Some critics have tried to hide, or at least to lessen the destruction of the couple Dib stages. Beïda Chikhi, for example, writes that Nafissa "nevertheless takes care of the household chores without a fuss" (59). The narrator does not think she does so in the above passage; in fact, he even thinks the children take pleasure in his panic over the crumbling couple. Tremaine writes of "Nafissa's role as a comforter and protector" (288) and Déjeux seems to hold a similar position: "Dib's thought is that woman helps man to reach his potential, for he remains a child for a long time. She helps him to escape his infantile nature, over-valued in his masculinity" (1977, 38). It is difficult to imagine how Nafissa can be read as comforter when the fire of her bombs spreads right into the conjugal bed. Instead, Dib seems to mine the couple, to portray it as one of the bomb sites of the novel. As Woodhull writes, "[f]ar from enshrining the married couple as refuge of traditional values in the inviolable space of the home, Nafissa functions here to reconfigure the conjugal relation as rubble encumbering the public space of the streets . . ." (1993, 61). In Dib's version of revolution, the couple and the patriarchal family explode along with the new city; patriarchy and the version of heterosexuality Fanon finds to be an improvement over it are destroyed along with colonialism.

Chapter Seven

THE HAUNTED HOUSE
OF THE NATION:
KATEB YACINE'S *NEDJMA*

In a scene from *The Battle of Algiers* (Pontecorvo 1966), a veiled figure passes by French soldiers in the medina. This seemingly normal occurrence is "unveiled," however, when the soldiers look down and notice the "woman" is wearing combat boots. A chase ensues during which they attempt to apprehend the urban guerrilla, who is, in a sense, doubly veiled, both wearing the actual veil and, therefore, disguised as a woman—in short, in drag. In Kateb Yacine's *Nedjma* (1956), as Rachid, one of the protagonists, is running from the police, he asks a prostitute for a veil. The discussion that follows can only be read as a parody of the one described above, even though Kateb's novel precedes the film by ten years. The prostitute responds with mockery: "[C]omme si une femme publique était obligée d'avoir un voile! . . . Va donc lui chercher un drap, si ça peut servir à son enterrement, et il a la chance d'être fou, sans quoi . . ." (36, Kateb's suspension points). ("[A]s if a prostitute had to have a veil! . . . Go find him a sheet, maybe he can get buried in it, and he's lucky to be crazy or else . . ." [49].) Before denouncing him to the very police he is attempting to flee, she continues, "après ça, j'espère qu'il m'achètera quelque chose, et il pourrait même me remplacer si je tombais malade, s'il tient tant que ça à jouer les ménagères, le fils de chien" (36) ("now I hope he'll buy me something, he could even take my place when I'm sick if he likes playing house[wives] so much, the son of a bitch" [49]). Unlike the revolutionary's veiling in *The Battle of Algiers,* Rachid's veil threatens to be more than a mere disguise; it threatens to turn him into a "woman," i.e. into the passive partner in sexual intercourse with men.

If for Renan, there is a forgotten violence at the Nation's origin, and for de Certeau, history (read: national history) is haunted by the ghosts of the past it seeks to inter, the specter of sodomy in the above passage points to a more collective haunting of the Nation. Rachid's veiling also parodies another, that of the eponymous character, Nedjma, who is kidnapped and taken to the site of national origins, only to be kidnapped from her kidnappers and veiled by force. This veiling, in the paradigm outlined by Renan, is the forgotten violence at the Nation's origins. When the ghosts of Sindibad's past return, a spring gushes forth as an alternate source for national identity. As it is often said that springs, sources of water, and *hammam* are haunted by *djnoun,* the spring/source of national identity is haunted in Kateb's writing of the Nation. He brings these ghosts back to haunt the Nation's present, and this haunting continues long after the novel's publication, even after Kateb's death. Woodhull (1993) argues for "a reading of *Nedjma* . . . that takes account of Algerian women's present situation as historical subjects" (2), a reading that serves as a warning against the actual outcome of the revolution as lived by women in the late 1980s and the '90s. Woodhull's interpretative strategy might also be said to conjure up Nedjma's ghost; and this specter is also that of a Queer Nation that must make room for those whom nationalist discourses attempt to conjure away.

Nedjma was published two years after the insurrection began in Algeria on 1 November 1954. One of the novel's central events is the 8 May 1945 demonstrations in Sétif that, brutally repressed by French authorities, turned into riots and then into a massacre at the hands of the French. This rebellion was a moment of awakening for the national movement whose consciousness *Nedjma* is often read as articulating. Nedjma, whose name means "star" in Arabic, is desired by the novel's four protagonists, Rachid, Mourad, Lakhdar, and Mustapha. They all end up together around Nedjma in Bône immediately following the Sétif rebellion. Later, they work together in a quarry in Constantine, where Lakhdar is arrested after striking their boss Ernest in a dispute. At the wedding of Ernest's daughter Suzy and the bus driver Ricard, Rachid kills Ricard for beating an Arab domestic servant. He is arrested, and the other three protagonists (Lakhdar has by now escaped) go their separate ways. The novel begins with these events at Constantine and ends with a retelling of the characters' parting. At a certain point, Rachid and Si Mokhtar, who is of Rachid's father's generation, set off on a pilgrimage to Mecca that they never complete. Later (how much is unclear), they kidnap Nedjma to take her to the Nadhor, land of their common ancestor Keblout.

The novel has long been interpreted as a narrative of national identity. It is often said that Nedjma *is* Algeria, or represents Algerian identity; the quest for Nedjma, and desire for her, allegorizes the quest/desire for a nation no longer under French control. The back cover of the novel reads, "Nedjma, c'est l'objet d'un amour d'enfance, c'est la femme éternelle, c'est l'Algérie. Nedjma, c'est l'obsession du passé, la quête de l'inaccessible, la résurrection d'un peuple. Nedjma, c'est la femme-patrie." (Nedjma is the object of a childhood love, she is the eternal woman, she is Algeria. Nedjma is the obsession with the past, the quest for the inaccessible, the resurrection of a people. Nedjma is the woman-homeland.) In a lecture, however, Kateb once questioned the symbolic valence often attributed to Nedjma: "You can't push a symbol too far. A symbol is always fragile; if you try to literalize it, it is destroyed. If you wish, Nedjma ends up symbolizing Algeria. This flower can also symbolize Algeria if you begin to contemplate the phenomenon of the flower" (Gontard 12). While admitting the possibility of reading Nedjma as Algeria, Kateb warns against reading every element of the novel figuratively. As much as the novel has been read as an allegory of the awakening of national identity, it is also an allegory of the failure of any narrative to write the Nation without marginalizing or doing violence to a portion of its citizens. *Nedjma* involves a return to national origins that fails to rejoin Nedjma and the ancestral space or origin. Its strategic deployment of nationalism thereby seeks to avoid any exclusion linked with a cult of origins. Yet, when the ancestors abduct and veil Nedjma, does this enclosure of a woman mark the text's sensitivity to the relation between a nationalist cult of origins and patriarchy? Or, in personifying the Nation as a woman surrounded by the desiring gazes of four young men, is the text "guilty" of reproducing the patriarchal enclosure of women?

Roots

Part of *Nedjma*'s challenge to nationality is its challenge to narrativity. Khatibi (1968) has described Kateb's mixing of genres as a "technique terroriste qui brise la structure propre au roman et qui crée un langage éblouissant fusant de toutes parts et se surpassant indéfiniment" (103) (a terrorist technique that shatters the structure inherent in the novel and

creates a dazzling language that fires off rockets in all directions and sur-
passes itself indefinitely). In his introduction to the English edition of
Nedjma, Bernard Aresu writes also that the novel "poetically explodes a
plot whose elements cohere only in synchrony" (xl). A major part of *Nedjma's* violence is thus its disruption of chronology. Beginning and ending
with the same event, the novel simultaneously seems to rely on the more
traditional sense of chronology at work in historiographical narratives
(with its implications of cause and effect). Critics have attempted to re-
construct this implied chronology, but often actually disagree on the exact order. The novel's editors include a plot summary at the beginning of
the novel, Marc Gontard narrates his own version, complete with a
graphic representation (38), and Jacqueline Arnaud challenges some aspects of Gontard's account (2: 320–26). The novel's event most contested
in terms of its placement in a "real" order of events is the very one most
central to the novel as a national allegory: the return to national origins
at the ancestral space of the Nadhor. While some sense of real order is
probably necessary to understand the narrative, this real order, ultimately
at least partially undecidable, could never be completely reconstituted
once and for all. Likewise, any attempt to reconstitute the real order of
events that the novel "messes up" also undoes what the novel carries out
so adamantly, a violence against narrative and a challenge to nationality
as a narrative form.

Taking Nedjma to the Nadhor would join the embodiment of national identity (and personification of the Nation) with national origins
located at the site of Keblouti resistance to colonial rule. Nedjma would
then be rooted at the source of national identity:

> [L]'inceste est notre lien, notre principe de cohésion depuis l'exil du pre-
> mier ancêtre; le même sang nous porte irrésistiblement à l'embouchure du
> fleuve passionnel, . . . Nedjma menant à bonne fin son jeu de reine fugace
> et sans espoir jusqu'à l'apparition de l'époux, le nègre prémuni contre
> l'inceste social, et ce sera enfin l'arbre de la nation s'enracinant dans la
> sépulture tribale. . . . (186–87)

> [I]ncest is our bond, our principle of cohesion since the first ancestor's
> exile; the same blood irresistibly bears us to the delta of the passional
> stream, . . . Nedjma concluding her stratagem, a queen fugitive and with-
> out hope until the husband's appearance, the black man forearmed against
> the social incest, and this at last will be the nation's tree taking root in the
> tribal sepulcher. . . . (249–50)

At work in this passage (as well as others in the novel) is a complex system of poetic associations used by many Maghrebian authors. The first image is that of water (with all its life-sustaining qualities), associated with its source or spring, which can also represent the source of national identity. A return to national origins and search for national identity are often described as a quest for roots, hence the image of the Nation's tree, which is planted near this source from which it drinks. This use of water also includes the sea (*mer*) and its homonym, mother (*mère*). The mother as the source of life, associated with amniotic fluids, is thus equated with the Nation's source or origin. A return to the national origins, then, can parallel a return to the womb or to childhood. Combining the Nation's story with that of its citizens, the novel similarly tells the tales of its four protagonists' childhoods as well as their fathers' stories. In addition, as an allegory of the birth of Algeria, *Nedjma* also narrates Nedjma's conception and birth. The story of Nedjma's conception, however, is shrouded in mystery, for her father is unknown. Like Nedjma, her mother is surrounded by four men, two of whom could be Nedjma's father.

The roots of national identity also recall the roots of another tree, the family tree. Alex Haley's search for "roots" involved uncovering his genealogy in addition to a return to the Africa of his ancestors. *Nedjma* involves a similar coincidence of genealogy and quest for origins, but its genealogy (because of the prevalence of endogamy among its characters) hardly resembles a tree and is as confusing as the novel's plot.[1] Due to questions about her paternity, Nedjma also represents a gap in the family tree, especially the patrilineal one. Because of her mixed origins (her mother was a French Jew), she could never embody an Algerian purity, free of all influence by the colonizer; for she is Jewish by Jewish definitions and Muslim by Muslim ones, as well as part French, part colonizer. In addition, the journey of return to national identity is a failure. Kidnapped by Rachid and Si Mokhtar, Nedjma is kidnapped in turn by those of the tribe still remaining on the ancestral lands. Calling Rachid and Si Mokhtar traitors for having abandoned the Nadhor, members of the tribe take away their object of desire, Nedjma, symbol of a free Algeria. This kidnapping of national identity parallels the kidnapping of the revolution described by Djaout, a kidnapping whose consequences for women Kateb also considers.

---

1. Gontard provides a chart of this genealogy (40).

Haunted Roots

Nedjma is a haunted novel: "Surmontant un patio de maison hantée (on s'y suicida en famille avant la guerre), la villa Nedjma est entourée de résidences qui barrent la route du tramway . . ." (65). ("Rising above a haunted patio (before the war, a whole family committed suicide here), the Villa Nedjma is surrounded by residences which cut across the street-car tracks . . ." [86].) Here Nedjma's house, by metonymy, becomes Nedjma—Kateb writes "la villa Nedjma" instead of "la villa *de* Nedjma"—and Woman and house carry the same name. This house is associated with the haunted, and by extension, *Nedjma* as house/novel is also haunted with the ghosts of history:

> [C]e sont des âmes d'ancêtres qui nous occupent, substituant leur drame éternisé à notre juvénile attente, à notre patience d'orphelins ligotés à leur ombre de plus en plus pâle, cette ombre impossible à boire ou à déraciner,—l'ombre des pères, des juges, des guides que nous suivons à la trace. . . . Ce sont nos pères, certes; des oueds mis à sec au profit de moindres ruisseaux, jusqu'à la confluence, la mer où nulle source ne reconnaît son murmure: l'horreur, la mêlée, le vide—l'océan—et qui d'entre nous n'a vu se brouiller son origine comme un cours d'eau ensablé, n'a fermé l'oreille au galop souterrain des ancêtres, n'a couru et folâtré sur le tombeau de son père. . . . (97, Kateb's suspension points)

> [W]e have ancestors' spirits in us, they substitute their eternal dreams for our childish expectations, our orphan patience bound to their paling shadow, that shadow impossible to dissolve or uproot—the shadow of the fathers, the judges, the guides whose [traces] we follow. . . . Yes, those are our fathers; every wadi ransacked, even the smallest brook sacrificed to the confluence, the sea where no springs recognize their own sound: agony, aggression, the void—the ocean—haven't we all seen our origins blurred like a stream in the sand, closed our ears to the underground gallop of our ancestors, played on our fathers' graves. . . . (127–28)

The protagonists are haunted by their ancestors' souls and bound to their shadows or shades. They must resurrect these ancestors or their ghosts/silhouettes, "ressusciter sans sortir de la terre ni revêtir leurs silhouettes oubliées" (97) ("resuscitate without even coming out of the ground or assuming their forgotten outlines" [128]). This task of resurrecting is also the one taken on by the novel.

The above passage also shares the poetic associations of trees and water with the Nation's origins (represented by the ancestors). Yet these origins are at least partially beyond reach, because the protagonists, though tied to their ancestors, are orphans and therefore disconnected from their fathers in the patrilineal family tree. Their fathers, then, are shadows or ghosts, and nothing more. The paths to national identity are clouded by wind-carried sand, and the rivers of national identity, also blurred by sand, mix with other rivers in the sea. Any attempt to narrate an Algerian identity separate from the neighboring nations, even the colonizer, will find that the course of that identity also flows into the Mediterranean, into a common identity shared by the Maghreb, southern Europe, and eastern Mediterranean countries: "Que le flux et le reflux se jouent de ce pays jusqu'à brouiller les origines par cette orageuse langueur de peuple à l'agonie, d'immémorial continent couché comme un molosse entre le monde ancien et le nouveau . . ." (183, Kateb's suspension points). ("Let the tide's ebb and the flow play with this country until its origins are blurred by the stormy languor of a people in agony, the immemorial continent lying like a watchdog between the old world and the new . . ." [245].) This confounding of sources, much exacerbated by colonialism's attempt to sever the Maghreb from its past, nonetheless has much earlier roots, even in the precolonial past of the Maghreb. Nevertheless, this blurring of origins—one way in which Kateb queers the Nation—and these attempts to fell the tree of the Nation,[2] only further root the sense of national identity in the conscience of the colonized.

History's course is the course of a river (*un cours d'eau*). This river is, like other bodies of water, a source of national identity. Nedjma, herself, is compared to a river:

> Car l'oued évadé qui coule au littoral n'est qu'un pseudo-Rhummel devenu le Grand Fleuve, l'Oued El Kebir, en souvenir de l'autre fleuve perdu: le Guadalquivir, que les Maures chassés d'Espagne ne pouvaient transporter avec eux; Guadalquivir, Oued El Kebir, le fleuve abandonné en Espagne se retrouvait au delà du Détroit, mais vaincu cette fois, traqué sous le Rocher comme les Maures chassés d'Andalousie, les pères de Rachid, et Rachid lui-même, revenu lui aussi d'une évasion sans issue au port où

2. Cf.: "[M]ais la conquête [française] était un mal nécessaire, une greffe douloureuse apportant une promesse de progrès à l'arbre de la nation entamé par la hache; comme les Turcs, les Romains et les Arabes, les Français ne pouvaient que s'enraciner, otages de la patrie en gestation dont ils se disputaient les faveurs . . ." (102). ("[B]ut the conquest was a necessary evil, a painful graft promising growth for the nation's tree slashed by the foreign axe: like the Turks, the Romans and the Arabs, the French could only take root here, hostages of the fatherland-in-gestation whose favors they quarreled over . . ." [135].)

l'attendait l'adversité faite femme—Nedjma l'Andalouse—, la fille de la Française qui avait opposé entre eux quatre soupirants, dont trois de la même tribu, les trois descendants de Keblout, car c'était la mère de Nedj-ma, la Française, c'était elle qui avait fait exploser la tribu, en séduisant les trois mâles dont aucun n'était digne de survivre à la ruine du Nadhor. . . . (178, Kateb's suspension points)

For the escaped wadi is only a false Rhummel that has become the Great River, the Wadi El Kebir, in memory of the other lost river: the Guadal-quivir, the river the Moors driven out of Spain could not take with them; Guadalquivir, Wadi El Kebir, the river abandoned in Spain was recovered beyond the Strait, but this time vanquished, tracked down under the Rock like the Moors driven from Andalusia, Rachid's fathers, and Rachid him-self, he too returned from a futile escape to the harbor where adversity in the form of a woman waited for him—Nedjma the Andalusian—the daughter of the Frenchwoman who had set the four suitors against each other, three from the same tribe, the three descendants of Klebout, for it was Nedjma's mother, the Frenchwoman, who had caused the tribe's downfall by seducing the last three males none of whom was worthy to survive the ruin of the Nadhor. . . . (237–38)

In her currents, Nedjma, like the Rhummel, carries the history of an Arab, or North African, presence in Europe and marks a time when part of present-day Spain belonged to the Maghreb. She thus represents the deconstruction of the difference between Europe and Maghreb, Europe and Orient, East and West. Though the Maghreb is troped as Oriental in French colonial discourse, the word itself refers to the western part of the Arab world, and most of the Maghreb is actually to the west of France.

The role of haunting national identity played by the ancestors' ghosts is also the role of history, which scatters its ruins across the novel's land-scape. Reflecting on the failure of the attempt to reconnect Nedjma and the ancestral space, Rachid, who has lived in Bône and Constantine, near the ruins of the Roman cities Hippo and Cirta, describes another kind of "ruines en filigrane de tous les temps, celles que baigne le sang dans nos veines, celles que nous portons en secret" (174–75) ("ruins water-marked from all time, the ruins steeped in the blood of our veins, the ruins we carry in secret" [232]). This blood could be the blood spilt by North Africans during a long history of invasions. The marks or traces, left in turn by Romans, Arabs, Turks, and the French, by Numidians and "Barbary" pirates, are not just the constructions of their architects. A history of suffering is carried in the veins of North Africans and is a crucial part of North African identity. The racial connotations conjured up by the image of blood might give this identity an essential, even biological, quality. Yet this identity is not straightforward; North Africans do not experience it as presence but carry it is as a hidden secret. The French, "descendants Romains," or *Roumis* as Maghrebians call them pejoratively (thereby assimilating the French to the former Roman conquerors), have built "new cities" on the ruins of the old, attempted to cut Maghrebians off from their histories. But this history remains, secret, hidden, ghostly, waiting to be reclaimed. *Nedjma* thus takes as its task "remettre en avant les Ancêtres" ("to set the Ancestors forward") and uncover "le germe indestructible de la nation écartelée entre deux continents" ("the indestructible germ of the nation spread between two continents"). This is the "enjeu du passé" (what is at stake in the past [my trans.]), which will grant Algeria the victory over the *Roumis* denied to Jugurtha, leader of the ill-fated Numidian rebellion against Rome, which might be seen as prefiguring the Algerian Revolution (174–75; 232–33 in trans.).

Traces

This notion of writing history as conjuring up ghosts from the past and returning to origins that turn out to be haunted ends up transforming nationalist visions of the past. In response to the conundrum between the necessity of narratives of origins in the struggle against the colonizer and the exclusion they carry out, *Nedjma* rewrites the nationalist paradigm of return by multiplying sites of origin. Describing Algerian literature's "nomadic characteristics," Raybaud (1993) similarly defines it as "a space of traces, objects of the dispersal of tribes and the provoked disintegration of collective memories, which is, at the same time, a space of obsessions, to the extent that the visible traces are points of emergence, and of passage, and of pressure, of a zone of repressed memories, crushed strength, denigrated or forbidden impulses . . ." (150). He cites *Nedjma* as an example of "nomadism between the archaic and the modern," a concept that refers to a heterogeneous space that is not only the novel or narrative but also the Nation (151). This notion of nomadism would then replace the origin as endpoint of a return with its traces ("l'ombre des pères, des juges, des guides que nous suivons à la trace"). One might search for a beginning, a prelapsarian origin, but it can only be present as an absence (above as an "âme," "ombre," or "silhouette"), in the impure traces it has left. As Bonn (1985) writes, this multiplicity of voices is not only a means of production of historical meaning, it is meaning itself. For if I have seen in Nedjma the novel's particularly fertile absent center, if Nedjma appears to her lovers as always fleeing their advances, it's because no identifying discourse could completely figure her out. Nedjma, who gives her name to the novel, the star symbolizing the fatherland, cannot be restricted to one meaning alone. *Nedjma*'s ultimate lesson, if there could be only one, would therefore be that there cannot be just one meaning or definitive answer. That's why Kateb is aware, according to his famous formula, of making his revolution within the political revolution, of being "disruptive in the midst of upheaval" [au sein de la perturbation, l'éternel perturbateur]. (67)[3]

Kateb, by being eternally disruptive within the disruption of the Algerian Revolution, guards Nedjma from any interpretive closure that would define Algerian national identity once and for all and pave the way for homogenizing the Nation. Nedjma, therefore, constitutes the novel's "center" (under erasure) and the "ungrounded ground"[4] of Algerian identity. To use Kateb's expression, *Nedjma* blurs national origins; rather than being defined through exclusion, his Algeria, embodied as a child of *métissage,* is remarkably *in*clusive.

Women at the Root of Nationalism

One manifestation of the novel's inclusiveness is the sexual freedom embodied by Nedjma, an unruly woman who cannot be controlled by her husband. Like her mother, she has four "lovers," the exact number of wives allotted to men by Islamic law; Nedjma therefore also marks a reversal in the sexual order. What does it mean to personify Algerian identity as a sexually liberated woman who is only partially Algerian and whose Muslim identity is contested? In *Nedjma,* where the family tree and Nation's roots are planted near the *source/mer/mère,* a number of tropes surround the symbolization of the Nation as Woman. Ahlem Mosteghanemi points out that, in Maghrebian literature, this sort of symbolization of Woman, whether as Nation, femme fatale, or mother earth, is unique to male writers (181). In its symbolization of Algeria in the figure of a woman character, *Nedjma* thus parallels the official discourses of Algerian nationalism: "The Algerian woman's role as the guardian of the collective patrimony made her the most living symbol of the fatherland

3. Bonn quotes Kateb from an interview in *L'Action* 28 April 1958.
4. The expression is Butler's (1992, 16).

and Algerian identity. At each stage of the struggle, this symbol takes on the traits of the prevailing situation in the country" (173). Bruno Etienne describes a similar role played by Woman in Algerian nationalist discourse, which deployed three main embodiments of nationalist values: the *moudjahid* or freedom fighter as symbol of historic legitimacy, the *fellah* or peasant as symbol of authenticity and keepers of the land, and women, guardians of tradition, honor, and national virtue (144–68). Nedjma, however, would hardly satisfy this third role: she is portrayed as a liberated woman and veiled only by force. In his choice of a woman to represent Algeria, Kateb contradicts official nationalist discourse on feminine virtue, even though he resorts to an exclusively male technique in his practice of symbolization. Whereas Mosteghanemi points out the exclusively male nature of this technique, she lauds rather than criticizes Kateb for using it (43). She also credits him with opposing nationalist discourses that dismiss feminist demands with the argument that women's liberation flows naturally from that of the Nation (112). Arnaud as well defends Kateb's symbolization of women, suggesting that Nedjma puts on the veil to participate in the national struggle: "The novel's unveiled woman, the libertine, takes back the veil and returns to a traditional role, and her transformation is subordinated to that of her country" (2: 312). This reveiling, however, is not chosen by Nedjma, but forced on her. Arnaud adds, "Veiled again, Nedjma leaves behind a false freedom to reimmerse herself among her people and participate in their struggle" (312). Arnaud's conception of women's struggle is quite problematic in that she repeats the role assigned to women in national struggle and Fanon's description of that role in "Algeria Unveiled."[5]

Many critics have questioned Fanon's assumption that women's liberation naturally coincides with national liberation. Woodhull (1992) writes: "For Fanon as for Kateb, the monolithic group 'women' stands for the nation as a whole, and for both writers the possibility of imagining a cohesive (though not unitary) national group relies on reducing the multiplicity and heterogeneity of women to a single figure, woman" (58). She also describes Nedjma's danger in a manner that resembles Nafissa's: "Already evident in these scenes, however, is an element that threatens to contain Nedjma's whirling revolutionary force, namely her terrifying power over the young men, particularly Lakhdar, who is alternately paralyzed by Nedjma and moved to paralyze her as a way of neutralizing the

5. Woodhull (1993) also points out how Arnaud misreads Fanon (31).

power he attributes to her" (55). The sexual danger posed to men by Nedjma as a "liberated" woman thus parallels the revolutionary force needed to kick out the colonizers. The nationalist struggle can then harness that force to liberate the Nation. One might, however, see how "using women" in such ways could have antifeminist implications. Though women were active participants in the Algerian Revolution up to a certain point and, in this struggle, also advanced the women's struggle, the Algerian Revolution is notorious for not only not furthering women's struggle, but also rolling back previous gains. John Ruedy writes, "Amidst the euphoria of liberation during the summer of 1962, FLN militants roamed the streets intimidating single women. A woman accompanied in public by a man other than a relative was liable to be hurried off to a forced marriage or jailed if she refused" (229). Here, the term *liberation* is contradicted by the description that follows it.

In Bouthaina Shaaban's collection of interviews with Arab women, several Lebanese women cite Algeria as the perfect example of what feminists should avoid by assuring that participation in national movements does not sacrifice feminist demands (101–4). In contrast, the Algerian women Shaaban interviews give more varied responses. While all agree that women played a great role in the revolution, the respondents who actually participated in the revolution tend to be more optimistic about how much the revolution brought in terms of women's liberation. Younger women are more pessimistic, as is evidenced by the following exchange between Farida and her mother Mme Almnowar, who fought in the revolution:

> Here Farida turned to her mother, saying, "I feel that the Algerian men used the Algerian women in the revolution. They used you as they used their weapons. You didn't get anything from the revolution; you got absolutely nothing."
> "No," said her mother. "I don't agree at all. Had we not fought the revolution you would not be here now doing an MA in English!" (186–87)

Farida goes so far as to say, "I think the Algerian male is going backwards rather than forwards. I believe my father is better than my husband and my husband better than his son" (187). Even Mme Almnowar negatively compares women's rights in Algeria to those in Morocco and Tunisia, where women did not fight in full-blown revolutions (191). But Farida's notion of women being used as weapons is an interesting one, for it resembles the woman hidden beneath Fanon's veil as well as the *femme-*

flamme Nafissa personifies. Harnessing women's force could preclude women's liberation in favor of that of the Nation. Given the actual outcome of Algeria's independence with respect to Algerian women, who, veiled or unveiled, are caught today in the crossfire between the ruling elite and its fundamentalist opposition, it is especially important to reconsider alternative visions of revolutionary anticolonial struggle such as Dib's.

When Kateb veils Nedjma at the source of the Algerian nation, on the surface he may seem to submit women's liberation to the national struggle as Fanon does when describing women who put the veil back on to hide weapons. Because Nedjma is kidnapped from her first kidnappers while bathing at the source of national identity, coming to national identity, narrated as a return to ancestral traditions, would require enclosing a woman and controlling the political and sexual danger she represents. As Woodhull (1992) remarks, however, rather than advocating such an unquestioning return to origins, "*Nedjma* constitutes a powerful articulation of the promise and the perils of [Algeria's] search [for identity as a modern nation] with respect to women" (57). *Nedjma* thus "exposes the risks of using women in this way, underlining the costs *to women*," because "the text's (and Nedjma's) unceasing mobility guards against a totalizing fixation upon a single, 'pure' national origin in order to forestall the designation of a scapegoat—woman—as the single origin 'of all the social ills from which Algeria is suffering'" (1993, 25, 28). *Nedjma,* instead of doing what occurs in the narrative (veiling a woman to carry out a narrative return to national origins), does the opposite by unveiling feminism as a danger to the Nation constructed by official discourse. Although Kateb performs the same return to national origins official discourse uses to kidnap women, in his rewriting there remains the possibility of a feminist Nation. When the ancestors kidnap Nedjma, they also kidnap the Nation. By unveiling this kidnapping, Kateb envisions the possibility of feminist roots of the Nation.

Reopening the question of national origins for possible resignification emphasizes the fact that Nedjma's origins—her place in the family tree (i.e. which father she is to be inscribed under) and, therefore, her exact link to the ancestor Keblout in a patrilineal tracing of descent (both possible fathers are, we remember, part of the Keblouti tribe)—are never clearly established. The lack of narrative closure in the novel thus corresponds to a lack of closure in the narrative of Nedjma's sexual origins— her conception resulting from a heterosexual sexual union—and serves as an allegory for uncertain national origins: origins covered over by colonial history and complicated by the presence of a series of invaders from foreign lands (and thus of different origins) on Maghrebian soil, origins now present only as traces, as the marks left by their absences. Maghrebian origins have been complicated over the course of history (hence Kateb's image of history as the flow of a river's currents clouded by sand) by the introduction of foreign origins inextricably mixed with a hypothetically pure Maghrebian identity. Using another of Kateb's images, one could also say the river of Maghrebian identity flows into a sea of *métissage,* where the waters, once mingled, can never be separated.

In *Le blanc de l'Algérie,* Kateb is one of the writers Djebar resurrects by describing his funeral, which practically turned into a political demonstration. The singing of the "Internationale" almost prevented the Imam from delivering the eulogy and reciting prayers. (Kateb was an atheist and, at one time, a communist.) Berber cultural activists showed up with pro-Berber political slogans written in the Berber alphabet, and the funeral service ended with more political slogans shouted by an unruly crowd (175–93). Even at his funeral, Kateb continued to disturb, to haunt. Beyond his burial, his corpus has also become a source of specters. In a way, Woodhull's interpretative strategy of reading Nedjma through the current situation in Algeria, brings back Kateb's ghost as a critical tool for understanding the present. In this way, Kateb's wish, to be "au sein de la perturbation, l'éternel perturbateur," continues to come true after his death. The disturbance he represents within nationalist discourses is even more eternal than he might have hoped.

Part Three

THE FEMINIST

MENACE

Qu'ils tremblent, les prêtres, on va leur *montrer* nos sextes.
—Hélène Cixous, *La jeune née*

Let them tremble, those priests; we are going to *show* them our *sexts*!
—Hélène Cixous, *The Newly Born Woman*

Chapter   Eight

B E C O M I N G   A   W O M A N :
T A H A R   B E N   J E L L O U N ' S
A L L E G O R Y   O F   G E N D E R

If *Nedjma* tells a story of Nation and of coming to national identity, both allegorized through a woman, Ben Jelloun's *L'enfant de sable* (1985) and *La nuit sacrée* (1987) tell the story of a character who, raised as a boy, later becomes a woman. This two-novel sequence, however, tells not only the story of one individual's becoming a woman, but also the story of gender, a narration of the process through which gender is stamped onto the bodies and minds of those belonging to "the second sex." Anderson claims that one has a nationality as one has a gender, and Slimane Zéghidour points out that, in Arabic, "the words for nationality (*djinsiya*) and a person's sex (*djinss*) share the same linguistic root" (152). Ben Jelloun's allegory of gender demonstrates that at the origin of gender, as at the origin of Renan's Nation, there is a violence that must be forgotten for gender to be naturalized. By uncovering this violence, he also narrates the deconstruction of gender. Given the parallel between narratives of gender and of Nation, *L'enfant de sable* and *La nuit sacrée,* when read as national allegories, rewrite the Nation as founded not on the subordination of one gender to another but on gender insubordination.

L'enfant de sable tells of a man who, after his wife has given birth to seven daughters, decides that his eighth child will be a boy, *no matter what.* The eighth child, Ahmed, born female, is raised to be a man through the apprenticeship of masculinity. Ahmed embodies the gender s/he was trained into until his/her father's death, when s/he begins to deviate from manliness.[1] One possible interpretation of this turn of events would be

---

1. Throughout this chapter, I shall use Ahmed and the pronouns s/he, him/her, his/her when reading *L'enfant de sable*—even though Ahmed takes the name Zahra by the end—to emphasize the

that Ahmed's upbringing covers over his/her natural sex, which is repressed until it returns. After his/her father's death, Ahmed ceases to live as a man. But Ahmed, not quite/not a man before his/her father's death, remains not quite/not a woman afterwards. On the one hand, s/he begins to "discover" his/her female body through masturbation and in two erotic encounters with women. On the other, s/he has a beard and a flat chest, which function as "biological" contradictions to his/her feminine hips.

In the two erotic encounters s/he has with (other) women, this contradiction becomes evident. The first encounter begins when a woman asks her in the street, "Que caches-tu sous ta djellaba, un homme ou une femme, un enfant ou un vieillard, une colombe ou une araignée?" (113). ("What are you hiding under your jellaba, a man or a woman, a child or an old man, a dove or a spider?" [84].) When Ahmed answers, "Je ne le sais pas moi-même" ("I myself don't know"), the woman throws herself at him/her:

> Comme j'hésitai, elle se précipita sur moi et, de ses mains fortes, déchira ma djellaba, puis ma chemise. Apparurent alors mes deux petits seins. Quand elle les vit, son visage devint doux, illuminé par un éclair troublant où se mêlaient le désir et l'étonnement. Doucement, elle passa ses mains sur ma poitrine, approcha de moi sa tête et posa ses lèvres sur le bout du sein droit, l'embrassa, le suça. Sa bouche n'avait pas de dents; elle avait la douceur des lèvres d'un bébé. Je me laissai faire puis réagis violemment, la repoussant de toutes mes forces. Elle tomba et je pris la fuite en essayant de refermer ma djellaba.
>
> Cette rencontre n'eut pas de suite, du moins pas dans l'immédiat. Cependant, ce qui se passa après me troubla beaucoup. Dois-je en parler? J'ai du mal à l'écrire. Je veux dire, j'ai honte. Je sens mes joues rougir à l'idée de me souvenir de cette journée où tout se précipita dans mon esprit et où mes émotions furent secouées. La sensation physique que j'éprouvai aux caresses de cette bouche édentée sur mon sein fut, même si elle ne dura que quelques secondes, du plaisir. J'ai honte de l'avouer. (114–15)

Since I hesitated, she threw herself on me and, with her strong hands, tore off my jellaba, then my shift. When she saw my two small breasts, her face became gentle, illuminated by a disturbing light in which desire mingled with surprise. She gently moved her hands over my chest, then put her lips to the nipple of my right breast, kissed it, sucked it. Her mouth was

---

fact that Zahra is taken on as a stage name. I reserve Zahra and feminine pronouns for reading *La nuit sacrée*. Though my practice breaks with previous criticism, it has the advantage of marking the change that occurs between the novels and emphasizing that, even by the end of *L'enfant de sable*, some accounts of the ending revert back to the name Ahmed.

toothless; it had the softness of a baby's lips. At first I did not stop her; then I reacted violently, pushing her aside with all my strength. She fell over and I took to my heels, trying to close up my jellaba.

This encounter had no consequences, at least not immediately. However, what happened afterward disturbed me a great deal. Must I speak of it? I find it difficult to write about it. I mean, I'm ashamed of it. I can feel my cheeks redden at the mere thought of that day, when everything in my mind was turned upside down and my emotion churned up. The physical sensation I felt as that toothless mouth caressed my breast was pleasurable, even if it lasted only a few seconds. I am ashamed to admit it. (84–85)

To settle the doubt concerning Ahmed's *gender,* the woman proceeds to uncover his/her body. The answer to gender ambiguity lies in the *sex* of the body. Yet the erotics of this search for the proof of Ahmed's gender leads to another ambiguity, the possibility of lesbian desire. The passage hints at future repercussions of the incident. Lesbian pleasure elicits shame, embarrassment (the word "honte" appears twice), and Ahmed wonders whether s/he should confine the experience to silence. The "trouble" the encounter provokes can thus be managed by keeping it secret.

The second encounter has a purpose similar to the first, that of settling a doubt. It occurs between Ahmed and one of his/her future employers, Oum Abbas, mother of Abbas, his/her other employer:

> Je compris vite qu'elle ne cherchait ni argent ni bijoux. Ses mains tâtaient mon corps comme pour vérifier une intuition. Ma poitrine minuscule ne la rassura point, elle glissa sa main dans mon séroual et la laissa un instant sur mon bas-ventre, puis introduisit son médium dans mon vagin. J'eus très mal. Je poussai un cri qu'elle étouffa en mettant l'autre main sur ma bouche, puis me dit:
> —J'avais un doute.
> —Moi aussi! dis-je entre les lèvres. (118)

> I soon realized that she was looking neither for money nor for jewelry. Her hands roamed over my body as if to verify an intuition. My tiny breasts did not reassure her; she slipped her hand into my trousers and left it for a moment on my sex, then inserted her middle finger. It hurt. I uttered a cry, which she stifled by putting her other hand over my mouth, saying, "I wasn't sure."
> "Nor was I!" I said between my teeth. (88–89)

On one level, this (homo)sexual encounter could be said to settle this doubt. When Oum Abbas's finger finds Ahmed's vagina, there is no

longer a doubt concerning his/her womanhood. But for this interpretation to be valid, the vagina must be understood as the essence of womanhood; Oum Abbas puts her finger on exactly what makes Ahmed a
woman. And yet, what exactly the doubt concerns is itself in doubt. Regardless of whether Oum Abbas doubts Ahmed is a woman, what could
be the subject of Ahmed's doubt? Perhaps his/her doubt refers back to
the ambiguity of the first encounter: s/he doubts whether s/he enjoys/
finds pleasure in the examination.

Abbas and Oum Abbas finally employ Ahmed in a circus sideshow.
His/her feminine name, Zahra, is taken on as part of this employment.
The image of a circus sideshow, with all the exploitation of the "freaks"
it puts on display, provides an interesting turn to Butler's theory. Whereas
she describes the performance of heterosexual gender roles as an "intrinsic
comedy" (1990b, 122), *L'enfant de sable* offers the possibility that this comedy might sometimes only be fit for the stage of the sideshow. The sideshow implies titillation, satisfaction of a desire for the unusual that seems
to exist at the margins of any gender system, as Abbas implies when in-
structing Ahmed on how to perform his/her role:

> [T]u te déguiseras en homme à la première partie du spectacle, tu disparaî-
> tras cinq minutes pour réapparaître en femme fatale . . . Il y a de quoi
> rendre fou tous les hommes de l'assistance. Ça va être excitant . . . , je vois
> ça d'ici . . . , un vrai spectacle avec une mise en scène, du suspens et même
> un peu de nu, pas beaucoup, mais une jambe, une cuisse . . . , c'est dom-
> mage, tu n'as pas de gros seins . . . Ici les hommes adorent les grosses poi-
> trines et les gros culs . . . Tu es trop mince . . . Ce n'est pas grave! . . . On
> va travailler les gestes et les sous-entendus! Tu commences demain. Il arrive
> parfois que des hommes s'excitent et jettent sur la danseuse des billets de
> banque. Tu les ramasses et tu me les donnes. Pas d'histoire! (121, Ben Jel-
> loun's suspension points)

> [Y]ou'll dress up as a man in the first part of the show; then you'll disap-
> pear for five minutes and reappear as a *femme fatale*. . . . There's enough
> there to drive all the men in the audience wild. It'll be very exciting. I can
> see it now—a real show, with proper staging, suspense, and even a bit of
> nudity, not much, just a leg, a thigh. . . . It's a shame your breasts aren't
> very big: the men around here love big breasts and buttocks. You're too
> thin, but it doesn't matter. We'll have to work on the gestures and innuen-
> does! You'll begin tomorrow. Sometimes men get excited and throw bank
> notes at the dancer. You'll pick them up and give them to me. No fooling
> around! (91)

This particular spectacle of gender consists in a continued unmasking of cross-dressing. In a way, Ahmed repeatedly reveals his/her history of dressing and passing as a man on the stage of the freak show. Yet what is revealed here is less important than how it is performed; that Ahmed's anatomy is unwomanly by male standards will matter less than "les gestes et les sous-entendus." Ahmed enacts the spectacle of womanliness for men, and this performance constitutes his/her employment. An audience of men decides what constitutes a good performance; for the good performance satisfies *their* desires. The requirement that s/he hand over his/her tips to his/her employer parallels the relation between a prostitute and her pimp. Performing woman, in this vision of gender, means doing so for the profit of a pimp.

The story of Ahmed's gender is narrated by a storyteller on a public square. This setting for his/her story is consistent with Ben Jelloun's stated desire to publicly disclose sexual secrets:

> Le secret est là, dans ces pages, tissé par des syllabes et des images. Il me l'avait confié juste avant de mourir. . . . Je sus alors que j'étais en possession du livre rare, le livre du secret, enjambé par une vie brève et intense, écrit par la nuit de la longue épreuve, gardé sous de grosses pierres et protégé par l'ange de la malédiction. Ce livre, mes amis, ne peut circuler ni se donner. Il ne peut être lu par des esprits innocents. La lumière qui en émane éblouit et aveugle les yeux qui s'y posent par mégarde, sans être préparés. Ce livre, je l'ai lu, je l'ai déchiffré pour de tels esprits. Vous ne pouvez y accéder sans traverser mes nuits et mon corps. Je suis ce livre. Je suis devenu le livre du secret; j'ai payé de ma vie pour le lire. (12–13)

> The secret was there, in those pages, woven out of syllables and images. He entrusted it to me just before he died. . . . I was in possession of a rare book, a book containing a secret, spanning a brief, intense life, written through the night of a long ordeal, hidden under large stones, and protected by the angel of malediction. This book, my friends, can be neither borrowed nor loaned. It cannot be read by innocent minds. The light that comes from it will blind those who are unprepared. I have read this book. I have deciphered it for others. You can gain access to it only by traversing my nights and my body. I am that book; I have paid with my life to read its secret. (5)

Here, the duty of the storyteller is to reveal a secret as it is contained in a written text. At the end of the passage, he becomes one with the text he reads/tells to his public. Unveiling the secret in the text is thus a self-unveiling; the secret contaminates whoever reveals it, which is perhaps at least partly why it is so dangerous. Within Ahmed's story, the secret is also associated with his/her mother, who becomes its receptacle when Ahmed's father tells her, "[T]u seras le puits et la tombe de ce secret" (23). ("You . . . will be the well and tomb of this secret" [13].) At Ahmed's birth, his/her mother cries because she has given birth to a girl: "Sa femme s'était voilé le visage pour pleurer" (26). ("His wife veiled her face to weep" [16].) This veil hides more than tears; it hides the secret they would reveal. The storyteller's function is one of unveiling, of removing this veil: "Il . . . sentait [la lumière] passer sur son corps comme une flamme qui brûlerait ses masques, une lame qui lui retirerait lentement le voile de chair qui maintenait entre lui et les autres la distance nécessaire" (7). ("He felt [the light] pass over his body like a flame threatening to burn away his mask, or like a blade slowly tearing away the veil of flesh that maintained the necessary distance between himself and others" [1].) Revealing Ahmed's secret risks burning the storyteller and anyone who reads his/her story.

In *L'enfant de sable,* the narrative of sexual identity is disrupted by challenges to the very narration of that identity. At various moments of the telling of Ahmed's story, the storyteller's version is contested by his audience. At one point, he remarks, "C'est le vent de la rébellion qui souffle! Vous êtes libres de croire ou de ne pas croire cette histoire" (43). ("The wind of rebellion blows among you! You are free to believe or not to believe this story" [28].) A man who claims to be Fatima's brother asserts:

> Notre conteur prétend lire dans un livre qu'Ahmed aurait laissé. Or, c'est faux! Ce livre, certes, existe. Ce n'est pas ce vieux cahier jauni par le soleil que notre conteur a couvert avec ce foulard sale. D'ailleurs ce n'est pas un cahier, mais une édition très bon marché du Coran. . . . Le journal d'Ahmed, c'est moi qui l'ai. . . . (70)

> Our storyteller is pretending to read from a book that Ahmed is supposed to have left behind him. That is untrue! Of course the book exists, but it is not that old notebook, yellowed by the sun, which our storyteller has covered with that dirty scarf. Anyway, it isn't a notebook, but a cheap edition of the Koran. . . . I am the one who has Ahmed's diary. . . . (49)

Before the story is finished, the storyteller disappears, and various would-be storytellers attempt to replace him by offering opposing versions of the story's ending. But the effect of this multiplicity of endings, however, is one of a lack of narrative closure—in *L'enfant de sable*, the story of gender has no closure, cannot be interpreted once and for all. The plotting of gender, like Kateb's plotting of Nation, renders multiple possibilities.

L'enfant de sable, however, has a sequel, *La nuit sacrée*, in which Ahmed—called Zahra from here on—is hired by a woman to care for her blind brother (the Consul) and ends up in a sexual relationship with him. Though this relationship is unconventional in that it is not sanctified by marriage, it would be possible to read it as the closure *L'enfant de sable* lacks. *La nuit sacrée* is a first-person narrative told by Zahra herself and resembles a more traditional narrative; it is linear, has an ending, and does not contain competing versions of events or an audience to contest the story. It would seem that Ahmed's search for being in *L'enfant de sable* is resolved in *La nuit sacrée* as s/he takes on a woman's name (and the name of woman)[2] as part of a heterosexual relationship, in Ahmed/Zahra's "becoming-woman" (Orlando 123). In this case, the consolidation of heterosexuality and closure would be one and the same. The French literary establishment seems to have placed its stamp of approval on the heterosexual closure *La nuit sacrée* might seem to provide. *La nuit sacrée* was awarded the Prix Goncourt and was the basis for the film version of both novels where the events of *L'enfant de sable* appear as flashbacks to the narrative in *La nuit sacrée*. This rereading of *L'enfant de sable* through the lens of *La nuit sacrée* uses the latter to answer questions left unresolved by the former and eliminates the challenges posed by the former to the narrative of gender. My reading of the two novels does the opposite, reading *La nuit sacrée* through the lens of *L'enfant de sable* and reopening questions that *La nuit sacrée*, at first glance, might seem to close.

In many ways, *La nuit sacrée* reads like the liberation of a woman repressed through the imposition of the "wrong" gender:

> Ma surprise fut grande: je retrouvais une élégance innée! Mon corps se libérait de lui-même. Des cordes et des ficelles se dénouaient peu à peu. Je sentais physiquement que mes muscles perdaient de leur fermeté. La métamorphose se faisait en marchant. Je respirais mieux. Je passais ma main sur mes petits seins. Cela me faisait plaisir. Je les massais dans l'espoir de les voir grossir, sortir de leur trou, pointer avec fierté et exciter les passants. . . . Je touchai mes seins. Ils émergeaient lentement. . . . Je faisais mes premiers pas de femme libre. (44–45)

---

2. Cf. the title of Riley's *"Am I That Name?": Feminism and the Category of "Women" in History*.

I was rediscovering a surprising innate elegance. My body was breaking free of itself. Cords and strings were unraveling, and I could feel my muscles loosening. [The metamorphosis occurred as I walked.][3] I breathed more easily. I ran my hand over my small breasts. It felt good. I massaged them, trying to make them bigger, to make them jut out proudly and excite passersby. . . . I touched my breasts. They were swelling slowly. . . . These were my first steps as a free woman. (40–41)

Woman's liberation, here, is a biological matter. The female body, bound (literally tied up with ropes and string) by the social conventions of the masculine gender, is released. Zahra becomes weaker, her breasts grow (even though she is already fully an adult at the time of the experience). This return of repressed biology has a heterosexual goal, "exciter les passants," gendered masculine, even though this goal never involves reproduction. A number of critics have interpreted this passage as describing Zahra's liberation. John D. Erickson describes Zahra's male drag as a veil: ". . . Ahmed the male serves as mask/veil . . . for Zahra" (60). And Abbes Maazaoui equates abandoning this drag with an unveiling: "[T]hese three acts of physical liberation (the removal of the cloth strips binding her breasts, the development of the sense of touch, and the acceptance of the body's sensual demands) are only possible if the body is unveilable, strippable [dévoilable, dénudable], in the concrete sense of the word. Woman's liberation seems to require a rejection of the veil and clothing" (70). This figurative use of the veil becomes quite problematic when one considers the way it masks the very literal veil Zahra might wear as a woman. Ben Jelloun himself has given authority to these interpretations in an interview: "[W]hat I wanted to show was the process of an emancipation . . . a woman's struggle to become what she should have been had she not been the victim of an aggression against her sexuality and all her being" (cited in Gaillard 44; my trans.). When read closely, however, L'enfant de sable and La nuit sacrée challenge the very interpretation Ben Jelloun seems to authorize.

Becoming a woman, for Zahra, involves the work of forgetting: "Le travail de l'oubli se faisait à mon insu et je m'installais de plus en plus dans l'histoire de l'Assise et du Consul" (113). (The work of forgetting was happening without my realizing it, and I was more and more a part of the Seated Woman and Consul's story.)[4] To become a woman, Zahra

---

3. This sentence is not translated in the English translation.
4. This sentence is not translated in the English translation.

must forget (repress) her manhood; since man and woman are in a relation of difference, self-identity depends on forgetting that relationship.[5] One might also say she must forget how Woman is inscribed as Law in a system of compulsory heterosexual gender roles. The first event in Zahra's journey to womanhood is her rapture by a knight veiled in blue, who takes her on a journey to the south. Zahra could even be said to arrive at the source of womanhood in a way that resembles the source of national identity that awaits those who complete the return to the Nation's origin:

> Avant d'arriver dans cette ville, j'ai eu la chance et le privilège de me baigner dans une source aux vertus exceptionnelles. L'une de ces vertus est vitale pour moi: l'oubli. L'eau de cette source m'a lavé le corps et l'âme. Elle les a nettoyés et surtout elle a remis de l'ordre dans mes souvenirs, c'est-à-dire qu'elle n'a gardé que très peu de chose de mon passé; seuls trois ou quatre souvenirs ont été maintenus. (104)

> Before I came to this town, it was my privilege and good fortune to bathe in a spring of exceptional qualities. One of them—the ability to wipe out memories—is vital to me. The waters of that spring cleansed me, body and soul, wiping my memories clean and reordering what little remains of my past, three or four memories. (96–97)

If *La nuit sacrée* is understood as a search for the roots of gendered identity paralleling the search for national identity, then this source can be read as the source of gender. Bathing in the source of gender is associated with forgetting. Is the source of gender to be understood as the more biological category of sex? By bathing in the source of gender, does Zahra wash off, remove what Wittig (1989) describes when she writes, "Language casts sheaves of reality upon the social body, stamping it and violently shaping it" (43–44)? Does she cleanse herself of her father's imposition of manliness onto her body?

Given Ben Jelloun's subversion of the narrative return to national origins in *La prière de l'absent,* one must ask whether the same sort of subversion is possible in *La nuit sacrée.* What if, as Butler (reading Wittig) suggests, sex as a biological category only comes to have meaning through gender (1990b, 112–13)? It is my contention that, instead of narrating the liberation of a female from the imposed gender of man, instead of narrating the return to the roots of womanhood, *La nuit sacrée* is about the impossible task of such a narrative. By positing that forgetting is an essen-

---

5. I owe this formulation to Ross Chambers.

tial part of this return, *La nuit sacrée,* when considered with Renan's description of the forgetting at the Nation's origin, begs the question: What violence at the origin of gender must be forgotten for one to become a woman? In Zahra's case, it could be the violent imposition of the wrong gender, having her breasts bound, being punished as a child when s/he cried "like a girl." In short, it could be the violent stamping of the body by language. Near the end of her story, Zahra's body is violently stamped (and not just with words) when she undergoes a forced clitorodectomy and infibulation as punishment for impersonating a man (158–60), but as a woman, she also faces another violence.

In one version of the conclusion to *L'enfant de sable,* Abbas rapes Ahmed, and s/he ceases to be a woman who dresses as a man and repeatedly unveils her "true" gender:

> Zahra n'était plus «princesse d'amour»; elle ne dansait plus; elle n'était plus un homme; elle n'était plus une femme, mais une bête de cirque que la vieille exhibait dans une cage. Les mains attachées, la robe déchirée juste au niveau du torse pour donner à voir ses petits seins, Zahra avait perdu l'usage de la parole. (142)

> Zahra was no longer Princess of Love; she no longer danced; she was no longer a man or a woman, but a circus animal whom the old woman exhibited in a cage. With her hands tied, her dress torn to the waist to reveal her small breasts, Zahra had given up the use of speech. (108–9)

Here, not having a gender is equated with imprisonment and being tied up. (Bathing at the source of gender, becoming a woman, we remember, is associated with an untying.) Not having a gender also means not having a voice. If subjectivity must be gendered, if to speak, a subject must use a gendered "je," this loss of voice becomes understandable. Abbas finally kills Ahmed (in this version) when he rapes him/her again after s/he places razor blades in his/her vagina to cut up his penis, and he dies from this experience as well. In *La nuit sacrée,* the knight who takes Zahra on her journey to the origin of gender also rapes her. At the origin of Zahra's becoming a woman, therefore, is a rape. Yet this violent past she tries to forget is never completely forgotten; it seems to come back to haunt her: "[M]on histoire, celle qui fit de moi un enfant de sable et de vent, me poursuivrait toute ma vie" (*La nuit sacrée* 172). ("[M]y story, which had made me a child of sand and wind, would pursue me all my life . . ." [163].) One of the memories that comes back is that of teasing the neighborhood girls:

Habillée en garçon je taquinais les petites filles autour de cette balançoire, jusqu'au jour où le frère d'une de ces filles me fit tomber. J'avais le visage en sang, je pleurais. Le frère qui était plus âgé que moi me dit avant de s'enfuir: «Si tu avais été une fille, je t'aurais fait autre chose!» (127)

Dressed as a boy, I would tease the little girls, until one day the brother of one of them knocked me out of the swing. My face was covered with blood, and I cried. The brother, who was older than me, said before running off, "If you were a girl, I'd have done something else to you." (118–19)

Here, a girl is defined as someone who can be raped.

In "Fighting Bodies, Fighting Words" (1992), Sharon Marcus describes a tendency among feminist antirape writings to suggest that "rape has always already occurred and women are always either already raped or already rapable" (386). The boy in the above passage seems to hold such a view. Marcus counters this essentializing vision of woman as (potential) rape victim with the notion of a "rape script" through which "social structures *inscribe* on men's and women's embodied selves and psyches the misogynist inequalities which enable rape to occur":

These generalized inequalities are not simply prescribed by a totalized oppressive language, nor fully inscribed before the rape occurs—rape itself is one of the specific techniques which continually scripts these inequalities anew. . . . Masculine power and feminine powerlessness neither simply precede nor cause rape; rather, rape is one of culture's many modes of feminizing women. A rapist chooses his target because he recognizes her to be a woman, but a rapist also strives to imprint the gender identity of "feminine victim" on his target. A rape act thus imposes as well as presupposes misogynist inequalities; rape is not only scripted—it also scripts.

She argues that "we can see rape as a *process* of sexist gendering which we can attempt to disrupt" (391). Marcus's way of viewing the "rape script" as both preexisting and being written through individual incidents of rape parallels Butler's description of gender roles, which both exist as Law and are constantly rewritten through their repetition. In fact, Marcus conceives of rape as one of many ways in which gender is instituted and turned into Law on a continual basis. Her conception of rape as both scripted and scripting points out that Butler's notion of gender as performance can have violent consequences (as opposed to reducing gender to endless play as some critics have suggested). The "rape script" could also be viewed as a concrete example of how gender is stamped onto bodies. Rape, then, is one of the forms of violence that must be forgotten for gender to be naturalized. Or rather, what must be forgotten is its scripted nature and institutional incorporation into scripts of gender, that these scripts have been scripted, are constantly rescripted, and therefore can be rescripted in feminist ways.

If, as Simone de Beauvoir stated, "[o]n ne naît pas femme: on le devient" (2: 13) ("[o]ne is not born, but rather becomes, a woman" [267]), part of the violence that must be forgotten is the violence of that becoming. For the gender system to work, gender as performance must be forgotten, replaced by gender naturalized and joined to its source, biology. It is thus paradoxical that the joining of gender to its source, involving a narrative of return to this origin, involves forgetting the source and rewriting a new one. Gender connected to its source through narration is therefore a fictional category. *La nuit sacrée,* instead of naïvely assuming the source to which Zahra returns is firmly rooted in her biology, seems to make visible the very narrative mechanisms by which this fictional return is naturalized as truth. Zahra's naming is naturalized through an invocation of the supernatural: "Tu es une femme. . . . La Nuit du Destin te nomme Zahra, fleur des fleurs, grâce, enfant de l'éternité . . ." (32). ("You are a woman. . . . The Night of Destiny names you Zahra, flower of flowers, grace, child of eternity" [26].) Yet this very same name was given to her in *L'enfant de sable* in a freak show. In the first novel, taking on the name of woman means performing as such in a sideshow. To what extent does becoming woman, naturalizing the name of woman, require forgetting that the category is performed as part of a sideshow?

At one point, Zahra pretends to be a woman, not herself, but a prostitute. With the pretense of helping the blind Consul choose a prostitute, Zahra accompanies him to the brothel. She secretly dismisses all the prostitutes, describes herself to him as one who left so that she can make love with him while he thinks she is a prostitute. Yet this "comédie du bordel" (130) ("brothel charade" [121]) is fully understood by the Consul. Like the circus sideshow, it can be read as an allegory of heterosexuality. In some ways the "comédie du bordel" parallels the freak show, in which Ahmed performs Zahra for the profit of his/her employer. At the sideshow, s/he disguises him/herself as a man and then unveils him/herself to be a woman. Yet, to say that Ahmed performs Zahra is also to say that the reverse is also true, that a man performs as woman. In the "comédie du bordel," however, Zahra disguises herself as (another) woman to perform as a prostitute. To what extent is performing as prostitute part of performing as woman? To what extent does the "comédie du bordel" have a script that, like Marcus's "rape script," genders its performers? Though *La nuit sacrée* perhaps does not establish *once and for all* that heterosexuality is or must be like prostitution, or is or must be based on rape, I would suggest that a careful reading of the novel at least raises questions as to whether heterosexuality as currently performed and instituted as a compulsory system in the Maghreb (or in the West, for that matter) can exist separately from these two practices.

The final disturbing aspect of Zahra's becoming a woman is what happens to her official identity in the process. In *L'enfant de sable*, Ahmed is fully recognized as a male citizen. Zahra, in becoming a woman, must dispose of this identity; she does so as she buries a number of her personal belongings with her father:

> Je vidai très vite le sac qui contenait presque tout ce que je possédais, une chemise d'homme, un pantalon, un extrait d'acte de naissance, une photo de la cérémonie de la circoncision, ma carte d'identité, l'acte de mariage avec la malheureuse Fatima. . . . Au moment de fermer la tombe, je m'accroupis pour bien tasser les objets et j'eus mal à la poitrine. Quelque chose me serrait les côtes et le thorax. Les bandelettes de tissu étaient encore autour de ma poitrine pour empêcher les seins de sortir et de grossir. Je retirai avec rage ce déguisement intérieur composé de plusieurs mètres de tissu blanc. Je le déroulai et le passai autour du cou du mort. Ensuite je serrai très fort et fis un nœud. J'étais en sueur. Je me débarrassais de toute une vie, une époque de mensonges et de faux-semblants. (*La nuit sacrée* 56–57)

> I emptied the bag, which contained almost everything I possessed: a man's shirt, a pair of trousers, a piece of a birth certificate, a photograph of the circumcision ceremony, my identity card, the marriage certificate for me and poor Fatima. . . . Before filling in the grave, I squatted down to pack the objects in and felt a pain in my chest, as though something were squeezing my rib cage. My breasts were still wrapped tight to stop them from growing. In a rage I tore off the wretched disguise, several yards of white cloth. I unrolled it and wrapped it around the dead man's neck, then knotted it and pulled it tight. I was sweating. I got rid of all my life, a time of lies and deception. (50–51)

Changing gender identity, here, requires physically burying a number of papers and possessions, but even more, it requires putting the old identity to death, conducting a funeral, and placing it in a tomb. ("Burying" thus has two levels of meaning: the simple one of placing any object in the ground and covering it with earth, and the more ritualistic one of laying the dead to rest.) Ahmed dies as a man; Zahra is born as a woman. Becoming a woman therefore involves naturalizing this becoming as a birth: one is born a woman. The forgetting at the source of gender involves believing this fiction. This birth is marked, again, by the liberation and unbinding of female biology that accompanies the burial of the men's clothes that covered Ahmed's body, disguised it, and lied for him. This unbinding resembles the removal of strips of cloth from a mummy, as if Zahra were not becoming a woman, but merely resurrecting the female within her who had been put to death. Again, the social is shed off, and biology finds its rightful place. But what if this new identity is no less of a disguise? It does involve a number of performances—the sideshow, the "comédie du bordel." Heterosexuality, like womanhood, is not merely released: it must be learned. It is not learned once and for all, but must be repeated over and over. In the above passage, one could say that Zahra takes off the mask that was Ahmed. This unmasking might seem to imply that Zahra has now revealed her true face.

Yet as *La nuit sacrée* draws to its conclusion, Zahra is unmasked again . . . as Ahmed! The consul's sister finds Ahmed's uncle who can testify to his/her marriage to Fatima (the uncle's daughter), and Zahra kills the uncle and is sent to prison. Rather than finding a true self, free of disguise, Zahra changes one secret for another and takes on an even more blackmailable identity. Perhaps the most disturbing aspect of this change in identity is the loss of official identity it requires: "Après tout je n'étais qu'une étrangère, une vagabonde, sans papiers, sans identité, sans bagages, venant du néant et allant vers l'inconnu" (94). ("I was, after all, only a stranger[/foreigner], a vagabond with no papers, no identity, and no baggage, coming from nothingness and heading for the unknown" [86].) For Zahra, becoming a woman means losing her status as citizen in the Nation, becoming like a foreigner, being marginalized into exile in her own country. *La nuit sacrée* seems to suggest that this loss of citizenship necessarily accompanies becoming a woman.

Here, the two novels become narratives of national as well as gendered identity. As long as Ahmed performs as man, s/he is given full rights as citizen in the Nation, but when the performance ceases, those rights go away. In *L'enfant de sable,* the exact connection between Ahmed's gender and national identity is rendered explicit by the newspaper announcement of his/her birth, in which his/her father claims, "Cette naissance annonce fertilité pour la terre, paix et prosperité pour le pays. Vive Ahmed! Vive le Maroc!" (30). ("This birth will bring fertility to the land, peace and prosperity to the country. Long live Ahmed! Long live Morocco!" [19].) The novel adds:

> Cette annonce dans le journal fit beaucoup jaser. On n'avait pas l'habitude d'étaler ainsi publiquement sa vie privée. Hadj Ahmed s'en moquait. L'important pour lui était de porter la nouvelle à la connaissance du plus grand nombre. La dernière phrase fit aussi du bruit. La police française n'aimait pas ce «Vive le Maroc!» Les militants nationalistes ne savaient pas que cet artisan riche était aussi un bon patriote. (30–31)

> This announcement in the newspaper set tongues wagging: people did not usually display their private life so publicly. Hajji Ahmed cared not a fig. For him the important thing was to bring the news to the knowledge of as many people as possible. The last sentence also caused a stir. The French police did not at all care for the "Long live Morocco!" The nationalist militants did not know that this rich craftsman was also a good patriot. (19–20)

His/her father becomes a model citizen in the Nation being born as he furnishes a new male citizen. Being a good citizen means performing gendered (i.e. private) identity on the public stage. Becoming a woman, however, means withdrawing from the Nation's stage to the domestic sphere. *Domestic,* here, takes on additional meaning when one considers that, as Zahra becomes a woman, she gains employment as a domestic servant, *une domestique* in French. Becoming a woman thus means changing from citizen to maid. When Fanon (1959) praises the role of the modern couple in the new Nation, he makes a slip that marks a similar change: "The Algerian couple, in becoming a link in the revolutionary organization, is transformed into a unit of existence. *The mingling of fighting experience with conjugal life deepens the relations between husband and wife and cements their union. There is a simultaneous and effervescent emergence of the citizen, the patriot, and the modern spouse [du citoyen, du patriote et d'un époux moderne]*" (114; 106 in original). In the first sentence, it is the couple that is the building block of the revolutionary organization. The third sentence, however, is about citizenship; that is, once the revolution has succeeded and the new Nation has become reality, one half of the couple is dropped and only the man, the "époux," gains status as citizen.[6] Only the man is entitled to the blossoming and growth, to the fulfilling potential of revolution.

Lisa Lowe suggests the possibility of reading *L'enfant de sable* as a

---

6. Thanks to Nancy K. Miller for this reading of Fanon's passage.

national allegory and points to the newspaper ad as a signal of the novel's allegorical nature (54–55). Her reading, however, might seem to imply the notion of Zahra's becoming a woman as liberation that I question above. Ahmed, cross-dressed as a man, would thus allegorize the travesty of Moroccan identity under the imposition of French control. Indeed, Ben Jelloun himself has suggested such an interpretation: "Les épreuves que subit Zahra pourraient aussi bien être celles d'un peuple en lutte pour sa libération" (cited in Gaillard 44). (Zahra's trials and tribulations could also be those of a people struggling for their liberation.) Yet Lowe does not see Zahra's becoming a woman as escaping transvestism, but as replacing one form of drag with another: "In this sense, Ahmed/Zahra devises an *alternative* transvestism, one which does not comply with the father's enforced transvestitism which expressed the power of men over women under patriarchy, but which is rather a *representation of cross-dressing* which both exhibits this logic of forced transvestitism, and ultimately makes use of further cross-dressing to deride the patriarchal logic" (56). She uses the image of nomadism, of traveling between two locations, to describe Ahmed/Zahra's search for gendered identity: "In this sense the protagonist's nomadic vacillation between the positions of male identity, female identity, male-as-female and female-as-male, suggests an analogous irresolution for the struggles of the Moroccan nation . . ." (56). This search for gendered, even sexual, identity thus parallels and allegorizes the search for national identity narrated in other novels as a quest for the Nation's origin.

In Lowe's concept of "sexual allegories of postcolonialism" (60), which rely on a "dialectic between the subject and collective struggle" (61), the Nation's origin is not the end point of a journey but one of two poles between which postcolonial identity oscillates, "the opposed poles of colonialism and nativism" (57). What Lowe calls nativism could also be called a cult of origins. By traveling as nomads between these two poles, Lowe's postcolonial subject both resists colonialism and avoids the nationalism that empowers national bourgeoisies. Lowe's concept of "literary nomadics" thus constitutes one way of disrupting narratives of return to national origins. I am especially interested in what Lowe describes as "narrative displacements of the categories themselves" (44). This is perhaps related to what she describes as "an *alternative* transvestism." In Lowe's nomadics, the journeying to the nativist pole, or what I would call national origins, would then involve a performance of national identity that both uses the origin of official nationalist discourse and disrupts the centrality of that origin. National identity, still useful in this concept, becomes a sort of drag. When Ben Jelloun unveils Ahmed's secret, he disrupts the version of Nation implied in the newspaper ad. The Nation becomes one composed of sand children, whose identities, like Kateb's rivers of national identity, are clouded with sand.[7] Ben Jelloun's model of the performance of gendered identity is thus simultaneously a model of national identity, where the Nation involved is inescapably queer. In this vision of becoming/performing woman, the relation between Nation and Woman is one of exclusion. The more Zahra becomes woman, the more she is denied an officially recognized identity. Ben Jelloun's narrative of becoming (in Beauvoir's sense) a woman, read as national allegory, asks an important question: What happens to woman (*que devient la femme*)[8] in nationalist discourse? Will, she, like Nedjma, be forced back under the veil, kidnapped, and cloistered? If for Dib, woman is dangerous to the colonizer and male subjectivity, for Kateb, she is dangerous to the Nation. This danger can be controlled, or, as the works by Maghrebian women writers will demonstrate, it can be liberated.

7. Cazenave writes, "[T]he child is made of sand, and . . . just like sand, one cannot grasp it and hold it firmly. In other words, the protagonist is an evanescent character with no firm substance" (448).

8. As opposed to Beauvoir's notion of becoming a woman.

Chapter Nine

PERSONALIZING THE POLITICAL, POLITICIZING THE PERSONAL: ASSIA DJEBAR'S FEMINIST REWRITING OF HISTORY

Anne McClintock describes the kind of gendered violence explored in *L'enfant de sable* and *La nuit sacrée* as being central to nationalism and nation-building:

> All nationalisms are gendered; all are invented; and all are dangerous—dangerous . . . in the sense that they represent relations to political power and to the technologies of violence. As such, nations are not simply phantasmagoria of the mind; as systems of cultural representation whereby people come to imagine a shared experience of identification with an extended community, they are historical practices through which social difference is both invented and performed. Nationalism becomes in this way constitutive of people's identities through social contests that are frequently violent and always gendered. . . . [D]espite many nationalists' ideological investment in the idea of popular *unity*, nations have historically amounted to the sanctioned institutionalization of gender *difference*. (89)

She thus marks the violence Renan describes at the Nation's origin as a gendered violence and asserts that gender performance ("social difference . . . both invented and performed") is foundational in nationalist discourses on national identity. Ben Jelloun's allegory narrates its own deconstruction by revealing the *gendered* violence at the Nation's origin. As McClintock points out, by showing how nationalist discourses on "popular *unity*" cover up the "institutionalization of gender *difference*," this gendered violence must also be forgotten to nationalize the Nation as a foundation of identity. Uncovering this violence is thus one way feminism can challenge dominant discourses on national identity.

Aamir Mufti and Ella Shohat have described feminism as dragging skeletons out of the closet in a manner similar to the one described by Ben Jelloun: "[F]eminist critique . . . has tried to free itself from the 'dirty linen' defensiveness about not publicly criticizing one's 'home' community—national, racial, ethnic—'in public' lest that be viewed as betrayal" (6–7). One may thus relate gender insubordination (the feminist menace) to sexual dissidence and marginal sexualities in their resistance to homogenizing nationalist discourses (or not so homogenizing, since as McClintock points out, this homogeneity relies on gender difference). In *L'amour, la fantasia* (1985), Assia Djebar articulates a model for writing history that also resurrects ghosts and brings them back to haunt the present. What she digs up, however, are women's role in history as well as their suffering and resistance, which have, like the queer ghosts examined in previous chapters, been hidden from history in colonial and nationalist historiographies. Whereas Nedjma is veiled at the Nation's origin, Djebar's task is to unveil women at the source of national identity. Her unveiling, however, is even more complicated than Boudjedra's; for Djebar is careful not to equate unveiling with women's liberation in a simplistic manner and acknowledges that unveiling can often replace an old veil with a new one. Djebar also connects the more figurative uses of the term "unveiling" with its more literal meaning for women. Her feminist rewriting of the Nation thereby disrupts in its own ways national family values and the Nation's dependence on heterosexual repronormativity.

Trained as a historian (Zimra 1993, 124), Assia Djebar was severely criticized by nationalists for her first two novels, because they supposedly focused on the concerns of a middle-class *évoluée* and totally ignored the political realities of Algeria at the time (Zimra 1992, 68). Indeed, these novels were published during the Algerian Revolution and yet contain no reference to the war and barely acknowledge a colonial presence. Clarisse Zimra (1992), however, has argued for a rereading of these earlier novels in a way that makes them consistent with her entire oeuvre and thereby challenges early nationalist criticism of Djebar's work. Danielle Marx-Scouras has written, "If Djebar was stigmatized for 'conjuring away Algerian reality,' . . . it was due to the fact that she was writing as a woman and voicing her sexual difference" (172). Khatibi (1968), as well, has defended Djebar against such accusations: "Algerian revolutionaries found it indecent that Djebar would only be preoccupied in this novel with the sexual problem while Algeria was in the grasp of a horrible war. Hadn't they understood that *La soif*'s character's discovery of her body was also an important revolution?" (62). The debate over Djebar's early novels, written in the midst of the nationalist struggle, is thus a paradigmatic example of the feminist menace to nationalism. Djebar tried to join the maquis[1] on the Tunisian border in 1958 but was told that women were no longer allowed in combat (Zimra 1992, 119). After criticism of her early novels, her work became more political. A ten-year silence then followed, which she ended with *Femmes d'Alger dans leur appartement* (1980). *L'amour, la fantasia, Ombre sultane* (1987), and *Vaste est la prison* (1995) constitute the first three volumes of what Djebar has called a quartet.

L'amour, la fantasia consists of three parallel and often simultaneous narratives: the invasion of Algeria by the French in 1830 and subsequent resistance to both this invasion and early French colonial rule, the Algerian Revolution, and a girl's childhood narrative. In the first two narratives, Djebar carries out the work of the feminist historian as described by Fatima Mernissi (1975):

> Man-written history is what constitutes our "national" or "cultural" heritage, in spite of the claim by the theocracies that it is of divine origin. We know that it is very difficult for a woman to design for herself a past. Ironically, any other task, including designing a future, seems more feasible, and definitely more rewarding. Writing the past is a highly coded and serious act, thought of, up to now, as an exclusively male endeavor, burden, and privilege. (xii)

Designing for herself a past is the task Djebar takes on in her more recent novel, *Loin de Médine* (1991), in which she writes the history of the beginning of Islam from the point of view of the women who participated in it as well as the view of those women who opposed its spread, women who, in both cases, often took up arms. Designing for herself a past is also the task Djebar takes on in *L'amour, la fantasia,* in which history and autobiography are intermeshed. When writing the history of colonial invasion, she has recourse only to the writings of French men who participated in or followed the military expeditions in Algeria. Writing the history of Algerian women during this period happens through inferring, questioning, and perhaps fictionalizing. To construct a history of the role of women during the Algerian Revolution, Djebar has recourse to women participants who are still alive. Since many of these women are illiterate and can leave no written history, Djebar must convert and translate their

---

1. The ALN, Armée de Libération Nationale or armed wing of the FLN.

oral histories in dialectal Arabic and Berber into written histories in French.

The third form of narrative Djebar includes is that of a girl's childhood, which resembles Djebar's in many ways and, for this reason, is often read as autobiographical. The childhood narrative tells the story of an Algerian girl who, through education in a French school, escapes veiling and sequestering. Like the other two narratives, the childhood narrative is a tale of resistance and liberation. Its presence in the novel marks the irruption of the personal into the political and offers a narrative of revolution in which women's liberation is consistent with the Nation's, whereas Kateb and Dib only point out the friction between the two struggles, even though from possibly feminist perspectives. On the one hand, unlike Fanon, who subordinates women's struggles to the national one, Djebar does not suggest that women's liberation flows naturally from that of the Nation. Instead, she articulates a heterogeneous battlefield where struggles are many and multipronged. On the other hand, she does not cover up the potential friction between various struggles. It is, after all, through her French education that the girl escapes the veil and the *harem*.[2] This ambiguous relation to the French language, which both serves as a channel of the girl's liberation and marks her colonization, is also present in the narratives of colonial invasion, of resistance to it, and of the Algerian Revolution.

In writing the history of the colonial conquest of Algeria, Djebar reveals acts of violence that accompanied the French invasion. She details, for example, the French practice of *enfumade*, or setting fire to caves sheltering Algerians who were fleeing French atrocities. Through such revelations, Djebar carries out the task the historian Abdallah Laroui calls for: "dévoiler l'histoire du Maghreb" (1: 10) (unveiling Maghrebian history), an unveiling that might also be associated with his call to "décoloniser l'histoire" (2: 67) (decolonize history). Djebar, however, gives this unveiling its fullest feminist possibilities, as well as its more literal implications:

2. The *harem* and *harem* fantasies are clichés of European Orientalist fiction and painting. In most European versions, the *harem* resembles a seraglio. Every house, however, has a *harem*, that is, a women's space where male nonrelatives are traditionally not allowed to enter, especially if the women are unveiled. According to Chebel (1995), *harem* "[d]esignates the private space that is women's sanctuary. . . . It has the same root as *harâm*, 'forbidden,' the principal figure of the intimate home" (295). He adds that "the interior of the *harem* is forbidden to all individuals not related to the family" (296). I use the word here in its strictest meaning, without the connotations European discourses often associated with the *harem*. Though Djebar describes her escape from the *harem* in the autobiographical mode, she also often describes the *harem* as a women's space, a safe space similar to what many North American feminists sought to establish in the 1970s.

in some cases, French soldiers actually stripped women of their clothes. In writing the history of the French invasions, Djebar cites many eyewitness accounts, often those written by French men—the enemy from both nationalist and feminist perspectives. In the writings of male colonizers, she finds traces of Algerian women's resistance and suffering. To articulate a feminist account of national origins in resistance to the colonizer, she must also look for traces of roots in colonial writings. In an interview, Djebar described history in *L'amour, la fantasia* as a "quête de l'identité [, i]dentité non seulement des femmes mais de tout le pays" (Mortimer 1988, 201) (a search for identity, not only women's identity, but also the whole country's). In her reading of the Baron Barchou de Penhoën's impressions of the invasion of Algeria, she writes, "Barchou la rapporte d'un ton glacé, mais son regard, qui semble se concentrer sur la poésie terrible ainsi dévoilée, se révulse d'horreur: deux femmes algériennes sont entrevues au détour d'une mêlée" (*L'amour* 28). ("Barchou's tone is ice-cold, but he seems to be transfixed with revulsion by the terrible poetry of the scene [unveiled] before his eyes; he had caught sight of the bodies of two Algerian women, lying a little apart from one group of skirmishers" [18].) In this passage, Djebar uses the notion of unveiling (which is not translated in the English version) to describe Barchou's writing. But in addition to reading his version of history, she also reads the historian. She steals his account from the camp of the colonizer to use it in the service of anticolonialism. She ventures into enemy territory like a spy to unveil hidden history and "design for herself a past." The importance of uncovering traces of women's resistance to colonial invasion in relation to the struggle for national independence is made clear in the third portion of the novel, in which Djebar describes the role of women in the Algerian Revolution. The novel situates national struggle within an anticolonial history uncovered by the nationalist historian. The Algerian Revolution, in this narrative, has roots in a history of resistance to colonial invasion.

Joan Nestle (1992) has stressed the importance of steering clear of two opposing dangers in the writing of lesbian history, "the dangers of romanticizing losses while at the same time aggrandizing little victories" (273). The first danger would involve reducing lesbians of the past to their oppression, seeing their oppression as governing their lives at the expense of neglecting their resistance to it, the ways they innovatively managed to live often fruitful lives in the face of their oppression. The second danger would consist of stressing their resistance at the expense of belittling their oppression. In writing Algerian women's history, Djebar seems to

negotiate this double bind, at once revealing atrocities committed by
French soldiers against Algerian women and uncovering Algerian wom-
en's heroic resistance to colonization in spite of the capitulation of the
Algerian male political elite. She also reveals the sexist mode of colonial
invasion by describing the letters of French captains as projecting the
fantasy of conquering "une Algérie-femme impossible à apprivoiser" (69)
("Algeria as a woman whom it is impossible to tame" [57]) and viewing
colonization as rape:

> Ce monde étranger, qu'ils pénétraient quasiment sur le mode sexuel, ce
> monde hurla continûment vingt ou vingt-cinq années durant, après la
> prise de la Ville Imprenable. . . . Y pénètrent comme en une défloration.
> L'Afrique est prise malgré le refus qu'elle ne peut étouffer. (70)

> This alien world, which they penetrated as they would a woman, this
> world sent up a cry that did not cease for [twenty or twenty-five]
> years . . . after the capture of the Impregnable City. . . . Penetrated and
> deflowered; Africa is taken, in spite of the protesting cries that she cannot
> stifle. (57)

The description of colonial invasion as the rape of an Algerian woman is
far from being unique to feminist writers; it is a trope of many male
nationalist writings, including Fanon's "Algeria Unveiled." Among male
writers, however, this tendency equates the "violation" of Algeria with a
"violation" of male honor. It is then up to men to defend this honor as it
is embodied by Algerian women as if the worst effects of colonial violence
to women were suffered by colonized men. Djebar, however, recounts the
suffering of women not merely as a metaphor for that of the entire country. She uncovers the consequences of colonization to individual women
and to women as a group. She points to "[l]e viol ou la souffrance des
anonymes" (69) ("the rape or suffering of the anonymous victims" [57]),
women whose names will never be known.

In the third section of the novel, "Les voix ensevelies" (Buried Voices
[my trans.]), Djebar uncovers or exhumes the voices of women who participated in the Algerian Revolution, voices buried by official accounts of
the revolution and also buried because these women could leave no written account by themselves. One of her informants says, "Hélas! nous
sommes des analphabètes. Nous ne laissons pas de récits de ce que nous
avons enduré et vécu!" (168). ("Alas! We can't read or write. We don't leave
any accounts of what we lived through and all we suffered!" [148].) Again,
Djebar relates both their suffering (being tortured by the French, for ex-

ample) and their heroic participation in the revolution. She combines the roles of novelist and historian by collecting oral histories through interviews with women fighters (Mortimer 1988, 204; Woodhull 1993, 80). These accounts give voices to the Algerian women whose names have been erased by history. At the same time, however, Djebar also recognizes that a complete recovery of these voices is impossible. As Spivak argues in her essay "Can the Subaltern Speak?" Djebar emphasizes the importance of acknowledging the ways in which subaltern women have been silenced by history "by *measuring* silences, if necessary—into the *object* of investigation" (Spivak 1988, 296). Feminist historians must therefore be attentive to the "eloquence of silence"[3] in order to show how the traces left by women's erasure from history speak volumes.

In some cases, the experiences of women in the maquis involved not only combat with the colonizer, but also resistance to sexism among male nationalists. For many male fighters, a single woman in the maquis ran the risk of being dishonored and therefore of becoming unsuitable for marriage; she also represented a temptation. Djebar interviews a woman who successfully resisted attempts by her male comrades to force her to get married (149), and her account of women's resistance to colonial invasion and participation in the revolution offers a counterdiscourse on the compatibility of women's struggles with the national one. Many male nationalists urged feminists to concentrate on liberating the Nation and promised that women's liberation would follow, a promise history has shown to be rarely if ever kept. Other nationalists accused feminists of being traitors, of adopting the ideals of the colonizers against Muslim traditions. Still other nationalists supported women's liberation as a prerequisite for national independence. But even among this last group, women's liberation was seen to be good mainly as a means, not in and of itself, and feminism was deployed as a weapon by men to further their own goals. In contrast, Djebar narrates a vision of national struggle that coexists with women's movements, a vision of the Nation that has room for feminists. For Djebar, feminism, as Khatibi points out, is itself a revolution as important as the national one against colonial rule, and is thus, to use Kateb's expression, "au sein de la perturbation, l'éternel perturbateur."

Djebar's unveiling of women's history is paralleled in the childhood

---

3. Cf. the title of Lazreg's *Eloquence of Silence.*

narrative of a girl who goes to French school, a narrative in which Djebar relates escaping the veil to writing:

> Voilez le corps de la fille nubile. Rendez-la invisible. Transformez-la en être plus aveugle que l'aveugle, tuez en elle tout souvenir du dehors. Si elle sait écrire? Le geôlier d'un corps sans mots—et les mots écrits sont mobiles—peut finir, lui, par dormir tranquille: il lui suffira de supprimer les fenêtres, de cadenasser l'unique portail, d'élever jusqu'au ciel un mur orbe.
> Si la jouvencelle écrit? Sa voix, en dépit du silence, circule. (11)

> So wrap the nubile girl in veils. Make her invisible. Make her more unseeing than the sightless, destroy in her every memory of the world without. And what if she has learned to write? The jailer who guards a body that has no words—and written words can travel—may sleep in peace: it will suffice to brick up the windows, padlock the sole entrance door, and erect a blank wall rising up to heaven.
> And what if the maiden does write? Her voice, albeit silenced, will circulate. (3)

Even veiled, the girl who writes projects words beyond the veil or the walls of the *harem* into the public sphere. Djebar, in fact, describes three cloistered girls who write love letters to escape the *harem* (18–23). In this tale of Algerian girls' coming to writing, the notion of the postcolonial Maghrebian writer as a sort of public storyteller who unveils secrets on the public square is deployed in the service of feminism. Writing thus becomes a way of bringing women out into the public space of the Nation: "L'écriture est dévoilement, en public, devant des voyeurs qui ricanent . . ." (204, Djebar's suspension points). ("[Writing] is a public unveiling in front of sniggering onlookers . . ." [181].) Whereas Ben Jelloun associates writing with unveiling sexual secrets, Djebar finds in writing a way of unveiling women: "Le murmure des compagnes cloîtrées redevient mon feuillage. Comment trouver la force de m'arracher le voile, sinon parce qu'il me faut en couvrir la plaie inguérissable, suant les mots tout à côté?" (245). ("I shelter again in the green shade of my cloistered companions' whispers. How shall I find the strength to tear off my veil, unless I have to use it to bandage the running sore nearby from which words exude?" [219].) Djebar's unveiling also involves transgressing taboos: "Ecrire *devant* l'amour. Eclairer le corps, pour aider à lever l'interdit, pour dévoiler . . . Dévoiler et simultanément tenir secret ce qui doit le rester, tant que n'intervient pas la fulgurance de la révélation" (75). ("To write *confronting* love. Shedding light on one's body to help lift the taboo,

to lift the veil . . . To lift the veil and at the same time keep secret that
which must remain secret, until the lightning flash of revelation" [62].)
Unveiling, here, is related to secrets; the association of the veil and the
closet is thus strengthened by this understanding of Djebar's feminist
writing as a form of unveiling. Narratives queer the Maghrebian Nation
and make the Nation feminist through similar tactics: disclosure, uncovering, digging up, revelation, and unveiling both secrets and transgressions.

One of the modes of this unveiling is history; the other is autobiography:

> Tenter l'autobiographie par les seuls mots français, c'est, sous le lent scalpel
> de l'autopsie à vif, montrer plus que sa peau. . . . Parler de soi-même hors
> de la langue des aïeules, c'est se dévoiler certes, mais pas seulement pour
> sortir de l'enfance, pour s'en exiler définitivement. Le dévoilement, aussi
> contingent, devient, comme le souligne mon arabe dialectal du quotidien,
> vraiment «se mettre à nu».
>
> Or cette mise à nu, déployée dans la langue de l'ancien conquérant, lui
> qui, plus d'un siècle durant, a pu s'emparer de tout, sauf précisément des
> corps féminins, cette mise à nu renvoie étrangement à la mise à sac du
> siècle précédent. (178)

> To attempt an autobiography using French words alone is to lend oneself
> to the vivisector's scalpel, revealing what lies beneath the skin. . . . Speak-
> ing of oneself in a language other than that of the elders is indeed to unveil
> oneself, not only to emerge from childhood but to leave it, never to return.
> Such incidental unveiling is tantamount to stripping oneself naked, as the
> demotic Arabic dialect emphasizes.
>
> But this stripping naked, when expressed in the language of the former
> conqueror (who for more than a century could lay his hands on everything
> save women's bodies), this stripping naked takes us back oddly enough to
> the plundering of the preceding century. (156–57)

Djebar describes writing one's life story in a language other than one's
native tongue as a form of exile. But it is also through this crossing of
linguistic borders that unveiling becomes possible, through sharing secrets with "outsiders," washing the Nation's dirty laundry outside the Nation. Writing autobiography in French, for an Algerian woman, links her
story with the history of her Nation, because writing in the colonizers'
language bears the mark of her colonization. On the one hand, autobiography written in French represents an exile from the childhood past as it
was experienced in Arabic. On the other, by returning to the Nation's

roots at the site of resistance to colonial invasion, autobiography can also represent the story of the Nation told allegorically through the story of a woman's life. As these returns mobilize by consolidating national identity, Djebar seeks roots of a feminist consciousness that can be deployed in women's struggles:

> Ecrire en langue étrangère, hors de l'oralité des deux langues de ma région natale—le berbère des montagnes du Dahra et l'arabe de ma ville—, écrire m'a ramenée aux cris des femmes sourdement révoltées de mon enfance, à ma seule origine.
>
> Ecrire ne tue pas la voix, mais la réveille, surtout pour ressusciter tant de sœurs disparues. (229)

> Writing in a foreign language, not in either of the tongues of my native country—the Berber of the Dahra mountains or the Arabic of the town where I was born—writing has brought me to the cries of the women silently rebelling in my youth, to my own true origins.
>
> Writing does not silence the voice, but awakens it, above all to resurrect so many vanished sisters. (204)

Women's writing carries out a return to origins, and writing autobiography resurrects past struggles of women. In Djebar's case, this return brings back a history of women's resistance to haunt the present Nation of official (and therefore male) discourse.

Autobiography, thus written by a woman, is the story of a feminine "je," which in itself is a story that should remain unspoken: "Comment une femme pourrait parler haut, même en langue arabe, autrement que dans l'attente du grand âge? Comment dire «je», puisque ce serait dédaigner les formules-couvertures qui maintiennent le trajet individuel dans la résignation collective?" (177). ("How could a woman speak aloud, even in Arabic, unless on the threshold of extreme age? How could she say 'I,' since that would be to scorn the blanket-formulae which ensure that each individual journeys through life in a collective resignation?" [156].) Djebar is referring to the difficulty of asserting a female self or subjectivity before being a mother or grandmother. Yet, finding the roots of women's history in a woman's autobiography also means articulating a female subjectivity. Saying "I" means lifting a linguistic cover ("couverture") from women's bodies.

Like Bhabha's Nation, however, Djebar's autobiography also involves writing a fiction: "Ma fiction est cette autobiographie qui s'esquisse, alourdie par l'héritage qui m'encombre" (*L'amour* 244). ("My fiction is this attempt at autobiography, weighed down under the oppressive burden of my heritage" [218].) Through the following questions, de Man, as well, has associated autobiography with fiction:

> But are we so certain that autobiography depends on reference, as a photograph depends on its subject or a (realist) picture on its model? We assume that life *produces* the autobiography as an act produces its consequences, but can we not suggest, with equal justice, that the autobiographical project may itself produce and determine the life and that whatever the writer *does* is in fact governed by the technical demands of self-portraiture and thus determined, in all its aspects, by the resources of his medium? And since the mimesis here assumed to be operative is one made of figuration among others, does the referent determine the figure, or is it the other way around: is the illusion of reference not a correlation of the structure of the figure, that is to say no longer clearly and simply a referent at all but something more akin to a fiction which then, however, in its own turn, acquires a degree of referential productivity? (1979b, 920–21)

Djebar's autobiography, written as fiction, seems to answer de Man's rhetorical question by producing the life it supposedly describes referentially. Writing this fiction in French, however, is a form of veiling as much as unveiling:

> L'autobiographie pratiquée dans la langue adverse se tisse comme fiction, du moins tant que l'oubli des morts charriés par l'écriture n'opère pas son anesthésie. Croyant «me parcourir», je ne fais que choisir un autre voile. (243)

> Autobiography practised in the enemy's language has the texture of fiction, at least as long as you are desensitized by forgetting the dead that writing resurrects. While I thought I was undertaking a 'journey through myself,' I find I am simply choosing another veil. (216–17)

Coming to writing through autobiography as a form of unveiling, for Djebar, is thus not a simple operation of writing the body into the public sphere, is not a pure and simple liberation or breaking a silence. In other places, Djebar has more explicitly stated that writing is a form of veiling: "[C]ertains écrivent pour dévoiler, j'écris pour me cacher ('Some write to reveal/unveil; I write to hide')" (Zimra 1992, 76).

Whereas elsewhere, Ben Jelloun has characterized novelistic revelations of sexual transgression as acts of unveiling, in *L'écrivain public* (1983), he describes writing in a way similar to Djebar:

Je pris ainsi le parti d'écrire et de me cacher. (III)

I thus took on the task of writing and hiding myself.

Les autres se cachaient pour se masturber, moi je me cachais pour écrire. (102)

Others hid to masturbate, *I* hid to write.

Les mots sont un voile, un tissu fin, fragile, transparent. (104)

Words are a veil, a thin, fragile, transparent cloth.

L'exorcisme par les mots est mon bouclier, mon voile, ma demeure et ma passion. (162)

Exorcism through words is my shield, my veil, my abode, and my passion.

Writing therefore simultaneously veils and unveils. A number of critics have picked up on Ben Jelloun's notion of writing as (un)veiling,[4] which considerably complicates his position in "Défendre la diversité culturelle du Maghreb." The title of Erickson's essay, "Femme voilée, récit voilé dans *L'enfant de sable* de Tahar Ben Jelloun," published in English as "Veiled Woman and Veiled Narrative in Tahar ben Jelloun's *The Sandchild*," makes such a connection: "Just as Ahmed the male serves as mask/veil (that is, a veil donned out of volition) for Zahra, however, so the series of storytellers/narrators, who seemingly adapt to the demands of conventional narrative, serve as masks/veils for the postcolonialist author" (60). Erickson's reading also depends on the association of Ahmed's male drag with a kind of veil, as if this veil had implications more important than those of the more literal veil Zahra might have to wear upon becoming a woman. This citation underscores an important complication in Ben Jelloun's theory of postcolonial writing, a complication that is all the more important in that it allows us to better understand Djebar.

Erickson's reading, however, also points to the danger of this figurative use of the veil, because it relies on a number of clichés many Arab feminists have challenged: "The voiceless narrative of Zahra evokes the state of [almost universal—"presque universel" in the French] aphonia in which woman exists in traditional Arab society. . . . The woman in traditional Arab society is silenced and silent [réduite au silence]. . . . The sole gaze permissible is that of the male" (52–53; 290 in French). Homa

4. See Déjeux 1993, 285; Novén 163–66; and Erickson (quoted below).

Hoodfar has described "the orientalists' interpretation of the veil as a symbol of the Muslim woman's subordination and exclusion from all social spheres and even her loss of control over her own life" (104). In her study of reveiling in Egypt, she has challenged this interpretation by demonstrating the conscious decision by "the educated women of the urban lower income groups" (121) to reveil for economic, familial, and social reasons. By doing so, Hoodfar stresses that the veil cannot be understood except in specific social, historical, political, and economic contexts. Does Hoodfar's argument thereby discredit not only Erickson's but also Ben Jelloun's and Djebar's description of writing as (un)veiling? I would suggest that Ben Jelloun's and especially Djebar's association of writing with not only unveiling (an association that might retain what Hoodfar calls "the view that veiling equals oppression and exclusion" [104]), but also with veiling, carefully guards the ambiguities and complexities of women's choices to veil or unveil as well as of the implications of revealing or dissimulating sexual secrets. (Such a reading, however, need not necessarily exclude the possibility that writers in French have incorporated Western clichés of the veil *qua* women's oppression and exclusion.)

For Djebar, women's liberation does not involve breaking out of the social, cultural, and linguistic constraints that bind a woman's body (as a veil supposedly would). There is no natural body beneath the veil waiting to come out, no body outside of language. As Ahmed/Zahra—unbinding his/her body to free it of imposed manhood—learns that becoming a woman is not merely a matter of liberating a female body from its social fetters but must also involve the learning of new roles, Djebar's autobiographical subject is not simply unveiled through writing but, instead, entails writing new fictions, or more precisely, rewriting old fictions to create new ones. In her writing, unveiling involves taking on another veil. There is no woman that can shed the veil of cultural meanings scripted onto her body. Writing means rewriting the script of gender, rewriting older fictions.

This rewriting also involves negotiating between cultures. Writing postcolonial female subjectivity in the Algerian context requires dealing with at least two or three languages, and this crossing of linguistic borders even takes on sexual connotations: "Ecrire en la langue étrangère devient presque faire l'amour hors la foi ancestrale: le tabou, en Islam, épargne, en ce cas, les mâles, bien plus, les valorise" (Djebar 1985b, 25). (Writing in the foreign language becomes almost like making love outside the ancestral faith: taboo, in Islam, spares, at least in this case, males, even more, valorizes them.) For a woman writer, sexual crossings of linguistic borders are more taboo than for men, who can increase their standing in homosocial networks through sex with European women. In Algeria, even the law regulates interfaith sex for women: "A Muslim woman is prohibited from marrying a non-Muslim man, while a man is indirectly allowed to do so, since Article 49 states that a child must be brought up 'in the religion of his father'" (Lazreg 1994, 152). This "love in two languages"[5] is literalized in *L'amour, la fantasia* as the narrator recounts her adolescent love:

> Les mois, les années suivantes, je me suis engloutie dans l'histoire d'amour, ou plutôt dans l'interdiction d'amour; l'intrigue s'est épanouie du fait même de la censure paternelle. Dans cette amorce d'éducation sentimentale, la correspondance secrète se fait en français: ainsi, cette langue que m'a donnée le père me devient entremetteuse et mon initiation, dès lors, se place sous un signe double, contradictoire. . . . (12)

> During the months and years that followed, I became absorbed by [the love story], or rather by the prohibition laid on love; my father's condemnation only served to encourage the [plot]. In these early stages of my sentimental education, our secret correspondence is carried on in French: thus the language that my father had been at pains for me to learn, serves as a [procuress], and from now [on] a double, contradictory sign reigns over my initiation. . . . (4)

Here, writing love letters in French marks the transgression of paternal interdiction, which heightens the pleasure of what it is supposed to forbid. Rather than revealing, love letters were supposed to keep a secret, which Djebar nonetheless reveals in the pages of her novel. The unveiling that her novel carries out depends on a previous veiling with ambiguous and contradictory implications: writing in French, on the one hand, is the catalyst for a love affair, and on the other, "renvoie étrangement à la mise à sac du siècle précédent" (178) ("takes us back oddly enough to the plundering of the preceding century" [157]); that is, writing in French recalls the French invasion of Algeria.

In some ways, Djebar's autobiographical subject thus resembles Nedjma, a figure of national identity represented as a product of *métissage*. Kateb shows that the Nation and national identity are necessary yet rewrites official versions of these narratives to make them less available for the justification of oppression and exclusion. Djebar's autobiographical

---

5. Cf. the English title of Khatibi's *Amour bilingue*.

subject, rooted in the history of the Nation and women's resistance to both colonialism *and* patriarchal oppression, is also a fiction. Often considered *the* novel of national consciousness, *Nedjma* has also provoked a debate on the implications of its version of national identity for feminism, a rather substantial debate in the context of the criticism on Maghrebian literature. Nationalist discourse, in this context as well as many others, is an overtly masculinist space. Not that women or feminists cannot be nationalists; their inclusion in the political sphere of the Nation, however, has often been a matter of discussion, debate, and even controversy in ways that it never is for men as a category.

However, if Kateb points both to the problems of using women as symbols of the Nation and vessels of national honor and to the stakes for women in uncomplicated returns to national origins, Djebar envisions ways of writing women into the Nation in feminist ways. She rewrites male writings of national identity, not by rejecting the Nation, but by making it feminist. Like Kateb, she offers a model of narrative return to the Nation's origins that digs up history. Kateb has also described his writing of the Nation as an "autobiographie au pluriel,"[6] an expression that could have several meanings. Critics often stress that Nedjma represents a cousin Kateb was in love with in his youth, a cousin who was married to someone else. From this point of view, Kateb splits the autobiographical subject into four voices, the four protagonists of the novel. Each is Nedjma's cousin, each desires her, and each occupies the position of narrating subject at various points of the novel (to such an extent that it is often difficult to decipher who is speaking). *Nedjma* is an "autobiographie au pluriel" in another way. Each of the four protagonists is a descendant of the ancestor Keblout. The return to the Nadhor is therefore a return to individual roots as well as national ones; it is also a return to Kateb's own ancestors. Djebar, in a similar way, links a return to her childhood with the birth of a Nation. In Kateb's version of national identity, at the Nation's origin a woman (Nedjma) is kidnapped, sequestered, veiled. In Djebar's version, at the Nation's origin, a woman escapes seclusion and veiling, and women resist male visions of Woman's place in the Nation and nationalist struggles. In her study of Djebar, Jeanne Marie Clerc has described Djebar as operating "une véritable inversion du discours de Kateb" (9) (a veritable inversion of Kateb's discourse). Indeed, in *Le blanc de l'Algérie,* Djebar has questioned the fact that Algeria is always personified

---

6. Arnaud (2: 284) quotes the expression from an interview in *Jeune Afrique* 118 (21–27 Jan. 1963).

as a woman: "Ainsi, l'Algérie en homme, en homme de paix, dans une dignité rétablie est-ce pensable? Pourquoi pas, pourquoi toujours «ma mère», ma sœur, ma maîtresse, ma concubine, mon esclave Algérie? Pourquoi au féminin? (120–21). (So, Algeria as a man, as a man of peace whose dignity has been restored, is it thinkable? Why not, why does it always have to be "my mother," my sister, my mistress, my concubine, my slave Algeria? Why always in the feminine?) So, while Djebar is far from equating unveiling with women's liberation in a simplistic way, she does uncover silences left by women's absence in both colonial and male nationalist accounts of history. As we shall see in the next chapter, this uncovering also involves a haunting, for it brings women out of the Nation's closets to disturb and challenge the foundation of national unity on the exclusion of women from the public sphere.

Chapter Ten

WOMEN COME OUT
INTO THE NATION:
DJEBAR'S ALLEGORY OF MARRIAGE

If, in *L'amour, la fantasia,* feminist writing of both history and autobiography consists of a narrative form of (un)veiling, in *Ombre sultane,* Djebar literally (un)veils her protagonist Hajila. *Ombre sultane* is the story of Isma, who convinces her husband to take Hajila as a second wife. Isma manipulates the institution of polygamy, criticized by many Arab feminists, to obtain her own freedom by escaping from marriage, perhaps at Hajila's expense. Hajila, in turn, escapes from marriage by going out when the husband is not at home and removing her veil in the streets. *Ombre sultane* thus offers a point of comparison for the various types of unveiling discussed thus far. When used figuratively, especially by male writers, unveiling could tend to become separated from women's issues. *Ombre sultane* offers a way of reading unveiling that, though not inconsistent with earlier readings, is perhaps more nuanced and reveals more of their feminist potential. The novel articulates women's resistance to patriarchal marriage and, therefore, compulsory heterosexuality and challenges the status accorded to women within the Nation of official discourse. By coming out into the Nation, Isma and Hajila challenge the family as a building block of the Nation, articulate ways for women to exist in the Nation separately and independently of men, and envision a feminist nation that is also a queer nation. Resistance to compulsory heterosexuality comes with finding a healing space for women within the traditional space of the *hammam,* whose homoerotic potential Djebar explores, even if not explicitly.

Like *L'amour, la fantasia, Ombre sultane* contains a number of narratives: Hajila's outings and unveiling, the story of her marriage, Isma's memories of her own marriage, her accounts of her experiences after marriage, and the narrative of her childhood. The childhood narrative in *Ombre sultane,* similar to that of *L'amour, la fantasia,* links the two novels, as well as both novels' autobiographical narrative of escape, to the narrative of anticolonial struggle in *L'amour, la fantasia.* Many critics are willing to read *Ombre sultane* as a critique of polygamy in the Maghreb, but few would point out that the novel does not envision replacing polygamy with monogamy or replacing a non-Western family structure with a Western one. I would suggest that Djebar's observations on marital power structures might also apply to the Western institution of heterosexual monogamy.

The picture Djebar paints of Hajila's marriage is not a pretty one. The husband is never referred to by name but only as "the man," and his anonymity reinforces his abstract nature as the manifestation of power within a social structure. The novel describes him beating his wife, and in the end Isma takes her daughter out of this household, away from what she calls "le spectacle des cris, des coups, de l'invraisemblable bêtise sexuelle" (79) ("the sight of the shouting, the blows, the incredible sexual stupidity" [70]). The following passage describes their marital coitus:

> Le viol, est-ce le viol? Les gens affirment qu'il est ton époux, la mère dit «ton maître, ton seigneur» . . . Toi, tu t'es battue dans le lit en te découvrant une vigueur insoupçonnée. Sa poitrine t'écrase. Tu te glisses, tu tentes d'échapper au poids, tes bras serrés spasmodiquement contre tes flancs, tu te fais de plus en plus raide à l'intérieur de l'étreinte. Les bras de l'homme enserrent, se desserrent, tu plies les jambes sans oser frapper, sans tenter de fuir. La lutte est circonscrite au matelas, aux draps froissés qui s'enroulent . . . L'homme a éteint, profitant d'un suspens, d'une accalmie. Tu fermais déjà les yeux. La conclusion approche, tu reprends la résistance. (66, Djebar's suspension points)

> Rape! Is this rape? People assert that he is your husband, your mother always refers to "your master, your lord" . . . He has forced you down on to the bed, you try to fight him off, finding unsuspected sources of strength. You are crushed beneath his chest. You try to wriggle free from under the weight, you stiffen your arms convulsively against your sides, bracing yourself as he clasps you to him. The man's arms tighten around you, then relax their grip, you bend your legs, not daring to kick, not trying to escape. A battle fought out on a mattress in a tangle of crumpled sheets . . . The man has switched out the lamp, taking advantage of a temporary let-up, a brief breathing space. You were already closing your eyes. The [conclusion approaches], you resume your resistance. (57–58)

This family romance equates male orgasm with narrative closure, that which gives the story meaning and a *raison d'être*. Whether intercourse is rape remains a question in the above passage. The question is answered, however, when the following day is referred to as the "lendemain du viol" (71) ("the day after the rape" [62]). Here, marriage gives the husband the right to rape his wife. The above description equates marital coitus with a struggle, a "lutte . . . circonscrite au matelas," a man forcing intercourse, a woman fighting back; rather than a harmonious union, this marriage resembles war. Hajila even wonders, "« Le coït, est-ce vraiment cela, cette douleur de la chair, pour toute femme? » Aucune ne s'est révoltée?" (71–72). ("'Is this what coitus really is for every woman? this physical pain?' Has no woman ever rebelled?" [63].) Coitus, like the sexual mode of colonial penetration in *L'amour, la fantasia,* calls for resistance. When Djebar writes, "L'homme est vraiment sorti; l'homme, tous les hommes!" (*Ombre* 17) ("The man has really gone out; the man, all men!" [8]), she suggests that the marriage in *Ombre sultane* may not be a unique case; the novel may, in fact, be an allegory of marriage in general. In *Vaste est la prison,* Djebar returns to marriage as a site for *la lutte des sexes* when she describes a woman in the *hammam* saying, "L'ennemi est à la maison" (13). (The enemy is at home.) In reaction to the narrator's surprise, another woman points out, "Oui, « l'ennemi », murmura-t-elle. Ne sais-tu pas comment, dans notre ville, les femmes parlent entre elles? . . . L'ennemi, eh bien, ne comprends-tu pas: elle a ainsi évoqué son mari!" (14). (Yes, "the enemy," she whispered. Don't you know how, in our city, women speak among themselves? . . . The enemy, well don't you understand: that's how she evoked her husband!) Likewise, *Ombre sultane* seems to ask whether marriage as an institution is nothing more than an "invraisemblable bêtise sexuelle." Isma's descriptions of her marriage with the same man, however, contradict any generalization of this sort. Her memories of marital coitus involve more pleasant, more caring descriptions of heterosexual intercourse.

As Ben Jelloun's allegory of becoming a woman asks how much gender is connected to rape scripts and the "comédie du bordel," *Ombre sultane* seems to suggest that coitus has political and structural functions in the compulsory institution of heterosexual marriage. In *Intercourse,* Andrea Dworkin describes a similar function: "Sexual intercourse is not intrinsically banal, though popular culture magazines like *Esquire* and *Cosmopolitan* would suggest that it is. It is intense, often desperate" (21). She describes how sexual intercourse can function as a tool in the exploitation and oppression of women and challenges the notion that men have a right to heterosexual intercourse. In contrast, as a part of American feminisms' "sex wars," essays such as Joan Nestle's "My Mother Liked to Fuck" and Gayle Rubin's "Thinking Sex" have challenged what some have called antisex, antiporn feminism. Yet what may have been seen as the discrediting of Dworkin's work has often led to a dismissal of the questions she and others have raised about the way sexuality is institutionalized in normative structures. While not sharing the antisex implications of Dworkin's studies, *Ombre sultane* suggests that her descriptions of the institutional purpose of heterosexual coitus may not have been that far off the mark. This suggestion does not mean that women have not resisted the institutional effects of heterosex, that they have not found ways to have heterosex against the grain of its institutions in order to rewrite its compulsory role; it does not mean that sex with men must equal submission to patriarchal law. Isma's sexual experience of marriage, for example, is quite different; she also uses heterosexual pleasure to ground both her sexual and national identity.

Ombre sultane suggests that marital coitus can have certain institutional effects and purposes and that, at the same time, women can rewrite these narratives and resist the institutionalized violence of marriage. Nevertheless, in spite of her pleasant memories of coitus, Isma escapes; she leaves her husband for her own freedom: "[J]e l'ai quitté pour moi-même" (95). (". . . I left him for myself" [86].) While feminism and anti-homophobic theory should challenge obstacles to pleasure, sexual freedom, and even perversion, they should also not lose sight of how the institutionalization of pleasure reinforces the oppression of women and sexual dissidents. "My Mother Liked to Fuck," after all, is no pretty picture of a liberated sexuality; Nestle's mother pays for the joy of sex by often being the target of violence. In addition, the debt that queer theory owes to Dworkin's and Catharine A. MacKinnon's radical critiques of heterosexuality often remains unacknowledged.[1] Butler's theory of compulsory gender performances, for example, would be unthinkable without Adrienne Rich's description of heterosexuality as a compulsory institution. While Butler and other queer theorists acknowledge Rich, the connections between Rich on the one hand, and Dworkin and MacKinnon on the other, often remain unacknowledged, perhaps because many queer theorists have also criticized Dworkin and MacKinnon's antipor-

---

1. See MacKinnon 1987 and 1989.

nography efforts. Yet surely, even from prosex, anticensorship positions (indeed, ones that acknowledge the potential values of pornography), one could recognize, even incorporate, their critique of heterosexuality as a compulsory, even violent, institution. Such a recognition would retain their analyses of the institution of marriage and the hierarchies reinforced by much pornography as the basis of a strategy for carving out spaces of oppositional practices in porn spectatorship and coupling (heterosexual or other) and of rewriting pornography and heterosexuality into less oppressive practices.

Indeed, Hajila herself begins to escape marriage, which Isma narrates as if she, too, experienced the same freedom. Instead of staying at home while her husband is at work and the children at school, Hajila begins to go out into the streets ("sortir") and unveil. The Algerian Arabic word for *unveiled* is the same as that for *naked;* Hajila is, as the title of one section suggests, "au-dehors, nue" (35) ("naked in the world outdoors" [26]). Again, more complicated than a single encumbrance one might easily remove, the veil also represents the freedom obtained by putting it on: "C'était comme si, avec ce tissu, tu te préparais à concocter le mensonge. Comme si le voile emmagasinait dans ses plis ta future journée. Ton échappée" (27). ("It was as if this length of cloth helped you concoct your lie. As if the veil held your future days in its folds . . . Your escape" [18].) As Djebar writes in *Femmes d'Alger,* the veil "permet à celle qui le revêt et qui circule au-dehors sous son couvert, d'être à son tour voleuse possible dans l'espace masculin" (174) ("allows the one who wears it and who circulates outside underneath its cover, to be in turn a potential thief within the masculine space" [138]). Veiling first means seizing the freedom to circulate, and unveiling, here, represents a second liberation. As for Fanon and Dib, Djebar's unveiling unleashes woman's danger and represents an explosion: "Là, tu décides avec violence: «enlever le voile!» Comme si tu voulais disparaître . . . ou exploser!" (*Ombre* 39, Djebar's suspension points). ("There, you make your sudden decision to take off that veil! As if you wished to disappear . . . or explode!" [30].)

Hajila's outings provide her with the courage to resist marital coitus. Isma describes to Hajila the effects of remembering these outings during sexual intercourse:

> Faut-il céder? Non, rappelle-toi les rues, elles s'allongent en toi dans un soleil qui a dissous les nuées; les murs s'ouvrent; arbres et haies glissent. Tu revois l'espace au-dehors où chaque jour tu navigues. Quand le phallus

de l'homme te déchire, épée rapide, tu hurles dans le silence, dans ton silence: «non! . . . non!» Tu te bats, il te fouaille, tu tentes de revenir à la surface. «Laisse-toi faire!» susurre la voix à la tempe. La déchirure s'étend, les rues déroulées en toi défilent, les ombres des passants reviennent et te dévisagent, chaînes d'inconnus aux yeux globuleux.

Le phallus demeure, la brûlure s'avive, dans le noir qui tue en toi les images de défense. Tu ne perçois qu'un gargouillis. Le mâle s'est détaché, tes jambes pendent, lamentables; dans la lumière de la lampe qui a giclé, les yeux en larmes, tu considères le flot de sang qui coule sur les draps, sur le matelas dénudé . . . L'homme a disparu dans la salle de bains. Revenu, il te jette une serviette; elle gît sur tes jambes maculées.

«Il voit mes jambes! Il voit mon sang! Il en a acheté le droit! . . . » (67, Djebar's suspension points)

Must you surrender? No! Think of the streets, they stretch out within you, bathed in the sunshine that has dissolved the storm clouds; the walls open; trees and hedges glide past. You can see the space out of doors through which you sail each day. When the man's [phallus] ruptures you, with one rapid sword-thrust, you scream out in the silence, breaking your own silence, "No! . . . No!" You struggle against him, he castigates you, you try to return to the surface. "Just relax!" the voice murmurs, near your temple. You are being torn apart; the procession of streets unwinds within you, shadowy passers-by turn back and stare at you, steady streams of unknown people with bulging eyes.

The [phallus] is still in place, the burning pain spreads, the darkness blots out all your defensive visions. You are conscious only of this squelching sound. The man has withdrawn, your legs hang limply; in the sudden spurt of light from the lamp, you survey with tear-drenched eyes the blood spreading over the sheets, over the bare mattress . . . the man has disappeared into the bathroom. When he returns he tosses you a towel; it lies over your blood-stained legs.

"He can see my legs! He can see my blood! He has paid for this right! . . ." (58)

Again, marital coitus is experienced as a violence and a violation. But this violence is contrasted with an escape from the *harem* and the husband's sexual demands. By reliving her outings in the conjugal bedroom, Hajila continues *la lutte des sexes* and physically resists intercourse. Remembering her daytime unveilings at night also allows her to understand the financial exchange between men wherein her husband has bought the rights to her body. Djebar's telling of women's resistance to colonialism takes on new meaning here as marriage becomes a form of sexual expropriation. Isma's narration of the violence of marital coitus allows her to rewrite the institution of polygamy. Instead of a woman being exchanged among men, it is a man, "the man," who is exchanged from one woman (Isma) to another (Hajila). One might even wonder whether Isma derives pleasure, even sexual pleasure, from narrating another woman's intercourse with her former husband.

It would be quite easy to use *Ombre sultane* in a feminist critique of polygamy as allowed by Islamic law. Djebar was once asked in an interview, "Vous faites un procès contre la polygamie, n'est-ce pas?" (You put polygamy on trial, don't you?) She responded, "Un procès? Non. Un roman n'est jamais un procès" (Mortimer 1988, 205). (On trial? No, a novel is never a trial.) This exchange, I would argue, reveals the dangers of *certain kinds* of *Western* feminist readings of Maghrebian (and other "non-Western") feminist texts. It is quite easy to criticize what is sexist about cultures over which one's own exerts a neocolonial authority. Polygamy is one of the clichés that make up what Mohanty describes as "third world difference" (53), and reading *Ombre sultane* as a critique of polygamy and not monogamy ignores how the novel also critiques marriage as an institution in general. Such a reading fails to take into account the way in which *Ombre sultane* also criticizes Western monogamy as a compulsory heterosexual institution, ignores many of the novel's most radical implications, and recolonizes the text in the service of a certain Western feminism unwilling to examine the colonial history of its own heterosexual privilege. In other words, such a reading would deny *Ombre sultane*'s critique of heterosexuality and participate in the colonial history of heterosexualizing colonized peoples. Indeed, Djebar herself actively rejected such a reading, just as she has suggested that Western women have a lot to learn from Maghrebians. Her critique of marriage is one source from which "we" might learn a great deal.

Indeed, Djebar rewrites polygamy from within. In this context, the second wife is referred to as the first wife's wound: "*Derra:* en langue arabe, la nouvelle épousée, rivale d'une première femme d'un même homme, se désigne de ce mot, qui signifie «blessure»: celle qui fait mal, qui ouvre les chairs, ou celle qui a mal, c'est pareil!" (*Ombre* 100). ("*Derra:* the word used in Arabic to denote the new bride of the same man, the first wife's rival; this word means 'wound'—the one who hurts, who cuts open the flesh, or the one who feels hurt, it's the same thing!" [91].) She literalizes this wound in the "déchirure" Hajila endures during intercourse and the wound from being struck by her husband with a beer bottle. As the section title indicates, it becomes the image of women's suffering in marriage: "Toute femme s'appelle blessure" ("Every Woman's Name is 'Wound'"). In her interview, Djebar stated, "Obviously, man's power comes from the fact that, since he has the right to several wives, he creates a rivalry between them. Therefore, they wound each other. But what happens if these women unite, if they eliminate the rivalry in advance? One realizes that, as soon as both unite, the man loses his power. He is the one who is wounded in fact, because, having lost his power, he is no longer anything at all" (Mortimer 1988, 205). Djebar thus reconfigures the relation between wives in a polygamous marriage to transform competition into solidarity and turn this wound against the husband in resistance to marriage.

Hajila's psychological wounds are healed in a women's space. Isma instructs Hajila to demand her weekly visit to the *hammam* once her physical wounds heal. After a sickness, ritual purification is carried out in the *hammam,* which is also the place of purification after sexual intercourse. In Hajila's case, however, the wound that must heal is caused by sexual intercourse. She is doubly impure, and her visit heals the wound that results from marital coitus as well as marks the healing of the wound from the beer bottle. In fact, this women's space provides relief and refuge from any marriage or *harem:* "Hammam, seule rémission du harem . . . Le bain turc sécrète pour les séquestrées (comme autrefois le chant de l'orgue pour les nonnes forcées) une consolation à cette réclusion. Dissoudre la touffeur de la claustration grâce à ce succédané du cocon maternel . . ." (163, Djebar's suspension points). ("*Hammam,* the only temporary reprieve from the harem . . . The Turkish bath offers a secret consolation to sequestered wom[e]n (such as organ music offered in former times to forced religious recluses). This surrogate maternal cocoon providing an escape from the hot-house of cloistration . . ." [152].) It is also a site of return to the mother's body and a space where the various wives in a polygamous marriage meet:

> Deux femmes—ou trois, ou quatre—qui ont eu en commun le même homme (durant des mois, des années, ou une vie entière car dans ce prétendu partage, c'est la durée surtout qui lancine), si elles se rencontrent vraiment, ne le peuvent que dans la nudité. Au moins celle du corps, pour espérer atteindre la vérité de la voix; et du cœur. . . . Deux femmes, de part et d'autre d'une présence d'homme, frontière ambiguë. (159–60)

> If two women—or three or four—who have shared the same man (for months, or years, or a whole lifetime, for what really hurts in this so-called sharing is the length of time it lasts) are really to come face to face, it can

only be if they are naked and unadorned. At least, if physically naked, they can hope to hear the voice speak true; and then to hear the heart's truth. . . . Two women, on either side of that ambiguous frontier—a man's presence. (149–50)

In the *hammam,* these wives, not separated by clothing, can rewrite polygamy, and in the context of this nudity, the "frontière ambiguë" (or husband that is supposed to make them rivals) perhaps takes on a homoerotic tone.

Bouhdiba (1975) cites the *hammam* as a place of homosexual encounters (205, 209). Likewise, in *Ombre sultane,* there are several descriptions of what Woodhull (1993) calls "the ambiguous space of the bath" (86) that might be read as homoerotic:

> Chaque après-midi, les enfants pleurent et écoutent avec volupté leurs propres pleurs. Les mères s'essoufflent puis soupirent de béatitude; les vierges se laissent admirer dans des instants de nudité ou accidentelle, ou concertée; les matrones se font pétrir par la masseuse vieillie, trop fardée, seule parmi les baigneuses à rappeler la douceur captieuse de la mort. (159)

> Every afternoon, the place is full of wailing children, delighting in the sound of their own tears; their mothers gasp for breath, then sigh with satisfaction; virgins let slip their tunics accidentally or by design, revealing a glimpse of naked flesh to admiring eyes; matrons submit to the ministrations of the elderly masseuse, who, with her highly painted face, alone among the bathers hints at the deceptive sweetness of death. (149)

Here, "volupté," signs of beatitude, virgins who allow themselves to be admired nude (perhaps on purpose), and massages are not necessarily homoerotic. Virgins might wish to be seen by mothers looking for wives for their sons, an activity that occurs in the *hammam,* which provides a rare occasion for a man to gauge, through his mother's eyes, a prospective wife's physical appearance. Nevertheless, combined, these elements give the impression of letting go ("abandon" in French) to sensual pleasures that might be erotic. In another passage, Isma is implicated in this homoerotic potential: "Elle se proposa de me laver: m'étriller, me masser, m'asperger, me frotter le cuir chevelu, pour finir, me rincer et m'envelopper dans la laine «comme une nouvelle mariée», me promit-elle, tentatrice, presque entremetteuse. Je refusai" (162). ("She volunteered to wash me, promising to scrub and massage me, splash water over me, give me a thorough shampoo, ending with a good rinse then wrapping me in wool, 'like a new bride' as she temptingly proposed, as if she were a procuress.

I refused" [151].) As above, where a common husband provides the excuse for several wives to meet in the nude, here the pleasure of a massage is linked to marriage. In the *hammam,* heterosexual institutions seem to be mere excuses for women to share sensual pleasure in the absence of men. The *masseuse* tempts, but Isma cuts short her temptation with a refusal.

Femmes d'Alger includes another visit to the *hammam* with its own homoerotic aspects. One ambiguity occurs in a passage describing pubic-hair removal: "A l'autre bout de la salle chaude qu'elles quittaient, parmi des vapeurs épaisses sentant fortement le soufre, Anne aperçut deux ou trois baigneuses qui, ayant auparavant éloigné d'elles leurs enfants, se rasaient méticuleusement le pubis" (45). ("At the other end of the steam room they were leaving, amid thick clouds of steam strongly smelling of sulfur, Anne noticed two or three bathers who were meticulously shaving their pubic areas, having moved their children out of the way first" [31].) The use of the plural reflexive verb in French could suggest that each shaves her own pubic hair (not an unusual activity in this context) or that they shave each other's pubic hair (which is also not necessarily unusual). Another ambiguity occurs in the description of female bathers' bodies:

> Baya traduisit, en chuchotant, à Anne, les mains sur ses seins qu'elle ponçait et c'est alors que la Française ne demanda plus rien, contempla fascinée les corps usés autour d'elle. Bras d'une masseuse, dressée debout sur la dalle, qui s'agenouilla ensuite, ceinturait le corps d'une baigneuse, face, ventre et mamelles écrasés contre la pierre, les cheveux en masse rougeâtre, les épaules ruisselant des traînées du henné délayé.
>
> La masseuse entrouvrait les lèvres sur les dents en or qui luisaient; ses seins longs, traversés de vénules jusqu'à leur bout, pendaient. (43–44)

> Whispering, Baya translated for Anne, while she was rubbing her breasts with her hands; it was then that the Frenchwoman stopped asking questions, looking at the wasted bodies around her in fascination. Arms of a masseuse, standing straight up on the marble slab, then kneeling down, encircling the body of a bather whose face, belly, and breasts were crushed against the stone, her hair a reddish mass, her shoulders dripping with trails of watery henna.
>
> The masseuse opened her lips halfway, showing golden teeth that shimmered; her long, pendulous breasts were crisscrossed with little veins all the way to the tips. (30)

With minutely described female bodies, this passage testifies to a female gaze focused on other female bodies, a gaze that at least suggests a homo-erotic possibility. A number of critics have explored this potential in

Djebar's novels.[2] I would suggest that the scenes quoted above both could be and are not necessarily homoerotic. There seems to be no dividing mark between the homosocial space of the women's *hammam* and the homoerotic potential this space evokes. For Djebar, the *hammam* seems to be the space of what Rich calls the "lesbian continuum."

Rich maintains that "heterosexuality, like motherhood, needs to be recognized and studied as a *political institution*" (182). A number of practices she uses to characterize compulsory heterosexuality are noticeably non-Western: "the practice of suttee on widows in India" (180), "child marriage," "arranged marriage," "the harem," "female infanticide," "genital mutilation or . . . binding the daughter's feet (or mind) to fit her for marriage," "the veil," "geisha," and "*kisaeng* prostitutes" (184). Is it a coincidence that these practices are associated with the "Orient"? In some cases, "Oriental" practices become metaphors for the universal oppression of women, such as when foot-binding represents the binding of every girl's mind to make her suitable for marriage. Any use of Rich's essay to describe a Maghrebian form of compulsory heterosexuality must first come to terms with the way she uses "Oriental" metaphors of women's oppression without considering the cultural contexts in which such practices occur and the negative effects simply abolishing these practices might have for women. In addition, the practices Rich describes are not unique to heterosexuality as defined by constructionists. In fact, if one uses this strict definition, the "Oriental" forms of women's oppression might be said to have nothing to do with heterosexuality at all. Nevertheless, the concept of compulsory heterosexuality might be useful in contexts where it is more problematic to speak of heterosexuality as a dominant sexual identity (that is, in every context except the West of the late nineteenth and twentieth centuries); one might use it wherever marriage between members of the opposite sex is the dominant mode of institutionalizing sexuality and reproduction.

One aspect of Rich's essay that might be applicable to the Maghreb is that of the "lesbian continuum":

> I mean the term *lesbian continuum* to include a range—through each woman's life and throughout history—of women-identified experience; not simply the fact that a woman has had or consciously desired genital sexual experience with another woman. If we expand it to embrace many

---

2. Zimra (1992) has discussed homoerotic aspects of Djebar's early novels. Long and Sautman have discussed those of later works such as *Femmes d'Alger* and *Ombre sultane*.

more forms of primary intensity between and among women, including the sharing of a rich inner life, the bonding against male tyranny, the giving and receiving of practical and political support; if we can also hear in it such associations as *marriage resistance* . . . we begin to grasp breadths of female history and psychology that have lain out of reach as a consequence of limited, mostly clinical, definitions of "lesbianism." (192)

The "lesbian continuum" constitutes a wide range of behaviors and feelings among women that are not necessarily sexual. In *Between Men*, Sedgwick elaborates on this continuum by conceiving it as going from homosociality to homosexuality. She claims that, unlike for women (and here she accepts Rich without questioning her), there is a break in this continuum for men: male bonding (the homosocial) must constantly distinguish itself from the homosexual. She also claims that this break is not universal: if homosocial networking constitutes patriarchy, and if the break in the homosocial/homosexual continuum is the mark of homophobia, patriarchy does not require homophobia. The reverse is not true; all possible forms of homophobia would also be sexist, she argues, giving Ancient Greece as an example of a patriarchal society in which homosocial bonding did not preclude homosexual behavior.

I would like to revise Sedgwick's view. The institution of pederasty, which worked quite well within patriarchy, did not permit just *any* homosexual behavior, only specific ones. It was not acceptable for an adult, male citizen to be penetrated. In Ancient Greece, it is less the case that there was not a break than that the break between homosocial and homosexual lay in a different place along the continuum, closer to the homosexual end than in the modern English context Sedgwick describes. Likewise, Rich's assertion that there is no such break for women in Western societies is hard to fathom. If it were impossible to distinguish whether all nonsexual behaviors were homosocial or homosexual, there would be no way for lesbian bashers to select their targets. And if, in the U.S., for example, there are many behaviors that arouse homophobic suspicions when occurring between men but not women, this does not mean that there are no behaviors between women that arouse suspicion. It is less the case that there is a break in the continuum for men and not for women than that the break lies at a different point, and even among Western societies, the place of the break may vary. Certain expressions of homosocial affection that are commonplace among men in France, for example, arouse suspicion in the U.S. I would propose a notion of the continuum that is, in fact, a continuum of continuums and that would allow for this variety in which the break's location can vary widely from society to society. Indeed, within any given society, its place varies from group to group, class to class, sex to sex, and age to age; and within any given group, it may also vary according to individual differences and variations from the norm. Finally, within any individual, it may vary from context to context, age to age, and place to place along migrations.

Djebar moves along such a "lesbian continuum" with great agility. Rich describes "marriage resistance," "bonding against male tyranny," and "the giving and receiving of practical and political support" as activities on this continuum. These all occur inside Djebar's *hammam*,[3] and this homosocial sensuality is linked with resistance to compulsory heterosexuality. In the above scenes, *hammam* behaviors seem to lie before the break on the homosocial/homosexual continuum. Any homosocial behavior, however, could also be homosexual; it simply does not arouse suspicion as such. Djebar seems to approach the break as closely as possible and accumulate as many homosocial practices as possible that are *almost* homoerotic, that *almost* cross the barrier without ever actually doing so. Another passage in *Femmes d'Alger,* however, might be read as more overtly sexual: "[L]e couple des deux femmes installées sur la dalle, dominant les autres baigneuses, se renouait dans le rythme ahané, prenait forme étrange, arbre lent et balancé dont les racines plongeraient dans le ruissellement persistant de l'eau sur les dalles grises" (44). ("[T]he couple formed by the two women on the marble slab high above the other bathers, became entwined again in panting rhythm, taking on a strange shape, that of a slow well-balanced tree whose roots plunged down into the persistent streaming of the water on the grey stone" [30].) Ahmed Bouguarche, at least, reads this passage to affirm that "[f]emale homosexuality, outlawed or just taboo, is not absent from the *hammam* . . ." (215).

Interestingly enough, the image used to describe this female couple, which may or may not be making love, is that of a tree. In the *hammam,* therefore, women's resistance may have lesbian roots. As suggested above in the passage describing the *hammam* as a "cocon maternel," a trip to the *hammam* is also a trip back into time. Going there, for Isma, involves a return to childhood, to the mother's body: "Je retourne à la source, antre des vestibules d'hier, étuve d'enfance entretenue. . . . [J]e ne m'abîme que dans l'eau mère: hier, celle de la volupté, aujourd'hui ruisseaux d'enfance

---

3. Long uses Rich to characterize Djebar's *hammam* as homoerotic.

remémorée" (158). ("I return to the [source/spring], taking refuge in the antechambers of yesteryear, in the steam room where my childhood is preserved. . . . I can only let myself be submerged in mother[-water]: yesterday, that of sensual ecstasy, today the rivers of my remembered childhood" [148].) Brinda J. Mehta describes the role of "[f]emale remembrance" in *Femmes d'Alger* as being central in the *hammam* as a "liberating space for women." Mehta therefore roots women's liberation in a return to the past through memory inside the *hammam*: "The autonomy of the body is possible due to its inscription in the maternal concretized by the recurrent use of water imagery in the text. Water represents the archetypal mother principle, the source of rejuvenation and reconnection" (54–55). If the *hammam* provides a site of resistance to compulsory heterosexuality, this resistance is also rooted in the origins of the female autobiographical subject. Paradoxically, it is while sleeping with her husband that Isma finds similar roots:

> Mêler larmes et sourires dans l'embrasement de mille nuits et de leurs couloirs! Dans l'antre maternel, nous nous réinstallons, moi, l'épouse aux antennes inaltérées, lui, le fils que je tire loin, plus loin . . . J'ai recréé sa naissance ou je l'ai engloutie, je ne sais. Mais je t'en ai dépouillée, ô mère devant laquelle je m'incline, à laquelle je me lie, mais que j'écarte enfin de mon amour. (62, Djebar's suspension points)

> Mingling tears and laughter in the blaze of a thousand nights with their dark corridors! We make our home again in the mother's lair, I, the wife, as ever sensitive to every signal, he, the son, whom I draw further and further away . . . Have I let him be reborn? or have I engulfed him? I cannot tell . . . But I have stolen him away from you, O Mother, to whom I defer, to whom I am bound, but whom I finally separate from the man I love. (53)

The English translation specifies Isma's love as a man, thereby further heterosexualizing the text. In contrast with Hajila's experience of marital coitus, however, Isma finds a return to origins in the body of her husband's mother:

> Quand je m'endors, je prends la main de l'époux comme si, dans le sommeil où nous nous écoutons, nos doubles traversaient des landes dévastées. D'autres nuits, l'image de la mère s'insinue entre nous, à l'instant où la lassitude nous couvre de son amnésie. . . . Hantise de l'origine, épée droite fichée en l'homme, qui le blesse et le redresse. Moi, je renie la matrone omniprésente. Je la renie précisément lorsqu'elle nous réunit. (59)

As I drop off to sleep, I clasp my husband's hand, as if our doubles, ever conscious of each other's sleeping presence, were setting out on a nocturnal journey across devastated wastelands. On other nights, the mother's image steals between us, just as we wearily sink into oblivion. . . . This [haunting of] origins is a sword thrust into the man, wounding him, startling him to his feet. For my part, I repudiate the ubiquitous matron. I repudiate her just as she is uniting us. (51)

The omnipresent matron is her husband's mother, who constitutes a rival for Isma and, as the haunting of his origin, threatens to separate the couple. Whereas Hajila experiences intercourse as a sword ripping into her, Isma during intercourse returns her husband to his origin, which she uses as a sword to penetrate him. This origin, paralleling the one Djebar returns to through autobiography, wounds the husband as polygamy is intended to wound women. Djebar's feminist subject, rooted in a history of women's resistance to colonialism and sexism, rooted in her own story of who she is, turns the tools of male power against "the man," "the husband," "the enemy."

This return *to* origins is also a return *of* origins (as one would speak of the return of the repressed). The origins of female subjectivity return to the present to haunt it ("hantise de l'origine"). Allegorically, Isma's return to the origins of her subjectivity represents a return to national origins. The origins found within the *hammam* and in resistance to compulsory heterosexuality also become the origins of a feminist nation not constructed from the building blocks of heterosexual families and not based on the oppression of women. If the origins uncovered in *Ombre sultane* and *L'amour, la fantasia* are also the Nation's origins, the Nation is indeed a queer nation, founded on resistance to compulsory heterosexuality. Since the husband is reduced to a "frontière ambiguë" (*Ombre* 160) ("ambiguous frontier" [150]) separating his multiple wives inside the *hammam*, these roots may also be lesbian. The possibility that a man's wives may be a source of erotic pleasure for each other drives a wedge into the institution of marriage and, quite literally, queers polygamy.

As the following passage from *Vaste est la prison* demonstrates, homosexuality can bring marital coitus to a halt:

Il peut paraître dérisoire qu'une femme arabe, et trop longtemps amoureuse, et aimée—hélas aimée dans la malédiction d'aimer—décide un jour— «non, je ne ferai plus l'amour ainsi, parce que je viens d'apprendre que Pasolini a été tué! peu m'importe, ils peuvent ricaner, tu peux ricaner et me dire: "Un cinéaste homosexuel italien a été assassiné, et c'est toi qui t'imagines recevoir un peu du coup . . ." J'ajoutai: "Car ils vont s'empresser de cracher sur son cadavre, ils l'ont tué et ils vont prétendre le salir. Le bel ordre moral qui, sous tous les cieux, s'étale! . . ."»

. . . Pourquoi Pasolini? Ce fut ainsi, c'est tout . . . Moi, femme arabe, écrivant mal l'arabe classique, aimant et souffrant dans le dialecte de ma mère, sachant qu'il me faut retrouver le chant profond, étranglé dans la gorge des miens, le retrouver par l'image, par le murmure sous l'image, je me dis désormais: «Je commence (ou je finis) parce que, dans un lit d'avant l'amour, j'ai ressenti vingt-quatre heures après et une Méditerranée entre nous, la mort de Pasolini comme un cri, un cri ouvert.» (200–201)

It might seem preposterous that an Arab woman, one who has been in love for too long and has been loved—alas, loved in the curse of loving— would decide one day, "No, I shall no longer make love like that, because I just learned that Pasolini has been killed. I don't care; they can laugh, you can laugh and tell me, 'An Italian homosexual filmmaker was assassinated, and you are the one who imagines having shared his blow. . . .' I added, 'Because they will trip over each other to spit on his corpse, they killed him and they are going to claim to sully him. What a fine moral order that rears its head all over creation. . . .'"

Why Pasolini? That's just how it was. . . . I, Arab woman, who write classical Arabic poorly, who love and suffer in my mother's dialect, who know that I must rediscover the profound chant, strangled in the throat of my people, rediscover it through image, through the whispers beneath the image, I said to myself hereafter, "I begin (or finish) because, in a bed before making love, I felt, twenty-four hours later and with the Mediterranean between us, Pasolini's death like a scream, a wide-open scream.

The scream equated with marital love in *L'amour, la fantasia* (122–23) thus becomes a scream produced through the mourning of a European homosexual. If Djebar digs up Jean Sénac's homosexuality in *Le blanc de l'Algérie* to haunt the postindependence ruling elite, here she resurrects Pasolini to haunt the institution of heterosexual marriage. The haunting of marital coitus described in *Ombre sultane* might therefore be likened not only to the way homosexuality interrupts coitus here, but also to the "frontière ambiguë" that the husband becomes when women get together in the *hammam* with all its homoerotic potential.

The other figure of haunting represented in the novel is that of Hajila circulating veiled in the streets: "[T]u n'existes pas plus qu'un fantôme! . . . [T]u te réenveloppes du *haïk!* Dehors, te revoici fantôme et la colère grisâtre replie ses ailes sous la blancheur du drap" (37, 42). ("[You exist no more than a fantom. . . . Y]ou wrap yourself once more in the *haïk!* You emerge into the street, a ghostly figure once more, and under the white veil grey anger folds up its wings" [34].) As she circulates veiled through the public spaces of the streets, Hajila haunts the Nation. Through the narration of her story, Djebar articulates the feminist subject as a menace to the Nation. Whereas in Ben Jelloun's gendered allegory of the Nation, becoming a woman means losing identification papers, becoming a maid and a prostitute, being excised, and performing in a circus freak show, Djebar rereads this gendered narrative of nationality and returns women to the public sphere, where they haunt the institutions of male power, perhaps, as we shall see in the following chapter, to destroy them.

Chapter Eleven

ESCAPING
THE IDENTITY POLICE:
LEÏLA SEBBAR

"Shérazade échappa de justesse au contrôle d'identité" (Shérazade barely escaped an ID check [my trans.]); thus writes the Franco-Algerian writer Leïla Sebbar in *Shérazade: 17 ans, brune, frisée, les yeux verts* (1982), the first novel of a trilogy whose main protagonist is the novel's eponymous character (209). Shérazade is avoiding the police because her father has given them her description (hence the novel's title) after she ran away from home. The ID check, however, is not the only *contrôle* Shérazade escapes in the novel; she also thwarts all attempts to control her identity. She escapes her father as well as the police who would return her to him and who enforce her status as second-class citizen in France as an Arab. She defies both male heterosexual and Orientalizing gazes, successfully defends herself against an attempted rape by pulling a gun on her would-be rapists, and complicates any easy notion of roots or national origins. She is, I would argue, a model of feminist subjectivity and the embodiment of feminist resistance; she is, in short, the paradigm of an urban feminist guerrilla in *la lutte des sexes* as well as the struggle against racism in France.

In *Room for Maneuver*, Chambers makes a distinction between resistance—the project of overthrowing oppressive systems—and opposition—that of transforming them from within. He questions the possibility of completely resisting power (understood in Foucauldian terms) from without and points out that the history of revolutions suggests that using violence to overthrow oppressive regimes might only reproduce their systemic violence in the new regime. Although seeming to favor oppositional strategies over resistance, he acknowledges that the difference between the two may not always be that clear. Shérazade, as well, deconstructs the resistance/opposition distinction by incorporating both into her battle with the identity police.

Sebbar was born in Algeria of a French mother ("une Française de France"—as was often said in colonial Algeria—that is, a French woman born in France as opposed to a *pied noir*) and an Algerian father, both parents being schoolteachers (Sebbar 1985b, 8). Often referred to as a *Beur* writer, Sebbar does not quite fit the definition of the term *Beur*. In a letter to Nancy Huston, published in their coauthored *Lettres parisiennes,* she wrote: ". . . I am not an immigrant, nor a child of immigrants . . . I am not a Maghrebian writer writing in French . . . I am not a French woman with French roots . . . My native language is not Arabic. . . . But from now on I know that I must be able to say, declare, and affirm unequivocally and without guilt, . . . this peculiar situation of mine: I am French, a French writer whose mother is French and whose father is Algerian . . . , and the subjects of my books are not my identity . . ." (125–26). By including Sebbar in this study on Maghrebian literature, I do not mean to force her under a rubric ("Maghrebian writer") that she herself has refused, nor do I intend to de-emphasize her difference from (other) Maghrebian writers. Regardless of whether Sebbar can and/or should be considered a Maghrebian writer, however, her work is in dialogue with many of the trends of Maghrebian literature examined thus far. In a letter to Beur-literature specialist Michel Laronde, she also wrote, "I am in a somewhat peculiar situation, neither 'Beure' nor 'Maghrebian,' nor completely French . . ." (Laronde 166). She is not quite/not French and occupies a space that is in-between French, Maghrebian, and even Beur (which is already an in-between) identities. Sebbar's character, Shérazade, however, is a Beure who challenges dominant models of both French and Maghrebian national identities through feminist resistance *and* opposition. Although her strategy for queering the Nation uses techniques similar to those examined in previous chapters, she also serves as an example of how these strategies might be put into practice, thereby adding another important layer to the kind of rewriting of national identity carried out by (other) Maghrebian writers.

Shérazade begins after its protagonist has left home, probably because her father beat her. Paternal control organized around gendered violence serves the interest of the French police, agents of another, racist violence, even though in most other circumstances the Algerian father and the police might find themselves at odds. Shérazade moves into a squat with members of the post-1968 revolutionary left and other children of immigrants. The novel tells Shérazade's adventures as she circulates across the Parisian cityscape, both at home in France, the country of her acculturation, and in exile, that is, seen as Other by the French of European origins. Shérazade has what might be described as a romance with Julien, a *pied noir* Orientalist whose parents were teachers in colonial Algeria and supporters of the FLN. She shoplifts, participates in a burglary and an "auto-réduction" (i.e. a holdup) with her leftist friends, and finally ends up leaving Paris, supposedly to go to Algeria (in a return to her origins). Pierrot, her revolutionary roommate, agrees to take her part of the way in his car, loaded with weapons to be used in revolutionary armed struggle. They have an accident, and Pierrot is killed as the car explodes.

Les carnets de Shérazade (1985) picks up in Marseilles, where Shérazade got off the boat to Algeria at the last minute. As a return to origins, therefore, Shérazade's journey fails. She hitches a ride with a truck driver, Gilles, to whom she recounts her adventures in the manner of her homonym, the protagonist of the *Arabian Nights*. From a distance, she follows the route of the Beur March against racism in France. Narratively, as an alternative itinerary of identity, the Beur March replaces the return to Algerian origins. *Le fou de Shérazade* (1991) begins as a film crew is waiting for Shérazade to return. Julien has written a film script for her, and the set of the film is to be the HLM—the projects—where Shérazade's family lives. Shérazade, however, is being held hostage in Lebanon by Arab militants who are convinced she is a spy, working either for the Christians or Israel. (When Shérazade speaks Arabic, her captors are unable to understand her.) The trip to the Middle East, another attempt to return to her Arab roots, also ends in failure. She is finally released and comes home to complete the film, which, centered around a transported olive tree, narrates a notion of roots that are transplantable, of identity rooted in narrative fiction.

Feminist Resistance

One of Shérazade's characteristics is her resistance to compulsory heterosexuality, her refusal to submit to male domination. In *Shérazade,* she often gets invited to dinner or clubs by older white men who expect more than her company for dining or dancing. At a certain point, she stops being the sweet little girl of their expectations and gives them a taste of their own medicine:

> Pourquoi soudain devenait-elle méchante, grossière, vulgaire, c'était mal pour une jeune fille . . . Elle entendait susurrer ces moralités jusqu'au moment où elle se levait, traitait l'homme de—vieux porc dégoûtant et de vipère lubrique . . . C'est Basile qui lui avait appris cette injure de la Chine populaire maoïste, et elle partait droite et raide avant de se mettre à courir. (86, Sebbar's suspension points)

> Why did she suddenly turn nasty, coarse, vulgar, it didn't suit her . . . She'd listen to them murmuring these moral platitudes until she'd suddenly jump up, calling the man a disgusting old pig and a randy snake—it was Basile who had taught her this insult from Maoist Popular China—and then she'd stalk out stiffly before breaking into a run. (90)

The men who take her out expect a return on their investment: after dinner, or a drink, or cover charge to a club, they feel they have a right to her body. Shérazade, however, abruptly removes her body from the marketplace and associates her resistance to male property rights over her body with revolutionary struggle.

In *Carnets,* she actually uses a firearm to defend herself against rapists and says to her attackers, "Ceci n'est pas un viol . . . c'est un hold-up de campagne . . ." (212). (This isn't a rape . . . it's a country holdup. . . .) She then takes all their valuables, effectively rewriting the rape script her attackers came with the expectation of performing. She later explains her actions to Gilles, the truck driver who is giving her a lift:

> Ils m'auraient violée tous les trois, et deux d'entre eux seraient venus aider l'autre, ils m'auraient battue si j'avais résisté. Je suis sûre, tu m'entends, sûre qu'ils n'auraient pas hésité. Pour eux, un viol c'est la fille qui a cherché, ils ne se sentent pas coupables. Je t'assure. A Paris, j'ai assisté à un procès pour viol, les types pensaient pas qu'ils étaient des salauds, mais vraiment pas. Et ils battaient la fille, ça leur paraissait normal, ça se fait pas toujours en douceur . . . Ces gars-là pensaient que ça se passerait sans bagarre, sans violence, c'est ce qui les a rendus vulnérables et j'avais pas peur à cause du P 38 et parce qu'ils n'avaient pas de couteau. Il faut avoir l'air d'être consentante, ils perdent leurs défenses et là, c'est à la fille de trouver une ruse. (213)

> They would have raped me, all three of them, and two of them would have come to the aid of the other, they would have beat me up if I had resisted. I'm sure, sure you hear, they wouldn't have wasted a second. For them, a raped girl was looking for it, they don't feel guilty. I'm telling you.

In Paris, I attended a rape trial, the guys didn't think they were such pricks, they really didn't. And they beat up the girl, it seemed normal to them, it's not always that easy . . . These guys thought it would happen without a fight, without violence, that's what made them vulnerable, and I wasn't afraid because of the .38 and because they didn't have a knife. You have to seem like you're consenting, they drop their defenses and, then, it's up to the girl to find a ruse.

She explains how she uses their own assumptions against them, rewriting what Marcus calls "the rape script." She also reflects on the institutionalized aspects of rape, the role of the courts, how the rapists being tried are not abnormal men, distinguishable from all the other, supposedly good, men; any man is a potential rapist. At one point, Gilles—the supposedly nice guy, the guy who tries to convince his buddies that just because Shérazade is not under a man's control (father, boyfriend, husband, pimp, police), it does not mean that she is the common property of all men and, therefore, rapable (34–35)—reflects on why he has not raped Shérazade: "Mais tu es restée, tes yeux n'étaient pas noirs, tu as dit que tu me raconterais des histoires et c'est vrai, tu m'en as raconté comme Schéhérazade, pour m'empêcher de te tuer, de te violer? Peut-être bien, après tout . . ." (280). (But you stayed, your eyes weren't black, you said you would tell me stories and it's true, you told them to me like Shaharazad, to keep me from killing you, raping you? Maybe so, after all. . . .) And again, it is through rewriting scripts that she accomplishes her task. Her role model, Shaharazad of the *Arabian Nights,* tells tales to the Sultan to keep him from cutting off her head and taking another wife, who will lose her head in turn. Shaharazad risks her life and uses the power of words to save the lives of other women. Marcus's notion of the "rape script" provides a strategy for disconnecting rape from the Law of gender, of engendering men who are not rapists and women who are not rapable; Shérazade similarly uses her storytelling skills to rewrite the scripts of gender. As Ben Jelloun's storytellers are models for the Maghrebian writer, Shaharazad, as a storyteller, becomes a model for the feminist writer, who rewrites old fictions to create new ones. Rewriting rape scripts is not simply a matter of words, trying to talk the rapist out of raping, or trying to give him more confidence in himself (which would imply that the rapist is an insecure man, a deficient man, not man enough, unlike other men); Marcus's rewriting also involves self-defense, fighting back. Shérazade, after all, defends herself with a .38.

She also uses her gun to rewrite male narratives of revolution. At one point, Basile tries to impress Shérazade with his feminist vision of revolution:

> [I]l expliqua que les femmes allemandes et italiennes appartenaient à des groupes terroristes, qu'elles pouvaient aussi bien que les hommes se servir des armes, qu'elles n'étaient pas seulement bonnes à servir de boîte aux lettres, d'agents de liaison, que l'égalité commençait là et que si dans une révolution on utilisait les femmes comme secrétaires et infirmières on pouvait aussi leur donner du pouvoir, des responsabilités . . . Shérazade, si elle voulait pourrait très bien devenir chef de réseau. . . . Pierrot qui n'avait rien dit, cita les combattantes vietnamiennes et algériennes, d'autres aussi qui avaient participé à des guerres de libération et qui, à l'indépendance, s'étaient retrouvées privées de la liberté et de l'égalité pour lesquelles elles s'étaient battues . . . (45–46)

> [He] explain[ed] that German and Italian women belonged to terrorist groups and could handle weapons as well as the men, they were good for other things besides being used as letter-boxes, couriers, and this was the beginning of equality and if in a revolution women could work as secretaries and nurses they could also be given power, responsibility . . . If Sherazade liked, she could very well become head of a network. . . . Pierrot, who hadn't said a word, quoted the Algerian and Vietnamese women fighters, other women who had taken part in wars of liberation and who, when independence was won, found themselves deprived of the liberty and equality they'd fought for. . . . (44–45)

Basile and Pierrot, on one level, as self-proclaimed feminists, promise their revolution will not have the same consequences as the Algerian one. Shérazade responds with admiration: "Vous en savez des choses . . . si vous avez le pouvoir un jour, ce sera super pour les femmes. Je vais me battre pour ça" (46, Sebbar's suspension points). ("You do know a lot . . . if you're in power one day, it'll be super for women. I'll fight for that" [45].) Her response, perhaps ironic in its implication that women's liberation will result when "enlightened" male revolutionaries take state power, is, however, punctuated with a gunshot: "Elle jouait avec le P.38 de Basile. Le coup partit juste dans l'œil gauche de Che Guevara dont le poster jaunissait au mur depuis des mois. Basile poussa un cri et arracha le P.38 à Shérazade" (46). ("She was playing with Basile's .38. The shot went off smack into the left eye of Che Guevara whose poster had been yellowing for months on the wall. Basile yelled out and snatched the .38 out of Sherazade's hands" [45].) Shérazade reveals one of the dangers of armed women within revolutionary struggle: once armed, they might no longer accept just following male directives. She shoots Che Guevara in the eye, thereby proving her "marksmanship" and demonstrating that not even male revolutionaries will submit her to their control. Basile, for all his nice words on arming women, attempts to disarm Shérazade once she shows that she means business. She then changes from the role of pretty, innocent girl who stands by her man (a traditional role that many revolutionary movements have perpetuated rather than challenged) to that of a woman who will not be walked on. She says to Pierrot, "Et maintenant, ne me traite plus de minette ou je te démolis . . ." (46, Sebbar's suspension points). ("And now, don't ever [treat me like a cute chick] again or I'll do you in . . ." [45].) If, for Fanon, Algerian women do not liberate themselves upon the invitation of Charles de Gaulle, Shérazade affirms that, just as importantly, they do not liberate themselves upon the invitation of Mao or Che.

Destroying the Ethnographic Gaze

In addition to escaping the French police, her father, rapists, and other men who try to control her, Shérazade dodges male gazes that try to bind her to the *idées reçues* of femininity, especially "Oriental" femininity. At a party with her friends France and Zouzou, Shérazade is, as usual, appreciated by the Parisian chic uppercrust for her "exotic" beauty. However, when a photographer begins to take pictures of her without permission, she reacts violently:

> Shérazade arracha son appareil photographique à un professionnel qu'elle avait vu à l'affût depuis un certain temps, et qui profitait de ce moment de confusion pour la photographier. Elle lança l'appareil au sol à plusieurs mètres d'elle et partit avec Zouzou sans prendre garde à la crise qu'elle allait provoquer. L'appareil avait coûté une petite fortune. Shérazade l'avait jeté avec une telle violence qu'il s'était cassé. Le photographe en pleurait de rage «La salope, elle me le paiera, si je la coince, elle me le paiera . . . Ça vient où ça ne devrait pas, ça excite tout le monde, ça joue les allumeuses, ça pose avec les petites copines, des gouines encore celles-là et en plus ça détruit le matériel . . . C'est mon outil de travail . . . elle me le paiera . . . et qu'elles retournent dans leur pays ces petites garces» . . . (124)

> Sherazade snatched the camera from one photographer she'd seen snooping after her for some time who had taken advantage of the momentary confusion to take a shot of her. She hurled the camera on the floor a few yards away and went off with Zouzou without taking any notice of the

crisis she was provoking. The camera had cost a small fortune. Sherazade had thrown it down so violently that it had broken. The photographer was weeping with fury. "The bitch, I'll make her pay for it, let me just catch her, I'll make her pay for it . . . That sort turns up where they don't belong, gives everyone the come-on, just a bunch of prick-teasers, showing off with their pals, both lezzies, and then smashes people's property into the bargain . . . I need that for my work . . . I'll make her pay for it . . . And the little sluts can go back to their own country." (133–34)

Shérazade responds to the theft of her image by reappropriating it and showing that only she will control it; she seizes the means of production of Orientalist images to halt their production. The photographer, dazzled by Shérazade's beauty just minutes earlier, responds with a homophobic ("des gouines encore celles-là"), racist, and sexist ("qu'elles retournent dans leurs pays ces petites garces") tirade, thereby demonstrating how the uglier forms of racism and sexism can coexist quite comfortably with a so-called admiration of "exotic" beauty. His use of the neuter pronoun "ça" reinforces the thingness he sees in Shérazade, and his actions parallel those of her dates, who suddenly turn angry when they do not get what they expect.

In "Visual Pleasure and Narrative Cinema" (1975), Laura Mulvey describes the male gaze that characterizes Hollywood cinema: "In a world ordered by sexual imbalance, pleasure in looking has been split between active/male and passive/female. The determining male gaze projects its fantasy onto the female figure, which is styled accordingly. In their traditional exhibitionist role women are simultaneously looked at and displayed, with their appearance coded for strong visual and erotic impact so that they can be said to connote *to-be-looked-at-ness*" (19). It is precisely this "to-be-looked-at-ness" that Shérazade seeks to undo. In the title of one of her sections, Mulvey even describes "Destruction of Pleasure as a Radical Weapon" (15). At times, Shérazade seems to engage in such a destruction, by destroying the tools (cameras) with which men construct this paradigm.

In another passage, France, Zouzou, and Shérazade pose for a photographer. He dresses them in skimpy clothes to resemble animals in a jungle:

France tigrée et Shérazade zébrée en mini-jupe et short ultra-court, des bas résille noirs, les épaules dégagées, l'une en jaune et noir à rayures régulières, l'autre en blanc et noir à rayures irrégulières. Elles avaient les cheveux ébouriffés en crinière et de larges ceintures barbares comme Spartacus de-

vait en porter. Zouzou avait mis une tenue léopard dont le pantalon était
un short fendu et un débardeur qui dégageait presque les seins. (153)

France was a tigress in yellow and black regular striped mini-skirt; Sherazade a zebra in irregular black and white striped hot-pants; both wore
black fishnet stockings and off-the-shoulder tops. Their hair was teased to
look like a mane and they each had a wide barbarian's belt such as Spartacus was supposed to have worn. Zouzou put on a leopard outfit consisting
of split shorts and a top that barely covered her breasts. (165)

Posed in front of a camera by a man, these three women can be the object
of a desiring gaze only when seen in the context of the jungle as savages;
their beauty is an exotic, even animal beauty. As missionaries and colonizers worked in tandem to characterize native African sexualities as uncontrollable and perverse, the only sex the photographer can envision with
these women is "wild sex." He himself points out the parallels between
his activities and colonization:

On aime beaucoup les scènes de jungle et de forêt vierge en ce
moment . . . il manque une panthère, mais j'ai de quoi dans le coffre. Ce
sera pour tout à l'heure. Attendez, j'ai une idée, vous allez prendre chacune
une mitraillette comme des guérillères, j'en ai là, des vraies pas chargées.
Les jouets font toc, c'est mieux comme ça. . . . (154)

Jungle and virgin forest scenes are very popular at the moment . . . We
ought to have a panther as well, but I've got a suitable outfit in the chest.
We'll have that later. Wait, I've got an idea, each of you take a sub-
machine-gun, like guerrillas, I've got some there, real ones, unloaded. Toy
guns [look fake], these are better. . . . (165)

As Djebar describes the colonial invasion of Algeria as a penetration "qua-
siment sur le mode sexuel" and a "défloration," the photographer (like all
the men who will identify with his gaze when looking at these photographs) penetrates a virgin forest. By taking a picture (*prendre une photo*),
he takes (*prend*) *tout court,* with all the sexual implications of the verb
prendre. The photo shoot of exotic women becomes a safari during which
the photographer/hunter shoots women/animals. And he "takes" with an
action resembling colonial expropriation.

As Alloula described in *The Colonial Harem,* Shérazade's photographer seeks to reproduce the cliché of "Oriental femininity" by asking the
women to pose as lesbians for the sole purpose of exciting male desire:

Alors, voilà ce que vous faites, d'abord vous vous embrassez sur la bouche
vous pouvez faire semblant dès que je le dis—top—vous changez de par-

tenaire vous faites comme si vous dansiez dans une boîte—les bals de
femmes ça existe—et ensuite vous êtes allongées couchées l'une sur l'autre,
à tour de rôle, c'est simple. Mais dégagez-vous bien qu'on voie les seins,
les fesses, il faut pas être pudibondes. Si vous étiez dans un sauna ou un
hammam puisque c'est la mode, vous seriez toutes nues ça ne vous gênerait
pas, eh bien là, c'est pareil. (154–55)

Well this is what you do, first you kiss on the lips you can pretend as soon
as I say "Now" you change partners as if you were dancing in a nightclub—there really are discos just for women—and then you lie down one
on top of the other in turn, it's quite simple. But see that your tits and
bums are visible, you mustn't be prudish. If you were in a sauna or a Turkish bath since that's the thing now, you'd be starkers and it wouldn't worry
you, well now it's the same thing. (166)

Whereas the photographer gave the women guns to pose with, he himself
retained the weapon, his camera, to shoot (at) women. He made sure the
guns were not loaded so that the women, seemingly unarmed, would
remain the target, the exact word Sebbar uses to describe Shérazade while
in front of the photographer's gaze in *Les carnets de Shérazade:* "Lam prit
cinq rouleaux de photos de Shérazade. Depuis les séances chez Julien,
Shérazade n'avait plus servi de cible à un œil photographique" (193).
(Lam took five rolls of pictures of Shérazade. Since the sessions at Julien's,
Shérazade hadn't served as the target of a photographic eye.) As at the
party, in the photographer's studio, the three women turn the tables
against him and his exoticizing gaze by pulling out toy .38s (which he
thinks are real) and destroying the entire studio. Although the fantasy of
armed women guerrillas sexually excited the photographer, once armed,
they destroy his fantasy by refusing to pose in the fetishistic models he
has prescribed for them. They rewrite the script and turn the guns on the
shooter; they turn his fantasy against him by making it come true.
Whereas one might argue that the kind of emasculation Nafissa carries
out in *Qui se souvient de la mer* is totally in keeping with the dangers of
the omnisexual woman described by Aït Sabbah—a male fantasy that,
rather than challenging the status quo, actually contributes to its reproduction—Sebbar offers a way of turning even misogynist images of
women against their makers.

In *Primitive Passions* (1995), Rey Chow describes how Mulvey's paradigm has also been used to describe a European Orientalizing gaze:
"[T]he visual culture of postcoloniality is usually associated with European cultural hegemony—a hegemony, moreover, that is defined as Eu-

rope's dominating, exploitative *gaze*" (12). By describing "the West's sco-pophilia and . . . the passive objectified, fetishized status in which non-Western peoples and cultures have been cast" (12), Chow also suggests a parallel between Mulvey's critique of the male gaze and critiques, such as Mercer's, of racial fetishism. Nowhere is this connection, with its violent colonial implications, more apparent than in the passage where Shérazade looks through a colonial photo album, *Femmes algériennes 1960:*

> Les visages des femmes dévoilées devant l'appareil photographique que manipulait le Français soldat-photographe, pour le recensement de plu-sieurs villages de l'intérieur, ces visages avaient la dureté et la violence de ceux qui subissent l'arbitraire sachant qu'ils trouveront en eux la force de la résistance. Ces Algériennes avaient toutes devant l'objectif-mitrailleur, le même regard, intense, farouche, d'une sauvagerie que l'image ne saurait qu'archiver, sans jamais la maîtriser ni la dominer. Ces femmes parlaient toutes la même langue, la langue de sa mère.
>
> Shérazade feuilletait l'album photographique et les larmes coulaient, malgré elle. (220)

> Faces of women not wearing veils in front of a camera held by a French soldier, taking pictures for the census of several villages in the interior . . . these faces displayed the severity and violence of people who submit to arbitrary treatment, knowing they will find the inner strength to resist. These Algerian women all faced the lens as if they were facing a machine-gun shooting them, with the same intense, savage stare, a fierce-ness that the picture could only file for posterity without ever mastering or dominating. These women all spoke the same language, her mother's language.
>
> Sherazade turned the pages of the collection of photographs and in spite of herself the tears streamed down her face. (237–38)

She explicitly makes the comparison between photographing colonized women and containing the Algerian Revolution and, therefore, main-taining French colonial rule in Algeria. In *Les carnets de Shérazade,* the truck driver Gilles has also looked at photo albums of colonized women:

> — . . . J'avais pas pensé à ça. Elle aurait pu s'asphyxier là-dedans. J'aurais retrouvé un cadavre . . . J'aurais livré un divan avec une fille endormie, allongée comme les femmes des harems . . . le pantalon blanc trop large pour elle ressemble à un pantalon bouffant de femme arabe ou turque.
>
> Il a feuilleté des albums de photographies coloniales, des cartes postales où on voit des Mauresques nues qui posent sur des divans de maisons ottomanes. Parfois elles portent seulement un pantalon court qui dégage

la cheville. Dans les sex-shops, on propose souvent des négresses et des Orientales pour les amateurs . . . Des femmes et des petites filles. (89)

"I didn't think of that. She could have suffocated in there. I would have found a corpse. . . . I would have delivered a sofa with a girl asleep, stretched out like *harem* women . . . her oversized white pants look like the pantaloons of an Arab or Turkish woman."

He thumbed though albums of colonial photographs, postcards where one sees naked Moorish women posing on sofas in Ottoman houses. Sometimes they're only wearing a short pantaloon with their ankles showing. In the sex-shops, they often have Negresses and Oriental women to offer those who like them . . . Women and little girls.

As Gilles remembers colonial postcards to imagine Shérazade dead, both photographers in *Shérazade* fix Shérazade with their cameras as if she were dead (in French, *fixer* means both to stare and to fix, to freeze in place). Clichés of the Oriental *harem*, here, feed both colonial and male fantasies about women.

From these examples alone, one might argue that Sebbar, through Shérazade, offers a critique similar to Mulvey's. If the gaze in dominant paradigms of looking is male, the only way of remedying this dominance is to destroy the gaze, with violence if necessary. Shérazade seems to view such a destruction as one possible solution. Yet in other passages, she takes on the male Orientalizing gaze in other ways. She ridicules it, identifies with it, or sees possibilities of rewriting it through parody. In one passage of *Les carnets,* she happens upon a group of men watching pornographic movies. Instead of seeing men identifying with the camera-phallus and fantasizing about penetrating (along with the camera and male actor) the woman on screen, she looks at the screen, she sees a larger-than-life penis, and she laughs: "Shérazade écarta discrètement le rideau interdit et aperçut sur l'écran un phallus géant. Elle ne put s'empêcher de rire. Les hommes se retournèrent, furieux" (121). (Shérazade discretely opened the forbidden curtain and noticed a giant phallus on screen. She couldn't keep from laughing. The men turned around, furious.) Whereas some feminists, such as Dworkin and MacKinnon, have called for legal sanctions in their opposition to pornography, Shérazade deploys another strategy. She makes a mockery of the penis and phallic power, and the men are angry because she has uncovered a dirty little secret. The male fantasy involved in pornography is not just about naked female bodies; it is also about penises. In this homosocial setting where men are fantasizing about other men as well as about women, they are also fantasizing about the large penises they may or (more likely) may not have. In "The Force of Fantasy" (1990), Judith Butler criticizes Dworkin's antipornography position and elaborates on the work of Jean Laplanche and J.-B. Pontalis: "[F]antasy does not entail an identification with a single position within the fantasy; the identification is distributed among the various elements of the scene . . ." (109). If watching pornography could be considered as engaging in fantasy, then fantasizing about penises for heterosexual men involves not only an identification with them but also a desire for them. Fantasizing about heterosexual intercourse on the screen would then involve not only identifying with the man but also the woman. The irruption of a woman and a female gaze destabilizes the assumption that their homosocial behavior is in no way homosexual. In this way, Shérazade lashes (out at) men at the site of their vulnerability.

As Judith Mayne has written,

> [m]any critics have challenged or extended the implications of Mulvey's account, most frequently arguing that for women (and sometimes for men as well), cinematic identification occurs at the very least across gender lines, whether in transvestite or bisexual terms. However complex such accounts, they tend to leave unexamined another basic assumption common both to Mulvey's account and to contemporary psychoanalytic accounts of identification, and that is that cinematic identification not only functions to affirm heterosexual norms, but also finds its most basic condition of possibility in the heterosexual division of the universe. (127)

Along similar lines, Shérazade undoes any male monopoly of spectatorship and constitutes herself as a spectacle that returns the male gaze to its sender. On the one hand, Mayne's reading offers a critique of Mulvey's rigid dichotomies; on the other, such a notion of subverting the male gaze also relies on her paradigm. Though there can be dissident uses of the gaze Mulvey characterizes as male, though her dichotomies can be and often are deconstructed, though women can seize the gaze for their own pleasure, and though men can identify with the spectacle instead of the camera's gaze, the paradigm Mulvey describes and characterizes as insidious is still a dominant one and worthy of being destroyed. Shérazade, likewise, approaches the male gaze with a multipronged strategy. She criticizes dominant paradigms of the male gaze, suggests ways of dislodging the paradigms (by force, if necessary), and at the same time, suggests that they are not as all-powerful as they might seem, that even from a feminist perspective, one might find ambivalent ways of identifying with this gaze.

This rewriting, however, occurs not only at the symbolic level; it is also quite literal, involving as it does, pulling a gun on the proprietors of the male gaze, which is thereby subverted in a kind of holdup. Women literally rob men of their monopoly on scopophilia.

As Mayne challenges Mulvey's description of the male gaze, Chow problematizes the parallel description of an ethnographic one:

> Because it clearly establishes seeing as a form of power and being-seen as a form of powerlessness, this view of visuality, even though it is greatly reductive, has become the basis for much antiorientalist criticism. Ironically, however, such a view of visuality also leads antiorientalist critics to focus their attention excessively on the details of the European "gaze"—a gaze exemplified by film, ethnography, and tourism alike—and thus unwittingly to help further knowledge about *Europe* rather than the non-West, in a manner that is quite opposite to their moral intentions.
>
> Although they undoubtedly expose the fine turns of the European "gaze," the arguments that set up "West" and "East" in terms of spectator and exhibit inevitably dwarf the fact the "the East," too, is a spectator who is equally caught up in the dialectic of seeing. (12–13)

As critics have challenged Mulvey's paradigms by overturning the binary it relies on, Chow dislodges the associations of the "West" with spectatorship and the "East" with spectacle, associations with their own gendered implications. She even questions the negative connotations that the field of ethnography often has in much anticolonial discourse: "Supplementing Mulvey's argument with the anthropological situation, we may argue, in parallel, that vision bears the origins of ethnographic inequality. But we must go one step further: the state of being looked at not only is built into the way non-Western cultures are viewed by Western ones; more significantly it is part of the *active* manner in which such cultures represent—ethnographize—themselves" (180).

The full extent of Shérazade's ambivalent position vis-à-vis the male Orientalizing gaze is played out in her relation with Julien. Like the other men who desire Shérazade, Julien finds a paradigm for his gaze in Orientalist texts. Instead of the "low" forms of exotic pornography and colonial postcards, Julien's models are to be found in the "high" arts, especially Orientalist painting. As Gilles sees Shérazade's beauty through the Western *idées reçues* of the *harem*, Julien sees her through Orientalist paintings such as Delacroix's *Femmes d'Alger dans leur appartement* and Matisse's *Odalisque à la culotte rouge*. The following exchange occurs when they are looking at Delacroix's painting in a museum together:

—Mais c'est vrai. C'est incroyable! Mais oui. Tu as raison. Elle a les yeux verts.

Il avait regardé fixement Shérazade, la prenant aux épaules:
—Comme toi. (13)

"It's true. It's incredible! Yes, you're right. She's got green eyes."
He'd stared at Sherazade, putting his hands on her shoulders.
"Just like you." (9)

In the case of Matisse's painting, the red folds of the "Arab pantaloon," worn by the "Oriental" woman, function as a metonymy for her vagina, which, were it visible, would be positioned in the center of the painting, thereby inviting the penetration of the spectator's/voyeur's gaze. In few texts is the parallel between colonial and sexual penetration in Orientalist fantasies more clear. On the one hand, Shérazade resists Julien's gaze, his desire to fit her into an Orientalist stereotype of what Oriental beauty should be. Before leaving Paris, supposedly for Algeria, Shérazade leaves a note that directly refuses comparison with Matisse's vision of the Oriental Woman: "Sur un bout d'enveloppe que Julien ne découvrit que le lendemain matin, elle avait écrit «Je ne suis pas une odalisque»" (206). ("On a scrap torn off an envelope that Julien didn't discover till next morning, she'd written, 'I'm not an odalisque'" [222].) Like the photographer at the party and the quasi-pornographic photographer at the studio, Julien likes taking pictures of Shérazade and even wants to write a film script for her. She thwarts his efforts to freeze her as image by tearing up all the photographs except one. On the other hand, she does leave the photograph she likes and finally returns, in the final volume, to go before the camera's gaze in his film. Though she comes and goes in and out of Julien's life as she pleases, thereby thwarting any desire on his part for her to settle down, she does sleep with him before leaving Paris and tells him that she loves him.

Shérazade even harbors a peculiar attraction for the same Orientalist images she resists being compared to. While looking at Matisse's *Odalisque,* she experiences the following reaction:

Elle sent battre son cœur. Ça lui est arrivé pour les *Femmes d'Alger.* Shérazade revient sur ses pas, essaie de procéder par ordre, n'y parvient pas, recommence, regarde avec soin chaque tableau, à cause de Matisse, sans savoir encore pourquoi Matisse. (244)

She feels her heart beating faster. That happened with *The Women of Algiers.* Sherazade retraces her steps, tries to proceed in order, doesn't suc-

Henri Matisse (1869–1954). *Odalisque à la culotte rouge,* 1921. Oil on canvas. © 1999 Succession H. Matisse, Paris / Artists Rights Society (ARS), New York. Musée National d'Art Moderne, Centre Georges Pompidou, Paris. Art Resource, NY.

ceed, begins again, looks carefully at each picture, because of Matisse, without yet knowing why Matisse. (263)

Later, the narrator states, "Elle ne comprend pas pourquoi ça l'émeut" (245). ("She can't understand why it moves her" [264].) Before leaving Paris, she makes her rounds among Parisian museums to see Orientalist paintings of Oriental women, and she continues such trips to provincial museums in the second volume. Before leaving Paris, she buys up all the postcards of Matisse's *Odalisque.* When the salesperson asks, "Elle est plus belle sur l'original, vous ne pensez pas?" (246) ("She's more beautiful in the original, don't you think?" [265]), Shérazade, preferring the copy to the original, answers no. Just before embarking on a return to origins, Shérazade experiences this curious identification with, not her original roots, but a Western stereotype of her identity. In this sense, Matisse's painting is not the original (as the salesperson claims) for which Shérazade buys up all the copies; it is itself the copy of a Western *idée reçue.* She buys the copies of a copy and puts these copies into circulation across France.

The *Odalisque* postcards could be seen as the "high" version of the "lower," perhaps more pornographic postcards Gilles uses as the model for looking at Shérazade (though not because they show more skin—is the "high" thus exempt from being pornography?). There is no original Oriental woman behind Matisse's *Odalisque,* but Shérazade does not have access to the origin of her own identity any more than Matisse would. Her return to origins fails in the end; instead of returning to Algeria, she ends up repeating another journey, the march Beurs organized to combat racism in France, and her intended return to origins is replaced with an acknowledgment of *métissage.* It is also replaced by a sort of pilgrimage to various museums where other Orientalist paintings can be seen. In the final volume, when she returns to Middle Eastern roots, she, like Nedjma, is kidnapped. It is as if, after colonization and the resulting diaspora, no return to a precolonial authenticity or prediasporic experience can occur. As Djebar must rewrite colonial history to design for herself a past, Shérazade must negotiate between various colonialist images of who she is, come to terms with these stereotypes, destroy some of them, and construct an identity out of the ruins.

Oppositional Resistance

As when Shérazade replaces Matisse's *Odalisque* with a cheap copy, one of the ways she learns to escape these Orientalist stereotypes is by turning them into obvious cheap imitations of the real thing. In *Les carnets,* whereas Shérazade finds that "Loti était un maniaque grotesque" (161) (Loti was a grotesque maniac), her friend Marie

> trouvait que les caprices orientalistes de Loti étaient plutôt amusants et en tout cas innocents. Au moins, il ne se conduisait pas comme un bourgeois rochelais conformiste, plutôt comme un riche original. Marie ne comprenait pas la hargne de Shérazade. Ces orientaleries accumulées l'avaient exaspérée, pas Marie. —Un Orient de Prisunic . . . Il l'a trouvé dans Bonux . . . avait dit Shérazade en riant, avant de s'envelopper dans la soie, pour sa nuit exotique. (162)

> felt, rather, that Loti's Orientalist caprices were amusing and, in many ways, innocent. At least he didn't behave like a conformist bourgeois from La Rochelle, but rather, like an eccentric rich man. Marie couldn't understand Shérazade's vehemence. These accumulated Orientalisms had exasperated her, but not Marie. "A K-Mart Orient. . . . He found it at Wal-Mart . . . ," said Shérazade laughing, before wrapping herself in silk, for her exotic night.

Shérazade thus discovers the possibility of exaggerating Orientalist stereo-types to the point of transforming them into kitsch. As Anne Donadey writes, "[t]he Orientalist tradition, then, is absolutely necessary to her, since she has no other way of learning about her origins" (160). Woodhull as well writes, "Through the motif of the put-on, Sebbar's novel stages a series of struggles over the means of representation in French culture . . ." (1993, 117). Within this K-Mart Orient, there lies a number of possible identifications that derail any Orientalist attempt to pin down Shérazade into a fixed stereotype.

Chambers "make[s] a distinction . . . between 'opposition,' which works within the structure of power, and 'resistance,' which challenges the legitimacy of a given power-system and, perceiving it therefore not as 'power' but as *force,* seeks to overturn it by a counterforce. Revolution would be a case of resistance in this sense" (xv). He describes opposition-ality, as a tactic for transforming society, in the following way:

> So in order to understand how oppositionality works, one must be ready to conceive discourse, not as a representation whose power depends on its adequacy to a (preexisting) real, but as a mediating practice with the power to produce the real. Within the framework of that conception, I will de-scribe the discursive strategies—more precisely the tactics—of opposi-tionality under the general head of "irony," that is, as the production through reading of a meaning that is not said, a (mis-)reading that thereby appropriates the discourse of power—working the irony of that (mis-)appropriation—and makes it available to mediate "other" effects than those of power, the "discontinuous local effects" I describe as deflections of desire. The irony of reading causes the irony of (mis-)appropriation which enacts the ironical character of power, which is that the system of power produces change. And my definition of reading will consequently be as a "space" where there is room for oppositional maneuver in that the discursive practice of irony works seductively to shift desire. So the ques-tion becomes: how does an irony work (as) a seduction? (xvi)

This use of irony thus resembles, in many ways, that of Butler, who de-ploys it in her strategy for subverting the heterosexual gender system. Both their paradigms rely on a notion of textuality in which the script that is performed (in Butler's case) or read (in Chamber's case) is rewritten in the process. Ben Jelloun's rereading/rewriting of the Nation through Sindibad's minority discourse might be considered as a similar opposi-tional reading/narrative. If the Nation is narrative, then Chambers's tactic of "reading (the) oppositional (in) narrative" might be deployed in a similar rewriting, what I have called queering the Nation. What distinguishes Chambers's reading strategy from Butler's is the importance of seduction in his model of opposition. Genet was seduced into political solidarity with the Black Panthers and the PLO. Shérazade, as well, seems seduced by Matisse's Orientalist painting, indeed, by clichés of Oriental femininity, and this seduction is the starting point for her rewriting of Orientalist stereotypes into an identity she can claim as her own.

In spite of arguing that, unlike opposition, resistance does not change the structure of power, Chambers acknowledges that the opposition/resistance difference may not be as clear as one might think:

> [A]ll these distinctions are heuristic and of considerable fragility. That there is a very large gray area straddling the categories of resistance and opposition is demonstrated, for example, by guerrilla warfare à la Giap—a mode of resistance that relies on oppositional tactics—but also by the way oppositional behavior shades towards resistance as it becomes more self-conscious and/or in "tight" contexts where . . . it is *regarded* as a form of resistance. (12–13)

Shérazade similarly uses opposition one minute, resistance the next. She takes literally Malcolm X's revolutionary slogan "By any means necessary" even when the means she deems necessary might be less "revolutionary" than other possible choices. She chooses among tactics *and* strategies, between opposition *and* resistance according to the needs of the transformative task at hand, thereby demonstrating that resistance and opposition need not be an either/or decision and deconstructing the binary "opposition" between the two. While, as Chambers demonstrates, opposition runs the risk of strengthening the power system it works within to transform, and resistance risks institutionalizing the violence it deploys to overthrow the previous system (supposedly only as a means to a greater end), the possibility of cherishing opposition within resistance movements, like Kateb's eternal disturbance in the midst of upheaval, provides a possible solution to the dangers of both resistance and opposition by creating opposition with(in) resistance, resistance with(in) opposition, opposition to certain forms of resistance, and vice versa.

Theories Postcolonial and Queer Revisited

To understand more completely Shérazade's oppositional reading of Orientalist stereotypes of, among others, herself, it is perhaps useful to return to a dialogue between postcolonial and queer theories. Over a decade before Butler's or Bhabha's use of performance theory to describe the embodiment of gender or national identity, Luce Irigaray, in *Ce sexe qui n'en est pas un* (1977), attempted to carve out a space for women in language through mimicry. Denied the position of universal subject, women, defined by men as feminine object, are in a double bind: they can seize the position of subject, wrest it from male control, but in occupying this masculine position, they risk leaving behind their specificity. Likewise, reclaiming femininity means performing a male-written script for men. Irigaray's solution to this double bind is to mime femininity without fully occupying the feminine:

> To play with mimesis [Jouer de la mimésis] is thus, for a woman, to try to recover the place of her exploitation by discourse, without allowing herself to be simply reduced to it. It means to resubmit herself—inasmuch as she is on the side of the "perceptible" [sensible], of "matter"—to "ideas," in particular to ideas about herself, that are elaborated in/by a masculine logic, but so as to make "visible," by an effect of playful repetition [répétition ludique], what was supposed to remain invisible [occulté]: the cover-up of a possible operation of the feminine in language. It also means "to unveil" [dévoiler] the fact that, if women are such good mimics [si les femmes miment si bien], it is because they are not simply resorbed in this function. *They also remain elsewhere:* another case of the persistence of "matter," but also of "sexual pleasure" [jouissance]. (76; 74 in original)

Women who mimic the feminine are almost the feminine as defined by male discourse, but not quite. In the difference between their interpretation and the male script, there lies a space that can belong to women.

"Almost the same, but not quite," this is the expression Bhabha (1994) uses to define colonial mimicry: "[T]he discourse of mimicry is constructed around an *ambivalence;* in order to be effective, mimicry must continually produce its slippage, its excess, its difference" (86). Colonial mimicry is the name Bhabha assigns to the so-called white man's burden, his civilizing mission, the colonizer's desire to make the people he colonizes resemble himself, a desire to see sameness in the Other.[1] Total assimilation of the colonized into the colonizer's culture, however, is impossible for two reasons. First, "[i]f the differences between the Euro-

---

1. Fuss has also compared Irigaray's mimicry with Bhabha's: according to Fuss, whereas Irigaray's mimicry leads to resistance, Bhabha's is the precondition of domination. Nonetheless, Fuss seems to acknowledge the subversive potential of Bhabha's mimicry: "[T]he mimicry of subjugation can provide unexpected opportunities for resistance and disruption . . ." (147).

peans and the natives are so vast, then clearly . . . the process of civilizing the natives can continue indefinitely" (JanMohamed 87). Civilizing mission accomplished, the colonizer could no longer justify colonial rule; he would have to go home. The colonized must remain "[a]lmost the same [as the colonizer] but not white" (Bhabha 1994, 89), "not quite/not white" (92)—that is, not quite white, not quite not white, but nevertheless, not white. Second, the ambivalence that characterizes colonial mimicry, according to Bhabha, is double; mimicry's double is menace: "The ambivalence of colonial authority repeatedly turns from *mimicry*—a difference that is almost nothing but not quite— to *menace*—a difference that is almost total but not quite" (91). Conflicting with a colonial desire to assimilate the colonized, a racist stereotype tropes the colonized as totally different (or almost—for if the colonized were totally other, there could be no hope of assimilation, and the civilizing mission would still not justify colonialism).

The stereotype, in Bhabha's theory, operates through an ambivalence similar to that of colonial mimicry:

> [T]he stereotype, which is [the] major discursive strategy [of colonial discourse], is a form of knowledge and identification that vacillates between what is always "in place," already known, and something that must be anxiously repeated . . . as if the essential duplicity of the Asiatic or the bestial sexual licence of the African that needs no proof, can never really, in discourse, be proved. . . . For it is the force of ambivalence that gives the colonial stereotype its currency: ensures its repeatability in changing historical and discursive conjunctures; informs its strategies of individuation and marginalization; produces that effect of probabilistic truth and predictability which, for the stereotype, must always be in *excess* of what can be empirically proved or logically construed. (66)

Like the gender roles described by Butler, Bhabha's stereotypes can only be maintained through a constant repetition. If the stereotype were proven once and for all, it would not have to be repeated. Many of Bhabha's critics accuse him of delighting in the ambivalence they see him as finding everywhere in colonial discourse; these critics, however, have misunderstood Bhabha's use of the term "ambivalence." To expose the ambivalence of colonial discourse is not to claim that it is any less oppressive; ambivalence is a "process" for Bhabha, it is "productive" (66, 67). It is only through the constant repetition or discursive deployment of stereotypes that colonial discourse can remain effective and productive, producing the discrimination that keeps the colonizer in power.

Bhabha characterizes both colonial mimicry and the stereotype as a contradiction or, as he calls it, a "splitting": colonial mimicry is split between almost total difference and almost complete sameness, and the stereotype is split between being such a given that it need not be argued and so excessive that it must be constantly repeated. The excessive nature of the stereotype makes it oppressive and, as a result, productive of violence; its constant and excessive reproduction constitutes, at the least, discrimination, and, in harsher forms, racial terror. The same excess, however, can also prove to be the stereotype's weakness. If one could perform the stereotype according to Irigaray's paradigm of miming, one could repeat Orientalist clichés without being totally reduced to them. Likewise, Shérazade seems to find a space within fantasies of Oriental femininity to mime the clichés in a similar manner. Indeed, when others attempt to reduce her to such stereotypes, she pulls out her .38 and/or destroys the means of their production.

The Identity Police

Miming a prescribed identity while remaining elsewhere, it is precisely with such a notion that, in *Ecarts d'identité* (1990), Azouz Begag and Abdellatif Chaouite describe Beur "identity":

> Ce livre sur les écarts d'identité s'intéresse aux conséquences incontrôlées de la migration des hommes d'un lieu à un autre. Ce n'est pas un énième recueil sur les souffrances des immigrés en France ou sur les Beurs; les gens qui bougent dérangent et provoquent des désordres. Nous, les enfants de ces travailleurs-paysans qui ont quitté leur pays et leur vie, qui sommes-nous par rapport aux Français de souche, à nos parents? Comment nos mères et nos pères ont-ils pu accomplir des voyages aussi fabuleux, comment ont-ils fait pour vivre en France depuis trente ou quarante ans sans être vraiment dedans? Que nous restera-t-il de leur souvenir quand ils seront morts? (21–22)

> This book on sidestepping identity is interested in the unchecked consequences of the migration of men from one place to another. It is not an umpteenth collection on immigrants' or their children's suffering in France; people who move upset and set off disorder. We, the children of these peasant-workers who left their country and their lives, who are we in relation to the French by blood, to our parents? How did our mothers and fathers accomplish such fabulous journeys, what did they do to live in France for thirty or forty years without really being there? What will remain of their memory when they die?

The French expression used by Begag and Chaouite, "écarts d'identité," is most obviously a play on *carte d'identité* (ID card). It is therefore difficult to translate. It means "moving identity out of the way," "moving out of the way of identity," or even "a misuse of identity" (cf. *un écart de langage*).[2] For them, Beur identity is an identity in movement that occupies an in-between space escaping easy definition. Neither French nor Algerian, or not quite/not French but not Algerian, the Beur—always *écarté(e)* from any geographical referent of origin—has no place for rooted identity. In the glossary at the beginning of the study, they define "écarts d'identité" as the "différence de couleur entre un passeport vert et une carte d'identité jaune" (10) (difference in color between a green passport and a yellow ID card). The "écart d'identité" is thus somewhere in between the bureaucratic means of regulating or controlling identity by the "papers" required of a nation's citizens, residents, and even visitors. When Shérazade obtains a fake ID, not only does she recognize identity as a necessary fiction, but she also beats the cops at their own game. Unlike Sindibad, Yamna, Moha, and Zahra after becoming a woman, all of whom have no ID, Shérazade manages to find a way to demand recognition from the powers that be who would otherwise deny her status as citizen with full rights.

The final volume of the Shérazade trilogy offers the possibility of a rooted identity in spite of all this dodging of the identity police, in spite of this constant *écartement de l'identité*. This novel begins as a film crew digs up an olive tree, "l'arbre des Ancêtres" (9) (the Ancestors' tree), "un olivier centenaire gardé par une sorcière" (26) (an olive tree a hundred years old guarded by a witch). This tree is taken to the HLM where Shérazade grew up for the film she is to star in, and like the trees described by writers such as Kateb and Dib, whom Shérazade reads at the public library, it represents the roots of national identity. Meanwhile, Shérazade has left in search of roots in another region: "Pourquoi il a écouté cette fille et ses histoires d'olivier, il n'aurait pas dû la laisser partir, elle prétendait qu'elle jouerait mieux si elle allait sur les lieux mêmes, la terre des Ancêtres, quels ancêtres? (26). (Why did he listen to this girl and her olive-tree stories, he shouldn't have let her leave, she claimed she was going to the place itself, the land of her Ancestors, which ancestors?) Yet, like Nedjma, Shérazade has been taken hostage at the site of the origins of Arab identity, because she is not considered a "true" Arab. As Western

2. Many thanks to Ross Chambers for this third trans.

men tried to force her in front of the camera's gaze, her kidnappers usher her in front of television cameras to display her again on *Western* television in order to strengthen their demands. Yet again, a woman has been kidnapped to further the national struggle.

Throughout the third volume, the woman who guarded the tree before it was uprooted searches for it: "Arracher un olivier centenaire, c'est un crime . . . Faut-il, pour une image, détruire à la folie? Il ne sait pas que déraciner un olivier planté par les Ancêtres, c'est déraciner la vie, l'arracher au ventre des femmes . . ." (67). (Uprooting a hundred-year-old olive tree is a crime. . . . To create an image, do you have to destroy madly? He doesn't know that uprooting an olive tree planted by the ancestors is uprooting life, ripping it out of women's wombs . . .) When she finally reaches the tree, she says, "Maintenant, je peux mourir" (201). (Now, I can die.) Like Shérazade, this woman has been separated from the lands of her ancestors, her identity has been uprooted, and at the end of the novel, she returns to roots that have been transplanted. Read as a return to national origins, *Le fou de Shérazade* demonstrates that roots are not planted before the narration of return to origins. It is the narration itself that plants, replants, even transplants roots. Shérazade shows that in a world of uprootedness, of diaspora, of crossing borders, and of *métissage,* people manage to write roots for themselves, rewrite official narratives of return (which might otherwise exclude them) to include themselves, and articulate models of subjectivity in a postmodern, postcolonial, late-capitalist world where subjectivity is increasingly fragmented even for those (namely Western white men) who once held a monopoly on the models of subjectivity that were supposedly universal. Shérazade shows that a feminist subject can articulate a rooted identity even while fleeing attempts on the part of the powers that be to impose an identity from without. And from this position of agency she has created for herself, she shows that the feminist subject need not always be in flight. She can, in fact, become an urban guerrilla in the struggle to destroy the power relations that forced her to flee in the first place.

Part Four

ALLEGORIES

OF THE

QUEER NATION

Chapter Twelve

The Joy of Castration: Childhood Narratives and the Demise of Masculinity

"In Algeria," writes Nefissa Zerdoumi, "it is quite rare for adults to talk about their childhood" (274). According to her description of traditional Algerian milieus, the public remembering of growing up and, therefore, becoming men and women seems not to be a common practice. As Bonn (1974) remarks, however, Maghrebian literature is most noticeable as an exception to this rule (26). Remembering what should be forgotten, Maghrebian childhood narratives often recount the expulsion of boys from the world of women, experienced as violence, and bring it back to haunt adult subjectivity. To gain access to the domain of men and male privilege, a man must deny an identification with the feminine, a denial that is experienced as a loss that is nonetheless kept and internalized through a melancholic mourning of it. In contrast, many novels nourish and endlessly cherish the haunting of childhood memories that will not go away. They bring back a childhood past to infect the present of narration, and the masculinity of the adult male subject, when contaminated by his not-so-masculine past, cannot emerge unscathed. The disavowal or denial of femininity upon which adult male masculinity is predicated thereby becomes less absolute and less efficient. Three texts in particular, not only remember this loss and bring what is mourned back to haunt the melancholic male subject/narrator, but also offer hints as to how Maghrebian male childhood narratives might be read: Férid Boughedir's film *Halfaouine* (Tunisia, 1990), Albert Memmi's *La statue de sel* (Tunisia, 1953), and Dib's *Qui se souvient de la mer* together offer a paradigm for understanding the challenge to Maghrebian masculinity carried out through a cultivation of the joy of castration.

Halfaouine tells the story of Noura, an adolescent boy in Tunis at the threshold of manhood, and describes his expulsion from the space of women. When Noura shows off soft-core pornographic magazines stolen from his father to his older friends, they point out that he is still young enough to gain entrance to the women's *hammam* and encourage him to gaze at the female bodies inside and return with detailed descriptions. After Noura gets his mother to take him to the *hammam,* the attendant hesitates to let him in; she sees a different gaze in his eyes and claims he has become a man. In spite of the attendant's reluctance, however, his mother convinces her to let him in. When Noura returns to tell what he saw, his friends remain unimpressed because he managed to see only breasts and no genitalia that were not covered by bath gloves or water pots. They accuse him of being too much of a child to know which parts of female anatomy are the most important for a man to see and threaten him with exclusion from their all-"men's" group. Noura responds to their threat as a challenge and announces that, during his next visit to the *hammam* for the celebration of his younger brother's circumcision, he will manage to see all. Later, when Noura accompanies female friends and relatives to the *hammam,* his mother must again convince the attendant to allow him in. This time, however, once they are inside, the attendant's assistant surprises Noura gazing at a woman, waiting for her to uncover her genitals, and he is expelled. Having been chased out through the shouts and blows of women bathers, he finds refuge in his bedroom while the circumcision celebration continues outside. When the moment arrives, his brother is laid on a table, pants removed, legs spread. A barber pulls the foreskin, moves the scissors towards his penis. The film cuts to Noura grabbing his own groin as his brother screams in pain.

Bouhdiba (1975) describes both a Maghrebian boy's circumcision and his expulsion from the women's *hammam* as important rites that mark the passage from the world of women into the world of men: "The son's emancipation, the distances he must inevitably take vis-à-vis his mother represent an essential moment in life that circumcision and expulsion from the *hammam* have, among others, prepared, but in a way that seems terribly insufficient. The child is literally gobbled up [happé] into the masculine adult world . . ." (272). *Halfaouine* recounts such a gobbling up and juxtaposes Noura's expulsion from the women's *hammam* (the most concrete example of a women-only space) and his previous circumcision, which he relives during his brother's as the threat of castration. Noura's reaction to this brother's circumcision provides the key to understanding how a male subject might experience the memory of circumcision unleashed by being the spectator of another circumcision, whether real, imagined, or represented in film or novel. In particular, he suggests the possibility of a politics of identification between the spectator (particularly the male spectator) and himself. Many wince at the moment of circumcision, as if they shared Noura's (and his brother's) psychic anguish (and/or physical pain). In contrast, *La statue de sel* provides an alternative interpretation of Noura's anxiety, one that offers a paradigm for understanding the destabilizing potential of the specter of castration haunting Noura's passage into masculinity. In spite of religious differences between the circumcisions Boughedir and Memmi recount (Memmi's narrator is Jewish), Memmi stresses possible identifications across cultural differences and creates the possibility of experiencing the memory of circumcision and the accompanying castration anxiety as *jouissance,* the joy of castration. Dib describes a similar delight in emasculation resurrected through the narrative remembering of childhood. We have seen how the subjectivity of Dib's narrator is undone by his wife's involvement in guerrilla warfare. Yet the memory of his expulsion from the feminine sphere is as important in the demise of his masculinity as his wife's challenge to traditional gender roles. While *Halfaouine* shows how the memory of circumcision conjures up castration anxiety and Memmi turns this specter into a source of sexual pleasure, Dib emphasizes the narrative aspect of childhood memories and the fact that the act of narration is what produces emasculation for the male narrator. If narration has such a powerful transformative potential for the narrator, perhaps the reader (or spectator, in the case of the film) can benefit from this potential as well, particularly when s/he identifies with the narrator along the lines suggested by both Memmi and *Halfaouine*. Whereas castration anxiety constitutes a common trope of Western psychoanalytical discourses, these Maghrebian texts not only challenge the narrative of progress proposed by Freudian accounts of sexual development, but also offer models of understanding parallel (but not identical) paradigms of castration that do not require kinship structures based on the nuclear family or the Oedipal complex.

Albert Memmi and the Joy of Castration

Noura's gesture of grabbing his own groin at the moment of his brother's circumcision is best understood as an act of memory in which Noura returns to his own earlier childhood and circumcision. One finds a paradigm for interpreting this rememoration in *La statue de sel,* a childhood narrative in which the memory of circumcision provokes the threat of castration, experienced by the narrator as a form of *jouissance.* One day in a streetcar, the Jewish narrator, Alexandre Mordekhaï Benillouche, witnesses a scene involving a young Muslim boy. A Muslim stranger asks the boy's father whether his son has been circumcised and learns that he has not. The stranger then asks the boy how much his penis would cost. After the boy refuses higher and higher prices, the stranger puts his hand in the boy's pants to take the penis without paying. The boy must defend himself according to a well-known scenario:

> Visiblement, il connaissait la scène, déjà on lui avait fait la même proposition. Moi aussi, je la connaissais. Je l'avais jouée dans le temps, assailli par d'autres provocateurs, avec les mêmes sentiments de honte et de concupiscence, de révolte et de curiosité complice. Les yeux de l'enfant brillaient du plaisir d'une virilité naissante et de la révolte contre cette inqualifiable agression. Il regarda son père. Son père souriait, c'était un jeu admis. (186)

> Quite obviously, the boy knew this whole routine and had already heard the same proposition before. I too, knew it all, and had myself played the game some years ago, attacked by other aggressors and feeling the same emotions of shame [and sexual excitement, of revolt and complicitous curiosity]. The child's eyes sparkled with the pleasure of his awareness of his own growing virility, and with the shock of his revolt against such an unwarranted attack. He looked toward his father, but the latter only smiled: this was an accepted game. (167)

The men in the streetcar all get a good laugh, and the father is proud of his son who successfully defends his penis and (by association) phallic privilege and power at such an early age. The boy is rewarded with male approval for successfully enduring one of the trials that make up the apprenticeship of masculinity. His reaction, however, provokes a rather different one in Memmi's narrator:

> Lorsque l'enfant hurla, je sentis mon sexe frémir à l'appel brusquement resurgi du fond de mon enfance. . . . Oui, je le connais bien ce frisson désagréable et voluptueux. Avant d'aller à l'école primaire, je fréquentais un kouttab. . . . (188)

> When the boy in the streetcar screamed with fear, I felt my own sexual organs quiver as if in response to a scream that reached me suddenly from the depths of my own childhood. . . . Yes, I know well that unpleasant but voluptuous tremor. Before going to grade school, I used to go to the *kouttab.* . . . (169–70)

Memmi's narrator identifies with the threatened boy and this identification produces a physical sensation of pain as well as of sexual pleasure in the penis, the target of attack on the boy's body.

Like the Proustian madeleine, this sensation resurrects another one from the past. Alexandre remembers a childhood performance of circumcision at the *kouttab,* or religious school, one day, after the rabbi had left the classroom. An older boy played the rabbi and a younger one was chosen to play the "victim." At first the narrator fears being selected for the latter role, but once a younger student is chosen, he identifies with him: "Mais le risque m'avait lié à la victime, avait déclenché en moi les affres du calvaire. Je ressentais l'angoisse du tout petit tremblant, porté sur les épaules du surveillant, comme un agneau de sacrifice" (191). ("But the mere threat had bound me closely to the victim and made me feel all the terrors of a real calvary. I could feel the anguish of the small boy who, all trembling, was now being carried, like the sacrificial lamb, on the shoulders of our [monitor]" [172–73].) Like Noura at his brother's circumcision, Alexandre identifies with the boy being circumcised, and this identification produces a physical sensation whose site is the penis: "J'avais mal au bas-ventre, au même point, comme si le couteau allait me blesser" (193). ("[M]y groin ached[, at the same spot,] as if the knife were about to wound me too" [174].) Since the victim is already circumcised, a second circumcision can only evoke the threat of castration: "Mon coeur battait de peur et d'émotion confuse. . . . Allaient-ils vraiment lui couper le membre? J'en avais une douleur vague et cependant non désagréable au bas-ventre" (192). ("My heart beat faster, under the pressure of fear and [embarrassed] emotion. . . . Were they really going to cut off his penis? The mere thought of it gave me a vague but not unpleasant pain in my own loins" [173].) And as in the streetcar, the threat of castration elicits sexual pleasure as much as pain:

> La peur intolérable qui me tenait collé au mur, la honte devant cette nudité, se mêlaient de ce sentiment que je ne peux oublier: un plaisir complice et consentant. Je ressentais dans mon sexe cette peur voluptueuse se traduire en frissons électriques. Comment oublierais-je cette complicité? Oui, je participais à la cérémonie, à la pâture collective, ancestrale.
>
> Ce fut physiquement intolérable, et je me sentis défaillir lorsque la main droite du sacrificateur, armée du rasoir, descendit lentement vers le petit bout de chair blanche qui émergeait entre l'index et le majeur de sa main gauche.
>
> Brusque fut la délivrance, explosèrent d'un seul coup ma peur, ma

honte, ma jouissance, mon dégoût, et l'insupportable tension du silence
angoissé de tous: à bout de nerfs, la victime venait d'éclater en sanglots.
(193)

An intolerable fear kept me close to the wall, a feeling of shame before this
nakedness; all this was mingled with a feeling too that I shall never forget,
a pleasure at being accessory to the ceremony, accepting it all. Within my
own penis, I felt the pleasure of fear transformed into tremors like those
of an electric shock. How shall I ever forget my complicity? Yes, I was
playing my part in the ceremony, in the ancestral and collective ritual that
was food for the mind.

It was physically intolerable, and I felt truly faint when the High Priest's
right hand, armed with a razor, came slowly down toward the tiny bit of
white flesh that [protruded] between the index and the second finger of
his left hand.

But my sense of having been liberated was sudden, and all my fear
vanished explosively, together with my shame, my pleasure, my disgust,
and the unbearable tension that was born of the anguished silence of all
of us: unable to stand it any longer, the victim had just burst into tears.
(174–75)

In these passages, the operation of memory establishes a connection between an adult narrator and his own childhood. At the same time, this
connection takes the form of an identification on the part of the narrator
with another boy, with whom he shares an emotion that is at once painful, unnerving, and pleasant. In the streetcar as at the *kouttab,* the reaction constitutes a sensual oxymoron ("douleur . . . non désagréable,"
"honte . . . concupiscence," "plaisir . . . agression," and "peur voluptu-
euse"). In fact, one must assume the emotions are shared, because one
cannot be sure of the sensation experienced by the Muslim boy; the narrator has projected a sensation from his own childhood onto him. Again,
this projection targets and comes from a specific body part, the same for
both people, the penis, which is perhaps not quite what Pierre Nora had
in mind when he coined the term "lieu de mémoire" (site of memory).[1]

This identification, associated with a practice common to the experiences of the narrator and the boy, transcends differences between Muslim
and Jewish (even Maghrebian Jewish) practices of circumcision such as
the difference in ages at circumcision and therefore men's ability to re-

---

1. For Nora, who cites Proust's madeleine as an example (xxx), the "lieux de mémoire" are traces
(xxiv), the effect of the collapse of memory and history (xvii). An archive of "lieux de mémoire" must
therefore be created because we are cut off from the past (xxiv).

member it; all the men in the tramway identify with the young boy's performance: "Décidément, nous nous sentions en famille, entre Méditerranéens" (187). (Decidedly, among Mediterraneans, we felt like family [my trans.].) The Jewish narrator identifies with the threat of castration faced by the Muslim boy and reads into the boy's experience one from his own past. One difference in Jewish experiences of circumcision involves its function as a corporeal trace of a religious pact with God. Though Muslims are expected to follow the example of the Prophet, who was circumcised, the Qur'an does not mention circumcision. As Abraham (the first circumcised in the Judeo-Muslim tradition) is also considered to be the father of Muslims (or especially Arabs), this religious aspect of a pact with God cannot be totally absent in Islam. Yet circumcision as a sign of virility is much more important in an Arab or Muslim context. As the anthropologist Vincent Crapanzano writes, in the Moroccan context "[c]ircumcision is said to make a man and a Muslim of a boy" (51). Obviously, if a baby is circumcised almost immediately after birth, circumcision is less likely to mark the passage to masculinity.

When boys are old enough at their circumcision to remember it later, they often associate it with the threat of castration. Chebel (1988), for example, writes, "For the Maghrebian boy, the threat of castration always takes the realistic form of circumcision which is always imminent" (173). Crapanzano, in describing his Moroccan informant's circumcision, also associates it with a fear of castration: "Tuhami could feel nothing. He did not look down. He was afraid his penis had been cut off" (50). Circumcised in accordance with Jewish tradition, the narrator cannot remember his own circumcision as many Muslim men can. He can, however, remember a collective experience ("je participais à la cérémonie, à la pâture collective, ancestrale") whose memory is physically inscribed onto his body: "Pourrai-je jamais oublier l'Orient alors qu'il est greffé dans ma chair, qu'il me suffit de me toucher pour vérifier sa marque définitive?" (188). (How will I ever be able to forget the Orient since it is grafted into my flesh, that I need only touch myself to verify its permanent mark [my trans.].) Remembering is troped here as an autoerotic experience ("il me suffit de me toucher"), perhaps even as masturbation, but once the memory of pleasure becomes collective (in the all-male experience of circumcision), it also becomes homoerotic. While the homoerotic aspect of this act of memory is not necessarily what threatens masculinity in this cultural context, Dib offers a model for understanding other ways in which Memmi's memory of circumcision may have emasculating consequences.

Dib: Haunting Memories and the Demise of Masculinity

Dib's narrator remembers growing up *in* and belonging *to* a women's space, his expulsion from which, like Noura's, marks his becoming a man. He associates his childhood with his mother, whose presence he prefers to his father's: "Je jouais à côté de [mon père], c'est-à-dire que, sans bouger, sans attirer l'attention sur moi, j'allais retrouver mes amis. Une fois que j'avais assez joué, il m'était permis de rejoindre les femmes" (35). ("I played by [my father's] side, which is to say that, without a fuss, without attracting any attention to myself, I would go and find my friends. When I had played enough, I was permitted to rejoin the women" [19].) The narrator plays in a paternal space only because he has to, and after a minimum contact with his father, he can return to the female, maternal space he prefers. His father is an oppressive presence that disturbs the narrator whenever he must endure it:

> Mon père . . . m'écrasait sous la vigueur de ses sens et de ses muscles, son égoïsme naturel, l'inflexibilité de son caractère. . . . Aussi, dès que je me trouvais en sa présence, me troublais-je. Je demeurais sans défense contre la panique qui fondait sur moi; dans un tel tête-à-tête, le plus innocent abandon de conduite, comme le plus calculé, pouvait tourner à chaque instant à ma confusion. (77–78)

> My father . . . crushed me beneath the vigor of his senses and his muscles, his natural egotism, the inflexibility of his character. . . . Further, as soon as I found myself in his presence, I would become upset. I was defenseless against the panic that gripped me; in such an encounter, the most innocent behavior, or the most calculated, could at any moment lead me into confusion. (46)

In contrast with the father's harshness, distance, and even violence, the mother represents a soothing, comforting presence.

Like Kateb, Dib uses a number of poetic associations, most notably the homophony in French between *mother* and *sea* (*mère/mer*) to describe the domain of the feminine in which he grew up. In its very title, *Qui se souvient de la mer* associates remembering with the sea and therefore the mother, an association explicitly made in one passage in which woman, wife, mother, and sea all perform the same function: "Sans la mer, sans les femmes, nous serions restés définitivement des orphelins; elles nous couvrirent du sel de leur langue et cela, heureusement, préserva maints d'entre nous!" (20–21). ("Without the sea, without the women, we would have remained orphans permanently; they covered us with the salt of their tongue[s] and that, fortunately, preserved many a man among us!" [10].) Likewise, the following passage also attributes maternal and nurturing qualities to the sea: "Imperceptible, comme ce parfum d'algues et de sel, l'air reprit. *Berce mon corps, dissous mon ombre . . .*" (31). ("Imperceptible, like that [scent] of algae and salt, the tune returned. *Cradle my body, dissolve my shadow . . .*" [17].) The sea lulls, soothes (*bercer*) as the mother rocks the cradle (*bercer*); in French, one could say that *la mer berce comme la mère*. This image leads to another, that of the lullaby (*berceuse*), which the narrator explicitly mentions in another passage: "Je me mis à chanter à mon tour une vieille chanson, une berceuse, du temps de mon enfance" (63). ("I began in turn to sing an old song, a lullaby, from my childhood" [37].) This lullaby could be described as the "chant de la mer" (64) ("[t]he singing of the sea" [37]) or *de la mère*. The sea/mother's lullaby provokes an act of memory on the narrator's part, a return to the womb, the place where amniotic fluid combines water and mother as *source de la vie*. Again, this return to the womb, comforting at times, can also be threatening: "On dirait qu'il a été avalé par le vagin de la terre!" (135). ("It's as if he'd been swallowed up by the vagina of the earth!" [85].) The sea spits out dead bodies, victims of colonial violence, as well as it soothes. The remembering of the sea in the title brings peace and is also a haunting— "La mer vint me hanter une fois de plus" (114) ("The sea came to haunt me once again" [71])—just as a return to childhood may recall a comforting presence as well as torment: "[J]'étais tourmenté par ces souvenirs qui ne me lâchaient pas . . ." (125). (". . . I was tormented by these memories that would not leave me alone . . ." [78].)

Dib's associations of the mother, water, and memory (which returns as a haunting) allow us to better understand the role of the *hammam* in *Halfaouine*. Like Djebar, in her description of the women's *hammam*, Bouhdiba describes the *hammam* with the same aquatic images Dib associates with the mother:

> The *hammam* is an overly sexual place [un lieu surévalué sexuellement]. One can even say that it is a uterine environment. . . . One descends into the *hammam* as one descends into the underworld. One slides in, plunges in before going into the *mathara* or the *khilwaq*, the most intimate place as well as the most demonic. . . . It is also a place where both scalding streams and cool, refreshing streams flow. They come from the furnace. They flow into the depths of the ground. A mystery accompanies the "river" that comes from a hole, crosses a hole, plunges into a hole. Going

to the *hammam* means plunging into a mystery. It is a return in dream to the mother's bosom. (210–11)

He associates the *hammam* with the mother's body and amniotic fluids ("milieu utérin"). Going into the *hammam* involves going back to one's childhood; it is also like a return to the womb. Though this return to the mother's body has a comforting aspect ("le lieu le plus intime" and "retourner en rêve au sein maternel"), it is also marked very ambivalently as being infernal. The *hammam* is a mysterious place, a dark continent; it is haunted ("le lieu . . . le plus démoniaque"), not only by *djnoun* or spirits, but also by memories: "We are born as children in the *hammam*. And once we have become adults, we populate it with our memories, fantasies, and dreams, which is precisely how every Muslim relives his childhood through his experience at the *hammam*" (207). Going to the *hammam* as an adult involves a return to childhood:

> Suddenly the *hammam* will be an imaginary return to the former world, the lost world of yore that is found again with each visit. Each bath at the *hammam* bathes us in our childhood fantasies, evocations of the past, aspirations, desires, all mingled into the cold and hot steam that pacify the body and excite the mind. Vast *hammam,* a place haunted with so many memories, so many scenes, so many mixed visions wherein one's mother and sisters, charming cousins, the enigmatic women from next door make up this dream-like bouquet of femininity that each man carries within himself. (209)

For Bouhdiba, as in *Halfaouine,* the haunting of the *hammam* thus involves a resurrection of childhood memories as well as the feminine world of boyhood. The return to the *hammam* is a return to the source/spring of the mother's body. On the one hand, Bouhdiba acknowledges that this resurrection of the feminine affects adult male subjectivity, since every man carries within him "ce bouquet onirique de la féminité" represented by childhood memories. On the other, Bouhdiba controls dangerous memories of the feminine by situating them in a heterosexual relation to the male subject and confining them to the space of the *hammam*. (Although Bouhdiba discusses the existence of homosexuality in the *hammam* [205, 209], he attributes this behavior to a regression to the prepubescent stage.) This internalized femininity is projected onto the past so it can be mourned in the consolidation of masculinity. The male subject practically desires the women in his memories ("les charmantes cousines, les énigmatiques voisines").

One of the haunting memories Dib's narrator brings back is that of his separation from his mother at his father's order. The incident follows a childhood injury he incurs upon leaving the house for the first time. Unaware that the home's protection does not extend into the street, he goes out without shoes, steps on glass, and cuts his foot, which takes a year to heal. During this time, his mother cares for him in a manner consistent with her soothing attributes:

> Pourtant, je m'apercevais combien la présence de ma mère pouvait m'être bienfaisante, combien sa voix, douce, un peu monotone, allégeait ma souffrance, surtout à la tombée de la nuit, quand elle s'élevait à mon chevet dans la pénombre du crépuscule. Arrivant des chambres éclairées, maman venait ainsi me faire recommencer de longues heures de veille, aider le malade à affronter la nuit. Que n'accepterais-je de subir pour me retrouver sous cette patiente, cette bienveillante influence? (93)

> And yet I felt how much my mother's presence could be soothing to me, how her voice, soft, a little monotonous, lightened my suffering, especially at nightfall, when she sat at my bedside in the shadows of dusk. Coming to me from the lighted rooms, Mama thus was there as I began the long hours of vigil, helping the sick child to face the night. What wouldn't I agree to undergo in order to feel once again that kind, patient influence? (57)

However, at one point, the father intervenes and forbids her to comfort the narrator, thereby separating the two:

> Un soir, elle entra, comme elle en avait pris l'habitude, dans la pièce où j'étais couché. Mon père surgit derrière elle et lui demanda ce qu'elle faisait près de moi.
> —L'enfant n'est pas guéri. Je crains pour lui.
> —Tu crains toujours. Celui qui craint le mal, pour soi ou pour un autre, perd foi en la providence. Sois tranquille. Le Seigneur prévoit tout. Nous attendrons la fin.
> —Il souffre. Nous sommes les seuls à pouvoir le soulager un peu.
> —Laisse, femme.
> Ma mère dut repartir, cette fois. (93–94)

> One evening, as was her habit, she came into the room where I was lying. My father burst in behind her and asked what she was doing there with me.
> "The child is not healed. I'm afraid for him."
> "You're always afraid. He who fears evil, for himself or for another, loses faith in providence. Don't worry. The Lord foresees all. We'll await the end."
> "He's suffering. We're the only ones who can comfort him a little."
> "Drop it, woman."
> My mother had to leave me, this time. (57)

The separation of the narrator from his mother and therefore from the sphere of women is marked by a rupture or "symbolic wound."[2] This break (*coupure*) could also recall more physical cuts or wounds that separate the male child from his mother's body (cutting the umbilical cord) and from the childhood world situated within women's spaces (circumcision). The narrator's wound occurs almost as a punishment for venturing beyond the women's space; becoming a man is lived as yet another punishment administered by the father, and at that particular moment, is in no way seen as desirable or natural or as constituting a privilege.

A nostalgic desire to return to the mother's womb is certainly not unique to Maghrebian literature.[3] This longing for an impossible return to the womb may not in any way threaten more dominant models of male subjectivity and may be a melancholy for what must be lost and mourned in the consolidation of male subjectivity.[4] There may be reasons why an adult Maghrebian man might wax nostalgic on his childhood that are not incompatible with patriarchal privilege. Many accounts of boyhood point out that, since mothers are rewarded for giving birth to boys, boys receive privileged treatment in comparison to their sisters. This privilege, however, often does not disappear with adulthood since the wife supposedly replaces the mother in this respect. What distinguishes many Maghrebian childhood narratives from, say, familiar tropes of nineteenth-century French poetry, is that rather than mourning an irretrievable loss, these narrating subjects resurrect the past in a way that questions privilege rather than reaffirming it. By recalling his childhood, Dib's narrator reconstructs the female space he once belonged to and identifies with the child he used to be: "Au fond de moi, je demeure inconsolable comme un enfant perdu. Placé, de la sorte, brutalement en face de moi-même, je constate que mon attitude est d'ailleurs celle d'un

2. The term is Bettelheim's. While I find his notion of the symbolic function of circumcision useful, his argument that circumcision is not a mark of the violent imposition of gender but a *natural* result of the envy of each sex for the other (unlike Freud, Bettelheim believes that penis envy has a parallel in men) is totally contradicted by almost all Maghrebian texts on the subject.

3. In *La révolution du langage poétique,* Julia Kristeva characterizes Lautréamont's and Mallarmé's poetry—which she labels as avant-garde—as consisting of a language closer to the mother's body. The theme or trope of a return to the womb is also common in the works of other nineteenth-century French poets.

4. In her reading of Freud's "Mourning and Melancholia" and *The Ego and the Id,* Judith Butler describes what must be lost in the consolidation of gender identity: "Because identifications substitute for object relations, and identifications are the consequence of loss, gender identification is a kind of melancholia in which the sex of the prohibited object is internalized as a prohibition" (*Gender Trouble* 63). Bouhdiba's "bouquet onirique de la féminité que chaque homme porte en soi" could be described as such a melancholia.

enfant" (46). ("Deep inside, I remain inconsolable like a lost child. Placed brutally face to face with myself in this way, I notice that my attitude is like that of a child as well" [26].) This identification, like Alexandre's in *La statue de sel,* can be read as one source of the emasculation that the adult narrator is dealt by his revolutionary wife. The inclusion of a childhood narrative in *Qui se souvient* (a narrative of revolution) suggests (like Djebar's *L'amour, la fantasia*) that childhood narratives can be an integral part of combat literature. In Dib's novel, childhood narrative is inseparable from the demise of the narrator's masculinity carried out by his wife.

Memmi: Memory as Emasculation

"To be penetrated," writes Leo Bersani, "is to abdicate power" (212). He describes an "infinitely . . . seductive and intolerable image of a grown man, legs high in the air, unable to refuse the suicidal ecstasy of being a woman" (212). Though his description is of a homophobic stereotype of gay men in the time of AIDS, it might just as easily be applied to Dib's narrator, who also embodies what Silverman calls "male subjectivity at the margins." Like penetration for Bersani, Silverman's marginal male subjectivity involves "[s]aying 'no' to power" (3). In describing a "heterosexual association of anal sex with a self-annihilation," Bersani also marks being penetrated, for men, as disruptive of male subjectivity (222). We have already seen how a victory over male subjectivity accompanies the loss of authority experienced by Dib's narrator. As in Silverman's description, his narrator's experience of specularity when the fireball/Nafissa stares at the narrator ("la roue de feu m'aborda comme pour me dévisager") might also be associated with his joy of emasculation. Likewise, the *jouissance* Memmi's narrator experiences in identifying with the "victim" chosen for circumcision at the *kouttab* is based at least in part on his identification with the boy as object of the other boys' gazes. At the moment of the boy's "circumcision," the narrator cannot take his eyes off the victim's penis: "Pourquoi, pourtant, ne suis-je pas arrivé à tourner la tête, pourquoi mes yeux sont-ils restés fixés sur le minuscule membre blanc, que je devinais de loin, dans la lueur qui tombait des soupiraux verdis par les moisissures sans âge?" (193). (Why, then, was I not able to turn my head, why were my eyes glued to the tiny, white member, that I made out from a distance in the glimmer of light that fell from the moldy light vents turned green through the ages? [my trans.].) Since the victim not only risks castration but is also a spectacle and the object of other boys' gazes, the narrator must identify with his position as the object of a male gaze as well as with this fear of castration. The narrator's *jouissance* therefore results in part from an enjoyment of specularity. One might thus interpret Alexandre's joy of specularity and castration as a challenge to his male ego, similar to the more explicit one Dib's narrator experiences. In Memmi as well then, the resurrection of childhood memories, specifically those related to circumcision, have an emasculating effect on the novel's narrator who rereads the circumcision—which is supposed to separate him from the feminine—in a way that actually strengthens his connection to it.

In "This We Know to Be the Carnal Israel" (1992), Daniel Boyarin describes the erotic nature of circumcision as a bodily marker of belonging to a religious community: "The physical act of circumcision *in the flesh*, which prepares the male Jew for sexual intercourse, is also that which prepares him for divine intercourse. It is difficult, therefore, to escape the association of sexual and mystical experience in this [midrashic] text" (493). Likewise, Memmi emphasizes the erotic aspect of circumcision as a sign of alliance with God when he writes:

> Nous étions tous attirés par ce mystère auquel nous avions participé, malgré nous, dans l'inconscience de nos premiers jours, qui nous scellait dans la grande chaîne sacrée qui, à travers les siècles remontait jusqu'à Dieu. Ce mystère nous attirait par l'extraordinaire consécration qu'il promettait, nous troublait parce que l'alliance avec Dieu était sexuelle, nous effrayait parce qu'ils [*sic*] s'imposait à nous avec cette fatale nécessité, que nous voyions tous les jours enchaîner nos frères et voisins nouveau-nés. (190)

> We all felt attracted toward this mystery in which each of us had taken part, against his will and in the unconsciousness of his first days of life; it was indeed the act that bound us within the great and sacred chain which, throughout the centuries, went all the way back to God. The extraordinary promise of consecration contained within this mystery appealed to us and disturbed us because the covenant with God was of a sexual nature; at the same time, it terrified us because it imposed itself on us like a fatal necessity in[to] which we saw, each day, our [newly born] brothers and neighbors [dragged]. (171–72)

In his analysis of Rabbinical writings, Boyarin also describes circumcision as a feminizing procedure:

> Circumcision is understood by the midrash as feminizing the male, thus making him open to receive the divine speech and vision of God. . . . Israel is a female partner with respect to God, but many of the adepts in Israel

are male. An event must take place in their bodies that will enable them to take the position of the female, and that event is circumcision. . . . This transformation is still powerfully enacted at the ritual level today, when at a traditional circumcision ceremony the newly circumcised boy is addressed: "And I say to you [feminine pronoun!]: In your [feminine] blood, you [feminine] shall live." These texts strongly suggest the possibility that circumcision was understood somehow as rendering the male somewhat feminine, thus making it possible for the male Israelite to have communion with a male deity. (495–96, Boyarin's brackets)

Circumcision thus prepares man for intercourse with God, who, as the active partner, penetrates the man. Alexandre's joy of castration, therefore, might be just as related to being penetrated as that of Dib's narrator. On the surface, Boyarin's description of circumcision in midrashic texts might seem to contradict Muslim experience, which is supposed to make a man out of a boy. Boughedir's *Halfaouine,* however, will show that the separation from the feminine circumcision is supposed to mark cannot occur without the threat of castration, which also threatens to destroy the very same masculinity it supposedly allows.

Halfaouine: A Boy's Expulsion from the Feminine

Before his expulsion, Noura has the freedom to cross the divide that more or less separates the sexes. He hangs out with women at the circumcision celebration and is admitted into the *hammam* with women; in short, his presence in the space known as the *harem* does not threaten the women or the social order founded on gender distinction (and separation). His expulsion from the *hammam* is therefore, in a larger sense as well, an expulsion from the women's spaces he had access to as long as he was not (yet) a man, what Serhane describes as a "second *sevrage affectif*" (160) (second affective weaning). In Bouhdiba's version of a boy's expulsion from the women's *hammam,* the separation from the realm of women occurs with few regrets:

> This, as we have seen, is precisely the moment when the boy, excluded from the women's *hammam,* begins to make his way to the men's *hammam.* It is like a rite of initiation into the hitherto foreign world of men. Behavior in the *hammam* is restructured at the same moment one is taken from one's mother, so that the first visit to the men's *hammam* is like a consecration, a confirmation, and a compensation. It is the confirmation of one's membership in the world of men. . . . (208–9)

The typical boy is immediately welcomed into the men's *hammam,* where his father's friends congratulate him. He lives this first visit as a consolidation of his manhood. Bouhdiba describes the expulsion, which he discusses in two passages, as more private and much milder than the one in *Halfaouine:* "Il faudrait que le jeune homme se laisse aller à un geste inconsidéré ou à un propos déplacé pour que la tenancière vienne dire doucement à la mamam: «Ton fils a grandi, ne l'amène plus avec toi»" (206). (The young man would inadvertently have to make an inconsiderate gesture or an awkward statement for the attendant to come and say softly to the mother, "Your son has grown up, don't bring him with you anymore.") In the second passage, he writes, "[N]'a-t-on pas été rejeté par le hammam des femmes? N'a-t-on pas entendu la tenancière affirmer: «C'est un grand»? N'a-t-on pas reçu les félicitations des amis et compagnons du père que l'on rencontre maintenant pour la première fois en petite tenue . . . ?" (209). (Weren't we rejected by the women's *hammam?* Didn't we hear the attendant say, "He's a big boy now"? Weren't we congratulated by our father's friends and buddies, whom we met for the first time in scanty clothing . . . ?) Bouhdiba's remarks on the *hammam,* however, were originally published in a journal article titled "Le hammam: Contribution à une psychanalyse de l'Islam" (1964), in which he describes the expulsion as being considerably harsher. The earlier version of the first passage (which describes a simple, private, and polite request in the later version) actually describes an expulsion: "C'est alors l'expulsion, pas trop méchante d'ailleurs" (9). (Then comes expulsion, but not too mean.) The earlier version of the second passage describes the expulsion as occasionally violent: "[N]'a-t-il pas été rejeté et parfois même de manière violente du hammam des femmes?" (11). (Wasn't he rejected and sometimes even violently from the women's *hammam?*) This mention of violence, though perhaps contradicting the first version of the first passage ("pas trop méchante"), actually corresponds to Noura's experience of a traumatic experience carried out publicly.[5]

Childhood narrative represents a return to origins, the source of life, but also of subjectivity, which is always gendered. At the source of gender, there is a violence, and for gender to be naturalized, this violence must

---

5. According to Chebel (1995), boys of Noura's age are no longer permitted to bathe with their mothers: "There was a time when prepubescent boys of eight or nine years were allowed to enter the *hammam* without the women as a whole seeing a valid reason to complain, as long as the little boy displayed no sexual curiosity. Today it is no longer possible to convince the *hammam* attendant: boys more than five or six years old must go with the men" (457).

be forgotten (at least as a form of violence), in other words accepted as just the way things are. In Bouhdiba's subsequent rewriting of the boy's expulsion, he also seems to have forgotten the violence at the origin of manhood that consecrates the separation of the sexes. If the consolidation and self-assured embodiment of masculinity require forgetting the violence at the origin of gender, many Maghrebian texts insist on remembering this very violence. *Halfaouine* thus reveals a violence at the origin of masculinity in parallel with Ben Jelloun's account of the imposition of femininity. That circumcision would come into play in the remembering of this violence, I would suggest, is not a coincidence. As we have seen in *La statue de sel,* the possibility of a second circumcision can provoke the threat of castration. Bouhdiba (1975) also associates the fear of castration with a second circumcision in describing "la crainte qu'on ne la lui coupe s'il n'est pas encore circoncis ou qu'on ne recoupe ce qui reste après la circoncision" (224) (the fear that they will cut it off if he isn't circumcised and the fear they will cut off what's left after circumcision), and Crapanzano writes, "Boys are sometimes told that they will undergo a second circumcision if they are not good" (51). Noura, as well, is confronted with the possibility of a second circumcision as he lingers around women at the circumcision ceremony when a woman grabs him and jokingly informs him that he, too, will be circumcised. When Noura responds that he is already circumcised, his tormentor threatens the removal of the bit of penis he has left, thereby explicitly associating circumcision and castration. Another woman reproaches the first: now a man, Noura should be called Monsieur Noureddine.[6] The first woman replies that, with such a small penis, Noura cannot possibly be a man.[7] Instead of physically castrating him, she cuts him down to size, so to speak, and thereby denies his masculinity. *Halfaouine* makes clear the association of circumcision and castration when Noura's brother is circumcised and, just after his expulsion, Noura simultaneously grabs his own groin, thereby reliving his own circumcision. Since Noura is already circumcised, reliving circumcision can only take the form of castration. The women's threat at the party is thereby realized; Noura *is* circumcised a second time as he resurrects his first circumcision to experience it again. The memory of circumcision, if understood as a reliving, would be the equivalent of a

---

6. In Tunisia, Noura is a nickname for Noureddine, but it is also a woman's name. In becoming a man, Noura will therefore abandon the name of woman for the name of man.

7. "Noura" is also a diminutive in parallel with Noura's supposedly small penis. Many thanks to Hédi Abdel-Jaouad for information on the significance of this nickname.

second circumcision and, therefore, castration, which would explain Alexandre's anxiety and resulting *jouissance* both at the *kouttab* and in the streetcar.

At this point in the film, Noura's father enters, carrying a basket of vegetables. At first, the irruption of a man into a women's space interrupts the women's talk. The film cuts to very black, thick coffee boiling over, marking this male irruption as a contamination. But the breach of separation of the sexes does more than disrupt the women; it also disturbs the man, who casts his eyes downward during the entire period of his presence in the women's space.[8] The father then rushes out of the women's space as the women joke about the phallic shapes of the carrots, cucumbers, and eggplants in the basket.[9] He runs away from these women who, like Shérazade, are making a mockery of the penis, supposed site of manhood, as if his presence in this women's space could adversely affect his own masculinity. Mosteghanemi writes, "A boy instinctively learns to flee the world of women as if he feared being contaminated by this misfortune woman seems to have a knack for spreading around her" (54). Femininity is thus contagious, and it is perhaps this contagion that Noura's father flees. His father then forces him to repeat the following rules of being a man: (1) a man does not cry; and (2) a man does not hang around women's skirts. When Noura cannot remember the second rule (the precise rule he had been breaking), his father strikes him. Becoming a man here requires learning a script whose successful performance will grant access to male privilege. His father's punishment for forgetting his lines reinforces the association of castration with hanging around women. Noura therefore experiences his expulsion from this group of women, which parallels his subsequent expulsion from the *hammam,* as a form of punishment. To be a man, Noura can no longer frequent women's spaces. To do so would be to risk castration (as the women literally threaten him), contamination by the feminine, and the father's punishment. Manhood, therefore, exists because of a threat of punishment—castration.

Before Noura can become a man, he must be castrated. Manhood thus exists thanks to a double bind—castration could take away man-

8. Downcast eyes are often seen as a sign of women's respect for men. Cf. Ben Jelloun's *Les yeux baissés.*

9. A woman had just accused the first woman—who threatened Noura with castration—of taking out her frustrations on Noura. According to the former, the latter was only releasing her frustrations with her husband, who spends all his time away from her at work. Implying that her frustrations are sexual and hinting at the use of dildos, another woman added that the first woman's husband sold vegetables yet had no cucumber to offer her.

hood, but without castration, manhood cannot exist—and this double bind is especially evident at the moment of circumcision. Though "[c]ircumcision is *said* to make a man and a Muslim of a boy" (Crapanzano 51, emphasis added), as Chebel (1988) explains, the privileges of manhood are postponed until a later date: "For one must admit that if circumcision marks a stage in a boy's life, it is certainly not in favor of a true acceptance into the world of complete masculinity, which only happens at puberty. In fact, everything functions as if the boy paid the price by anticipation, long before the promised sexual enjoyment, as one sees, to take only one example, in African rituals" (174). He also describes what he labels as a typical exchange between father and son at the moment of circumcision. The father says, "«Voyons! Ne pleure pas, c'est la fille qui pleure.» L'enfant répond: «J'ai envie d'être une fille, une fille c'est mieux»" (177). ("Come on! Don't cry, only girls cry." The boy replies: "I'd rather be a girl, it's better to be a girl.") Circumcision is relived not as the attainment of a privilege, which is postponed, but as a trauma that, allowed to haunt the present of masculinity, even threatens the privilege it is supposed to give access to. Remembering a time when male privilege, put off until some faraway future time, did not seem to be worth its price seems to beg the question as to whether it is still worth it. In the case of Noura's brother (who is probably not older than three), it is clear that he will not be expelled from the female world immediately after circumcision, just as Noura has had continued access to the female sphere up until this point. Remembering childhood brings back the threat to masculinity that circumcision (with its accompanying fear of castration) poses to adult male subjectivity. Crapanzano discusses the connection between the memory of circumcision and the fear of castration: "Moroccan men often joke about circumcision, especially in the baths. They talk of the mutilated and those with jagged foreskins and those—they are actually very rare—who have lost their penises. There is much anxiety. The lines between manhood and womanhood, that great social-symbolic cleavage in the Arab world, is not very clear after all" (51–52). He associates this castration anxiety with definitional distinctions between masculinity and femininity that become more unclear when the topic of circumcision comes up. Interestingly enough, Crapanzano cites the *hammam* as the site of such anxiety. In *Halfaouine* as well, the *hammam* is not only the site of a definitional crisis in the distinction between masculinity and femininity, but is also related to anxiety about castration. Whereas for Bouhdiba, gender distinctions are consolidated by a boy's expulsion from

the *hammam* (which represents the triumph of masculinity), Noura lives
this expulsion more as a loss to be mourned.

Later, however, Noura like Bouhdiba seems to forget this violence:
after the expulsion, because he refuses to go to the men's *hammam* with
his father, his mother instructs the orphan girl she has taken in to wash
Noura at home while the other women go to the *hammam*. Upon returning, they find her undressed with Noura giving her a massage, and
Noura's parents decide to kick her out of their home. The night before
her departure, Noura goes to bed with her. After this first heterosexual
experience, he seems to recover from his loss and remembers the *hammam* as the idealized site of the complete satisfaction of his heterosexual
gaze, visually represented by the film through a flashback. Noura's memory, however, constitutes a rewriting that projects a young man's heterosexual desire back onto his supposedly preheterosexual boyhood. The
filmic text also contains the pre-expulsion *hammam* scenes that contradict Noura's postexpulsion fantasies of the *hammam* as a heterosexual
utopia. While the character Noura forgets that his heterosexuality was
violently imposed, the film does not: a character's forgetting thus inserted
in a text is therefore not forgotten (like the childhood described by Zerdoumi) but remembered.

In contrast with his subsequent idealization of heterosexual desire,
immediately after expulsion, Noura holds a grudge against his friends for
forcing him into heterosexuality. In a scene of homosocial bonding prior
to the expulsion, Noura's friends push him towards heterosexual desire,
which he seems to be discovering for the first time. The narrative of his
own heterosexual gaze would improve his standing in a group of young
men who have yet to affirm his masculinity. Because he always resisted
visits to the *hammam,* his mother reacts to his request for a bath with total
disbelief, which signals that, previously, Noura's trips to the *hammam* did
not elicit a heterosexual desire strong enough to motivate the visit. The
hammam attendant likewise detects the difference between man and boy
in the presence of Noura's heterosexual gaze.[10] Heterosexual desire, almost imposed in this scenario, comes into being at the urging of homosocial peer pressure and as a part of the apprenticeship of becoming a man.
In *Halfaouine,* the male role necessarily involves a performance of heterosexuality, and the apprenticeship of masculinity involves learning hetero-

10. In *Dreams of Trespass* (1994), Fatima Mernissi describes her cousin's expulsion from the wom-
en's *hammam,* which seems to have resulted from a similar gaze: "Then came the day that Samir was
thrown out of the *hammam* because a woman noticed that he had 'a man's stare'" (239).

sexual desire. After his expulsion, when Noura meets his friends in the street, they attempt to initiate homosocial bonding in which he can boast about heterosexual exploits, but he refuses to talk and runs away angry. At this moment, the loss that heterosexuality requires seems not to be worth the privilege it will later grant.

At the moment of his brother's circumcision, as well, the price of male privilege (both circumcision and expulsion) seems quite high indeed. This moment is also a key one for the spectator. In Memmi's performance of circumcision, the tension he describes consists in not knowing whether the performance will "only" be a performance, or whether the victim will be circumcised again and lose more than his foreskin (which is no longer there). Boughedir's film plays with a similar tension; because it is part of a filmic narrative, the circumcision scene in *Halfaouine* is also a performance. Will the boy actor playing the role of Noura's brother be circumcised in "real life" as the scene is filmed? Boughedir defers the moment of suspending the filming of the about-to-be-circumcised penis until the last possible second. Though the spectator does not actually see blood or the removal of foreskin, it is hard to image that the boy actor is not "actually" circumcised. In other words, the circumcisor's scissors seem to have already passed the "point of no return" before which circumcision might be stopped once the penis is no longer being filmed. Rather than the foreskin, however, the film is cut; through montage, the cut replaces circumcision on screen. *Halfaouine* toys with the danger, pain, and perhaps even pleasure of circumcision so as to provide spectators with the possibility of sharing Noura's identification with his brother as Alexandre identifies with the victim on stage. When read through other Maghrebian allegories of reading childhood narratives, however, the film allows spectators to turn Noura's pain into a pleasure similar to Alexandre's, the joy of castration. Memmi gives circumcision new meaning and rewrites narratives of coming to masculinity by using the very circumcision that grants access to manhood in order to bring about the demise of that same manhood. In its remembering of circumcision through performance, therefore, *La statue de sel* offers a paradigm through which to understand Noura's experience of his brother's circumcision as a remembering of his own. When, unlike Noura, the adult male subject no longer flees the feminine for fear of being contaminated or castrated, masculinity—which is predicated on this fear—can never be quite the same.

Chapter   Thirteen

ALLEGORIES   OF   THE   QUEER   NATION

Maghrebian literature offers a number of models of returning to the past. The interpretive strategy of returning to read the past through the present, as in Woodhull's reading of Kateb, has been this study's implicit project from the beginning. Understanding the subversive role of sexual dissidence, marginal sexualities, and gender insubordination in postindependence novels has allowed us to understand how the struggle represented in combat literature was sexual all along. In the previous chapter, I began to apply the revolutionary emasculation that Dib formulated to some of the earlier works of Maghrebian literature in order to show how even the texts that first began to articulate an anticolonial consciousness shared this project of emasculation. Dib's inclusion of a childhood narrative in the premier combat novel of the Algerian Revolution suggests that the narratives of return to male childhood examined in the previous chapter might also serve as national allegories. This chapter considers the final aspect of this return; for the paradigmatic return to roots can also serve as an allegory of reading that urges the reader to return to the origins of Maghrebian literature in order to deconstruct the Nation as narrative and reveal it as having been queer all along.

In Jameson's formulation of the genre of national allegory (1986), the "private" aspect of the "third-world" text "invested with a properly libidinal dynamic" is what "project[s] a political dimension" (69). The politicization of sexuality in Jameson's paradigm of reading offers interesting possibilities for queer readings of Maghrebian national allegories in the form of childhood narratives. He characterizes "first-world" culture as having "a radical split between the private and the public, between the poetic and the political, between what we have come to think of as the domain of sexuality and the unconscious and that of the public world of classes, of the economic, and of secular political power: in other words, Freud versus Marx" (69). In contrast, in "third-world" national allegory, the personal (and therefore the sexual) is indeed political; the very technique of using the private to allegorize the public bridges this split and deconstructs these binaries. As postindependence Maghrebian writers use revelations of sexual transgressions to "mess up" the political projects of national elites, in the earliest works of Maghrebian fiction, national allegory similarly carries out a sexual intrusion into the political.

The year 1950 saw the first publication of Mouloud Feraoun's *Le fils du pauvre*. Mouloud Mammeri's *La colline oubliée* and Mohammed Dib's *La grande maison* were published in 1952, and Memmi's *La statue de sel* in 1953. And in 1954 Driss Chraïbi's *Le passé simple* appeared. Though there was a Maghrebian literature prior to these works, literary histories that reread Maghrebian literature through the political outcomes of struggles for independence often set up these years as a foundational moment. In his description of "ethnographic" literature, Déjeux (1973) addressed political critiques of this early Maghrebian literature and inscribed it in a narrative of progress wherein combat literature would mark an advancement in political consciousness over its more "naïve" predecessors:

> A so-called "ethnographic" (or documentary) literature was written if not for the pleasure of the European reader, at least to enter his framework, in any case while taking him into account. Folkloric and regionalist themes are abundant as an immediate response to readers' curiosity. However, ethnographic details are not always retained by the writer to please the Other; certain authors describe their society and their life as a part of a search for identity, and their literature thereby takes on the meaning of unveiling and contesting. This so-called "ethnographic" literature, in fact, taps into the best and the worst, and Maghrebian critics today are doubtlessly wrong in tending all too often to hold it up *en bloc* to public ridicule [la vouer en bloc aux gémonies]. (37)

Déjeux includes, among others, Feraoun, Dib, and Mammeri in this category, while placing Memmi and Chraïbi in the category of "littérature de refus et de contestation" (38) (contestatory literature of refusal), but here, as in other accounts, ethnographic literature is closely associated with the early works of Maghrebian literature in French as well as with the childhood narratives that tend to characterize it. Although Déjeux chastises nationalist critics who reject this category "en bloc" and ques-

tions the link between writing "ethnographic" literature and the assumption of a European readership whose exoticizing gaze may or may not be
satisfied by it, his mention of regionalism especially stands out, since it
was a label often applied to Berber writers who wrote about Berber topics.
Both Feraoun and Mammeri fall into this category and were seen by some
as betraying the national cause because they stressed their specificity (i.e.
their difference from Arab culture). One might even wonder whether it
would have been possible for a Berber writer dealing with Berber subject
matters to escape these criticisms. One may also discern a peculiar parallel
between nationalist condemnations of ethnographic or regionalist literature and accusations that feminism and marginal sexualities betray the
national cause. This parallel, I would suggest, is not merely a coincidence:
Déjeux uses two words, "dévoilement" and "contestation," that also appear in Ben Jelloun's description of many Maghrebian novels' sexual politics. As well, in many of the early works of Maghrebian fiction, ethnographic representation works in tandem with representations of marginal
sexualities and the deconstruction of sexual difference to disrupt nationalist narratives of national identity.

In previous chapters, I have considered critiques that accuse Boudjedra and Ben Jelloun of being inauthentic or pandering to the pornographic and exoticizing desires of European readers. I have also mentioned parallel criticisms of Djebar's early work that accused her of
ignoring the political events of the Algerian Revolution. As Kaye and
Zoubir write, "Feraoun's treatment of traditional Kabylia was used [by
the French media] as a total vindication of the French 'civilizing mission.'" They also point out that "[f]or a long time Feraoun was seen as a
colonized writer . . ." (80). Khatibi (1968) adds, "Accused of romanticizing misery [Taxé de «misérabiliste»] during the Algerian war, Feraoun is
reincorporated after Independence, now that everyday life takes its re-
venge on political events" (51–52). In Chraïbi's case, it was his cavalier
treatment of sexuality and Islam that elicited a strong reaction from nationalist critics.[1] He was accused of betraying his nation, playing into
racist stereotypes of Moroccans, and collaborating with the colonizer.
After these criticisms, he even disavowed *Le passé simple*.

Farida Boualit notes that Feraoun and Mammeri "were accused, of-

1. See Yetiv (95–96, 107–8) and Basfao for an account of the "affaire du *Passé simple*." For an
additional account of the criticism of Mammeri and Chraïbi, see Khatibi 1968, 25–27.

ten without nuance, of being assimilationist writers, without however being associated with the Algerian writers of the '20s who were more obviously so" (26). Even the harshest critics of what, in the Maghreb at least, has been called the 1950s generation differentiated these writers from the pre-'50s generation. Fanon ([1959] 1962), eschewing the category of ethnographic literature altogether, also contrasts the '50s generation with an earlier so-called assimilationist literature:

> In the second phase we find the native [colonisé] is disturbed [ébranlé]; he decides to remember. . . . Past happenings of the byegone [*sic*] days of his ch[il]dhood [De vieux épisodes d'enfance] will be brought up out of the depths of his memory; old legends will be reinterpreted in the light of a borrowed estheticism and of a conception of the world which was discovered under other skies.
>
> Sometimes this literature of just-before-the-battle [cette littérature de pré-combat] is dominated by humor and by allegory. . . . (222; 162 in original)

As opposed to other critics who call this literature ethnographic, for Fanon, in his own specifically revolutionary reading of literary history, the '50s generation was already political. Interestingly enough, in addition to being a "replongée" (resubmersion [my trans.]) in childhood, this precombat literature also resorts to allegory. Nationalist critiques of "ethnographic" literature seem to have forgotten Fanon's inclusion of these works in an anticolonial literary history, just as recent debates on the validity of national allegory (including Jameson's own formulation of it) have forgotten Fanon's use of the genre to characterize precombat literature.

In his discussion of a Guinean novel that was subjected to similar criticism, Christopher L. Miller (1990) has written, "African readers are now less likely to demand explicit political content and are more attuned to the symbolic politics of *L'Enfant noir;* there is a greater willingness to see *L'Enfant noir* as a work of subtly *sublimated,* rather than *repressed* politics" (124). As the struggle for independence recedes further into the past, the same might also be said for these early works of Maghrebian literature. Ten years after the scandal set off by *Le passé simple,* when the Moroccan poet Abdellatif Laâbi rehabilitated the novel, Chraïbi retracted his earlier disavowal. In the passage quoted above, Khatibi points out that Feraoun's novel has been rehabilitated; it has also been consecrated as part of the canon by Algerian educational institutions (Achour 11–29), perhaps in part because the author was assassinated by the OAS during the final months of the revolution.[2] Feraoun was therefore a convenient candidate to be made into a hero by the new governing elite in the manner described and criticized by Djebar in *Le blanc de l'Algérie*. Reconsidering this criticism now, therefore, might seem somewhat like kicking a dead dog. However, one of the reasons why antiethnographic criticism is much less common today is that its nationalist revolutionary motives have also faded into the background. In a study whose project is to recuperate certain ideals of independence struggles and formulate an anticolonial but nonexclusionary nationalism, reconsidering this aspect of an earlier nationalist criticism is imperative.

Ethnography Queered: Mouloud Feraoun's *Le fils du pauvre*

Feraoun offers one of the most detailed fictional accounts of the Kabyle system of honor as well as the way this system is mapped onto the gendered topography of Kabyle society. Pierre Bourdieu, in "The Sentiment of Honour in Kabyle Society" (1966) articulated the classical account of this system, and it might be tempting to read Feraoun as literary evidence in support of Bourdieu's arguments. I shall sketch out such a reading here but concentrate on how Feraoun diverges from this account and how his novel might be read as a gendered allegory of French attacks on Algerian property structures. Because precolonial property structures are associated with a childhood past in a female sphere in this gendered allegory, Feraoun dislodges the economy of honor from its usual gendered associations in nationalist discourses that troped the French colonization of Algeria as an affront to male honor.

Bourdieu argues that "values of honour constitute the true basis of the Kabyle political order" (229). He begins by describing a number of cases in which the rules of honor were misinterpreted by Kabyles who had grown unaccustomed to the workings of the system of honor while living outside of Kabylia. To better understand the system's workings, Bourdieu paradoxically examines these examples of its breakdown due to an intrusion of external values. It is the third such case that is the most helpful in an "ethnographic" reading of Feraoun's novel:

2. The OAS (Organisation Armée Secrète) was a seditious faction of the French Army that attempted to maintain French control in Algeria even after the de Gaulle government had decided to grant independence. At one point, it also attempted to invade France and overthrow the metropolitan government.

In a third village a certain incident had pushed to its height the tension between the two moieties (*eçffuf*) which in their modern degenerated form appear more like leagues or factions. One of the *eçffuf*, fed up with the situation, went to visit an important member of the opposing moiety, accompanied by a whole train of dignitaries . . . whom he had transported, lodged and fed. To everyone except the person who was its object—a Kabyle who'd lived abroad and had little knowledge of local custom—this was a ritual. The custom was that, after kissing the negotiators on the forehead, one accepted their proposals and called for peace. (196)

This Kabyle, however, accused the dignitaries of siding with those who had fed them and offended all those present.

A fight breaks outs between the two *eçffuf* (written *çof* by Feraoun) in *Le fils du pauvre* when the novel's narrator, Fouroulou Menrad, refuses to back away from Boussad N'amer, who is crafting a basket in the *djema*, or public square. When Boussad's knife slips, Fouroulou is injured. Rather than explaining the incident as an accident, however, Fouroulou claims, "[I]l a voulu me tuer" (32). (He wanted to kill me.) The family's response is swift:

> Cela suffit. Mon oncle file comme une trombe. Instantanément, il a ima-giné la scène: ce Boussad, d'un çof rival, armé d'un couteau, se jette sur son neveu sans défense. Il veut tuer l'enfant, supprimer le dernier des Menrad . . . Mon oncle court, vole à la djema armé d'un gourdin. Une bouffée de haine lui monte du cœur à la tête. Il va venger son honneur, il va imposer aux gens le respect de la famille.
>
> Ma mère se précipite derrière lui, entraînant le reste de ma famille. (32, Feraoun's suspension points)

> That was sufficient. My uncle stormed out like a whirlwind. Instantly, he imagined the scene: armed with a knife, this Boussad, from a rival *çof*, jumped on his defenseless nephew. He wants to kill the child, eliminate the last of the Menrads . . . Armed with a club, my uncle runs, flies to the *djema*. A burst of hate rises from his heart to his head. He is going to avenge his honor, he is going to impose respect for the family on other people.
>
> My mother hurries behind him, dragging along the rest of my family.

Bourdieu explains, "[T]he slightest quarrels always threatened to become larger in scope, since the honour of all might be affronted in the honour of the individual and as soon as the incident occurred the moieties were mobilized" (201). Indeed, the fight in *Le fils du pauvre* becomes a veritable battle: "La djema se remplit de plus en plus de spectateurs et de lutteurs. Aucun spectateur n'est indifférent. Les vieilles inimitiés se réveilleront;

d'anciens comptes qui n'attendent qu'un prétexte peuvent se régler" (32). (The *djema* was filled by more and more onlookers and fighters. No onlooker is indifferent. Old hostilities will awaken; former grudges only waiting for a pretext can be settled.)

As opposed to Bourdieu's example, wherein one of the fighting parties requests the intervention of dignitaries, in *Le fils du pauvre,* the *amir,* or village leader, intervenes of his own accord and demands that the fighting cease. Bourdieu explains the dignitaries' role as follows: "In the midst of the discussion, mediators intervene: their task is to accuse and find fault with the party from whom pardon has been sought, so that a balance may be restored and that the supplicating party may avoid complete humiliation . . ." (196). In Feraoun's novel, however, as opposed to Bourdieu's example, there is no "supplicating party"; the dignitaries intervene to restore peace for the benefit of the entire village (and paradoxically, establishing peace means declaring enemies). Yet restoring peace does not mean restoring order, for the battle, rather than constituting a breakdown in social order, as it might seem to an outside observer, actually signifies its functioning perfectly: "These political and warlike leagues pursued their hostilities in the form of a strictly regulated game, of an ordered competition which, far from threatening social order, tended on the contrary to safeguard it by making it possible for the spirit of competition, the point of honour, the *nif,* to express itself in prescribed and institutionalized forms" (Bourdieu 201). The battle Feraoun describes represents social structuring along the lines of the code of honor and is the means by which the system of honor is inscribed upon village life.

The ordering of society through the rules of honor also occurs along gendered lines. The fight breaks out in the first place because Fouroulou, staking a claim to his male privilege, refuses to leave the *djema:* "J'ai ma place à la djema comme tous les autres. . . . Tous les marmots du village apprennent de bonne heure qu'ils ont leur place à la djema. Le moindre rejeton mâle y a autant de droits que n'importe qui" (30–31). (I have a right to the *djema* just like everybody else. . . . All the village brats learn at a young age that they have a place in the *djema.* The puniest male runt has just as much right to be there as anybody else.) Even the battle theater's *mise en scène* is choreographed through a separation of the genders: "A une dizaine de mètres plus loin, dans une ruelle sans issue, se déroule la bataille des femmes, bruyante et grotesque réplique. Elles forment, elles aussi, une grappe tumultueuse et multicolore où dominent le noir des chignons et le rouge des foutas" (32). (Ten or so meters away, in a cul-de-sac alley, the women waged their own battle, a noisy, grotesque retort. They, too, made up a tumultuous and multicolored bunch dominated by the black of hair buns and the red of scarves around their hips.) This gendered division of space, as Bourdieu points out, is not limited to battles: "In the Kabyle village the two areas are distinctly separate; the path that leads to the fountain avoids the domain of the men" (221). "The fountain," he adds, "is to the women what the *thajmaâth* is to the men. . . . [T]he house being the domain of women, the men are to some degree excluded from it. The place of the man is out of doors, in the fields or in the assembly, among other men. This is something taught very early to the young boy" (222).[3] Feraoun describes a similar sexual division of space: "Le fellah n'a guère l'habitude de passer ses heures de repos dans sa masure au milieu des femmes et de la marmaille. La djema est un refuge sûr, toujours disponible et gratuit" (16). (The *fellah* [or peasant] is not at all used to spending his resting hours in his hovel amongst women and young'uns. The *djema* is a safe refuge, always available and free.)

Both Bourdieu and Feraoun refer to a system of education within the system of honor, be it the male privilege of access to the *djema* that "[t]ous les marmots du village apprennent de bonne heure" or the distinction between house and *djema,* "taught very early to the young boy." Like Noura, Fouroulou is a student of masculinity, and much attention is devoted to his lessons: "Il est clair que mon oncle n'avait pas tort de vouloir me donner une éducation virile. Mais il y mettait trop d'enthousiasme et de parti pris. Je n'ai guère profité de ses leçons" (30). (It's clear my uncle wasn't wrong to want to give me an education in manliness. But he was too enthusiastic and partial about it. I didn't learn anything at all from his lessons.) Unlike the male narrators of other childhood narratives examined herein, Fouroulou most distinguishes himself by failing to embody masculine ideals. As his parents' oldest son and the extended family's oldest grandson, Fouroulou experiences the burden of additional expectations vis-à-vis his masculinity: "J'étais destiné à représenter la force et le courage de la famille. Lourd destin pour le bout d'homme chétif que j'étais" (25). (I was destined to represent the family's strength and courage. A heavy fate for the small bit of a frail man I was.) However,

---

3. Where Bourdieu writes "thajmaâth," Feraoun uses "djema," a French transliteration of the Arabic. In Feraoun's first uses of the word, however, he spells it "tadjemaït."

he can only disappoint his relatives' expectations: ". . . [M]es parents voy-
aient s'écrouler, peu à peu, leur rêve de faire de moi le lion du quartier,
plus tard le lion du village" (26). (Bit by bit, the dream of making me the
lion of first the neighborhood and later the village fell apart right before
my relatives' eyes.) Not unlike Noura, Fouroulou receives an "éducation
virile" that is regulated first and foremost through violence—the violence
he is allowed and/or expected to dish out as well as the violence he receives:

> Si j'avais affaire à un petit, [mon oncle] me permettait de lui donner la
> correction pourvu qu'après coup je me sauve ou me cache. Si on venait se
> plaindre, mon oncle me cherchait pour me punir, se gardait de me trouver,
> consolait l'enfant, promettait aux parents mon châtiment.
>
> S'il s'agissait d'un garçon de mon âge, je n'avais aucune raison de le
> craindre. Mon oncle faisait ressortir avec colère que l'avantage était de mon
> côté. . . . Par contre, il n'admettait pas qu'un garçon plus grand que moi
> me frappât ou me taquinât. (29)

> If I was dealing with someone young, my uncle allowed me to punish him
> as long as I ran away or hid afterwards. If anyone came to complain, my
> uncle looked for me to punish me, kept from finding me, consoled the
> child, promised the parents I would be chastised.
>
> If it was a boy my own age, I had no reason to be afraid of him. My
> uncle angrily pointed out that I had the advantage. . . . In contrast, he
> didn't allow an older boy to hit me or pick on me.

While not explicitly as a lesson or apprenticeship, this passage corresponds to one of the most important rules of honor. As Bourdieu explains, the "games" of honor can only be played among equals: "Whilst
the logic of disdain and humiliation brings together *a* freedom and *a*
nature, the dialectic of honour is exercised between two persons who,
by their very dialogue, recognize that they are each other's equals in hu-
manity and liberty" (198). Defending one's honor against someone who
is not one's equal paradoxically brings on one's dishonor: "To take
unfair advantage, to crush one's opponent, is to expose oneself to sharing
in the humiliation inflicted when some question of honour is really involved . . ." (199). In contradiction with Bourdieu's account, Fouroulou
is allowed to break these rules by beating up smaller and younger boys in
order to learn how to defend himself "like a man."

This rule also has a gendered exception that constitutes the greatest
contradiction both within the system of honor and between Bourdieu's

and Feraoun's accounts of it. Part of Fouroulou's "éducation virile" involves free reign in beating up his sisters:

> Je pouvais frapper impunément mes sœurs et quelquefois mes cousines: il fallait bien m'apprendre à donner des coups! . . . Pénétré de mon importance dès l'âge de cinq ans, j'abusai bientôt de mes droits. Je devins immédiatement un tyran pour la plus petite de mes sœurs, mon aînée de deux ans. (25)

> I could hit my sisters and, sometimes, my female cousins, without being punished: after all, I had to learn how to give punches! . . . Self-absorbed with my importance as early as five years old, I soon abused my rights. I immediately became a tyrant for my youngest sister, older than me by two years.

His training thus involves a behavior that should be considered dishonoring in this context, picking on girls and younger boys, who are not in a position to respond. There is one space, however, in which Fouroulou can escape the demands of masculinity. His unmarried aunt Khalti and his aunt Nana, whose husband lives in France, live together and are considered a part of the extended family. With his sister Baya, he spends a lot of time around them as they engage in women's work—weaving and making pottery. According to Bourdieu, "most tasks performed by women are held to be dishonouring for men" (225–26), but this female space seems to exempt Fouroulou from such concerns: "Nous formâmes bientôt une petite famille en marge de la grande, un cercle intime et égoïste" (42). (We soon formed a small family in the margins of the big one, an intimate, self-centered group.) When reread along the lines of the model provided by *Halfaouine*, Feraoun's presentation of this space can be situated in the narrative of becoming a man; the marginal space of Fouroulou's maternal aunts thus parallels the *hammam* from which Noura is expelled. Likewise, this space is brutally destroyed for Fouroulou when Nana dies during childbirth, and Khalti subsequently goes mad and eventually disappears.

Another gendered aspect of the system of honor is women's power to dishonor men: "She [the woman] must therefore be on her guard against acting in any way that might prejudice the prestige and reputation of the group" (Bourdieu 223). Likewise, when Khalti loses all sense of propriety during her madness, she spreads her legs, forcing men to look away. The greater fear of her leaving causes her family to lock her up: "Elle était jeune, elle pouvait aller en pays étranger, déshonorer la famille. Est-ce que des inconnus songeraient à épargner une folle?" (78). (She was young, she might have gone off to foreign lands, dishonor the family. Would strangers imagine sparing a madwoman.) Bourdieu explicitly describes how gender is mapped onto honor:

> What is *h'aram* (namely, taboo, in the exact sense), is essentially the sacred of the "left-hand," namely the intimate life, and more precisely, the feminine world, the world of the secret, enclosed space of the household, in contrast to the open world of the public square (*thajmaâth*), reserved for men. . . . The sacred of the "right-hand" is essentially "the rifles," that is to say the group of agnates, "sons of the paternal uncle," all those whose death must be avenged by blood and all those who are bound to carry out blood vengeance. . . . Thus, to the passivity of *h'urma*, continually threatened, and to the vulnerability of *h'aram*, of a feminine nature, is to be opposed the active susceptibility of *nif*, of a manly nature. (219)

It is precisely the *harem* that Fouroulou loses with Khalti's and Nana's deaths, which he describes as his "premier malheur" (70) (first misfortune).

The gendered system of honor is also mapped onto the narrative structure of *Le fils du pauvre*, which is divided into two parts, "La famille" (The Family) and "Le fils aîné" (The Eldest Son). The first part is framed by a narrator, who is not Fouroulou, and who presents it as Fouroulou's personal journal. The second part picks up where the journal leaves off and seems to be told by the same narrator who frames the entire novel with introductory prefaces to each part. The narrative of the first part supposedly exists in physical form, which the narrator takes out of Fouroulou's desk at the school in a Kabyle village where he teaches as an adult: "Tirons du tiroir de gauche le cahier d'écolier. Ouvrons-le. Fouroulou Menrad, nous t'écoutons" (10). (Let's take the schoolboy's notebook from the left drawer. Let's open it. Fouroulou Menrad, we're listening to you.) The first part, narrated in the first person, is associated with the left hand, explicitly labeled as feminine in Bourdieu's account.[4] If *Halfaouine* tells the story of a boy's expulsion from the feminine, *Le fils du pauvre* inscribes this separation onto the novel's structure.

---

4. This association between the left drawer of the notebook and Bourdieu's essay was made by Francesca Canadé Sautman in a graduate seminar on Maghrebian literature at the CUNY Graduate School. Many thanks for her permission to use this idea here.

In the previous chapter, I examined a number of accounts of male-subject formation, which requires a boy's separation from femininity. In *The Reproduction of Mothering*, Nancy Chodorow argues that in Western society, because of the sexual division of labor in raising children, girls are encouraged to identify with their primary caretakers (their mothers) as a part of the reproduction of motherhood. Female-subject formation therefore does not involve the same experience of separation from other subjects, particularly when that subject is the mother. Many male childhood narratives from the Maghreb parallel Chodorow's account of male-subject formation. The way Feraoun frames this story, however, contradicts the separation of the male-subject-in-formation from femininity. The subject "je" narrates only the first part of the novel, which not only describes Feraoun's growing up in a more female space, but is also structurally associated with the left-handed or feminine aspect of Kabyle society.

There is also a second way in which Feraoun's narrative is masculinized during the course of the novel. In the beginning, Fouroulou's family is headed not by a man, but a woman: "Ma grand-mère menait la maison avec une grande sûreté et se faisait obéir" (53). (My grandmother led the household with great self-assurance and was obeyed by all.) Though this fact may seem to make the family matriarchal by European standards, it could also be read as totally in keeping with Maghrebian patriarchal structures, since the head of the family, Tassadit, Fouroulou's grandmother, has acquired this status only after producing two sons and, with Fouroulou, a grandson; these men constitute the base of her power. When she dies, however, the family breaks up: "Il était donc bien vrai que ma grand-mère était le pilier de la communauté puisque l'une a cessé d'exister presque en même temps que l'autre" (54). (It was therefore quite true that my grandmother was the pillar of the community since the one ceased to exist almost at the same time as the other.) After her death, the rivalry between Fouroulou's mother Fatma, and his aunt Hélima, "originaire du quartier d'en haut" (19) (originally from the upper neighborhood) and therefore of the rival *çof,* forces the extended family to divide their property into two nuclear units.

Bourdieu explains such a division as a breach of the codes of honor:

> The fear of French justice, the weakening of the sentiment of family solidarity and the contagious effect of another system of values have often caused the Kabyles to give up the ancient code of honour. In former society, honour was indivisible, like the family land. Alongside the tendency

to break up the indivisibility of the family possessions, which has mani-
fested itself ever more and more strongly in the last twenty years, the feeling has developed that the defending of one's honour is a matter that concerns the individual alone. (238)

Bourdieu explains this breach as part of a general trend brought about by
French attacks on the precolonial system of honor, which was also a system of justice. While it might be tempting to articulate a reading of Feraoun that emphasizes only the idyllic aspects of Kabyle "traditions," the
novel hints at such a conflict between Kabyle and French notions of justice. After the fight, Fouroulou's mother, in a moment of anger, says "Il
faut . . . laisser [les blessés] tels qu'ils sont et que les roumis les voient
ainsi" (33). (We must leave the wounded as they are so the *Roumis* will
see them like that.) But once the dignitaries intervene, the *amin* says, "Il
est inutile d'aller à la justice française qui compliquerait tout" (38).
(There's no use going to the French authorities who would complicate
everything.) This attempt to avoid French interference in the "traditional" system of justice perhaps explains the difference between Feraoun's account of wars between the moieties and Bourdieu's (which pur-
ports to describe a precolonial society, even though the fieldwork was
conducted well into the twentieth century). The division of family property in *Le fils du pauvre,* I would argue, is not merely representative of a
trend brought about by the colonization of Algeria; it might also be read
as an allegory of the systematic destruction of the precolonial property
structures and system of honor.

In *The Emergence of Classes in Algeria* (1976), Marnia Lazreg describes
similar changes to the precolonial property system in Algeria. In spite of
the representation of the Algerian property system in colonial discourse,
"pre-capitalist Algeria was neither feudal nor communal. Neither was it
made up of nomadic tribes roaming through vast stretches of land, as
has been claimed" (26). Rather, "[t]he structure of Algerian property was
composed of three categories: *arsh* (private but non-alienable property);
melk (equivalent to private alienable property); and *habus* (or land do-
nated for religious or cultural proposes)" (26). Of the three types, only
melk could be sold, "but custom forbids selling it" (27). Lazreg writes,
"Soon after they invaded Algiers, the French embarked upon a policy
aimed at systematically destroying Algerian society for the purpose of realizing capital accumulation" (37). In 1844, "[t]he administration declared
the expropriation of all land that appeared to be uncultivated" (41). This

was easily accomplished because "[i]t was customary for Algerian tribes-men to leave part of their land fallow in order to avoid exhausting it" (26). In addition, "*habus* property was abolished" (41). Algerians were required to obtain French titles for uncultivated lands; when they did not, their lands were expropriated. After more decrees, some of which, ironically, were intended to protect Algerian property systems, even more land changed hands: "This forced transformation of the means of pro-duction inevitably led to the alienation of what had been, up to then indivisible property. Sales became more and more frequent. Those who could not sell their fields rented them out to Europeans. Gradually, the peasant who had once owned his land became a *khammes* or sharecropper on it . . ." (46). The division of family property in *Le fils du pauvre,* there-fore, parallels trends brought about by the French colonial presence as well as the more general dismantling of precolonial property structures.

In addition to this breakup of property previously worked by the extended family, Fouroulou's more immediate family (like the other half) suffers economic hardship because of the new distribution of land. Fou-roulou's father, like many other Algerians, is forced to immigrate to France in order to sell his labor and almost dies in a work-related "accident." Lazreg also describes the economic degradation experienced by the Alge-rian population due to changes in the property system: "A by-product of the application of French laws to Algerian property was the institution of usury. The need to borrow money to pay taxes and legal fees, a result of the registration of one's property or suits against the administration for expropriation and/or sequestration, attracted unscrupulous usurers and land speculators" (46). Likewise, Fouroulou's family becomes increas-ingly indebted:

> Lorsque le jeune homme se présenta au brevet, il fallut emprunter pour lui acheter un costume et payer ses frais de séjour à Alger. Ramdane hésita longtemps avant de s'adresser à un usurier. Mais quand la chose fut faite, il admit avec facilité les avantages d'une telle transaction qui tire si bien un homme de l'embarras. Il finit par prendre goût à ces emprunts à longue échéance et il se mit à s'endetter au fur et à mesure des besoins. Il en avait assez de lutter. Les temps devenaient de plus en plus difficiles; il se déchar-geait du poids de la famille sur le plus exigeant des créanciers. . . . (116)

> When the young man was to take his exams, they had to borrow money in order to buy him a suit and pay for his stay in Algiers. Ramdane was hesitant for a long time to go see a usurer. But once things were said and

done, he easily accepted the advantages of such a transaction, which gets
a man out of trouble so well. He ended up liking these long-term loans
and began to go into debt as need required. He had had enough of struggling. The times were becoming more and more difficult; he unloaded the
burden of the family onto the most demanding lenders. . . .

Feraoun's allegory of colonization is thus associated with the colonial
school system, which is, in part, responsible for the unbearable expenses
the new, more nuclear family must deal with. In an allegorical reading of
Feraoun, the French school system plays a complicit role in colonization,
and particularly in the expropriation of land. The *Bildungsroman* narrative of the progress represented by assimilation through French education
thus runs against the current of a simultaneous narrative of economic
degradation.

What then does the allegorical aspect of the novel have to do with
the gendered aspects of Feraoun's "ethnographic" discussion of the system
of honor and his childhood narrative of the apprenticeship of masculinity? The family breakup that allegorizes colonial expropriation of land
involves a transition from a single household headed by a woman to two
households headed by men. Whereas colonial discourses represent precolonial cultures as being more patriarchal than the colonizing one, the literal level of *Le fils du pauvre,* reread through the allegory it projects, associates colonization with an imposition of a specifically European form of
patriarchy, the nuclear family headed by men. Since colonization was also
a full-scale attack on the system of honor, which was, after all, the indigenous system of justice, it was, in this context, literally dis-honoring. The
association of colonization with dishonor is not unique to Feraoun's novel
and Bourdieu's essay; it is also a central trope of a certain male-centered
nationalist discourse, including that represented by Fanon's "Algeria Unveiled," which represents colonization through the metaphors of unveiling and rape: "Every veil that fell, every body that became liberated from
the traditional embrace of the *haïk,* every face that offered itself to the
bold and impatient glance of the occupier, was a negative expression of
the fact that Algeria was beginning to deny herself and was accepting the
rape of the colonizer" (42). Fanon also associates unveiling with prostitution: "An unveiled Algerian girl who 'walks the street' is very often noticed by young men who behave like young men all over the world, but
who use a special approach as the result of the idea people habitually have
of one who has discarded the veil. She is treated to unpleasant, obscene,
humiliating remarks" (53). Unveiling, rape, and prostitution, in these pas-

sages, represent the colonization of Algeria. The male response to the unveiled Algerian woman *qua* metaphor for her country is dismissed by Fanon as not only natural but also universal. Since unveiling, rape, and prostitution are considered dishonoring not only to the women they affect, but especially to their male guardians, the implicit message of Fanon's essay is that colonization has dishonored Algeria, and especially Algerian men. This male-centered nationalist discourse implies that the greatest victims of colonial violence against colonized women are, in fact, colonized men.

Feraoun implicitly rejects this version of nationalist discourse. He first sets up a parallel between precolonial gendered violence and the changes brought about in family and property structures by colonialism. Second, his allegory associates the female sphere of male childhood with a precolonial family structure that is, by European standards, more matriarchal than the colonial patriarchy that follows. Bringing back this premasculine femininity represents a return to precolonial roots. These roots, however, are not those of a male-centered nationalist discourse, for certain male privileges are questioned. Let us not forget, after all, that even if a young Fouroulou is allowed to beat up his sisters and is given twice as much food as them, these privileges are questioned and mocked by Fouroulou in his role of adult narrator.

Memmi's Allegory of Alienation

Feraoun's implicit association of the colonial school system and the French expropriation of Algerian property finds a more explicit parallel in Memmi's *La statue de sel.* In addition to bringing back a childhood past in a way that delights in the threat of a loss of masculinity, Memmi uses the separation from his mother to allegorize the alienation caused by his education in the French school system, which increasingly removes him from "traditional" practices and belief systems. Memmi wrote his first novel several years before his political essays "Portrait du colonisateur" and "Portrait du colonisé," which along with Fanon's writings and Aimé Césaire's *Discours sur le colonialisme,* constitute the most detailed philosophical and analytical condemnations of colonialism written in French. In many ways, *La statue de sel* reads like a case study in support of these essays; whereas the novel describes the alienation of an *évolué,* the politico-philosophical essays demystify this alienation in the context of a colonial system of economic expropriation that only used the civilizing mission as its own justification. Considering Feraoun's and Memmi's novels together thus reveals the economic foundation of colonial alienation in colonial expropriation. The narrator's separation from his mother (resembling as it does that of many other childhood narratives) then comes to represent his alienation from the "Orient." As Said points out, however, this "Orient" is itself a construction of colonial discourse; it will also become the site of the narrator's cultural resistance to assimilation.

At the literal level, colonial alienation in *La statue de sel* actually leads Memmi's narrator to reject his origins: "[J]'ai choisi vigoureusement la culture occidentale et je me moque de la Barbarie" (357). ("[S]o I vigorously opt[ed] for Western culture and try to ignore all that is barbarian" [325].)[5] His rejection of the Orient, however, is complicated by the fact that the West he has chosen rejects him in return: "J'avais refusé l'Orient et l'Occident me refusait" (352–53). ("I had rejected the East and had been rejected by the West" [321].) The resulting impossible situation described by the narrator is that of his alienation as a French-educated colonial *évolué:*

> Moi je suis mal à l'aise dans mon pays natal et n'en connais pas d'autre, ma culture est d'emprunt et ma langue maternelle infirme, je n'ai plus de croyances, de religion, de traditions et j'ai honte de ce qui en eux résiste au fond de moi. . . . [J]e suis de culture française mais Tunisien. . . . [J]e suis Tunisien mais juif, c'est-à-dire politiquement, socialement exclu, parlant la langue du pays avec un accent particulier, mal accordé passionnellement à ce qui émeut les musulmans; juif mais ayant rompu avec la religion juive et le ghetto, ignorant de la culture juive et détestant la bourgeoisie inauthentique; je suis pauvre enfin et j'ai ardemment désiré en finir avec la pauvreté, mais j'ai refusé de faire ce qu'il fallait. (364)

> I am ill at ease in my own land and I know of no other. My culture is borrowed and I speak my mother tongue haltingly. I have neither religious beliefs nor tradition[s], and am ashamed of whatever particle of them has survived deep within me. . . . I am a Tunisian but of French culture. . . . I am Tunisian, but Jewish, which means that I am politically and socially [excluded]. I speak the language of the country with a particular accent and emotionally I [am out of tune with what Muslims find moving]. I am a Jew who has broken with the Jewish religion and the ghetto, is ignorant of Jewish culture and detests the middle class because it is phony. I am

5. An alternative, probably more literal translation of the end of this sentence would be, "I could care less about Barbary."

poor but desperately anxious not to be poor, and at the same time, I refuse
to take the necessary steps to [get out of] poverty. (331)

This often-cited passage eloquently articulates the in-between Bhabha
qualifies as the "not quite/not white." The narrator is not quite a Tunisian, not even a Jewish Tunisian, any longer. In his efforts to assimilate,
he has irremediably separated from his Jewishness and his Tunisianness.
Yet France's refusal to accept him as her own—exemplified by his much-
admired philosophy teacher's refusal to hide him from the invading German army and, in turn, by the French army's request that he enroll under
a Muslim name after the Allied Forces' "liberation" of Tunisia—denies
him the possibility of being completely French. Even prior to colonization, the Jewish narrator would not have been completely Tunisian, and
thus Memmi complicates even Bhabha's paradigm. Not quite Tunisian.
Not French. Not quite/not Tunisian or French.[6] Yet, what I find interesting in the above passage is the "ce qui en eux résiste au fond de moi," that
part of his Tunisianness that resists colonial assimilation.

In another often-quoted passage, Memmi's narrator describes a similar resistance to his attempts to reject the Orient, for it is precisely colonial alienation that leads the narrator to reject his mother. In the chapter
entitled "La danse," he returns home early from school one day to find
his mother dancing in a trance as part of an exorcism ceremony for a sick
relative. At first he does not even recognize her, but once he does his
reaction to the sight of her is one of disgust:

> En cette femme qui dansait devant moi, les seins à moitié nus, livrée in-
> consciente à ces dérèglements magiques, je ne retrouvais rien, je ne com-
> prenais rien. Dans mes livres, la mère était un être plus doux et plus hu-
> main que les autres, symbole du dévouement et de l'intelligence intuitive.
> Comme ses enfants devaient se sentir reconnaissants et heureux, fiers
> d'une telle mère! Ma mère, à moi, la voici: Cette loque envoûtée par
> l'épouvantable musique, par ces musiciens sauvages, envoûtés eux-mêmes
> par leurs obscures croyances . . . ma mère, la voici, c'est ma mère . . . (180,
> Memmi's suspension points)

> And this woman who was dancing before me, with her breasts barely cov-
> ered, abandoning herself unconsciously to magical contortions, suggested
> to me nothing that was familiar or that I could understand. In the books

6. For the classical reading of alienation, see Yetiv, for whom Memmi, "l'aliéné au troisième
degré" (alienated to the third degree), represents the epitome of alienation due to his being both
Jewish in a Muslim society and colonized (143–201).

that I had read, the mother was always somebody more soft and human than all others, a symbol of devotion and of intuitive intelligence. How her children must be grateful and happy, proud of having such a mother! As for my own mother, here she was: this wretch . . . with a spell cast on her by the dreadful music, by these savage musicians, themselves under the spell of their dark and obscure beliefs. My mother? Well, here she was . . . (161)

The sight of his Oriental mother dancing before him corresponds in no way to the representations of motherhood in his French textbooks. In contrast, he sees his mother as abject: "Mon mépris, mon dégoût, ma honte se concentrèrent, se précisèrent" (180). ("My contempt and disgust and shame now became clearer, more concentrated" [161].) He even compares her to a snake and depicts her as inhuman:

[M]a mère obéit, son corps ondule comme désossé, lente danse du serpent fasciné. . . . Les musiciens accélèrent, accélèrent, poussés eux-mêmes par on ne sait quelle force, leurs yeux jaillissent, leurs veines gonflent, les figures tailladées atrocement grimacent, masques magiques qui brusquement se mettent à vivre. La danseuse explose, se déchire, jette ses membres dans toutes les directions. (181)

[M]y mother follows obediently, her body swaying as if boneless in the slow dance of the charmed serpent. . . . The musicians then begin to accelerate their pace, driven by some mysterious force. Their eyes bulge out of their faces, veins swell in their foreheads, their hideously incised faces grimace like magical masks that suddenly come to life. As for the dancer, she seems to explode, torn apart as her limbs begin to cast themselves wildly all around her. (162)

The narrator's initial response is one of violence, and his abjection of his mother allegorizes the othering of the Orient in colonial discourse.

In *Pouvoirs de l'horreur* (1980), Kristeva defines the abject as the mother's body from which the son must separate himself in a manner similar to the one described by Chodorow. As Kristeva argues that the abject is abject precisely because it is in some ways a part of our selves, Memmi's narrator cannot completely distance himself from his mother:

Elle m'était étrangère, ma mère, étrange partie de moi-même, plongée au sein des continents primitifs. C'est elle pourtant qui m'a enfanté. Quels sombres liens m'enchaînent à ce fantôme, arriverai-je à émerger du gouffre? (181)

She was a stranger to me now, my mother, a part of myself become alien to me and thrust into the heart of a primitive continent. Still, it was she who had given birth to me. What somber ties still bound me to this ghost, and how shall I ever manage to return from the abyss into which she is now dragging me? (162)

The abject is the mother from whom one must separate oneself but which is always a part of oneself; it constitutes a double bind. The Orient from which he has attempted to separate continues to haunt him, and this ghost has his mother's face. In the end, he is almost seduced by what he has attempted to abject:

Peut-être aurait-il fallu que je danse moi aussi jusqu'à l'étourdissement, que j'accepte ces rythmes, que je batte ma tête d'un geste saccadé, répété jusqu'à la perte de la conscience, que ma tête continue toute seule, vide comme celle des poupées à balancette plombée, que je disloque mon corps à toutes ses articulations, de sorte que pas un seul os, un seul muscle ne reste en place, que ma conscience évanouie, mon corps désintégré, je laisse le biniou se saisir de mes nerfs, le tambourin ordonner les battements de mon sang, les cymbales m'écarteler chaque membre épars aux quatre coins du ciel et de la terre: peut-être alors finirais-je par passer de l'autre côté? (181–82)

Perhaps I too should dance until I became giddy, until I lost consciousness after accepting these rhythms and beating my own head again and again with disjointed gestures, repeated until it continued to shake all by itself, as empty as a doll's head that moves as it follows its leaded pendulum, until my whole body became dislocated in all its joints, so that no longer a single bone, not a muscle, remained in its proper place, with all my consciousness vanished and my body disintegrated while I allowed the bagpipes to seize my nerves, the tom-tom to rule the beating of my heart and blood, and the cymbals to tear my limbs apart and scatter them north, south, east, and west, throughout the sky and the earth? Would I then manage in turn to get through to the other side . . . ? (162–63)

Although *La statue de sel* is not usually categorized as an ethnographic novel, this passage presents an almost clinical description of the physiology of the trance. Interestingly, when it comes to articulating such an ethnographic description, the narrator projects its effects onto his own body, further strengthening his identification with it in spite of his disgust. Through ethnography, therefore, Memmi articulates an identification with the Orient that resists assimilation and complicates both Kristeva's and Chodorow's paradigms by turning them into allegories of his own attempt at assimilation.

Memmi's Recovery of a Queer Orient

In contrast, however, as a personification of the Orient, his mother is not the only person Memmi's narrator attempts to distinguish himself from. The abjection of her Orientalness parallels his abjection of homosexuality. Without contradicting the definition of "Oriental sex" proposed by many Western scholars, Memmi rejects the opportunity to participate in the acts themselves:

> Jamais je n'avais pu accepter les jeux sexuels des garçons. Je refusai avec mépris et scandale lorsqu'on m'apprit qu'un grand élève s'offrait pour caresser précisément et jusqu'à la jouissance tous ceux qui le désiraient. Mes camarades organisaient ces parties de plaisir collectif dans un terrain vague non loin du lycée. Ils s'alignaient, paraît-il, le dos au mur et Giacomo passait devant chacun, à tour de rôle. Dans la salle des surveillants d'internat, j'étais le seul à refuser de raconter mes aventures, le seul à ne pas évoquer, à ne pas décrire avec complaisance les attributs féminins et masculins, mille fois par jour. Je trouvais cette promiscuité de fort mauvais goût et d'ailleurs je n'avais rien à raconter. Mais quelle que fût ma pudeur, je dus convenir que la solitude sexuelle, comme toutes les autres, me devenait insupportable, mon secret demandait à être partagé. (257–58)

> I had never been able to [accept] the sexual games of boys. When I was told that one of the older pupils offered to caress, with enough skill to cause an orgasm, anyone who wished, I refused with scorn and horror. My comrades organized these parties of collective pleasure out on a vacant lot not far from the school. Apparently, they all lined up with their back[s] to the wall and Giacomo passed [in front of them] one by one. I was the only one in the boarding-school common room not to talk of my adventures or to describe [with self-indulgence] the sexual attributes of men and women a thousand times a day. To me, such promiscuity was [in very bad taste]; besides, what had I to tell? Nevertheless, shy though I was, I was forced to admit that my sexual and general isolation were becoming unbearable and that my secret demanded to be shared. . . . (239–40)

At first glance, the narrator's main purpose for describing this example is to assure the reader that he has never participated in these homosexual "parties de plaisir." For something that he has never witnessed, however, he is aware of so many details that the "paraît-il" seems like an afterthought. What is perhaps striking about this example is that Memmi's narrator seems to be alone in his disgusted condemnation of a homosexual pleasure. Memmi's description involves a homosexual pleasure that any Oriental man might be capable of enjoying. The narrator's rejection of homosexuality is thus a rejection of a specific Oriental form of sexuality, as is constituted by the Western clichés of "Islamic" homosexualities. To become an assimilated colonized intellectual, therefore, the narrator must become heterosexual in the modern, Western sense. When he distances himself from the other schoolboys who engage in Oriental homosex, he distances himself not only from homosexuality, but also from the Orient. His rejection of homosexuality could thus be read as paralleling the various passages in which he rejects the Orient as well as his Oriental mother.

To further assert his heterosexuality, he follows up on this description of homosexual *jouissance* by narrating his first heterosexual experience in a brothel. The above passage, in fact, serves as the introduction to the chapter entitled "Le quartier," in which he discusses hiring prostitutes in Tunis's red-light district. After overcoming the embarrassing necessity of purchasing condoms, his first visit to a brothel ends in a failure; whereas "[il] attendai[t] vaguement quelque chose comme une communion, un tendre jeu à deux" (264) ("[he] had rather expected some sort of gentle communion, a game [they] would play together" [245]), the prostitute frustrates his desire for sentimentality by cutting short his small talk, and he ejaculates prematurely. The next visit with another prostitute, however, produces the desired results and reiterates the previous quotation: "J'avais enfin l'impression de communier sexuellement. Le secret allait être partagé" (272). (". . . I had, at last, a feeling of sexual communion and of sharing my secret" [251].) Although homosexuality is often constructed as a secret, here it is a frustrated heterosexual desire that must remain unspoken. Homosexuality, in contrast, at least in a male homo*social* space, is not a secret at all. Similarly, the previously discussed chapter, "Au kouttab," in which Memmi's narrator remembers the Hebrew-school boys' performance of a circumcision ceremony, is followed by a chapter entitled "Ginou." Here, in a manner paralleling his assertion of heterosexuality to compensate for any danger of homosexual contagion in "Le quartier," he describes his schoolboy crush on a French girl Ginou as a way of countering the emasculating dangers of the joy of castration. The narrator's heteroromance with a French girl also serves as an allegory of his alienated desire to pass as French and be assimilated into French culture. The narrator's desire for assimilation, however, is frustrated in the end; he is never totally accepted by Ginou as an equal, nor as a potential partner in romance. That the desire for colonial assimilation is allegorized through a heteroromance begs the question of the allegorical implications of the narrator's rejection of homosexual pleasure.

In the end, Memmi's narrator, unlike Memmi himself, refuses this assimilation. *La statue de sel* is framed narratively as the response written to a question in an examination the narrator takes at the end of his French education. After composing what is, for the reader, the narrative of the novel, the narrator does not turn in his response, thereby ending his career as a member of the French educated elite. The reader must then reread the narrator's rejection of Oriental homosexuality in light of both this failed attempt to abject his Oriental mother and his failure to assimilate completely. Is this Oriental homosexuality, like his mother and the Orient itself, an "étrange partie de [lu]i-même" that he will never be able to exorcise? In his abjection of the Orient and its homosexuality, does he end up like Boudjedra's narrator, who abjects both his mother and his French companion? Boudjedra's narrator attempts to sequester Céline as he attempts to confine both his brother's and his own homosexuality to the past in order to assert his own heterosexuality. Yet we have seen how the ghosts of a repressed past can return to haunt the present. To what extent does the queer Orient return to haunt the assimilated Maghrebian intellectual? "La danse," after all, directly precedes "Au kouttab"; the narrator's attempt to exorcise the Oriental from himself leads to the realization that the Orient's resistance to assimilation is sexual, for it is inscribed into his flesh. The resurrection of a feminine boyhood, involving as it does a recovery of the narrator's homoerotic *jouissance* through a pleasurable identification with the emasculation of other boys, thus parallels remembering boyhood episodes of homosex. The Orient's sexual resistance to colonialism is then grafted onto his body as the mark of his Jewishness, and in spite of his claim that he is "mal accordé passionnellement à ce qui émeut les musulmans," it is precisely through circumcision that he identifies with Muslims. In the streetcar scene, we remember, it is through the physical sensation of a homoerotic *jouissance* whose site is the penis that Memmi's narrator can claim to belong to the same family as the Muslims in the car. Could *La statue de sel* be suggesting that the model of Judeo-Muslim solidarity within a nonexclusionary nation is homoerotic sexual identification? If so, the Tunisian nation would be quite queer indeed.

Throughout this discussion of Memmi, I have referred to his origins in an unproblematic way as the Orient, mostly because this is how he describes them himself. *La statue de sel* was written almost three decades before *Orientalism* suggested that the Orient was not a geographical region but a figment of the Western imagination. What then does it mean for Memmi's narrator to refuse the "Orient" if it is a set of Western "idées reçues" or stereotypes? If for Irigaray, both subject and object positions are masculine, and both the masculine and the feminine are male constructions, the double bind of Memmi's narrator becomes even more complicated; both the Frenchness he desires and the Orient he rejects are products of colonial discourse. The Oriental homosexuality he rejects is likewise the Orientalist stereotype of the Orient as a polymorphously perverse space, or, as Said describes it, queer. Irigaray's solution to the double bind produced by male supremacy is mimicry. Sebbar as well produces a parallel oppositional rereading/rewriting of Oriental stereotypes that reincorporates them into a parodic performance of Orientalness. I would argue that, when reread through these later rereadings (not only Sebbar's, but also those of many of the novels examined in this study), *La statue de sel* offers glimpses of a similar rewriting of the Orient. The Orient's queerness in Orientalist discourse may be a mark of the production of the Orient as Other by a colonial discourse that is complicit with the colonization of what is supposed to be the Orient's geographical referent, but the Orient's queerness is also the trace of the heterosexualizing moves of colonialism and its propaganda. The "Orient," as a Western discourse, was deployed to attempt to heterosexualize not only North Africa, but also Europe. The production of the Orient as queer marked it as a site of sexual resistance to the institution of heterosexuality as a compulsory regime in the West. Some nationalist discourses have countered this Orientalist, and therefore colonialist, queering of the Orient with their own supposedly anticolonial heterosexualization of the Maghrebian Nation.

Memmi's narrative, however, attests to the fact that such a queerness, when repressed, can only return to haunt the nationalist discourse that has attempted to exclude it. What many of the examples considered in this study have shown is that this supposedly anticolonial strategy actually continues the work of the colonizer's sexual politics. Even Fanon, who warns against the indigenous elite's replacement of the colonizer in other political, social, and economic arenas, reproduces the colonizer's sexual politics vis-à-vis the family in *A Dying Colonialism*. As Memmi brings back a feminine past in his recollection of the joy of castration, which has its own homoerotic implications, he also brings back a queer

Orient that he has attempted to abject. Unlike the Orient of Orientalist discourse, however, Memmi's returns with an anticolonial force that offers a way out of the double bind of assimilation. For his queer Orient is an in-between space that marks the Orient's resistance to Orientalism, a site where the Orientalists' queer Orient is itself queered. Like Matisse's *Odalisque,* which Shérazade rewrites for herself as she circulates its multiple reproductions, Memmi's queer Orient exceeds the Orientalizing clichés that originally produced it. In this rewriting, queerness thereby constitutes a resistance to colonialism and not its product. In the precombat literature, the "replongée" described by Fanon, the "vieux épisodes d'enfance . . . ramenés du fond de [l]a mémoire," the "vieilles légendes" that root anticolonial struggle in a national consciousness, constitute a narrative return to queer origins. The roots of the Maghrebian Nation, like the roots of its literature, are thus indeed queer.

Abdel-Jaouad, Hédi. 1991. "The Dialectics of the Archaic and the Post-modern in Maghrebian Literature Written in French." *Studies in Twentieth Century Literature* 15, no. 1: 59–76.

———. 1996. "'Too Much in the Sun': Sons, Mothers, and Impossible Alliances in Francophone Maghrebian Writing." *Research in African Literatures* 27, no. 3: 15–33.

Abun-Nasr, Jamil M. 1971. *A History of the Maghrib.* Cambridge: Cambridge Univ. Press.

Achour, Christiane. 1986. *Mouloud Feraoun: Une voix en contrepoint.* Paris: Silex.

Ahmad, Aijaz. 1987. "Jameson's Rhetoric of Otherness and the National Allegory." Reprinted in *In Theory,* 95–122. See Ahmad 1992.

———. 1992. *In Theory: Classes, Nations, Literatures.* London: Verso.

Aït Sabbah, Fatna. 1986. *La femme dans l'inconscient musulman.* Paris: Albin Michel.

Alcalay, Ammiel. 1993. *After Jews and Arabs: Remaking Levantine Culture.* Minneapolis: Univ. of Minnesota Press.

Alloula, Malek. 1981. *Le harem colonial: Images d'un sous-érotisme.* Geneva: Slatkine. Trans. as *The Colonial Harem* by Myrna Godzich and Wlad Godzich. Minneapolis: Univ. of Minnesota Press, 1986.

Anderson, Benedict. [1983] 1995. *Imagined Communities: Reflections on the Origin and Spread of Nationalism.* London: Verso.

Apter, Emily. 1992. "Female Trouble in the Colonial Harem." *differences* 4, no. 1: 205–24.

———. 1994. "Acting Out Orientalism: Sapphic Theatricality in Turn-of-the-Century Paris." *L'esprit créateur* 34, no. 2: 102–16.

Arnaud, Jacqueline. 1986. *La littérature maghrébine de langue française.* 2 vols. Paris: Publisud.

Arteaga, Alfred. 1994. "Introduction: The Here, the Now." In *An Other Tongue: Nation and Ethnicity in the Linguistic Borderlands,* edited by Alfred Arteaga, 1–7. Durham: Duke Univ. Press.

Balzac, Honoré de. [1835] 1977. *La fille aux yeux d'or.* In *La comédie humaine,* vol. 5, 1039–1112. Paris: Gallimard, Bibliothèque de la Pléiade. Trans. as *The Girl with the*

Golden Eyes by Herbert J. Hunt. In *History of the Thirteen,* 307–91. New York: Penguin, 1974.

Barthes, Roland. 1970. *L'empire des signes.* Geneva: Albert Skira. Trans. as *Empire of Signs* by Richard Howard. New York: Farrar, Straus and Giroux; Hill and Wang, 1982.

———. 1987. *Incidents.* Paris: Seuil. Trans. as *Incidents* by Richard Howard. Berkeley: Univ. of California Press, 1992.

Basfao, Kacem. 1990. "Pour une relance de l'affaire du *Passé simple.*" In *Littératures maghrébines: Colloque Jacqueline Arnaud,* vol. 2. Spec. issue of *Itinéraires et contacts de cultures,* vol. 11, 57–66. Paris: L'Harmattan.

Beauvoir, Simone de. [1949] 1976. *Le deuxième sexe.* 2 vols. Paris: Gallimard, coll. Folio. Trans. and ed. as *The Second Sex* by H. M. Parshley. New York: Random House, Vintage Books, 1989.

Begag, Azouz, and Abdellatif Chaouite. 1990. *Ecarts d'identité.* Paris: Seuil.

Behdad, Ali. 1994a. *Belated Travelers: Orientalism in the Age of Colonial Dissolution.* Durham: Duke Univ. Press.

———, ed. 1994b. *Orientalism after "Orientalism,"* vol. 34, no. 2, of *L'esprit créateur.*

Bellamy, James A. 1979. "Sex and Society in Islamic Popular Literature." In *Society and the Sexes in Medieval Islam,* edited by Afaf Lutfi al-Sayyid-Marsot, 23–42. Malibu: Undena.

Ben Jelloun, Tahar. 1977. *La plus haute des solitudes: Misère affective et sexuelle d'émigrés nord-africains.* Paris: Seuil, coll. Points.

———. [1977] 1988. "Pour Jean Genet." In *Les nègres au port de la lune: Genet et les différences,* 11–12. Bordeaux: La Différence.

———. 1978. *Moha le fou, Moha le sage.* Paris: Seuil, coll. Points.

———. 1981. *La prière de l'absent.* Paris: Seuil, coll. Points.

———. 1981–82. Contribution to the "Dossier Jean Genet." In *Masques* 12: 27–28.

———. 1983. *L'écrivain public.* Paris: Seuil, coll. Points.

———. 1985. *L'enfant de sable.* Paris: Seuil, coll. Points. Trans. as *The Sand Child* by Alan Sheridan. New York: Ballantine, 1987.

———. 1987. *La nuit sacrée.* Paris: Seuil. Trans. as *The Sacred Night* by Alan Sheridan. San Diego: Harcourt Brace Jovanovich, 1989.

———. 1991a. "Défendre la diversité culturelle du Maghreb." In *L'état du Maghreb,* edited by Camille and Yves Lacoste, 271–72. Paris: La Découverte.

———. 1991b. *Les yeux baissés.* Paris: Seuil.

———. 1992. "Jean Genet avec les Palestiniens." In *Genet à Chatila,* edited by Jérôme Hankins, 75–83. Paris: Solin.

———. 1996. *Eloge de l'amitié: La soudure fraternelle.* Paris: Arléa.

Bersani, Leo. 1987. "Is the Rectum a Grave?" *October* 43: 197–222.

Bettelheim, Bruno. 1954. *Symbolic Wounds: Puberty Rites and the Envious Male.* Glencoe, IL: Free Press.

Bhabha, Homi K., ed. and intro. 1990. *Nation and Narration.* London: Routledge.

———. 1994. *The Location of Culture.* London: Routledge.

Bleys, Rudi C. 1995. *The Geography of Perversion: Male-to-Male Sexual Behaviour outside the West and the Ethnographic Imagination, 1750–1918.* New York: New York Univ. Press.

Bolt, Mary, and Agnes Poveda. 1994. "Sodomy and the Sandinistas: AIDS Education in Nicaragua Fifteen Years after the Overthrow of Somoza." Talk given at the CUNY Graduate School, New York, 19 July.

Bonn, Charles. 1974. *La littérature algérienne de langue française et ses lectures: Imaginaire et discours d'idées.* Sherbrooke: Naaman.

———. 1985. *Le roman algérien de langue française: Vers un espace de communication littéraire décolonisé?* Paris: L'Harmattan.

Boone, Joseph A. 1995. "Vacation Cruises; or, The Homoerotics of Orientalism." *PMLA* 110, no. 1: 89–107.

Boualit, Farida. 1996. "La logique chromatographique de la trilogie *Algérie.*" In *Mohammed Dib,* edited by Jacqueline Arnaud et al., 26–38. Paris: L'Harmattan.

Boudjedra, Rachid. 1969. *La répudiation.* Paris: Denoël, coll. Folio. Trans. as *The Repudiation* by Golda Lambrova. Colorado Springs: Three Continents, 1995.

———. 1979. *Les 1001 années de la nostalgie.* Paris: Denoël, coll. Folio.

———. [1981] 1982. *Le démantèlement.* Paris: Denoël.

———. 1987. *La pluie.* Paris: Denoël.

Boughedir, Férid (director). 1990. *Halfaouine.* Tunisia.

Bouguarche, Ahmed. 1995. "Le hammam: Sexualité, purification et régénérescence dans l'œuvre d'Assia Djebar." In *L'eau: Source d'une écriture dans les littératures [sic] féminines francophones,* edited by Yolande Helm, 209–26. New York: Peter Lang.

Bouhdiba, Abdelwahab. 1964. "Le hammam: Contribution à une psychanalyse de l'Islam." *Revue tunisienne de sciences sociales* 1: 7–14.

———. 1975. *La sexualité en Islam.* Paris: Presses Universitaires de France.

Bourdieu, Pierre. [1966] 1974. "The Sentiment of Honour in Kabyle Society." In *Honour and Shame: The Values of Mediterranean Society,* edited by J. G. Peristiany. Chicago: Univ. of Chicago Press, Midway Reprint.

Bousquet, G.-H. 1966. *L'éthique sexuelle de l'Islam.* Paris: G.-P. Maisonneuve et Larose.

Boyarin, Daniel. 1992. "'This We Know to Be the Carnal Israel': Circumcision and the Erotic Life of God and Israel." *Critical Inquiry* 18: 474–505.

Butler, Judith. 1990a. "The Force of Fantasy: Feminism, Mapplethorpe, and Discursive Excess." *differences* 2, no. 2: 105–25.

———. 1990b. *Gender Trouble: Feminism and the Subversion of Identity.* New York: Routledge.

———. 1992. "Contingent Foundations: Feminism and the Question of 'Postmodernism.'" In *Feminists Theorize the Political.* 3–21. See Butler and Scott.

Butler, Judith, and Joan W. Scott, eds. 1992. *Feminists Theorize the Political.* New York: Routledge.

Castle, Terry. 1993. *The Apparitional Lesbian: Female Homosexuality and Modern Culture.* New York: Columbia Univ. Press.

Cazenave, Odile. 1991. "Gender, Age, and Narrative Transformations in *L'Enfant de sable* by Tahar Ben Jelloun." *The French Review* 64, no. 3: 437–50.

Chambers, Ross. 1991. *Room for Maneuver: Reading (the) Oppositional (in) Narrative.* Chicago: Univ. of Chicago Press.

———. 1994. "Pointless Stories, Storyless Points: Roland Barthes between 'Soirées de Paris' and 'Incidents.'" *L'esprit créateur* 34, no. 2: 12–30.

Chebel, Malek. 1988. *L'esprit de sérail: Perversions et marginalités sexuelles au Maghreb.* Paris: Lieu Commun. Reprinted as *L'esprit de sérail: Mythes et pratiques sexuels au Maghreb.* Paris: Payot, 1995.

———. 1994. Untitled talk given as part of the session "Politique et ambiguïté: Sexualités marginales au Maghreb" at the Congrès Mondial du Conseil International d'Etudes Francophones, Quebec City, 14 April.

————. 1995. *Encyclopédie de l'amour en Islam: Erotisme, beauté et sexualité dans le monde arabe, en Perse et en Turquie.* Paris: Payot.

Chikhi, Beïda. 1989. *Problématique de l'écriture dans l'œuvre romanesque de Mohamed Dib.* Algiers: Office des Publications Universitaires.

Chodorow, Nancy. 1978. *The Reproduction of Mothering: Psychoanalysis and the Sociology of Gender.* Berkeley: Univ. of California Press.

Choukri, Mohamed. 1974. *Jean Genet in Tangier.* New York: Ecco.

Chow, Rey. 1995. *Primitive Passions: Visuality, Sexuality, Ethnography, and Contemporary Chinese Cinema.* New York: Columbia Univ. Press.

Chraïbi, Driss. 1954. *Le passé simple.* Paris: Denoël, coll. Folio. Trans. as *The Simple Past* by Hugh A. Harter. Washington: Three Continents, 1990.

Cixous, Hélène, and Catherine Clément. 1975. *La jeune née.* Paris: Union Générale d'Editions. Trans. as *The Newly Born Woman* by Betsy Wing. Minneapolis: Univ. of Minnesota Press, 1986.

Clerc, Jeanne Marie. 1997. *Assia Djebar: Ecrire, transgresser, résister.* Paris: L'Harmattan.

Clifford, James. 1988. "On *Orientalism.*" In *The Predicament of Culture: Twentieth-Century Ethnography, Literature, and Art,* 255–76. Cambridge: Harvard Univ. Press.

Cohen, Roger. 1997. "Divisions Deepen among Algeria's Secretive Military Rulers." *The New York Times,* 11 Sept., A8.

Crapanzano, Vincent. 1980. *Tuhami: Portrait of a Moroccan.* Chicago: Univ. of Chicago Press.

de Certeau, Michel. [1975] 1988. *The Writing of History.* Trans. Tom Conley. New York: Columbia Univ. Press.

Déjeux, Jean. 1973. *Littérature maghrébine de langue française: Introduction générale et auteurs.* Sherbrooke: Naaman.

————. 1977. *Mohammed Dib: Ecrivain algérien.* Sherbrooke: Naaman.

————. 1991. "Jeh'a ou la saillie (*nadira*)." In *Psychanalyse et texte littéraire au Maghreb,* edited by Charles Bonn, 106–21. Paris: L'Harmattan.

————. 1993. "Les romans de Tahar Ben Jelloun ou «Le territoire de la blessure»." In *Carrefour de cultures: Mélanges offerts à Jacqueline Leiner,* edited by Régis Antoine, 273–86. Tübingen: Gunter Narr.

Deleuze, Gilles, and Félix Guattari. 1972. *L'anti-Œdipe.* Paris: Minuit. Trans. as *Anti-Oedipus: Capitalism and Schizophrenia* by Robert Hurley, Mark Seem, and Helen R. Lane. Minneapolis: Univ. of Minnesota Press, 1983.

————. 1980. *Mille plateaux.* Paris: Minuit.

de Man, Paul. 1979a. *Allegories of Reading: Figural Language in Rousseau, Nietzsche, Rilke, and Proust.* New Haven: Yale Univ. Press.

————. 1979b. "Autobiography as De-facement." *Modern Language Notes* 94: 919–30.

Derrida, Jacques. [1993] 1994. *Specters of Marx: The State of the Debt, the Work of Mourning, and the New International.* Trans. Peggy Kamuf. New York: Routledge.

Dib, Mohammed. 1962. *Qui se souvient de la mer.* Paris: Seuil. Trans. as *Who Remembers the Sea* by Louis Tremaine. Washington: Three Continents, 1985.

Djaout, Tahar. 1984. *Les chercheurs d'os.* Paris: Seuil.

————. 1987. *L'invention du désert.* Paris: Seuil.

Djaziri, Eyet-Chékib. 1997. *Un "poisson" sur la balançoire.* Lille: Gai-Kitsch-Camp.

————. 1998. *Une promesse de douleur et de sang.* Lille: Gai-Kitsch-Camp.

Djebar, Assia. 1980. *Femmes d'Alger dans leur appartement.* Paris: des femmes. Trans. as

Women of Algiers in Their Apartment by Marjolijn de Jager. Charlottesville: Univ. Press of Virginia, 1992.

————. 1985a. *L'amour, la fantasia.* Paris: Jean-Claude Lattès. Trans. as *Fantasia: An Algerian Cavalcade* by Dorothy S. Blair. Portsmouth, NH: Heinemann, 1993.

————. 1985b. "Du français comme butin." *La quinzaine littéraire* 436: 25.

————. 1987. *Ombre sultane.* Paris: Jean-Claude Lattès. Trans. as *A Sister to Scheherazade* by Dorothy S. Blair. Portsmouth, NH: Heinemann, 1993.

————. 1991. *Loin de Médine: Filles d'Ismaël.* Paris: Albin Michel.

————. 1993. Untitled lecture given at the Congrès Mondial du Conseil International d'Etudes Francophones. Casablanca, 13 July.

————. 1995a. *Le blanc de l'Algérie.* Paris: Albin Michel.

————. 1995b. *Vaste est la prison.* Paris: Albin Michel.

Dollimore, Jonathan. 1991. *Sexual Dissidence: Augustine to Wilde, Freud to Foucault.* Oxford: Oxford Univ. Press, Clarendon Press.

Donadey, Anne. 1993. "Polyphonic and Palimpsestic Discourse in the Works of Assia Djebar and Leïla Sebbar." Ph.D. diss., Northwestern Univ.

Duberman, Martin Bauml, Martha Vicinus, and George Chauncey, Jr., eds. 1989. *Hidden from History: Reclaiming the Gay and Lesbian Past.* New York: Penguin, New American Library Books.

Duggan, Lisa. 1994. "Queering the State." *Social Text* 39: 1–14.

Dworkin, Andrea. [1987] 1988. *Intercourse.* New York: Macmillan, Free Press.

Dynes, Wayne R. 1983. "Homosexuality in Sub-Saharan Africa: An Unnecessary Controversy." *Gay Books Bulletin* 9: 20–21.

El Maleh, Edmond Amran. 1988. *Jean Genet: Le captif amoureux et autres essais.* Grenoble: La Pensée Sauvage; Casablanca: Toubkal.

Erickson, John D. 1993. "Femme voilée, récit voilé dans *L'Enfant de sable* de Tahar Ben Jelloun." In *Carrefour de cultures: Mélanges offerts à Jacqueline Leiner,* edited by Régis Antoine, 287–96. Tübingen: Gunter Narr. Published in English as "Veiled Woman and Veiled Narrative in Tahar ben Jelloun's *The Sandchild.*" *boundary 2* 20, no. 1: 47–64.

Etienne, Bruno. 1977. *Algérie, cultures et révolution.* Paris: Seuil.

Fanon, Frantz. 1952. *Peau noire, masques blancs.* Paris: Seuil. Trans. as *Black Skin, White Masks* by Charles Lam Markmann. New York: Grove, 1967.

————. [1959] 1962. *L'an V de la révolution algérienne.* Paris: Maspero. Third edition. Trans. as *A Dying Colonialism* by Haakon Chevalier. New York: Monthly Review Press, Grove, 1965.

————. [1961] 1987. *Les damnés de la terre.* Paris: Maspero, La Découverte. Trans. as *The Wretched of the Earth* by Constance Farrington. New York: Grove, 1963.

Fayolle, Roger. 1996. "Ecrivains, écrits vains?" In *Mohammed Dib,* edited by Jacqueline Arnaud et al., 9–18. Paris: L'Harmattan.

Feraoun, Mouloud. [1950] 1954. *Le fils du pauvre.* Paris: Seuil, coll. Points.

Flaubert, Gustave. 1973. *Correspondance,* vol. 1. Paris: Gallimard, Bibliothèque de la Pléiade.

Foucault, Michel. 1976. *La volonté de savoir.* Vol. 1 of *Histoire de la sexualité.* Paris: Gallimard. Trans. as *An Introduction* by Robert Hurley. Vol. 1 of *The History of Sexuality.* New York: Random House, Pantheon Books, 1978.

Fuss, Diana. 1995. "Interior Colonies: Frantz Fanon and the Politics of Identification." In *Identification Papers,* 141–72. New York: Routledge.

Gafaïti, Hafid. 1987. *Boudjedra ou La passion de la modernité.* Paris: Denoël.

———. 1996. "The Blood of Writing: Assia Djebar's Unveiling of Women and History." *World Literature Today* 70, no. 4: 813–22.

Gagnier, Regenia. 1986. *Idylls of the Marketplace: Oscar Wilde and the Victorian Public.* Stanford: Stanford Univ. Press.

Gaillard, Philippe. 1987. "Tahar le fou, Tahar le sage." *Jeune Afrique* 1404: 44–46.

Gautier, Théophile. [1857] 1966. *Le roman de la momie.* Paris: Garnier-Flammarion.

Geesey, Patricia. 1996. "Exhumation and History: Tahar Djaout's *Les Chercheurs d'os.*" *The French Review* 70, no. 2: 271–79.

Genet, Jean. [1958] 1979. *Les nègres.* In *Œuvres complètes,* vol. 5, 75–156. Paris: Gallimard.

———. [1961] 1979. *Les paravents.* In *Œuvres complètes,* vol. 5, 157–375. Paris: Gallimard.

———. 1964. "Jean Genet: A Candid Conversation with the Brazen, Brilliant Author of *The Balcony* and *The Blacks,* Self-Proclaimed Homosexual, Coward, Thief and Traitor." Interview with Madeleine Gobeil. *Playboy,* April, 45–53.

———. 1986. *Un captif amoureux.* Paris: Gallimard.

———. 1991. *L'ennemi déclaré: Textes et entretiens.* Paris: Gallimard.

Glissant, Edouard. 1981. *Le discours antillais.* Paris: Seuil.

———. 1990. *Poétique de la relation.* Paris: Gallimard. Trans. as *Poetics of Relation* by Betsy Wing. Ann Arbor: Univ. of Michigan Press, 1997.

Godfrey, Sima. 1980. "The Fabrication of *Salammbô:* The Surface of the Veil." *Modern Language Notes* 95: 1005–16.

Goitein, S. D. 1979. "The Sexual Mores of the Common People." In *Society and the Sexes in Medieval Islam,* edited by Afaf Lutfi al-Sayyid-Marsot, 43–61. Malibu: Undena.

Gontard, Marc. [1975] 1985. *"Nedjma" de Kateb Yacine: Essai sur la structure formelle du roman.* Paris: L'Harmattan.

Grant, Rena, Maxine Wolfe, and Jim Fouratt. 1991. "Gays and Lesbians in Radical Struggles." Teach-in held during the student occupation of the CUNY Graduate School, New York, 16–25 April.

Greenberg, David F. 1988. *The Construction of Homosexuality.* Chicago: Univ. of Chicago Press.

Haley, Alex. 1976. *Roots.* New York: Bantam Doubleday Dell.

Halperin, David M. 1990. *One Hundred Years of Homosexuality and Other Essays on Greek Love.* New York: Routledge.

———. 1998. "Forgetting Foucault: Acts, Identities, and the History of Sexuality." *Representations* 63: 93–120.

Hodges, Tony. 1982. *Historical Dictionary of Western Sahara.* Metuchen, NJ: Scarecrow.

Hoodfar, Homa. 1991. "Return to the Veil: Personal Strategy and Public Participation in Egypt." In *Working Women: International Perspectives on Labour and Gender Ideology,* edited by Nanneke Redclift and M. Thea Sinclair, 104–24. London: Routledge.

Houchins, Sue. 1994. "A Family Matter: Blood/Bluhd-Sisters/Sistahs." A paper delivered at the African Literature Association Conference, Accra, Ghana, 28 March.

Huston, Nancy, and Leïla Sebbar. 1986. *Lettres parisiennes: Autopsie de l'exil.* Paris: Barrault.

Irigaray, Luce. 1974. *Speculum de l'autre femme.* Paris: Minuit. Trans. as *Speculum of the Other Woman* by Gillian C. Gill. Ithaca: Cornell Univ. Press, 1985.

———. 1977. *Ce sexe qui n'en est pas un*. Paris: Minuit. Trans. as *This Sex Which Is Not One* by Catherine Porter. Ithaca: Cornell Univ. Press, 1985.

Jameson, Fredric. 1971. *Marxism and Form: Twentieth-Century Dialectical Theories of Literature*. Princeton: Princeton Univ. Press.

———. 1986. "Third-World Literature in the Era of Multinational Capitalism." *Social Text* 15: 65–88.

JanMohamed, Abdul R. [1985] 1986. "The Economy of Manichean Allegory: The Function of Racial Difference in Colonialist Literature." In *"Race," Writing, and Difference,* edited by Henry Louis Gates, Jr., 78–106. Chicago: Univ. of Chicago Press.

Kateb, Yacine. 1956. *Nedjma*. Paris: Seuil, coll. Points. Trans. as *Nedjma* by Richard Howard, intro. by Bernard Aresu. Charlottesville: Univ. Press of Virginia, 1991.

Katz, Jonathan Ned. 1995. *The Invention of Heterosexuality*. New York: Penguin, Dutton Books.

Kaye, Jacqueline, and Abdelhamid Zoubir. 1990. *The Ambiguous Compromise: Language, Literature and National Identity in Algeria and Morocco*. London: Routledge.

Khatibi, Abdelkebir. [1968] 1979. *Le roman maghrébin*. Rabat: SMER.

———. 1982. *Amour bilingue*. Casablanca: Eddif. Trans. as *Love in Two Languages* by Richard Howard. Minneapolis: Univ. of Minnesota Press, 1990.

———. 1983. *Maghreb pluriel*. Paris: Denoël; Rabat: SMER.

———. 1987. *Figures de l'étranger dans la littérature française*. Paris: Denoël.

Khawam, René R., trans. and intro. 1986–87. *Les Mille et une Nuits*. 4 vols. Paris: Phebus.

Kristeva, Julia. 1974. *La révolution du language poétique: L'avant-garde à la fin du XIXe siècle: Lautréamont et Mallarmé*. Paris: Seuil, coll. Points.

———. 1980. *Pouvoirs de l'horreur: Essai sur l'abjection*. Paris: Seuil, coll. Points. Trans. as *Powers of Horror: An Essay on Abjection* by Leon S. Roudiez. New York: Columbia Univ. Press, 1982.

———. 1988. *Etrangers à nous-mêmes*. Paris: Fayard.

———. 1990. *Lettre ouverte à Harlem Désir*. Paris: Rivages. Trans. as *Nations without Nationalism* by Leon S. Roudiez. New York: Columbia Univ. Press, 1993.

———. 1992. "La question nationale aujourd'hui." Lecture given at New York Univ., 20 October.

Laronde, Michel. 1993. *Autour du roman beur: Immigration et identité*. Paris: L'Harmattan.

Laroui, Abdallah. [1970] 1975. *L'histoire du Maghreb: Un essai de synthèse*. 2 vols. Paris: François Maspero.

Lauten, Kathryn Marie. 1997. "Ex-Hum(aniz)e/Re-Hum(aniz)e: Disturbing Bodies in 'Post-Colonial' Francophone Literature and Film." Ph.D. diss., Univ. of Michigan.

Lazreg, Marnia. 1976. *The Emergence of Classes in Algeria: A Study of Colonialism and Socio-Political Change*. Bolder: Westview.

———. 1994. *The Eloquence of Silence: Algerian Women in Question*. New York: Routledge.

Lionnet, Françoise. 1989. *Autobiographical Voices: Race, Gender, Self-Portraiture*. Ithaca: Cornell Univ. Press.

Long, Diane. 1993. "Sexualité cachée, désir voilé dans la littérature maghrébine." Paper read at the Congrès Mondial du Conseil International d'Etudes Francophones, Casablanca, 16 July.

Lowe, Lisa. 1993. "Literary Nomadics in Francophone Allegories of Postcolonialism: Pham Van Ky and Tahar Ben Jelloun." *Yale French Studies* 82: 43–61.

Ludlam, Charles. 1989. *Salammbô*. In *The Complete Plays of Charles Ludlam,* 845–76. New York: Harper and Row, Perennial Library.

Maazaoui, Abbes. 1995. *"L'Enfant de sable* et *La Nuit sacrée* ou le corps tragique." *The French Review* 69, no. 1: 68–77.

MacKinnon, Catharine A. 1987. *Feminism Unmodified: Discourses on Life and Law.* Cambridge: Harvard Univ. Press.

———. 1989. *Toward a Feminist Theory of the State.* Cambridge: Harvard Univ. Press.

Mameri, Khalfa. 1988. *Abane Ramdane.* Paris: L'Harmattan.

Mammeri, Mouloud. 1952. *La colline oubliée.* Paris: Plon.

La marche verte ou la philosophie de Hassan II. 1977. Paris: PAC.

Marcus, Sharon. 1992. "Fighting Bodies, Fighting Words: A Theory and Politics of Rape Prevention." In *Feminists Theorize the Political,* 385–403. See Butler and Scott.

Marrouchi, Mustapha. 1990. "Breaking Up/Down/Out of the Boundaries: Tahar Ben Jelloun." *Research in African Literatures* 21, no. 4: 71–83.

Marx-Scouras, Danielle. 1993. "Muffled Screams/Stifled Voices." *Yale French Studies* 82: 172–82.

Maupassant, Guy de. [1885] 1959. *Bel-Ami.* Paris: Garnier. Trans. as *Bel-Ami* by H. N. P. Sloman. Baltimore: Penguin, 1961.

Mayne, Judith. 1991. "Lesbian Looks: Dorothy Arzner and Female Authorship." In *How Do I Look?: Queer Film and Video,* edited by Bad Object-Choices, 103–43. Seattle: Bay Press.

McClintock, Anne. 1997. "'No Longer in a Future Heaven': Gender, Race and Nationalism." In *Dangerous Liaisons,* 89–112. See McClintock et al.

McClintock, Anne, Aamir Mufti, and Ella Shohat, eds. 1997. *Dangerous Liaisons: Gender, Nation, and Postcolonial Perspectives.* Minneapolis: Univ. of Minnesota Press.

McCubbin, Bob. [1976] 1979. *The Gay Question: A Marxist Appraisal.* Atlanta: World View.

McKenna, Andrew J. 1988. "Flaubert's Freudian Thing: Violence and Representation in *Salammbô*." *Stanford French Review* 12, nos. 2–3: 305–25.

Mehta, Brinda J. 1994. "Proclaiming a New Order: Daughters in Action in the Mother-Daughter Dyad in Tahar Ben Jelloun's *L'enfant de sable* and *Les yeux baissés*." *Revue francophone* 9, no. 1: 39–58.

Memmi, Albert. [1953] 1966. *La statue de sel.* Paris: Gallimard, coll. Folio. Trans. as *The Pillar of Salt* by Edouard Roditi. Boston: Beacon, 1992.

Mercer, Kobena. 1994. *Welcome to the Jungle: New Positions in Black Cultural Studies.* New York: Routledge.

Mercer, Kobena, and Isaac Julien. 1988. "Race, Sexual Politics, and Black Masculinity: A Dossier." In *Male Order: Unwrapping Masculinity,* edited by Rowena Chapman and Jonathan Rutherford, 97–164. London: Lawrence and Wishart.

Merini, Rafika. 1992. "The Subversion of the Culture of Voyeurism in the Works of Leïla Sebbar and Assia Djebar: A Socio-Literary Study." Ph.D. diss., SUNY, Binghamton.

Mernissi, Fatima. [1975] 1987. *Beyond the Veil: Male-Female Dynamics in Modern Muslim Society.* Bloomington: Indiana Univ. Press.

———. [1987] 1991. *The Veil and the Male Elite: A Feminist Interpretation of Women's Rights in Islam.* Trans. Mary Jo Lakeland. Reading, MA: Addison-Wesley.

———. 1994. *Dreams of Trespass: Tales of a Harem Girlhood.* Reading, MA: Addison-Wesley.

Miller, Christopher L. 1990. *Theories of Africans: Francophone Literature and Anthropology in Africa.* Chicago: Univ. of Chicago Press.

———. 1993. "Nationalism as Resistance and Resistance to Nationalism in the Literature of Francophone Africa." *Yale French Studies* 82: 62–100.

Miller, Nancy K. 1991. *Getting Personal: Feminist Occasions and Other Autobiographical Acts.* New York: Routledge.

Mimouni, Rachid. 1982. *Le fleuve détourné.* Paris: Robert Laffont.

Mohanty, Chandra Talpade. [1984] 1991. "Under Western Eyes: Feminist Scholarship and Colonial Discourses." In *Third World Women and the Politics of Feminism,* edited by Mohanty, Ann Russo, and Lourdes Torres, 51–80. Bloomington: Indiana Univ. Press.

Mortimer, Mildred. 1988. "Entretien avec Assia Djebar, écrivain algérien." *Research in African Literatures* 19, no. 2: 197–205.

Mossman, Carol A. 1989. "*Salammbô*: Seeing the Moon through the Veil." *Neophilologus* 73: 36–45.

Mosteghanemi, Ahlem. 1985. *Algérie, femme et écritures.* Paris: L'Harmattan.

Mouliéras, Auguste, trans. and ed. 1892. *Les fourberies de Si Djeh'a: Contes kabyles.* Paris: Ernest Leroux.

Mufti, Aamir, and Ella Shohat. 1997. "Introduction." In *Dangerous Liaisons,* 1–12. See McClintock et al.

Mulvey, Laura. [1975] 1989. "Visual Pleasure and Narrative Cinema." In *Visual and Other Pleasures,* 14–26. Bloomington: Indiana Univ. Press.

Murray, Stephen O. 1997. "Some Nineteenth-Century Reports of Islamic Homosexualities." In *Islamic Homosexualities,* 204–21. See Murray and Roscoe 1997.

Murray, Stephen O., and Will Roscoe. 1997. *Islamic Homosexualities: Culture, History, and Literature.* New York: New York Univ. Press.

Nestle, Joan. [1981] 1987. "My Mother Liked to Fuck." In *A Restricted Country,* 120–22. Ithaca: Firebrand Books.

———. [1992] 1997. "I Lift My Eyes to the Hill: The Life of Mabel Hampton as Told by a White Woman." In *Queer Representations: Reading Lives, Reading Cultures,* edited by Martin Duberman, 258–75. New York: New York Univ. Press.

Nora, Pierre. 1984. "Entre Mémoire et Histoire: La problématique des lieux." In *Les lieux de mémoire,* vol. 1, xvii–xlii. Paris: Gallimard.

Novén, Bengt. 1996. *Les mots et le corps: Etude des procès d'écriture dans l'œuvre de Tahar Ben Jelloun.* Upsala: Upsala Univ.

O., Rachid. 1995. *L'enfant ébloui.* Paris: Gallimard.

———. 1996. *Plusieurs vies.* Paris: Gallimard.

———. 1998. *Chocolat chaud.* Paris: Gallimard.

"On the Question of Homosexuality and the Emancipation of Women." 1988. *Revolution* 56 (Spring): 40–55.

Orlando, Valery Key. 1996. "Beyond Postcolonial Discourse: New Problematics of Feminine Identity in Contemporary Francophone Literature." Ph.D. diss., Brown Univ.

Al-Qur'an: A Contemporary Translation. 1984. Trans. Ahmed Ali. Karachi: Akrash.

Parker, Andrew, Mary Russo, Doris Sommer, and Patricia Yaeger, eds. 1992. *Nationalisms and Sexualities.* New York: Routledge.

Plant, Richard. [1986] 1988. *The Pink Triangle: The Nazi War against Homosexuals.* New York: Henry Holt, Owl Book.

Pontecorvo, Gillo (director). 1966. *La battaglia di Algeri* (The Battle of Algiers).

Proust, Marcel. [1913–27] 1987–89. *A la recherche du temps perdu.* 4 vols. Paris: Gallimard, Bibliothèque de la Pléiade. Trans. as *In Search of Lost Time* by C. K. Scott Moncrieff and Terence Kilmartin, revised by D. J. Enright. 6 vols. New York: Random House, The Modern Library, 1992–93.

Raybaud, Antoine. 1993. "Nomadism between the Archaic and the Modern." *Yale French Studies* 82: 146–57.

Renan, Ernest. [1882] 1947. "Qu'est-ce qu'une nation?" In *Œuvres complètes,* vol. 1, 887–906. Paris: Calmann-Lévy. Trans. as "What Is a Nation?" by Martin Thom. In Bhabha 1990, 8–22.

Rich, Adrienne. [1980] 1983. "Compulsory Heterosexuality and Lesbian Existence." In *Powers of Desire: The Politics of Sexuality,* edited by Ann Snitow, Christine Stansell, and Sharon Thompson, 177–205. New York: Monthly Review Press.

Riley, Denise. 1988. *"Am I That Name?": Feminism and the Category of "Women" in History.* Minneapolis: Univ. of Minnesota Press.

Roumani, Judith. 1983. "Mohammed Dib's *Qui se souvient de la mer:* Literary Technique and the Drama of Algeria." *Revue CELFAN/CELFAN Review* 2, no. 2: 8–11.

Roussillon, Alain. 1990. "Le débat sur l'orientalisme dans le champ intellectuel arabe: L'aporie des sciences sociales." *Peuples méditerranéens* 50: 7–39.

Rubin, Gayle. [1984] 1989. "Thinking Sex: Notes for a Radical Theory of the Politics of Sexuality." In *Pleasure and Danger: Exploring Female Sexuality,* edited by Carole S. Vance, 267–319. New York: HarperCollins, Pandora.

Ruedy, John. 1992. *Modern Algeria: The Origins and Development of a Nation.* Bloomington: Indiana Univ. Press.

Russo, Vito. [1981] 1987. *The Celluloid Closet: Homosexuality in the Movies.* New York: Harper and Row.

Said, Edward W. [1978] 1979. *Orientalism.* New York: Random House, Vintage Books.

———. 1986. "Orientalism Reconsidered." In *Literature, Politics and Theory: Papers from the Essex Conference 1976–84,* edited by Francis Barker et al., 210–29. London: Methuen.

Saigh Bousta, Rachida. 1992. *Lecture des récits de Tahar Ben Jelloun: Ecriture, mémoire et imaginaire.* Casablanca: Afrique Orient.

Sautman, Francesca Canadé. 1994. "Gynosociabilité et la femme-homme: Politique d'un espace érotique féminin dans cinq œuvres de Ben Jelloun, Djebar et Emna Bel Haj Yahia." Paper read at the Congrès Mondial du Conseil International d'Etudes Francophones, Quebec City, 14 April.

Schild, Maarten. 1990. "Islam." In *Encyclopedia of Homosexuality,* edited by Wayne R. Dynes, vol. 1, 615–20. New York: Garland.

Schmitt, Arno, and Jehoeda Sofer, eds. 1992. *Sexuality and Eroticism among Males in Moslem Societies.* New York: Haworth, Harrington Park.

Sebbar, Leïla. 1980. *Le pédophile et la maman: L'amour des enfants.* Paris: Stock.

———. 1982. *Shérazade: 17 ans, brune, frisée, les yeux verts.* Paris: Stock. Trans. as *Sherazade: Missing: Aged 17, Dark Curly Hair, Green Eyes* by Dorothy S. Blair with intro. London: Quartet, 1991.

———. 1985a. *Les carnets de Shérazade.* Paris: Stock.

———. 1985b. "La langue de l'exil." *La quinzaine littéraire* 436: 8–10.

———. 1991. *Le fou de Shérazade.* Paris: Stock.

Sedgwick, Eve Kosofsky. 1985. *Between Men: English Literature and Male Homosocial Desire.* New York: Columbia Univ. Press.

———. 1990. *Epistemology of the Closet.* Berkeley: Univ. of California Press.

Serhane, Abdelhak. 1995. *L'amour circoncis.* Casablanca: Eddif.

Shaaban, Bouthaina. [1988] 1991. *Both Right and Left Handed: Arab Women Talk about Their Lives.* Bloomington: Indiana Univ. Press.

Shohat, Ella. 1988. "Sephardim in Israel: Zionism from the Standpoint of Its Jewish Victims." *Social Text* 19/20: 1–35.

Silverman, Kaja. 1992. *Male Subjectivity at the Margins.* New York: Routledge.

Spear, Thomas. 1993. "Politics and Literature: An Interview with Tahar Ben Jelloun." *Yale French Studies* 83: 30–43.

Spivak, Gayatri Chakravorty. [1984] 1990. "The Post-modern Condition: The End of Politics?" In *The Post-colonial Critic: Interviews, Strategies, Dialogues,* edited by Sarah Harasym, 17–34. New York: Routledge.

———. [1987] 1990. "Practical Politics of the Open End." In *The Post-colonial Critic,* 95–112.

———. 1988. "Can the Subaltern Speak?" In *Marxism and the Interpretation of Culture,* edited by Cary Nelson and Lawrence Grossberg, 271–313. Urbana: Univ. of Illinois Press.

Szyliowicz, Irene L. 1988. *Pierre Loti and the Oriental Woman.* London: Macmillan.

Toso Rodinis, Giuliana. 1994. *Fêtes et défaites d'éros dans l'œuvre de Rachid Boudjedra.* Paris: L'Harmattan.

Tremaine, Louis. 1988. "Psychic Deformity in Mohammed Dib's *Qui se souvient de la mer.*" *Research in African Literatures* 19, no. 3: 283–300.

Warner, Michael. 1995. "Something Queer about the Nation-State." In *After Political Correctness: The Humanities and Society in the 1990s,* edited by Christopher Newfield and Ronald Strickland, 361–71. Boulder: Westview.

White, Edmund. 1993. *Genet: A Biography.* New York: Alfred A. Knopf.

Wittig, Monique. 1980. "The Straight Mind." *Feminist Issues* 1, no. 1. Reprinted in *The Straight Mind and Other Essays,* 21–32. Boston: Beacon, 1992.

———. 1989. "On the Social Contract." *Feminist Issues* 9, no. 1. Reprinted in *The Straight Mind and Other Essays,* 33–45. Boston: Beacon, 1992.

Woodhull, Winifred. 1992. "Rereading *Nedjma:* Feminist Scholarship and North African Women." *SubStance* 69: 46–63.

———. 1993. *Transfigurations of the Maghreb: Feminism, Decolonization, and Literatures.* Minneapolis: Univ. of Minnesota Press.

Yetiv, Isaac. 1972. *Le thème de l'aliénation dans le roman maghrébin d'expression française: De 1952 à 1956.* Sherbrooke: CELEF.

Zéghidour, Slimane. 1990. *Le voile et la bannière.* Paris: Hachette.

Zeraoui, Fouad. 1992. "Algérie 1952–1962: Colons gay, l'autre histoire." *Illico,* 21–26 July.

Zerdoumi, Nefissa. 1970. *Enfants d'hier: L'éducation de l'enfant en milieu traditionnel algérien.* Paris: François Maspero.

Zimra, Clarisse. 1992. "Writing Woman: The Novels of Assia Djebar." *SubStance* 69: 68–84.

———. 1993. "'When the Past Answers Our Present': Assia Djebar Talks about *Loin de Médine.*" *Callaloo* 16, no. 1: 116–31.